PATTON'S PEERS

PATTON'S PEERS

THE FORGOTTEN
ALLIED FIELD ARMY COMMANDERS
OF THE WESTERN FRONT, 1944–45

John A. English

STACKPOLE
BOOKS

Published by
STACKPOLE BOOKS
5067 Ritter Road
Mechanicsburg, PA 17055
www.stackpolebooks.com

Printed in the United States of America

10 9 8 7 6 5 4 3 2 1

FIRST EDITION

Library of Congress Cataloging-in-Publication Data

English, John A. (John Alan)
   Patton's peers : the forgotten allied field army commanders of the Western Front,
1944–45 / John A. English.
        p. cm.
   Includes bibliographical references and index.
   ISBN 978-0-8117-0501-1
   1. World War, 1939–1945—Campaigns—Western Front. 2. World War, 1939–1945—
Biography. 3. Generals—Biography. I. Title.
   D756.E54 2009
   940.54'120922—dc22
                                        2008036406

For Valerie, the love of my life,
and our daughters,
Shannon and Laura,
with love forever

Contents

Preface

In 1982, while serving with Central Army Group headquarters in Heidelberg, Germany, I made a pilgrimage to the Luxembourg grave of Gen. George S. Patton Jr. I found that it had been moved to the front of the cemetery since countless visitors had beaten a path across the manicured grass to pay their respects at the original location. The new location created the impression that Patton, even in death, still led his Third Army. At the Combat Training Centre in Gagetown, Canada, I later heard distinguished military historian Martin Blumenson suggest that the greatly admired Patton was as much a poet as a soldier. Later still, at a U.S. Naval Institute conference in Wheaton, Illinois, I listened to former war correspondent Andy Rooney express a far less flattering view of Patton as a commander of American troops. The contrast was thought-provoking and reminded me that while I had visited the grave of Patton and even that of Canadian war poet John McCrae, who wrote "In Flanders Fields," I had not made the effort to visit the grave of the commander of the First Canadian Army, which fought in line with Patton's Third.

I also realized that the reason that Patton was so often compared to Bernard Law Montgomery and Omar Bradley—even though both commanded army groups one level above Patton—was simply because Patton was the only field army commander popularly perceived to be noteworthy. Having attended and conducted numerous battlefield tours of Normandy with the Canadian Land Forces Command and Staff College, this struck me as somewhat unfair since other field army commanders won the beachhead and created the conditions for the advance into Germany. Such discrepancy prompted me to undertake a series of research trips to write a book about the less universally hailed commanders who led Allied field armies to victory on the Western Front in World War II.

Lt. Col. Dr. John A. English
Honorary Lieutenant Colonel,
The Brockville Rifles
Milton on the St. Lawrence
Kingston, Ontario

Introduction

Seven Allied field armies bore the brunt of the fighting against the forces of the Third Reich on the Western Front during the last two years of World War II. As eventually deployed from the English Channel to the Swiss border, they were the First Canadian Army, the British Second Army, the U.S. Ninth Army, the U.S. First Army, the U.S. Third Army, the U.S. Seventh Army, and the French First Army.[1] Of the seven officers who commanded these armies, however, only Gen. George S. Patton Jr. of the U.S. Third Army has truly been remembered. Whereas Patton is almost a household name, the other field army commanders—Harry Crerar, Miles Dempsey, William Simpson, Courtney Hodges, Alexander Patch, and Jean de Lattre de Tassigny—are hardly recognized. Historians have written numerous books about Patton, and publishers appear eager to produce even more, but there is only one published biography of Patch, one just released on Crerar, and none yet on Dempsey or Simpson. A biography of Hodges did not appear until 2006.[2] De Lattre has rated several biographies in French, but only one in English. That Patton has been so highly celebrated compared to his peers has been partly explained by the assertion that members of the press, usually war correspondents, first establish military reputations in their wartime reporting. Only later, with some perspective, do historians judge performances and sustain or revise earlier impressions.[3] This book aims to offer some perspective on the performances of those generals besides Patton who led field armies across Western Europe.

This work will focus on Patton's peers—the forgotten Allied field army commanders of the Western Front—and the battles and campaigns they fought with their armies in the Allied coalition. Their early development and military advancement will be recounted briefly, along with the growth and structure of their respective field armies. Their method and style of operational command, such as how they handled their staffs and subordinates, will then be examined against the battlefield performance of their armies. In addition to encouraging interest in field army commanders who have remained in the shadows for so long, this operational focus should illuminate the achievements of troops in the six field armies other than Patton's Third.

Before scrutinizing individual field army commanders it is necessary to review the organization and functional responsibilities of the various levels of Allied land and air forces on the Western Front. Some discussion of the importance of general staff systems is also required to understand how large, modern ground forces actually carried out their operations. A brief look at the development and structure of the Anglo-American alliance should also serve to place the coalition operations of Allied field armies in context. Finally, the relative strengths of Allied forces deployed on the Western Front will be examined to determine their effect on the implementation of military strategy.

ALLIED ORGANIZATION

By the end of the war in 1945, three Allied army groups operated on the Western Front. From north to south, these were the Anglo-Canadian 21st Army Group under Field Marshal Bernard Law Montgomery, the U.S. 12th Army Group under Gen. Omar N. Bradley, and the U.S. 6th Army Group under Gen. Jacob L. Devers. Army groups, which were not used in the Pacific or Southeast Asian theaters, were unique to the European theater, reflecting German field formation structure for large-scale continental operations.

The 21st Army Group had been set up in July 1943 to plan and execute Operation Overlord. After the battle of Normandy, it controlled the operations of Dempsey's British Second and Crerar's First Canadian Armies. The 12th Army Group, formed on 1 August 1944, directed Hodges's First, Patton's Third, and later Simpson's Ninth Armies. The 6th Army Group came into being on 15 September 1944, following the U.S. Seventh Army's invasion of southern France, its junction with the Third, and the concurrent establishment of the French First Army. Under Supreme Headquarters Allied Expeditionary Forces (SHAEF), the theater-level command headed by Gen. Dwight D. Eisenhower, army groups directed operations on a scale considered too large for a single field army headquarters to handle.

In the Anglo-American terminology of the day, theater operations fell into the military strategic realm below national grand strategy. Army groups directed military strategic operations below theater level. In doing so, they assigned zones of action to field armies, attaching or detaching corps and divisions to support specific operational plans, but they played little part in army supply and administration except to estimate the means required, allocate resources, and provide general supervision. The principle was that field armies administered themselves according to procedures set by theater headquarters, drawing supplies directly from Communications Zone installations. Although army groups were intended to guide field armies through small, mobile, and flexible headquarters, the headquarters of the 21st and 12th Army Groups tended to duplicate theater and field army functions, which naturally increased manpower and inhibited mobility. For example, Bradley exercised close control over his armies—to the point of moving specific divisions—and saw his staff swell from 200 to 900 officers, more than the officer strength of an infantry division. In comparison, the 6th Army Group limited its headquarters to 311 officers and 1,221 enlisted personnel, largely because of Devers's insistence that it should be patterned after a corps and function with fewer staff than an army headquarters.[4]

In theory, army group commanders directed military strategic operations but did not carry them out. This was the responsibility of field army commanders, who executed broadly stated tasks or missions assigned by group commanders. The size and composition of field armies varied with circumstances, generally fitting the nature of the operation to be undertaken. Seen as the fundamental unit of strategic maneuver by the Americans, the field army's only permanent structure was its headquarters. As a rule of thumb, a field army usually had half its personnel in combat divisions and the other half in army- and corps-level ancillary troops to support and sustain the combat divisions. Ancillary troops usually consisted of signal, engineer, intelligence, military police, ordnance, and other specialist arms and services.

Army-level responsibilities included determining objectives and priorities, developing plans and concepts of operations, and assigning achievable objectives to corps along with sufficient resources to attain them. This involved allocating divisions and supplementary fighting assets, the most important of which were brigaded heavy and medium artillery regiments, engineer bridging units, and specialized armored vehicles such as flamethrowers and flail tanks. Other army-level responsibilities included supporting corps administratively and logistically, providing high-level intelligence, arranging the application and control of air support, and coordinating operations that involved two or more corps. Beyond supervising corps operations, a field army commander could influence the battle through the commitment of reserves and additional artillery, air strikes, boundary adjustments, shifting and regrouping formations, operational maneuver, and personal inspiration. To do this, he had to develop a feel for battle, position himself where he could best obtain information and personally communicate with subordinates, and have a sound grasp of terrain and time factors associated with force deployments. He also had to know the strengths and weaknesses of his own forces as well as those of the enemy.

The primary responsibility of the field army commander was to think and plan as far ahead as rationally possible, to focus not on the close battle *being* fought, but on the distant battle *to be* fought. This meant looking well beyond operations currently in progress to those he intended to conduct in the future, along with all the associated logistical support requirements. His main role was to plan as much as two or three operations in advance and issue orders not hours ahead, but days and even weeks in advance. Yet if the immediate operational situation demanded, it was his duty to intervene directly in the conduct of the ongoing battle.[5]

In at least one respect, the field army commander's role in the provision of high-level intelligence was unique. With the exception of the French First Army, army commanders and their closest advisors enjoyed access to Ultra, the British naval code-name for intelligence derived from the decryption of high-grade ciphers from different sources but most notably from radio messages sent by German Enigma enciphering machines. Dedicated signals liaison units headed by Ultra officers fed army commanders decrypts of the Germans' most secret communications, which, if confirmed by another source, could be released downward to corps commanders. So far as is known, the only two corps commanders with direct access to Ultra were Maj. Gen. Lucian K. Truscott, who had received such intelligence at Anzio, and Lt. Gen. Guy G. Simonds, who commanded the First Canadian Army during the Battle of the Scheldt.

Although Ultra produced certain intelligence coups—for example, locating a panzer group headquarters in Normandy and detecting the German withdrawal from southern France on 17–18 August 1944—it normally had to be corroborated with other sources in order to determine enemy strengths and dispositions. The Germans rarely discussed tactical plans in wireless transmissions, and because of changing situations in the field, they often modified the broad higher-level plans that the Allies intercepted through Ultra. Since Ultra alerts commonly arrived twelve to twenty-four hours after the event, they were usually too late to be of any value to divisions and smaller units, especially during fluid operations; Bradley pointed to Ultra's discovery of the German attack at Mortain as such a case.

While insufficient evidence exists to cross-compare how Ultra affected the decisions of the field army commanders under discussion, it does appear that commanders who relied too heavily on Ultra ran as much risk as those who depended too little on it. Truscott's overly cautious reaction to the announced presence of the 11th Panzer Division east of the Rhone on 22 August 1944 stands as an example of the former. Overreliance on Ultra may also have skewed intelligence estimates before the Battle of the Bulge when Ultra predictions seemed to indicate an attack in the Aachen area rather than through the Ardennes.[6] Still, Ultra could increase an army commander's confidence by providing him with more battlefield knowledge than his subordinates.

Another unique function of a field army commander was the coordination and allocation of air support. To ensure the best use of resources, air assets were commanded at the highest possible level, and like artillery, they were controlled through a functional chain of command. Air force commanders enjoyed coequal status with their army counterparts. Until the end of the Normandy campaign, the Allied Expeditionary Air Force under Air Chief Marshal Sir Trafford Leigh-Mallory controlled all tactical air operations on the Western Front, where each Allied army group and field army was supported by an affiliated air formation.[7] Air Marshal Sir Arthur "Maori" Coningham's 2nd Tactical Air Force, which consisted of No. 2 (Bomber) Group and two composite air groups of fighters and fighter-bombers, worked with the 21st Army Group. No. 84 Group, Royal Air Force (RAF), commanded by Air Vice-Marshal L. O. "Dingo" Brown and later by Air Vice-Marshal E. C. Hudleston, supported the First Canadian Army. No. 83 Group, RAF, under Air Vice-Marshal Harry Broadhurst, supported the British Second Army.[8]

Lt. Gen. Hoyt S. Vandenberg's U.S. Ninth Air Force supported the 12th Army Group. The U.S. First Army received air support from the IX Tactical Air Command under Maj. Gen. Elwood R. "Pete" Quesada and the U.S. Third Army from the XIX Tactical Air Command under Brig. Gen. Otto P.

Allied Land-Air Affiliations

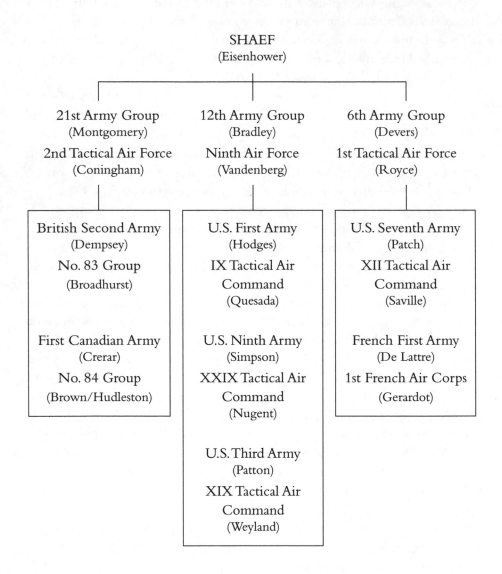

SHAEF
(Eisenhower)

21st Army Group (Montgomery)	12th Army Group (Bradley)	6th Army Group (Devers)
2nd Tactical Air Force (Coningham)	Ninth Air Force (Vandenberg)	1st Tactical Air Force (Royce)

British Second Army (Dempsey)	U.S. First Army (Hodges)	U.S. Seventh Army (Patch)
No. 83 Group (Broadhurst)	IX Tactical Air Command (Quesada)	XII Tactical Air Command (Saville)
First Canadian Army (Crerar)	U.S. Ninth Army (Simpson)	French First Army (De Lattre)
No. 84 Group (Brown/Hudleston)	XXIX Tactical Air Command (Nugent)	1st French Air Corps (Gerardot)
	U.S. Third Army (Patton)	
	XIX Tactical Air Command (Weyland)	

Weyland.[9] After 1 October 1944, Brig. Gen. Richard E. Nugent's XXIX Tactical Air Command supported the U.S. Ninth Army. Around the same time, U.S. Maj. Gen. Ralph Royce's multinational 1st Tactical Air Force (Provisional) began coordinating air support for the 6th Army Group since the French First Army started receiving dedicated air support through General Gerardot's 1st French Air Corps. All the while, from August 1944, Brig. Gen. Gordon P. Saville's (later Brig. Gen. Glenn O. Barcus's) XII Tactical Air Command provided air support to the U.S. Seventh Army.[10] Ideally, the closest possible association between field army and air headquarters was warranted in order to ensure optimal tactical air coordination.* All requests for strategic heavy bomber support from RAF Bomber Command and the U.S. Eighth Air Force also had to be processed at field army level through supporting air headquarters.

In order to direct operations, a field army commander had to maintain the closest possible continuous contact with his corps commanders. He also had to stay in touch with his division commanders. One level below a corps, the division was essentially the building block of the corps and the largest single fighting formation with a fixed structure and permanently established strength. According to Gen. James Gavin, it was the division that "cut the mustard," carrying out the tough job of fighting tactical engagements while keeping troop morale up in the face of heavy losses and adverse conditions.[11]

Frontline divisions fell into two basic categories, infantry and armored, the first akin to a sledgehammer, the second to a weapon of opportunity.[12] Both types were structured to include only those elements thought to be essential to their operations in order not to dissipate fighting personnel by dispersing them too widely. An infantry division contained three brigades or, in the U.S. Army, three semipermanent regimental combat teams, along with supporting arms and services. An armored division consisted of an armored brigade and an infantry brigade or, in the U.S. Army, three tank battalions and three infantry battalions. In action, the American armored division usually split into three combat commands—Combat Command A (CCA), Combat Command B (CCB), and Combat Command Reserve (CCR)—each a tailored mix of tank, infantry, and artillery battalions with reconnaissance, engineer, tank destroyer, antiaircraft, and supporting services. The British and Canadian armored division similarly proved most effective when formed into four battle groups (two under each brigade, which coordinated artillery support), each consisting of an armored regiment (equivalent to an American battalion) and infantry battalion.

---

* For details, see Appendix.

Each division's artillery was structured to support only one brigade or regimental attack, allowing artillery brigades to be pooled at army level for more flexible and concentrated distribution to corps and divisions as the tactical situation dictated. The same principle governed the use of armor, engineer, and other combat-support assets, with independent armored brigades being assigned to add punch to Anglo-Canadian infantry divisions and independent tank battalions to American infantry divisions.[13]

Since single-division attacks against the Germans generally were not productive, the fighting power of a corps was required. If the division was the great combat unit, ventured American general Walton Walker, the corps was the great operations unit.[14] Unlike a division, a corps consisted of only a permanent headquarters and, like a field army, was task-organized for the specific operation to be undertaken. For reasons related to the ease of working together, however, certain ancillary troops—such as heavy artillery not integral to divisions, antiaircraft batteries, artillery survey units, medium armored car reconnaissance, engineer companies, supply transport columns, and ordnance workshops—became permanently affiliated with individual corps.

The corps was the highest tactical level of command and the key headquarters for employing all combat elements in proper tactical combinations. As a general rule, while divisions fought the close-in battle looking forward roughly twenty-four hours, corps looked forward about three days, always keeping in mind that divisions needed twelve to eighteen hours to execute an order. Although the number of divisions allocated to a corps varied according to the tactical situation, any corps headquarters was expected to handle efficiently up to three infantry divisions, three armored divisions, or any combination of the two types. In certain instances, several corps controlled more than three divisions.[15]

A corps usually operated within a territorial corridor covering the line of communication along which it moved. The task of the corps commander, who could easily make or break an operation, was to plan the battle with the forces at his disposal, issue orders, and then supervise their execution. In consultation with his principal staff and artillery, engineer, air support, and logistics advisers, the commander initially worked out the battle plan, which included plans for maneuver and fire, alternative courses, and counterbattery fire. Upon finishing the plan, the commander conferred with his divisional commanders to fine-tune the details and then gave his orders.[16]

GENERAL STAFFS

Staffs are so important to the exercise of the effective command of ground forces that they warrant more than just passing mention. As Napoleon discovered in Russia, there were definite limits to the size of an army that could be controlled by one person. Military genius—always rare—was no longer sufficient to shore up the generalship of increasingly large forces. First instituted by Prussians to compensate for lack of competence among aristocratic commanders appointed more for social reasons than military ability, a general staff system provided field commanders with specially trained advisors capable of offering expert counsel and overseeing the detailed execution of orders. This general staff differed qualitatively and functionally from all previous military staffs, which were often little more than personal suites or retinues of commanders.

Within the Prussian army, general staff officers acting as chiefs of staff at field army and corps levels became so effective that they gained the institutionalized right to share in the operational decision-making process. Empowered to communicate directly with the chief of the general staff at the side of the kaiser, they not only advised their respective commanders, but also assumed joint accountability for decisions taken. Unlike normal subordinates who tended to give as little offense as possible in their advice to superiors, the chief of staff was duty-bound to press his candid, unsolicited advice on his commander and urge him to make a rational decision based on the facts. Established convention further obligated the commander to listen to this advice before making a decision, which the general staff officer then adopted as his own. The commander was not similarly obliged to listen to any other staff officer.

This system, which to the uninitiated appeared to countenance insubordination, had the wider effect of elevating function and knowledge over hierarchy; it was not uncommon for junior general staff members to give orders to higher-ranking officers and have them obeyed.[17] Even though general staff officers eventually occupied most command positions, it remained an unwritten rule for some time that corps chiefs of staff could enter their opinions in war diaries when they fundamentally disagreed with the responsible commander's decision.[18] By the end of World War I, highly competent chiefs of staff actually commanded the armies of princes and nobles. The importance of the chief of staff had been most famously underscored by the German victory at Tannenberg in 1914, which many argued had been won by the chief of staff, Maj. Gen. Erich Ludendorff, rather than the field army commander, Col. Gen. Paul Hindenburg.[19]

The organizational institution of the general staff was arguably the greatest military innovation of the nineteenth century. Rooted in staff and war colleges that provided a higher level of military education and training than cadet schools like Sandhurst, Saint-Cyr, and West Point, the general staff grew into a collective brain that developed a more systems-oriented approach to waging war in which no individual was indispensable. The staff and war colleges, nurseries of the general staff, dispensed practical expertise and taught a common doctrine for fighting, ensuring that both commanders and staffs would be capable of responding promptly and logically to most situations on the battlefield.[20] To ease transfers and compensate for casualties, every general staff officer had to be able to take over the work of another and apply to it the same body of basic ideas and principles of operational and tactical thought. When applied to the employment of all arms and services, such uniformity of doctrine and practice facilitated command efficiency and made possible massive field army deployments.

The increasingly complex problems of large modern armies related to the movement and concentration of personnel and materiel for combat also increased the need for staff to obtain factual information and prepare and issue plans and orders in the commander's name. As general staff officers inevitably rose to assume command positions because of their superior military knowledge, it also became easier for higher commanders to grant similarly indoctrinated subordinate commanders greater initiative and freedom of action in the execution of operations. In turn, such decentralization reduced inherent bureaucratic friction and encouraged innovation at lower levels, which permitted the army at large to adapt more quickly to changing circumstances.[21] As the introduction of the general staff considerably raised the knowledge threshold of armies, the staff and war colleges also became the most important stepping-stones along the path leading to high field command.

Although the French and Americans emulated the Germans in establishing army general staffs, the structures of their systems varied from the model. In the German system, a chief of staff coordinated staff work at army and corps levels, but below corps, the Ia (principal general staff officer), looked after operational and training matters and supervised the Ic, who was responsible for reconnaissance and intelligence, and the Ib, who headed up logistics. In comparison, after the Franco-Prussian War in 1870–71, the French established an *état-major général de l'armée* organized into three bureaus—the first for personnel and supply, the second for intelligence, and the third for operations and training. Because of the huge increase in materiel and ammunition required in World War I, a fourth bureau for logistics, which subsumed the supply function of the first bureau, was introduced in 1917. At all levels, a chief of staff coordinated the work of the four bureaus.

Like the French, war experience convinced the Americans of the need for a general staff. As a result of the Spanish-American War, the U.S. Congress in 1903 adopted an almost exact copy of the general staff system established by the Prussians. In the course of World War I, however, the Americans switched to the French variant. By 1918, the American Expeditionary Force's staff had five sections: administration and personnel (G1), intelligence (G2), plans and operations (G3), supply (G4), and training (G5). Three years later, the U.S. Army formally adopted this system, omitting the G5 section, which was later reintroduced to assume the civil-affairs function of G1. By World War II, the chief of staff in an American divisional headquarters coordinated the work of four assistant chiefs of staff—each heading G1, G2, G3, and G4 sections—and various artillery, engineer, signal, finance, ordnance, chemical, medical, and quartermaster advisers. In its essential features, this system also prevailed at corps headquarters. At army level, the headquarters establishment eventually increased to 330 officers and 740 enlisted personnel, which the chief of staff controlled through two deputies: a deputy chief of staff for operations who supervised the G2, G3, and G4 sections and a deputy chief of staff for administration who supervised the G1 section and administrative special staff.[22]

The British Army's general staff established after the Boer War in 1899–1902 presented yet another variant. The general staff system introduced in 1906 intentionally rejected the German model for fear that it would produce a too powerful chief of the general staff within the British government. Thus, the British general staff was not unified like the German, French, or American models in which field formation staff branches reported to one chief of staff (or Ia). In fact, the original British staff system appeared to give greater power to administration and logistics than operations. An army council chaired by the secretary of state for war headed the staff system and comprised civil, financial, and four military members. The first military member was the chief of the general staff (renamed chief of the imperial general staff, or CIGS, from 1909), who as *primus inter pares* assumed responsibility for staff coordination and operational matters (G), including intelligence, training, and doctrine. The second military member, the adjutant general, looked after administrative matters (A), including personnel, mobilization, and army schools, while the third military member, the quartermaster general, took care of facets pertaining to material needs (Q), such as supply, quartering, and movement. A fourth military member, the master general of ordnance (MGO), retained responsibility for armament, fortification, and procurement. With the exception of the MGO, staff representation on the army council was projected down throughout the field army, with Q discharging MGO's responsibilities. The appointment of staff officers to A and Q branches jointly rather than separately after 1913 further enabled senior administrative (AQ) appointments to supervise the work of both.[23]

During World War II, the senior G staff officer in a British Commonwealth division was a general staff officer, grade 1 (GSO1), in the rank of lieutenant colonel; his assistants were a GSO2 and a GSO3 in the ranks of major and captain, respectively.[24] The senior administrative-quartermaster staff officer was the assistant adjutant and quartermaster general, who had under him a deputy assistant quartermaster general and a deputy assistant adjutant general. At corps headquarters, the senior operations staff appointment was the brigadier, general staff (BGS). Assisting him was a GSO1 who supervised the work of two GSO2s for operations, a GSO2 for intelligence, a GSO2 for air, a GSO2 for staff duties, a GSO2 for liaison, and several GSO3 staff officers. The senior corps administrative-quartermaster staff officer was the deputy adjutant and quartermaster general, also in the rank of brigadier, who was assisted by administrative staff officers exclusively responsible for administrative and quartermaster matters.

Since Montgomery had been a believer in the German chief of staff system since 1918 and had always employed it in his commands, he formally introduced the "chief of staff principle" within the 21st Army Group.[25] Its stated purpose was to authorize the chief of staff to make all decisions in implementing the commander's policy, thereby relieving him of the task of coordinating the work of the staff so that he could devote his full attention to the prosecution of operations. The result was that at corps level, the BGS was redesignated the chief of staff. At field army level, with roughly 200 officers in the headquarters establishment, the chief of staff coordinated the staff work of the operations branch, which was headed by a BGS, and the administrative-quartermaster staff, which was headed by a deputy adjutant and quartermaster general. Army headquarters, like corps and divisional head-quarters, was also physically divided into forward operations staff and rear-ward administrative-quartermaster staff components. Within the operations staff, the BGS supervised the G sections for operations, air, intelligence, and staff duties while the chief of staff directly supervised the plans, liaison, and administrative-quartermaster sections.[26]

Except for differences in nomenclature and the organizational position of intelligence, the American and Montgomery-modified British staff systems were quite similar, with operations and administrative heads reporting to one chief of staff.[27] Both recognized that given the complexity of modern war-fare, no commander was likely to prevail without a competent staff, but a good staff could conceivably save a less-than-competent commander. In sug-gesting that an average divisional commander would always do well if he had a good GSO1, Montgomery expressed a common view.[28] Although neither incorporated the unique role of the German general staff officer, both placed a high premium on the selection of competent chiefs of staff and attempted to balance personal strengths and weaknesses in the appointment of com-manders and their principal staff officers. Both staff systems also warned against the danger of a staff officer being a yes-man but stressed that once command decisions were taken, they were to be loyally implemented.

As set forth by Bradley to his U.S. First Army headquarters in 1944, the staff had three chief purposes: first, to advise the commander with frank-ness and honesty; second, to implement the decisions made by the com-mander; and third, to serve the troops by visiting subordinate units and looking for ways to help them.[29] Like Bradley, Crerar expected the staff officer to be frank in offering advice, even if it entailed arguing against a commander, though, one suspects, not as forcefully as a German general staff officer. For the most part, this called for intelligent anticipation and entailed gathering timely and accurate information to enable the com-mander to analyze, decide, and give direction. Ideally, the commander's decision flowed from an appreciation or estimate of the situation that logi-cally determined the best course of action. Neither Crerar nor Simpson, however, was above asking staff officers to produce appreciations or esti-mates for operations. This, too, required complete loyalty, and Crerar in par-ticular viewed a disloyal staff officer as thoroughly pernicious. If one were out of sympathy with his commander, Crerar stressed, the only course to follow was to resign or keep one's mouth shut.[30]

COALITION WARFARE

The American and British staff systems employed on the Western Front in World War II were meshed at the very top by a coalition infrastructure that reflected America's deliberate choice to deal with Britain above all others. The roots of Anglo-American staff integration can be traced back to secret American-British Conversations (ABC) that took place in Washington between January and March 1941. The British representatives carefully referred to themselves as the United Kingdom delegation, but the Americans deliberately chose to call them British and considered them representative of the Commonwealth as a whole, thus formally excluding Canada and other British dominions. The conversations resulted in a plan, called ABC-1, stipulating that in the event of American involvement in a two-ocean war, the priority of both Allies would be to defeat Germany first.[31]

The development of ABC-1 and the congressional passage of Lend-Lease on 11 March 1941 effectively marked the beginning of the grand alliance between the United States and Great Britain. Under the terms of the agreement that traded American destroyers for British bases in the Western Hemisphere, signed in London on 27 March 1941—the same day that the ABC conference concluded—the United States established a security zone in the western Atlantic. On 7 July, fifteen days after Germany attacked the Soviet Union, U.S. Marines relieved British Commonwealth garrisons in Iceland, Trinidad, and British Guiana. In September 1941, as agreed by President Franklin D. Roosevelt and Prime Minister Winston Churchill at Argentia, Newfoundland, the United States assumed strategic control of the western Atlantic. The U.S. Navy thus moved beyond protecting only American commerce to escorting ships of other flags in Atlantic convoys. Since the U.S. Navy had effectively joined the North Atlantic convoy system coordinated by the Royal Navy's Western Approaches Command, the Royal Canadian Navy's Newfoundland Escort Force fell under the strategic direction of the commander in chief of the U.S. Atlantic Fleet.[32] Arguably, this transfer of the major part of a belligerent navy to American command signalled the entry of the U.S. into the European war.[33]

After Pearl Harbor ignited a truly global war, the U.S. State Department drafted an initial plan that called for a supreme war council of representatives from the United States, Great Britain, China, and Russia. Roosevelt rejected the plan on the grounds that only Britain and the United States could formulate and implement a truly global strategy and, more practically, determine the allocation of resources worldwide. Besides, the Soviet Union was not at war with Japan, and China was not at war with Germany.[34] At the Arcadia Conference held in Washington from 22 December 1941 to 14 January 1942, Roosevelt and Churchill accordingly approved the formation of the Combined Chiefs of Staff Committee, which would have the responsibility for determining the strategic direction of the Allied war effort.[35] The Combined Chiefs of Staff consisted of the British Chiefs of Staff and the American Joint Chiefs of Staff.[36] They made their most important decisions during a series of major conferences at which Roosevelt and Churchill jointly presided. The Combined Chiefs of Staff met in permanent session in Washington, with the heads-of-service delegations of the British Joint Service Mission representing their respective British chiefs. The head of the British mission, Field Marshal Sir John Dill, represented Churchill and the British Chiefs of Staff, which Churchill chaired as minister of defence.[37]

Perhaps because of the firmness with which the Joint Chiefs of Staff rejected Australian and New Zealand pleas for representation on the Combined Chiefs of Staff, the Canadian government never applied for membership and willingly left the strategic direction of the war to Roosevelt and Churchill, who eventually allowed Canada to send one officer to represent the Canadian Cabinet War Committee at the Combined Chiefs of Staff. A Canadian military officer thus represented a national political authority in front of a largely military authority.[38] The result was that Canada was almost entirely excluded from deliberations. The Canadian government received no advance warning of the invasion of Sicily despite the involvement of Canadian troops, and although Canadian forces constituted 20 percent of the Normandy invasion force, Canadian prime minister Mackenzie King learned of D-Day only when a Royal Canadian Mounted Police constable roused him from his sleep early on 6 June 1944.[39]

Most nations strive to have their own interests served in any alliance, and the Americans demonstrated considerable strategic acumen before and after Pearl Harbor in this regard. For the first time, the United States undertook strategic consultations with an ally prior to the start of hostilities.[40] So long as it looked as though Britain might fall or make a separate peace, the U.S. focused on shoring up the defense of the Western Hemisphere, but after the Battle of Britain, the Americans felt emboldened enough to contemplate action abroad. Yet it was not until after Germany attacked the more formidable Soviet Union on 22 June 1941 that the Americans assumed an openly belligerent role in

the North Atlantic and began sinking German submarines. Allying more intimately with the British Empire than any other power gained the Americans
privileged access to a quarter of the world's land surface without having to be
concerned about such things as port entry and fly-over rights. The British also
offered a matchless array of world-ranging air, naval, and ground forces and
bases. The establishment of Supreme Headquarters Allied Expeditionary Forces
(SHAEF) without effective staff representation from any Dominion or other
minor power participating in Operation Overlord further helped ensure eventual American dominance on the most decisive Allied front.

SIZE OF ALLIED FORCES

The United States could not have fought a two-ocean war and Eisenhower
could not have carried out his broad-front strategy without British, Commonwealth, and French forces.[41] In fact, the United States could only have
replaced them with the twenty-one U.S. Army and six U.S. Marine divisions it
sent to fight in the Pacific. Recognition of this reality and concerns about
shipping more American forces to Europe figured prominently in the American decision to equip and field French forces for operations on the continent.

The numbers of non-American forces deployed on the Western Front
speak for themselves. Following the invasion of Normandy, the British and
Canadians fielded four corps of ten infantry and three armored divisions by 1
July, while the Americans had four corps with eleven infantry and two
armored divisions. By 15 September, Eisenhower commanded three army
groups, seven field armies, an Allied airborne army, and fifty-five divisions on
the Western Front. Four of the armies and twenty-eight divisions were
American. Three of the armies and twenty-seven divisions were non-American and included fourteen British (excluding the 79th), three Canadian, one
Polish, and eight French divisions. On 3 January 1945, American ground
force strength totaled forty-nine divisions, but other Allies still fielded twelve
British (two having been disbanded), three Canadian, one Polish, and eight
French divisions. At the end of the war, Eisenhower commanded ninety-one
divisions, of which sixty-one were American, fifteen British, five Canadian,
one Polish, and nine French (an additional French division screened the Italian border and another operated in the area of Bordeaux). Of 28,000 combat
aircraft, 13,155 were non-American.[42]

However one compares coalition contributions, it is difficult to escape the
conclusion that the United States' coalition partners were more important to

the advancement of American interests than commonly perceived. According to Western Front strength returns of 30 April 1945, the Americans fielded 2,618,023 troops, compared to 835,208 British, 183,421 Canadians, 413,144 French, and 34,518 other Allies. From 6 June 1944 to 7 May 1945, the Americans suffered an estimated 135,576 combat dead, the British 30,276, the Canadians 11,695, the French 12,587, and other Allies 1,528. Even in the end, non–Americans provided more than a third of the forces that contributed to victory on Western Front.[43]

Although British divisional counts often include the 79th Division—which was a parent organization for special armor rather than a fighting division and therefore not counted here—such figures almost never take into account the eight independent armored brigades that roughly equaled three extra divisions.[44] Moreover, Anglo-Canadian divisions were larger fighting entities than American divisions. An Anglo-Canadian infantry division establishment totalled 18,347 troops as compared to 14,253 in a U.S. infantry division; with four instead of three rifle companies per battalion, Anglo-Canadian divisions contained some 8,400 infantrymen, compared to 5,211 in American divisions. Unlike U.S. infantry divisions that were pared down to 14,037 in January 1945, Canadian infantry divisions retained their large structure, which the army attempted to maintain at full strength.

An Anglo-Canadian infantry division also had a seventy-two-gun divisional artillery, compared to the forty-eight guns supporting a U.S. infantry division.[45] The British 25-pounder gun-howitzer was as good as or better than the U.S. 105mm howitzer. According to later observations of the veteran combat commander Gen. James A. Van Fleet, British Commonwealth divisional artillery could bring all of its fire to bear on a single target in seconds, which American artillery could not do.[46] The British Firefly, a modified U.S. Sherman, was furthermore the only Allied tank capable of matching heavy German panzers since its 17-pounder gun could easily penetrate the 100-millimeter frontal armor on the Tiger at 2,000 yards. Anglo-Canadian armored divisions, with 14,964 troops and 246 medium and 44 light tanks, were also larger than their American equivalents, which had 10,937 troops and 186 medium and 77 light tanks.[47]

In the following chapters, the forgotten Allied field army commanders will be considered in the order of their initial SHAEF deployment from north to south on the Western Front. On the left of the line, the northernmost

First Canadian Army became operational in Normandy on 23 July 1944, with fifty-six-year-old Harry Crerar as its commanding general and Canadian national commander. Crerar assumed command of the First Canadian Army in March 1944, after it had been assigned a follow-up role similar to that of Patton's U.S. Third Army. As the head of Canada's first field army, Crerar was acutely conscious that he followed in the footsteps of the highly competent Gen. Sir Arthur Currie, who had led his celebrated Canadian Corps from victory to victory in World War I. Unfortunately, Crerar got off to a bad start when he attempted to fire his sole corps commander, British lieutenant general John Crocker, the day after the First Canadian Army became operational. Crerar went on to liberate the Channel ports, but temporary illness compelled him to sit out the Battle of the Scheldt. Arguably Canada's greatest contribution to Allied victory in Europe, the protracted struggle to open the Scheldt Estuary to shipping fell to his innovative subordinate, Lt. Gen. Guy G. Simonds, who conducted First Canadian Army operations with creative brilliance. Crerar nonetheless later directed nine British as well as his own Canadian divisions in the Battle of the Rhineland—almost half a million troops, more than any Canadian in history.

Miles "Bimbo" Dempsey, who led the British Second Army ashore in Normandy was a World War I veteran like Crerar. At age forty-eight, he was the youngest and longest continuously serving Allied army commander on the Western Front. Yet while Dempsey commanded Britain's greatest field army in World War II, he remains an enigma and stands among the least well known of his peers. An outstanding map reader who had commanded a brigade and corps in combat, he epitomized the decent, quiet type of practical leader who easily gained the confidence of subordinates with whom he interacted regularly. He was highly respected by the Canadians, with whom he had served as a corps chief of staff. In operations from Normandy to the Baltic, Dempsey further displayed a good "fingertip" feel for battle and, always forward, did not hesitate to intervene in corps operations when he thought it necessary. The seldom acknowledged 300-mile advance of his British Second Army from Falaise to Brussels in ten days compares favorably with Patton's dash of more than 400 miles in twenty-six days.

Courtney Hodges, commanding general of the U.S. First Army, was one year older than Crerar and also a World War I veteran. Hodges went ashore in Normandy as Omar Bradley's deputy commander in the First and replaced him as commander on 1 August 1944, when Bradley ascended to command the 12th Army Group. Patton thought little of Hodges, but Marshall, Eisenhower, and Bradley all praised him. Hodges's reputation as a field army commander nonetheless suffers because of his conduct of the Battle of the Huertgen Forest. Here, in an "American Passchendaele," he persisted in fighting the Germans on ground of their own choosing with tunnel vision reminiscent of the worst of World War I generals. By mid-December, just before the Battle of the Bulge, his First Army had been bled white, with five divisions rendered combat ineffective. Although Hodges has also been criticized for his exercise of command during the Battle of the Bulge, he appears to have been saved by the performance of his staff and army at large. The lucky seizure of the undestroyed Ludendorff railway bridge at Remagen later served to salvage a reputation tarnished by these earlier struggles. In the end, Marshall selected Hodges and his headquarters for further service in the Pacific theater.

Bill Simpson, whose U.S. Ninth Army became operational on 5 September 1944, appears to have been a more affable figure than Hodges, though he remains the least well known of the four American army commanders on the Western Front. Significantly, Simpson had not been a first choice for field army command, and in August 1944, Eisenhower had even recommended selecting combat-experienced corps commanders over him.[48] Simpson's greatest sin may have been that he got along far too well with the British as part of the 21st Army Group and remained under their shadow too long. Originally, Simpson's Ninth Army deployed between the U.S. First and Third Armies, but when it looked as though Hodges's First might be placed under Montgomery, Bradley switched the Ninth to the northern flank of his 12th Army Group. As a consequence of the Battle of the Bulge, from mid-December 1944 to 4 April 1945, Simpson's 300,000-strong Ninth Army operated as part of Montgomery's 21st Army Group. A West Point classmate of Patton's and a World War I veteran the same age as Crerar, Simpson conducted Operation Grenade, the meticulously planned and well-executed southern pincer that complemented Crerar's Operation Veritable thrust from the north in the Battle of the Rhineland. After Grenade, Simpson's Ninth Army carried out the northern envelopment of the Ruhr pocket and, on reverting to 12th Army Group command, raced to the Elbe. To the end, Simpson maintained that he could have beaten the Russians to Berlin, though in what relative strength remains uncertain.

In his modest, earthy demeanor, Simpson somewhat resembled Alexander "Sandy" Patch, who, like Dempsey, considered it unprofessional to seek publicity. Patch had commanded a corps on Guadalcanal and, at age fifty-four, followed in the footsteps of Patton as commander of the U.S. Seventh Army, but his exploits remain largely unsung. Probably the least healthy Allied army commander, he suffered from a lung ailment that put him in his grave a month before Patton. Some also suspected that his intense grief over the death of his only son in action in October 1944 might have adversely affected his ability to command. When Patton dashed off to his greatest glory in the Bulge, thereby escaping the dead end of fame in the mud of Lorraine, Patch's Seventh Army took over twenty-five miles of the Third Army's front. This was a lucky break for Patton, but too bad for Patch, who was actually in a position at the time to cross the Rhine. The supreme irony was that Patton's dash left his old Seventh Army, now commanded by Patch, very much on the sidelines. Patch's earlier execution of Operation Dragoon, the almost perfect amphibious landing in southern France, nonetheless remained an impressive achievement, as did his almost unnoticed defense against the last German counteroffensive, Operation *Nordwind,* in January 1945.

For Operation Dragoon and the subsequent advance up the Rhone Valley, Patch had French forces under his command. Indeed, French Army B under fifty-five-year-old Jean de Lattre de Tassigny constituted two-thirds of the Seventh. With the creation of the 6th Army Group on 15 September, Army B was redesignated the French First Army. Of all Allied field army commanders, de Lattre attained the highest distinction, being made a Marshal of France posthumously, but his performance on the Western Front has often been unfairly maligned. Inspired by the iconic Napoleon, de Lattre's dramatic and unpredictable command style sorely tested his staff and American allies, but his capture of Toulon and Marseilles and subsequent drive through the Belfort Gap represented laudable feats of arms. His was the first Allied field army to reach the Rhine. Although closing the Colmar pocket later posed a problem, the overall performance of the French First Army proved relatively impressive for a formation that had to resort to maneuver for lack of artillery and deal with structural problems not faced by other Allied armies. De Lattre also led his army as a political instrument, using it to secure France's postwar position as a great power.

With this introductory background covered, we can now turn to the individual Allied field army commanders.

CHAPTER ONE

In the Shadow of Sir Arthur

GEN. H. D. G. CRERAR, FIRST CANADIAN ARMY

Gen. H. D. G. "Harry" Crerar stares out of historical photographs a stranger to most observers. Barely remembered in his own country, he has been even more forgotten internationally. His place in history has nonetheless been assured since he commanded the first and last field army ever deployed by Canada. Like Patton's U.S. Third Army, the Allies designated the First Canadian Army as a follow-up force for the invasion of Normandy. It became operational on 23 July 1944 and fought to the end of the war on the coastal flank of Bernard Montgomery's 21st Army Group from the area of Caen up to the Weser River in Germany. Except for the period from 27 September to 7 November 1944, when Lt. Gen. Guy Simonds assumed his duties and fought the Battle of the Scheldt, Crerar directed the First Canadian Army's operations until the end of the war. Arguably, he was the most important Canadian general of the war; no one else had such a profound effect on the raising, fighting, and eventual disbanding of the greatest land force ever fielded by Canada.[1] Crerar's performance as a field army commander—while favorably assessed in terms of his uniqueness as a Canadian[2]—has been criticized from an operational perspective. His exercise of field command as Canada's highest-ranking general also contrasted sharply with British and American practice, which saw top-ranked generals such as Sir Alan Brooke and George Marshall remain at seats of government to advise political leaders.

The field command pattern followed by Crerar mirrored that of World War I, in which Canada's most senior general, Sir Arthur Currie, led the

Canadian Corps into legend. The creation of the First Canadian Army on Easter Monday, 6 April 1942, was highly symbolic, for it was on Easter Monday, 9 April 1917, that the Canadian Corps under British general Sir Julian Byng captured the heavily fortified bastion of Vimy Ridge. In the darkest year of the war, this small but spectacular Canadian victory provided a bright ray of hope. On the heights of Vimy Ridge, Canada built its greatest memorial to its 60,000 war dead.

The remarkable fighting performance of Canadian troops in World War I convinced official historian Col. C. P. Stacey that "the creation of the Canadian Corps was the greatest thing that Canada had ever done."[3] In fact, the Canadian Corps, with its larger, permanently allocated divisions, was the equivalent of a shock army within British imperial forces. Currie, the first Canadian-born commander, went on to lead the corps through the so-called Hundred Days of Victory from 8 August to 11 November 1918, cracking some of the strongest points of the German line. From the surprise attack at Amiens on 8 August 1918—"the black day of the German army"—the field forces of the British Empire, employing artillery, tanks, and aircraft in support of infantry, advanced relentlessly across sixty-two miles to break the back of the German Army on the Western Front. To an extent perhaps greater than any other fighting formation, the Canadian Corps spearheaded this last great British imperial offensive that sent the kaiser's army reeling back, to be saved from ultimate destruction only by the eleventh-hour armistice.

Crerar wanted the Canadian Army of World War II to emulate and even surpass the success of Currie's illustrious Canadian Corps.[4] Born in Hamilton, Ontario, to a well-connected family on 28 April 1888, Crerar had served in the Canadian Corps with distinction. Educated in private schools in both Canada and Switzerland—among them elite Upper Canada College—he attended the Royal Military College in Kingston, Ontario, graduating in 1909. When World War I broke out, he was a lieutenant in the non-permanent active militia. Trooping overseas in 1914 as a captain with the 3rd Brigade, Canadian Field Artillery, he saw action with the 1st Canadian Division at Ypres. In 1915, Crerar took command of a battery and, two years later, commanded the 3rd Brigade as an acting lieutenant colonel. Awarded the Distinguished Service Order in June 1917, he assumed the appointment of brigade major of the 5th Canadian Divisional Artillery after completing a staff course in England. In the course of his duties, he became a close friend of the corps' counterbattery staff officer, Lt. Col. A. G. L. "Andy" McNaughton, who would rise to become chief of the general staff after the war. In 1918, McNaughton saw to it that Crerar went to corps headquarters to understudy and later succeed British lieutenant colonel Alan Brooke, who was then staff officer, Royal Artillery, in the Canadian Corps and would become the chief of the Imperial General Staff in World War II. As staff officer, Royal Artillery, Crerar planned artillery support during the Hundred Days, and promoted to brevet lieutenant colonel, he later took over from McNaughton as counterbattery staff officer.[5]

On repatriation to Canada, Crerar opted to stay in the army's tiny permanent-force artillery as a major. Initially an artillery staff officer in Ottawa, he passed staff college preparatory examinations and entered the British Army Staff College, Camberley, in 1923. After graduation, he assumed a post as a general staff officer, grade 2, in the War Office in London, where he was placed in charge of a section dealing with home defense. Returning to Canada in 1927, Crerar served as commander of B Battery of the Royal Canadian Horse Artillery and, briefly, as a professor of tactics at the Royal Military College. When Major General McNaughton became chief of the general staff in 1929, he called Crerar to National Defence Headquarters to take on several general staff appointments dealing with army reorganization and defense planning. In 1932, Crerar served as military adviser to the Canadian delegation at the Disarmament Conference in Geneva. Two years later, he attended the Imperial Defence College in London, where he again studied under Brooke. On returning to Canada in 1935, he assumed the duties of director of military operations and intelligence in the rank of colonel and, on promotion to temporary brigadier in August 1938, took over as commandant of the Royal Military College.

Called back to Ottawa at the outbreak of war in order to put the finishing touches on the army's mobilization plans, he began to lobby superiors and politicians for overseas duty. When selected to be brigadier, general staff (BGS), at Canadian Military Headquarters in Britain, he also asked to be promoted to major general so he could deal with his British comrades on a more equal footing. Although authorities in Canada denied the request, McNaughton, who had taken the 1st Canadian Division to Britain in December 1939 and was now the senior Canadian commander overseas, considered it more favorably, and in late January 1940, Crerar was promoted to the rank of acting major general.[6]

As BGS, Crerar handled the initial organization of Canadian Military Headquarters and implemented reception arrangements for quartering and training Canadian troops in Britain. After the cataclysmic fall of France in June 1940, however, the minister of national defence, on the advice of McNaughton, decided to recall Crerar to Ottawa and appoint him chief of the general staff. The Cabinet War Committee had meanwhile authorized the formation of a Canadian Corps of three divisions. Faced with the prospect of a longer war after Dunkirk, the government further announced that a fourth division would be recruited. Passed by Parliament in June 1940, the National Resources Mobilization Act also introduced conscription for home defense, but to placate public opinion in Quebec, service overseas remained voluntary.

To his lasting credit, while others focused narrowly on home defense and looked to the United States for protection, Crerar maintained a strategic emphasis on taking the war to the enemy by supporting embattled Britain. In his view, this called for expanding the Canadian Expeditionary Force from corps to army size. On 11 August 1941, he estimated that sufficient man-power existed in Canada to field an overseas army of two corps—each with one armored and two infantry divisions—for a war period of more than six years. In the event, the Overseas Army Programme for 1941–42 called for the creation of an overseas field army headquarters to command and administer a Canadian corps of three divisions and a Canadian armored corps of two divisions. The inclusion of two additional independent army tank brigades, however, came close to meeting Crerar's original proposal. Largely because of his political and military maneuvering as chief of the general staff, Head-quarters, First Canadian Army, came into existence in April 1942, with McNaughton as its commanding general.[7]

Crerar's efforts appear all the more remarkable because the Canadian government's policy gave priority to the air force, navy, and war industry. Prime Minster William Lyon Mackenzie King personally opposed fielding a large army for fear of triggering conscription for overseas service. Possibly for reasons related to this, he also opted not to play a strategic role in the war, discouraging all proposals to form an Imperial War Cabinet and Common-wealth Committee of Prime Ministers as established during World War I. He later agreed to leave the higher strategic direction of the war to Churchill and Roosevelt through the Combined Chiefs of Staff.[8]

Canadian public opinion had nonetheless demanded the deployment of the Canadian Army overseas to serve in operations with British forces. By the end of 1943, the overseas army reached a peak strength of nearly a quarter of a million men.[9] The provision of ancillary troops posed a major problem, however, since they constituted a personnel commitment equal to the fighting elements of the 1 and 2 Canadian Corps.* With a Royal Canadian Navy of 92,000 and Royal Canadian Air Force of 215,000 battling for manpower from the same volunteer pool, the First Canadian Army was never able to operate as an entirely Canadian entity. To ensure the completion of its rear-echelon services, the British War Office contributed more than 9,000 men per division as a permanent commitment. Since the Canadian Army did not possess any heavy artillery, British regiments also had to be attached to the 1 and 2 Canadian Army Groups Royal Artillery as required.[10]

While in Ottawa fighting for the expansion of the Canadian Army overseas, Crerar continued to press for personal promotion,[11] this time to the rank of lieutenant general by virtue of his office. His unbridled ambition, alleged vanity, and manner by which he quite correctly insisted on being consulted on all matters of military policy also apparently rubbed the minister of national defence, Col. James L. Ralston, the wrong way. Indeed, on one occasion, Ralston said that he hated Crerar and despised the Canadian general staff from top to bottom, but he was sorely pressed to think of a replacement chief of the general staff.[12]

As things turned out, Crerar's ambition to command an army field formation solved the minister's problem. Before he left for Canada in July 1940, Crerar had made plain to McNaughton that he wished to command a division. On learning in late 1941 of plans to remove the commander of the 2nd Division because of age, Crerar asked and received permission from both McNaughton and Ralston to replace him. After Crerar's promotion to lieutenant general finally came through on 19 November 1941, he offered to take a reduction in rank to command the division. This did not prove necessary, however, since McNaughton—because of illness or "breakdown" brought on by nervous strain—went on sick leave between November 1941 and March 1942.[13] Since command of the 1 Canadian Corps had devolved temporarily to Maj. Gen. George R. Pearkes of the 1st Canadian Infantry Division, Crerar, on the recommendation of the departing McNaughton, passed over divisional command to take direct charge of the corps in an acting capacity. He had meanwhile turned over his duties as chief of the general staff to his friend Maj. Gen. Kenneth Stuart, whom the minister

---

* I have used Arabic numbers to denote Commonwealth corps per custom at the time.

apparently found much more to his liking.[14] As Canada's top-ranking general and national commander overseas, Crerar nonetheless continued to play a powerful and influential role at National Defence Headquarters.

From 23 December 1941, when he returned to Europe, Crerar enjoyed unbroken corps command until he took over the First Canadian Army on 20 March 1944. As commanding general of the 1 Canadian Corps, he initially came under the command of Bernard Montgomery, who was then heading Home Forces Southeastern Command. One of Crerar's first acts, taken on the advice of his good friend Brooke, was to allow Montgomery to review his corps. This produced a purge of officers with which Crerar readily concurred.[15] Unquestionably, Crerar learned a great deal from Montgomery, who approved of Crerar's handling of the 1 Canadian Corps in subsequent exercises. Crerar's performance on Exercise Spartan in March 1943 drew special praise from Brooke, who noted that he had improved his corps beyond all recognition.[16]

In marked contrast, McNaughton's poor performance as commander of the First Canadian Army on the same exercise later cost him his job. Crerar hastened his exit by more than once complaining to Brooke and others about his patron's utter inability to command a field army. Significantly, Crerar and McNaughton also differed on the deployment of the First Canadian Army. Whereas McNaughton adamantly insisted that it be kept together and fight only as a complete entity, Crerar favored getting it into action as soon as possible. Having had a hand in sending Canadian troops to Hong Kong in November 1941 and mounting the Dieppe raid in August 1942, Crerar did not oppose splitting the army.[17] The Canadian government's dispatch of the 1st Canadian Infantry Division and 1st Canadian Army Tank Brigade to Sicily in July 1943 finally settled the matter, and McNaughton relinquished command in December 1943. In the meantime, the 5th Canadian Armoured★ Division and Crerar's corps headquarters had also been sent to Italy, ostensibly to gain battle experience but reflecting, as well, Mackenzie King's growing suspicion that casualties in the projected invasion of Normandy could be heavy and might be avoided by sending troops elsewhere.[18]

Up to this point, the First Canadian Army had been designated an assault army for the invasion of France, but now, reduced to only one national corps, it was reinforced by a British corps and relegated to a follow-up role as an

---

★British spelling will be preserved in the names of British, Commonwealth, and Polish units.

Anglo–Canadian field army. Until the last two months of the war, the First Canadian Army boasted more British troops than Montgomery's Eighth Army had at Alamein in 1942.[19] By agreement, it was also to have British staff officer representation not exceeding 50 percent. Crerar officially learned in Italy that he was to command the First Canadian Army. Unfortunately, although the 1 Canadian Corps took over an active sector of the front in February 1944, he was unable to acquire any real operational experience beyond coordinating patrols.

On return to England after a month in the line, Crerar had little more battle experience than when he had left. He had nonetheless managed to upset many of the officers and men of the 1 Canadian Corps by flooding the unit with paperwork and insisting on rigorous adherence to dress regulations in a British imperial army that took perverse pride in ignoring regulation dress.[20] A perceived personal slight also caused him to clash with Guy Simonds, who had won his battlefield spurs as commander of the 1st Canadian Infantry Division and now led the 5th Canadian Armoured Division. Unhappy that the younger rising star had also sacked a Canadian brigadier without seeking his concurrence, Crerar expressed reservations to Montgomery about Simonds's suitability for higher command. He also took the extraordinary step of having his senior medical officer and a visiting army psychiatrist examine Simonds's correspondence to determine his mental competence.[21]

Crerar's complaints about Simonds failed to sway Montgomery, who retained the highest confidence in the younger Canadian, but they did sow doubts in the British general's mind about Crerar's fitness for field army command.[22] In contrast to Montgomery, who constantly strove to reduce complexity to simplicity, Crerar tended to dwell on staff detail that a higher commander might have been well advised to avoid. Methodical and precise to the point of pedantry, Crerar typically put everything on paper. C. P. Stacey described his austere and rather frigid personality as peculiarly Canadian, "grimly cold as a codfish on a slab," and one that did not endear him to his troops. Of average height at 5 feet, 8 inches, and somewhat withdrawn, Crerar cut more of a professorial than military figure in Canadian battledress uniform. Yet while Montgomery had once referred to him as an awfully nice chap, though dull and stodgy, there was an element of terror in Crerar's manner of command. Stacey personally witnessed him publicly berate his light aircraft pilot, much to the embarrassment of many observers within earshot.[23]

This certainly accorded with Maj. Gen. Harry Foster's assessment that on the surface Crerar appeared to be a gentlemanly, inoffensive sort of man, but there was an unpleasant mean streak in him.[24]

Crerar's long-established role as kingmaker in the promotion and appointment of officers to senior command positions also made him a formidable bureaucratic force in the Canadian Army at large. His heavy involvement in Canadian national administrative matters further buttressed his personal power but absorbed so much of his time that it clearly demonstrated that a field commander should not be burdened with such responsibilities. That Canadian National Defence Headquarters felt compelled to seek Crerar's approval on army matters at home and abroad was also misguided. Canada's top-ranking general should have been in Ottawa looking after national strategic interests and absolving field commanders of all concerns except fighting.[25]

As a corps commander, Crerar established a specific headquarters routine for receiving information and making decisions. At approximately 0700 hours each day, he telephoned the general staff duty officer to obtain reports of any incidents of importance during the night. Following this, he received briefings at breakfast from his BGS and deputy adjutant and quartermaster general on items to be discussed at the daily operations and administrative-quartermaster conference at 0830. After the conference, the BGS and the deputy adjutant and quartermaster general reported to him to settle any business that arose at the meeting. Conditions permitting, Crerar would then usually go forward to visit subordinate headquarters and units at locations arranged by his aide-de-camp. On returning to corps headquarters around 1600, he received further briefings from his BGS and deputy adjutant and quartermaster general on actions carried out or pending and advised them of any orders he had issued during his visits. He then dealt with paperwork until dinner around 2000. Before or after dinner as necessary, the BGS—accompanied by the general staff officer, grade 2 (intelligence), and general staff officer, grade 1 (operations)—again met with Crerar to discuss troop dispositions, intentions, and actions.

Crerar also established a drill so that no time would be lost in the preparation of appreciations leading to the development of operational plans.[26] As a first step, he gave the BGS and deputy adjutant and quartermaster general the objective he wanted to attain. The BGS thereupon collated and coordinated the appropriate information as well as the responses of various general staff officers and the deputy adjutant and quartermaster general relating to factors affecting the attainment of the objective; in the standard format of an appreciation, the BGS submitted these to Crerar. Based on the information received, Crerar then personally selected the alternative courses of action, weighing the arguments for and against each. Following this, Crerar chose the plan he believed was best suited to the attainment of the objective. Thereafter, detailed orders and instructions coordinated by the BGS were issued to everyone concerned. Prior to their issue, Crerar also endeavored to address commanders on the aim, operational objectives, and, in general, the means and methods available.[27]

Crerar adhered to an almost identical routine within the First Canadian Army headquarters, which has been described as smooth-functioning, relatively happy, and comfortable. Here, "Uncle Harry" Crerar seems to have been more popular with his senior staff than with his forward troops.[28] Comprising approximately 200 officers, the headquarters was almost entirely Canadian, with the number of British staff officers never exceeding 15 percent (let alone the authorized 50 percent ceiling). Largely self-contained, the headquarters deployed into main (operational) and rear (administrative) elements. Crerar's tactical headquarters included nine officers and eighty-nine other ranks,* but he rarely strayed far from main in the exercise of command, often preferring to fly to reduce transit time.[29]

At main, Crerar's chief of staff, Brig. C. Churchill Mann, directly supervised the staff duties, plans, and liaison sections, while Col. G. E. Beament (later BGS) headed the general staff branch comprising the operations, intelligence, and air sections. Crerar's rear headquarters—under the deputy adjutant and quartermaster general, Brig. A. E. Walford and later J. F. A. Lister—coordinated administrative and quartermaster activities.[30] Armored, artillery, engineer, signals, survey, camouflage, and chemical warfare sections attached to the general staff were also located at rear headquarters. Significantly, Mann's role as chief of staff seems to have been somewhat undercut since Crerar tended to immerse himself in the details of staff work. Beament later alleged that Crerar did not really want a chief of staff, just a good managing clerk to see that everything ran smoothly at headquarters. Crerar also

---

* In British and Commonwealth militaries, "other ranks" generally refers to those soldiers who are not commissioned officers.

relied heavily upon Lt. Col. G. F. C. Pangman, general staff officer, grade 1, for plans, whose six-officer section drew up copious appreciations for imminent and future operations to help the army commander formulate his plans. When Beament once suggested to Crerar that it was a commander's responsibility to make his own appreciation, the latter reportedly blew his top.[31]

From 12 August 1944, No. 84 Group, RAF, commanded by South Africa–born Air Vice-Marshal Leslie "Dingo" Brown, provided tactical air support for the First Canadian Army. Before this time, No. 84 Group had remained under the operational control of No. 83 Group, RAF, commanded by Air Vice-Marshal Harry Broadhurst and principally affiliated with the British Second Army. Along with No. 2 (Bomber) Group, these composite air groups of fighters and fighter-bombers made up the bulk of Air Marshal Sir Arthur "Maori" Coningham's 2nd Tactical Air Force, which had been formed to work with the 21st Army Group. Although nearly half the squadrons in No. 83 Group were Canadian, none in No. 84 Group was.[32] Out of twenty-six Spitfire, Mustang, and Typhoon attack squadrons, five were Polish, three Czech, three French, two Norwegian, one Belgian, and one New Zealand.[33] Arguably, this "united nations" composition accorded with the multinational makeup of the First Canadian Army, which regularly included a British corps, a Polish division, and at various times Belgian, Dutch, and Czech brigades.[34]

The routine collocation of No. 84 Group headquarters with that of the First Canadian Army as well as the establishment of a joint battle room further encouraged a close army-air relationship that streamlined the air support request system.[35] Decisions about sorties to be flown were made the previous evening at joint conferences between senior representatives of each service. In addition to requests for air support emanating from the various staff sections at the First Army headquarters, those originating from the field were forwarded through air support signal unit channels from visual control posts (VCPs) located near the front. The response time of the tactical air support system, fine-tuned since June 1944, could under ideal conditions be as quick as fifteen minutes.[36] Still, in Mann's view, relations between air group and army headquarters "were only on a cordial basis superficially" and deteriorated after Coningham relieved Brown in November 1944 for allegedly being too cooperative with the army. Australia-born Air Vice-Marshal Edmund Hudleston, who took over on 10 November 1944, apparently proved less cooperative, though he had extensive experience in tactical air support operations in the Mediterranean theater.[37]

Crerar's First Canadian Army did not become operational until 23 July 1944, seven weeks after D-Day and twelve days after Simonds's 2 Canadian Corps had deployed under the British Second Army. By this time, the 3rd Canadian Infantry Division Group, which included the 2nd Canadian Armoured Brigade, had been in action for forty-eight days. Having landed on D-Day as part of Lt. Gen. John T. Crocker's British 1 Corps, it had advanced farther inland than any other Allied division, attacked Carpiquet in Operation Windsor on 4 July, and participated in the capture of Caen in Operation Charnwood from 8 to 10 July. On 11 July, the 2 Canadian Corps took the 3rd Canadian Infantry Division and 2nd Canadian Armoured Brigade under its command and, with the 2nd Canadian Infantry Division and 2 Army Group Royal Artillery, launched a secondary attack code-named Atlantic on 18 July in support of Operation Goodwood, an attack delivered by the British 8 Corps. Operation Atlantic called for the 3rd Division to clear the industrial outskirts of Caen east of the Orne while the 2nd Division advanced south from Caen to seize the area of Verrières Ridge. Dogged German resistance and counterattacks brought Atlantic to a standstill, however, with the 2nd and 3rd Divisions suffering 1,149 and 386 casualties, respectively. On 25 July, the 2 Canadian Corps struck again, this time in support of Operation Cobra, a major attack delivered by the U.S. First Army. The object of the Canadian attack, Operation Spring, was to apply pressure to prevent the seven panzer divisions facing the British front from reinforcing the two panzer divisions facing the American front farther to the west.[38]

The 2 Canadian Corps did not revert to the command of the First Canadian Army until 31 July 1944, in accordance with Montgomery's plan to delay the introduction of Crerar's army. Until the British Second Army gained sufficient space to the northeast, east, and southeast of Caen, there was neither sufficient frontage nor depth for the deployment of another army. The Second Army's battle area could accommodate the 2 Canadian Corps as a fifth corps, but not all the ancillary troops that would accompany Head-quarters, First Canadian Army. Instead, Montgomery decided to bring in Crerar's headquarters and army troops after the arrival of the 2 Canadian Corps and have them take over the eastern sector of the 21st Army Group— initially with the British 1 Corps and later with the 2 Canadian Corps under command.[39] Such an arrangement ensured that Simonds commanded all Canadians in France for a period, a desirable situation since Montgomery considered Simonds far and away the best Canadian general, "the equal of any British corps commander, and . . . far better than Crerar."[40] Perhaps because of his experience with Crerar in Italy, Montgomery had lost faith in the commander of the First Canadian Army. On 7 July, he wrote to Brooke expressing "grave fears that Harry Crerar will not be too good; however, I am keeping him out of the party as long as I can." Brooke, for his part, still believed in his old friend Crerar and, more fully attuned to Dominion sensitivities, replied, "It is evident that the Canadians are very short of senior commanders, but it is equally clear that we shall have to make the best use of the material we have. . . . I want you to make the best possible use of Crerar. . . . You can keep his army small and give him the less important role."[41]

As if to reinforce Montgomery's fears, on the day after the First Canadian Army became operational, Crerar attempted to fire Crocker, his only corps commander. The dispute centered on command and tactics and revealed the nature of working relationships at the higher levels of command where disagreements between superiors and subordinates have been neither uncommon nor necessarily unhealthy.[42] Montgomery, who had been drawn into the affair by Crerar's request to remove Crocker, was forced to sort the matter out. While allowing that Crocker could be a somewhat difficult subordinate, he reproached Crerar for using formal orders rather than persuasion to harness Crocker's proven experience. A World War I veteran, Crocker had fought in France in 1940 and commanded the 6th Armoured Division and 9 Corps in North Africa. Montgomery declined to transfer Crocker, but he agreed to speak with him to straighten out the relationship. Montgomery then counseled Crerar that an army commander should give his corps commanders a task and let them decide how to carry it out. While keeping in touch, he must stand back from the detailed tactical battle—the province of his corps commanders—and intervene only if he thinks the effort is not going to succeed. To reinforce this point, Montgomery warned that in an army of only one corps—in which he might not have enough to do—the higher commander might be inclined to command that corps himself and become involved in details that are the province of his subordinates. Montgomery further suggested—no doubt in direct reference to Crerar's written instruction to Crocker—that the best results were obtained by dealing verbally with corps commanders, who could then present their views. In Montgomery's view, Crocker was a very experienced fighting commander who had to be led rather than driven.[43] This turned out to be sound advice as Crerar and Crocker later got along very well.[44]

With the Crocker dispute behind him, Crerar advised Simonds on 29 July to commence planning a thrust down the Caen-Falaise road to coincide with projected operations by the U.S. First and British Second Armies. On 4 August, Montgomery followed with a formal order for the First Canadian Army to launch a heavy attack from the Caen sector in the direction of Falaise no later than 8 August and, if at all possible, the day before. The main object of this operation, code-named Totalize, was to cut off the enemy forces facing the British Second Army as it advanced from the west.

The promise of this undertaking and especially the historic nature of the date were not lost on Crerar, who clearly envisioned it as an opportunity for Canadian arms to conduct a decisive attack similar to that delivered by the Canadian Corps at Amiens in 1918. On 5 August, in an address to senior officers that suggested that the potentially decisive period of the war had been reached, Crerar stressed his firm conviction that "a highly successful, large-scale operation, now carried out by one of the Armies of the Allied Expeditionary Force, favourably placed for that purpose, will result in the crushing conviction to Germans, even of the S.S. variety, that general defeat of the German Armies on all fronts has become an inescapable fact." Expecting a quick termination of the war to follow, Crerar entertained high hopes that the results of Totalize would be historically decisive. He expressed little doubt that the First Canadian Army could make 8 August 1944—the anniversary of the decisive Battle of Amiens—an even blacker day for the Germans than that same date twenty-six years before.[45]

Crerar later claimed that he established the basic plan for Totalize and that the tactics adopted for it were based on an earlier directive he had issued.[46] He did, however, credit two innovations to Simonds: the night employment of strategic bombers on targets close to friendly troops on each flank of the attacking front and the use of improvised infantry armored personnel carriers. Crerar stressed that if 8 August 1944 were to become another historic date, all ranks had to firmly grasp the vital importance of maintaining the momentum of the attack. He went on to underscore the importance of keeping the initiative, condemning the general tendency to consider objectives on the ground an end rather than a means of killing the enemy. He further cautioned that on reaching an objective, everyone must swiftly prepare for a quick but determined small-scale tank-infantry counterattack by the Germans. Warning that to surrender to German SS troops was to invite death, Crerar exhorted the infantry to drive on using their own weapons in the absence of "laid on" support. He criticized the far-too-prevalent attitude that without a colossal scale of artillery or air support, continued advance of the infantry was impossible.[47] Despite such exhortations, however, Crerar gave quite another impression to Montgomery, who commented that the desperately anxious Crerar, worried about fighting his first battle at the head of the first Canadian field army, had "gained the idea that all you want is a good initial fire plan, and then the Germans all run away!"[48]

The developing operational situation gave credence to Crerar's assessment that a golden opportunity lay before the First Canadian Army. Following the successful breakout of the U.S. First Army from St. Lô on 27 July, the German Seventh Army on 6 August launched a major five-division counterattack toward Mortain in order to stem the rapidly accelerating American advance through Avranches. A subsequent Canadian advance to the area of Falaise would thus have caught the Germans in full stride as they struck west, rupturing the right rear flank of the Seventh Army and sealing off its main body around Mortain. In any case, Totalize forced enemy logistical elements to withdraw southward, which deprived the Seventh Army of its rear installations and necessitated resupply to be provided by the Fifth Panzer Army. The commander in chief in the west, Field Marshal Günther von Kluge, also quickly grasped that his Seventh Army risked being cut off at the base by Totalize. On 8 August, he remarked that a breakthrough had occurred near Caen the like of which he had never seen.[49] For these reasons as well as the tantalizing prospect of what might have been, this particular operation is likely to continue to attract the attention of Canadians.

Despite Crerar's claim to basic authorship of Totalize, however, the weight of evidence indicates that it was largely the brainchild of Simonds. In response to Crerar's direction of 30 July, Simonds produced a remarkable written appreciation and outline plan for mounting an armored night attack in the wake of strikes by strategic bombers during darkness, using armored personnel carriers to transport infantry.[50] Much has been written on Totalize, often in excruciating antiquarian detail, but only its most salient aspects need be discussed here. The plan ultimately submitted to Crerar by Simonds called for a corps attack by three infantry and two armored divisions; two armored brigades; two complete Army Groups Royal Artillery plus the support of two more; a searchlight battery for movement lighting in the event of low cloud cover; four squadrons of special armor with flail tanks, engineer assault vehicles, and flamethrowing Crocodiles; and the whole of the available air effort.

Noting that the enemy front was manned by the 1st SS Panzer Division on the right and the 9th SS Panzer on the left, each disposed with one infantry regiment back and one forward with all tanks and self-propelled guns in support, Simonds expected very heavy fighting. The presence of the 12th SS Panzer Division in close reserve also meant that a counterattack was likely on the eastern flank. Simonds thus envisioned one "break in" phase to penetrate the foremost defensive zone along May-sur-Orne–Tilly-la-Campagne–La Hogue and a second to pierce the partially prepared position to the rear along Hautmesnil–St. Sylvain. Given the open nature of the ground—ideally suited to German long-range antitank weaponry—he deduced that the defense would be most handicapped by bad visibility, smoke, fog, or darkness when the advantage of long range was minimized.[51]

The first phase called for a night attack on the Fontenay-le-Marmion–La Hogue position by two infantry divisions in armored personnel carriers, each supported by an armored brigade, under the cover of a rolling barrage. The task of the 2nd Canadian Infantry Division, committed west of the Caen-Falaise road with the 2nd Canadian Armoured Brigade under its command, was to secure the line Caillouet-Gaumesnil and ensure the "mopping up" of St. Andre, May-sur-Orne, Fontenay-le-Marmion, and Rocquancourt. East of the road, the 51st (Highland) Division, with the 33rd British Armoured Brigade under its command, was to capture the areas of Lourguichon Wood, Garcelles-Secqueville, Cramesnil, St. Aignan de Cramesnil, and Secqueville-la-Campagne. There was to be no preliminary artillery bombardment during the first phase, though commencing at H-Hour, RAF Lancaster bombers were to obliterate the areas of May-sur-Orne, Fontenay-le-Marmion, and La Hogue–Secqueville.

The second phase, expected to commence after noon the following day with a massive air strike, called for the 4th Canadian Armoured Division to dash southward along the Caen-Falaise road to seize Point 206 between Fontaine-le-Pin and Potigny. Simultaneously, the 1st Polish Armoured Division was to pass through the 51st Division and advance directly east of the Caen-Falaise road to take Point 159 overlooking and dominating Falaise. Each armored division was to have one medium artillery regiment under its command and the support of medium bombers and fighter-bombers to deal with possible threats from the 12th SS Panzer Division. To enable them to blast their way forward, two Army Groups Royal Artillery, each with five medium regiments, were also made available, one to each division. This phase was to be heavily supported by fighter-bombers, medium bombers, and American B-17 heavy bombers.

While the 2nd Canadian Infantry and 51st (Highland) Divisions secured the right and left flanks around Bretteville-sur-Laize and Cavicourt, respectively, the 3rd Canadian Infantry Division was to remain in reserve north of Caen, prepared to move on Simonds's order to take over the areas of Hautmesnil, Bretteville-le-Rabet, and Point 140 east of the Caen-Falaise road. New intelligence that the powerful 1st SS Panzer Division had been relieved by the 89th Infantry Division and fallen back to the second German defensive line (in fact, it had left to participate in the Mortain offensive) served to accentuate the importance of carrying out bomber strikes before launching the ground attack in phase two.[52]

Crerar's role in all of this, while touching on intelligence, artillery, and logistical matters, centered heavily on arranging air support since it was the one area in Totalize planning that remained the sole prerogative of the First Canadian Army. In the event, two VCPs coordinated close air support for the 2 Canadian Corps. Because strategic bombing support had to be requested through No. 83 Group and the Allied Expeditionary Air Force headed by Air Chief Marshal Sir Trafford Leigh-Mallory, making the case for the tactical employment of strategic bombers—which many top airmen considered a misuse of air power—required considerable effort.[53] Crerar's chief of staff had to spend two days in England presenting the arguments.[54]

Heavy bomber strikes in darkness raised concerns about troop safety and initially left the commander in chief of Bomber Command, Air Chief Marshal Sir Arthur Harris, cool to the idea. He would agree to carry out the task only if his "master bombers" were satisfied that red- and green-colored concentrations fired by 25-pounders could be clearly identified in the dark. It took a trial on the night of 6 August to confirm that targets indicated by colored marker shells could be satisfactorily identified at night. H-Hour for the commencement of the first phase of Totalize would thus remain 2300 hours on 7 August, from which time both flanks of the 2 Corps armored-infantry thrusts would be protected by heavy bombing. Air support for the second phase, now estimated to start at 1400 hours on 8 August, was more comprehensive and, because of a last-minute change, became largely the responsibility of the U.S. Eighth Air Force, with coordination to be effected through No. 83 Group. The overall effect of entrenching air support timings meant, of course, that all land force movement would be contingent on bomber strikes.[55]

In the heat and dust of 7 August, Simonds's maneuver elements formed up in concentrated columns of tanks, special armor, and armored personnel carriers. An armored and infantry brigade constituted the main assaulting force in both the 2nd and 51st Divisions. After dark, all columns rolled closer to the start line, and at 2300 hours, 1,020 Lancaster and Halifax bombers commenced to drop a total of 3,462 tons of bombs on flank targets identified by red artillery marker shells in the east and green in the west. At 2330 hours, both divisions crossed the start line in their respective formations. Fifteen minutes later, a rolling barrage began, fired by 360 guns in nine field and nine medium regiments, advancing 100 yards a minute in 200-yard lifts to a depth of 6,000 yards. Altogether, 720 guns, each with up to 650 rounds, supported the attack. To assist the columns in keeping direction, a Bofors tracer barrage coordinated by corps was fired over divisional thrust lines. Artificial moonlight and wireless radio directional beams, two per divisional front, were also employed. Although the movement of the armored columns by night proved a harrowing experience despite all navigational aides, it nonetheless worked brilliantly, and within hours, chaos produced success.

The rapid advance of the 51st (Highland) Division took it past Tilly to secure Lorguichon by 0445 hours, Garcelles-Secqueville by 0530, and Cramesnil by 0730. With the exception of Tilly, which, though bypassed, held out until 1200 hours, the division had seized all of its first-phase objectives, including St. Aignan-de-Cramesnil, and was ready for the 1st Polish Armoured Division to pass through. Similar success attended the 2nd Division's attack, which rolled around Rocquancourt southward into the debussing area between Cramesnil and Caillouet. By 0600 hours, leading elements of the 2nd and 51st Divisions were fighting in the vicinities of their first objectives and had nearly cleared them.[56] While mopping-up operations against rearward enemy pockets continued, the first phase of Totalize was successfully completed for the relatively light total of 380 casualties. Though many did not know it, the road to Falaise also lay open.[57]

The first phase of Totalize had also been a resounding success in terms of timing, and Crerar rushed forward to offer congratulations.[58] Simonds's decision to pause for six hours before the initiation of the second phase, however, guaranteed the loss of momentum that Crerar had specifically sought to avoid. Indeed, the pause invited the Germans to mount the counterattacks that Simonds had feared and hoped to avert by striking deep into the German defenses in phase one. The commanders of the 4th Canadian and 1st Polish

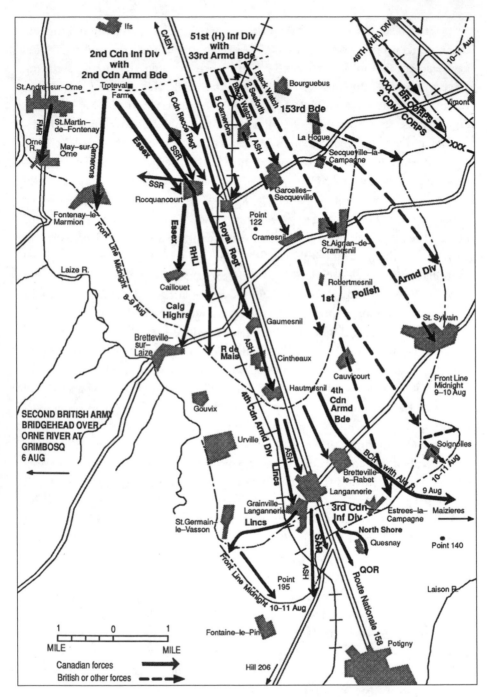

Operation Totalize, 7–10 August 1944

Armoured Divisions had also warned him of the potential danger of such a long pause between phases. Simonds, under the erroneous perception that the formidable 1st SS now defended the second German defensive zone, nonetheless insisted that the armored divisions await the support of heavy bombers. He apparently did not want a repeat of Atlantic, during which he had decided to exploit a successful advance by launching a follow-up offensive against seemingly light German opposition only to receive a bloody nose from the counterattacking 1st SS. Similarly vicious German reactions during Spring likely reinforced his decision to pause. Yet as Crerar so correctly pointed out, losing the momentum of the attack was something that should have been avoided at all costs—especially when in this case, the loss was self-imposed and not forced by enemy.[59] Waiting for the second bomber strike guaranteed a loss of momentum. The limitation on forward reconnaissance imposed by the bomb line further highlighted the wisdom of Simonds's earlier admonition that there was nothing more dangerous than to sit down in front of the Germans and not know what they were up to.[60]

The best time to have launched a second attack upon the Germans was when they were reeling and disorganized, unable to recover immediately because of severe disruption. This opportunity presented itself on the morning of 8 August, when the shattered German defense was in turmoil, but it was a fleeting moment that should have been seized by continuing to press the attack. The inescapable fact remains that the momentum of the first-phase attack, which exceeded expectations, could have been maintained only by keeping up the pressure in phase two. Every passing minute allowed the Germans time to catch their breath and regroup. That neither Simonds nor Crerar actually knew that the route to Falaise lay open was of less consequence than recognizing the historical reality that breakthroughs have not always been easily discernible.

Vague and imprecise information about the enemy should never preclude fighting for information or quick and aggressive action by reserves. In Operation Cobra, for example, the U.S. VII Corps commander, Maj. Gen. J. Lawton Collins, ordered one division to pass through another despite the risk of congestion and generally chaotic conditions. His later decision to commit the 3rd Armored Division was even based on bad information. Yet his unleashing of exploiting forces before breakthrough elements had secured their immediate objectives turned out to be one of the vital decisions of the Cobra operation.[61]

Maintaining similar momentum in Totalize would have necessitated either moving the bomb line and launching air strikes farther south—an almost impossible task given coordination and time constraints—or canceling the bombing attack altogether to enable the armored divisions to strike directly toward their assigned objectives.[62] Although target timings had been confirmed with the U.S. Eighth Air Force, canceling the bombing should have been no more difficult than it was around 1330 hours when Simonds personally called Crerar to stop all bombing since it was also falling on friendly forces.[63] Had the armored divisions attacked mid-morning rather than in the afternoon, they would have encountered far less coordinated resistance and beaten serious German counterattacks to the punch.

Clausewitz, in his often overlooked but still perceptive analysis, had a great deal to say about the consequences of waiting. Waiting was not just the main characteristic of defense, but its chief advantage, the very method by which defense approaches its goal. Time permitted to pass unused naturally accumulates to the credit of the defender. Any omission on the part of an attacker, whether from poor judgment, fear, or neglect, tends moreover to accrue to the benefit of the defender in the sense that he "reaps what he did not sow."[64] Nowhere was this better illustrated than in Totalize, when German countermoves escalated to serious counterattacks north of the bomb line between 1230 and 1340 hours. Although these ripostes, centered on St. Aignan-de-Cramesnil, were beaten back, they served as spoiling attacks that shook Canadian confidence and morale. The German forces so engaged also fell back on cohesive defensive positions along the general line Gouvix–Hautmesnil–St. Sylvain, which had meanwhile been better prepared by rearward German troops frantically digging in and coordinating defensive arcs of fire. Plans to strengthen the German defense had also been set in motion with the reassignment of the 12th SS Panzer Division's *Kampfgruppe Wünsche* from the area of Grimbosq, where it had been fighting the British Second Army, to the heights west and northwest of Potigny and the narrow passage between the Laison and Laize Rivers.

When Simonds's armored divisions finally attacked at 1355 after bomber strikes between 1226 and 1355 (roughly the period of German counterattacks north of the bomb line), they got nowhere. Within an hour, the Poles lost forty tanks to enemy antitank and tank fire, and by 1600, their advance stalled completely with a paltry gain of not quite a mile and a quarter. The 4th Canadian Armoured Division did not fare much better, barely getting to

Hautmesnil for an advance of just under two and a half miles.[65] On the basis of the evidence on German countermoves and deployments, it is hard to imagine that Canadian arms could have done any worse had they opted to cancel the bombing and attack earlier. By maintaining the momentum of the attack, they would at least have stood a chance of forcing the situation to develop to their advantage, rather than waiting to let it develop to the advantage of the defenders.

Excuses have been made for the lackluster performance of Simonds's armored divisions during the second phase of Totalize. Inexperience has arguably topped the list,[66] though much has also been made of the road congestion and enemy fire from pockets of resistance that reportedly held up the forward deployment of divisional artilleries integral to attacking armored divisions. The realization that the attack was not to go in until about 1400 hours, after heavy bombing strikes, did not induce any sense of urgency that may have goaded these divisional artilleries into more aggressive forward movement. That gunners expected predesignated gun positions to be perfectly sanitized and clear of all enemy mortar and machine-gun fire was also unreasonable in the circumstances. Artillery incurred only 8 percent of casualties, as compared to the infantry's 76 percent, and should have been forced to accept greater risks and clearance tasks in gun position areas.[67] As for congested road movement, it could have been greatly diminished by restricting the forward movement of the rear and administrative echelons of first-phase assault divisions and giving priority to the forward movement of the attacking armored divisions in the second phase. Had the strike been waived and high command attention turned to the staff problem of getting fighting troops and supporting artillery forward, the tempo could have been sustained. The roughly six-hour wait for the commencement of phase two, however, contributed to the tendency of the first-phase assault divisions to tidy up the battlefield and bring their rear echelons forward, increasing congestion. The armored divisions had meanwhile been standing by on notice to move and, given the relatively short distances involved, should have been able to get their fighting echelons forward before the congestion increased.[68] Again, all of this would have required a greater degree of urgency and staff attention that could have been ordered in the circumstances.

The supreme irony is that the bombing was hardly worth the wait since it proved largely ineffective and partly counterproductive. Because of enemy antiaircraft fire and heavy clouds of dust and smoke, only 70 percent of the

U.S. Eighth Air Force's bombers managed to attack, and only three of four targeted areas were adequately bombed. Moreover, of the 492 bombers that attacked, two 12-plane groups mistakenly bombed elements of the 2nd Canadian Armoured Brigade, 2 Canadian Army Group Royal Artillery, 9 Army Group Royal Artillery, and the 1st Polish and 3rd Canadian Divisions, killing 65 soldiers and wounding another 250.[69]

Although this friendly fire did not prevent the 1st Polish Armoured and 4th Canadian Armoured Divisions from crossing the start line for the attack on time, the American bombing had not fatally crippled the now-recovered German defenses. Contrary to popular belief, the bulk of roughly eighty 88-millimeter antitank guns—most of them belonging to three Luftwaffe flak regiments—were deployed south of Potigny; only the divisional batteries were forward. It was thus mainly the 12th SS Panzer Division's resourceful handling of its tanks that stemmed the 2 Canadian Corps' attack.[70]

The additional irony was that at 1830, Simonds attempted to regain the momentum lost during the pause by directing the 4th Armoured to press on through the night to secure Bretteville-le-Rabet and Point 195, the highest feature before Falaise. Although this ended in disaster for the Worthington Force battle group (named for the commander of the 28th Canadian Armoured Regiment, which was accompanied by three companies from the Algonquin Regiment) sent to secure Point 195, it also demonstrated just what might have been accomplished by an aggressively handled armored force headed in the right direction. Setting out at 0200 on 9 August, Worthington Force drove deep into German territory and, five hours later, arrived not on Point 195 but, because of a nighttime map-reading error, roughly four miles to the east on Point 140, where it was annihilated. Had the force been unleashed in daylight at 1100 hours on 8 August, it might well have been on Point 195 by 1600 hours or even earlier.[71]

To argue that Totalize had to turn out as it did is tantamount to accepting the inevitability of history. Crerar was the only one who could have overruled Simonds, and had he been a more experienced field army commander, perhaps he would have done so, opting to hit the enemy immediately to ascertain his true strength while seeking to shape a more favorable development of the situation. That Simonds should have been overruled is reasonably clear, but it would have taken a field army commander with the requisite *Fingerspitzengefühl,* or fingertip feel, to do it. Crerar was certainly aware of the adverse implications of the loss of momentum in an attack, but he obviously did not think that he could do much to influence matters.[72] Simonds did not therefore receive the counseling or prodding that might have been expected from a field army commander.

Having expended so much effort in arranging strategic bomber support, the one area of Totalize planning that was solely the prerogative of the First Canadian Army headquarters, Crerar may also have been reluctant to request a cancellation for fear of jeopardizing future support from "Bomber" Harris, with whom he had developed a cozy relationship.[73] His recent dispute with Crocker may additionally have disposed him to refrain from interfering in corps operations. As he later remarked, under normal conditions, he as army commander would not give a direct order to a division or tell Simonds which troops should be employed to carry out assigned tasks, though "he might suggest that, say, the P.A.D. [Polish Armoured Division] seemed to be well placed to do the job."[74] The result was that Crerar gave loose rein to his corps commanders. Yet the essence of Montgomery's counsel centered on when a field army commander should and should not interfere in corps operations.

Arguably, Crerar could have directed Simonds to smash straight through immediately or outflank the Germans from the west via Claire Tizon, as was eventually done by the 2nd Division. According to the former operations officer of the 12th SS, Hubert Meyer, it may also have been wiser to send the reserve 3rd Division to outflank the Germans to the east. Crerar instead blamed the Poles, charging that the 4th Armoured Division's advance had been checked by the "dog fight" that developed between the 1st Polish Armoured Division and German elements in Quesnay Wood. Had the Poles contained the enemy there and pushed on with the bulk of their strength, they would have widened the front and increased the depth for a tactically decisive advance. As it was, when dark came, they had advanced less than a few hundred yards south of the start line.[75]

The failure of Totalize necessitated mounting another corps attack, Operation Tractable, which under cover of smoke rather than darkness thundered down the Caen-Falaise road in daylight. This time, Crerar ensured that he would be unable to influence the battle by opting to fly back and forth along the west side of the Caen-Falaise road, attempting to "escort" heavy bombers and prevent them from bombing short as occurred in Totalize. As Tractable dismally disappointed in this respect[76] and also failed to meet operational expectations, the initiative that had momentarily resided with the

Canadian Army passed into other hands. It now reacted to higher direction in an increasingly fluid situation as four Allied armies converged upon the Falaise Gap. The withdrawal of German forces through the gap reached full flood on 18 August, the day Falaise finally fell to a right hook by the 2nd Canadian Division from the area of Clair Tizon.

Following the closure of the gap itself on 21 August, the First Canadian Army raced toward the Seine in concert with its sister Allied formations.[77] While Crocker's northernmost British 1 Corps drove on Honfleur and the Seine north of Rouen, Simonds's 2 Canadian Corps advanced through Bernay toward Elbeuf and the Foret de la Londe southwest of Rouen. On 26 August, the Canadians made their first crossing at Elbeuf, establishing contact with U.S. First Army forces who were already there. In the Foret de la Londe, however, the considerably understrength 2nd Canadian Infantry Division battled stiff German rearguard resistance for three days. The 2nd had suffered exceptionally heavy losses in Normandy and was still deficient by 1,910 other ranks despite receiving numerous reinforcements. The shortage lay mainly in trained infantrymen, but this did not stop the division's commander from throwing in battalion after battalion. By the end of the fighting in the Foret de la Londe, the South Saskatchewan Regiment's four rifle companies mustered only sixty men. The British 1 Corps had meanwhile closed up to the Seine and, on crossing at Caudebec-Caux and Duclair, found that the enemy had withdrawn. By 30 August, the 3rd Infantry and 4th Armoured Divisions of the 2 Canadian Corps had pushed north and east out of the Elbeuf bridgehead, enabling the 9th Canadian Infantry Brigade to take Rouen from the east.

On the same day, Crerar issued a new directive to his corps commanders, giving the 2 Canadian Corps the immediate task of capturing Dieppe while advancing along the main army axis running through Neufchatel to Abbeville on the Somme River. This was in keeping with Montgomery's order of 26 August that listed the tasks of the 21st Army Group as follows: operate northward and destroy enemy forces in northeast France and Belgium, secure the Pas de Calais area and airfields in Belgium, and secure Antwerp as a base with the eventual aim of advancing on the Ruhr. The order also directed Dempsey's British Second Army to cross the Seine with all speed and drive through the industrial region of northeast France into Belgium. The tasks given to Crerar's First Canadian Army were to secure the ports of Le Havre and Dieppe and quickly destroy all enemy forces in the coastal belt up to

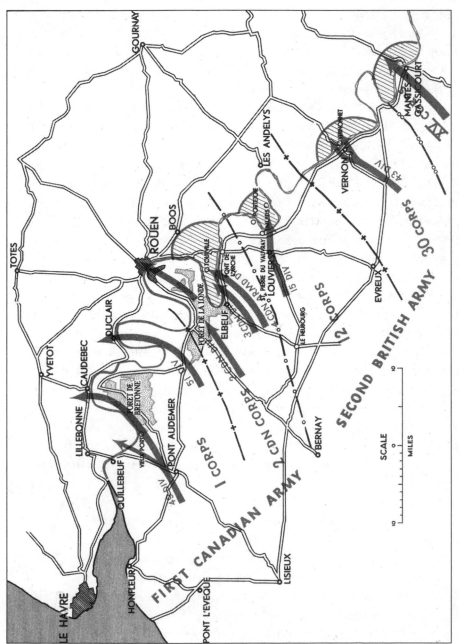

The 21st Army Group's Crossing of the Seine

Bruges. Accordingly, on the morning of 31 August, the 2 Canadian Corps commenced a pursuit through the zone of German flying bomb launch sites from Rouen to the Pas de Calais while the British 1 Corps turned north to envelop Le Havre. Crerar's headquarters followed along the main army axis, collocating with the headquarters of No. 84 Group, RAF, from 2 September until the end of the campaign in Europe.[78]

Since British Second Army elements had already reached Amiens by the morning of 31 August and were reportedly advancing downriver on Pont Remy and Abbeville in the 2 Canadian Corps' sector, Montgomery directed Crerar to relieve British forces in these locations the next day so that the Second Army would be free to push on to Arras and St. Pol. Within the 2 Canadian Corps, the 4th Armoured Division, which had been slated for four days' refit, spearheaded this movement, and despite colliding with the British, it reached the outskirts of Abbeville early on 2 September.

The 2nd Canadian Infantry Division had meanwhile been deliberately earmarked to capture Dieppe, where it had incurred especially heavy losses in a raid on 19 August 1942. This was accomplished without opposition on 1 September, and the following day, the 51st (Highland) Division, in a similarly symbolic action, took St. Valery–Caux, where the division's main body had been surrounded and forced to surrender in June 1940. On learning that the 4th Armoured Division was to refit east of Abbeville and the 2nd Division in the Dieppe area, however, Montgomery signalled that with the Second Army nearing the Belgian frontier, this was not the time to stop for maintenance. As this was a pursuit, he urged Crerar to push his two armored divisions, the 1st Polish and 4th Canadian, forward with all speed to St. Omer and beyond. Failing to note that Montgomery referred mainly to armored divisions, Crerar testily replied that reinforcement was essential for the 2nd Division and that there was no lack of push or rational speed on the part of his army. He had also planned to go to Dieppe to attend a remembrance parade in honor of the Canadian dead of the 1942 raid.[79]

If the capture of Dieppe was nationally important to Crerar, it was also logistically important to the Allied effort. From 7 September, the First Canadian Army received 60 percent of the tonnage offloaded at the port, which eliminated serious Canadian supply problems by mid-September.[80] This accorded with Overlord plans that originally reserved the Channel ports for the British and Canadians. The exception was Le Havre, which was later earmarked for the Americans—whose far more serious supply problems ulti-

mately determined the employment of First Canadian Army.[81] Much responsibility for this lay with Eisenhower and SHAEF, which in the hope of capturing Channel ports—and even Rotterdam and Amsterdam—decided on 3
September to abandon plans to use the Brittany ports of Lorient, Quiberon
Bay, St. Nazaire, and Nantes. On 14 September, a similar decision was made
regarding Brest; the Germans had surrendered the port, like Cherbourg, in a
thoroughly demolished state that from a planning perspective could only have
been expected in the case of Antwerp.[82] The rapid capture of Antwerp by
Dempsey's Second Army on 4 September had caught the Germans completely off guard, with the result that the dock facilities of Europe's second
largest port were left entirely intact. Unfortunately, the continued presence of
German forces in the heavily dyked "polder" country (reclaimed land below
sea level) of Walcheren, Beveland, and the west bank of the Scheldt from
Knocke-sur-Mer to Terneuzen rendered Antwerp inaccessible from the sea
and hence limited its logistical value to the Allies. Montgomery's fixation
with the Ruhr and his desire to establish a bridgehead over the Rhine before
winter further complicated the opening of the port. With the German Army
reeling all along the Allied front in early September, his preferred choice was
to thrust immediately into the German heartland rather than risk being be
drawn into a potentially protracted struggle on a flank.

The result was Operation Market Garden, which Eisenhower enthusiastically approved, specifically authorizing Montgomery to defer the clearance of
the Scheldt. Given the green light, Montgomery signaled Crerar on 6 September that he needed Boulogne for the rapid development of his plan, since
Antwerp seemed to be unusable for some time since the mouth of the
Scheldt remained in German hands. By 9 September, he had also calculated
that it would be possible to advance to Berlin on the basis of supplies arriving
at Dieppe, Boulogne, Dunkirk, and Calais, supplemented by 3,000 tons of
cargo per day through Le Havre. He further estimated that with one good Pas
de Calais port, an extra 1,000 tons of airlift per day, and an additional allotment of motor transport, it would be possible to reach the Rheine-Münster-
Osnabrück area.

The tasks assigned to the First Canadian Army on the ninth thus gave first
priority to the capture of the Channel ports and placed secondary emphasis
on the destruction of the enemy east of the Ghent Canal. On 12 September,
however, the Combined Chiefs of Staff telegraphed their concern about
Antwerp to Eisenhower, and Montgomery received a message from Brooke

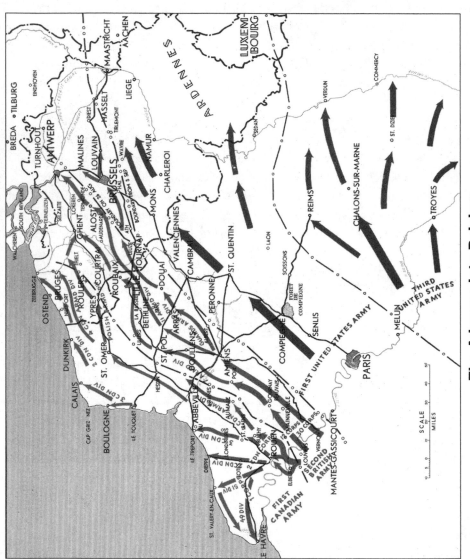

The Advance into Belgium

stating that he considered the early opening of Antwerp and clearance of the Scheldt likely to be of great importance.[83] That morning, Montgomery signaled Crerar that the early opening of Antwerp was daily becoming increasingly important and requested his views on how he would go about tackling such an operation. The next day, Montgomery advised the Canadian general that while the capture of Boulogne, Dunkirk, and Calais remained desirable, operations to open Antwerp were probably more important. As a helpful hint, Montgomery further suggested that to ensure maximum concurrent activity, Crerar should use one of his corps headquarters to control operations from Boulogne to Dunkirk and the other to plan and execute the opening of Antwerp. In a supplementary message the same evening, Montgomery added that the early use of Antwerp was so urgent that he was prepared to give up operations against Calais and Dunkirk and settle for Boulogne. He also asked, "If we do this, will it enable you to speed up the Antwerp business?"[84]

Crerar at first offered only tentative comments, explaining that his staff had not had adequate opportunity to analyze and present to him the various issues involved. He also asked for more resources, specifically the temporary transfer of the British 12 Corps currently in the Antwerp area. Alternatively, he suggested that his British 1 Corps take over the 53rd (Welsh) Division from the 12 Corps and assume responsibility for the city of Antwerp. The development of operations along the Breda-Tilburg axis would then become a Canadian Army responsibility.[85] Why Crerar proposed the latter role for the 1 Corps, instead of following Montgomery's advice and designating it to control operations from Boulogne to Dunkirk while using Simonds's 2 Corps headquarters for the opening of Antwerp, is not entirely clear and may have been an error on Crerar's part. Certainly, it was an opportunity to *commit* elements of the First Canadian Army that Montgomery would have had difficulty expropriating for other tasks later. In any case, special armor used in the siege of Le Havre had to be moved to support Boulogne operations. Ironically, as neither the 12 Corps nor the 53rd Division could be spared from Market Garden, Montgomery seized on Crerar's alternative suggestion and ordered him to move the British 1 Corps and its subordinate 49th (West Riding) Division, using 51st (Highland) Division transport, to relieve the 53rd Division in Antwerp as soon as possible. The 51st Division thus remained grounded without vehicles at Le Havre, which had been captured by the 1 Corps on 12 September after a brilliant two-division attack launched forty-eight hours earlier.[86]

Following further discussion with Crerar on 14 September, Montgomery issued his directive on the Arnhem operation, which also formally assigned the clearance of the Scheldt to the First Canadian Army as a top priority. The next day, Crerar forwarded his own directive to his two corps commanders, assigning the Scheldt operation to the 2 Canadian Corps. As a first step, he ordered the 2nd Canadian Infantry Division, now relieved from the task of taking Dunkirk,[87] to take over the city of Antwerp from the 53rd Division of the 12 Corps by 18 September. Crerar initially detailed two supporting missions to the British 1 Corps: first, mount a deliberate attack on Calais in the event it did not fall easily to the 2 Corps; and, second, in the event Calais did surrender quickly, take over the right front of the First Canadian Army to protect the right flank of the 2 Corps while it engaged in operations to open Antwerp. On 19 September, however, Crerar decided to make the 2 Corps exclusively responsible for the eventual reduction of Calais and, at same time, ordered the 1 Corps to take over the 12 Corps' Antwerp sector near Turnhout with a view to developing operations along the Breda-Tilburg axis. Although the reasons for this change were apparently not recorded, it is likely that given the exigencies of Market Garden, Montgomery may have taken Crerar up on his earlier suggestion that the 1 Corps assume responsibility for operations along the Breda-Tilburg axis.[88]

The effect of this directive left the four divisions of the 2 Canadian Corps stretched between Boulogne and Antwerp.[89] On 12 September, Simonds had directed the 1st Polish Armoured Division to clear the Ghent-Antwerp-Terneuzen triangle up to the West Scheldt. The 4th Canadian Armoured Division was at the same time directed to clear the area west of the Ghent-Terneuzen Canal, making its main thrust along the line Moerbrugge-Maldegem-Breskens. The 8th and 9th Infantry Brigade Groups of the 3rd Canadian Infantry Division in the meantime prepared to attack Boulogne on 17 September. The remaining brigade of the division, the 7th, supported by the 7th Reconnaissance (Tank) Regiment, continued to invest Calais and the great German cross-Channel gun batteries at Cape Gris Nez. After the reduction of Boulogne on 22 September, the 8th Brigade joined the 7th to participate in an assault upon Calais while the 9th captured Cape Gris Nez.

Following the capitulation of Calais on 1 October, Crerar expected his 2 Corps to thrust northward toward Roosendaal and Bergen op Zoom in order to establish a firm base to the east of South Beveland from which that objective could be attacked.[90] That Crerar held a protracted series of conferences to effect these actions left several commentators to observe that the clearance of the coastal belt and ports by the First Canadian Army was ponderous and slow. Two Canadian military historians have even charged that Crerar conducted operations so poorly that had he been a British rather than Canadian general, he would most likely have been sacked.[91] The sixteen days that passed between Montgomery's request of 6 September to get Boulogne and its actual capture are at particular issue. Although the German garrison defending the port city was only slightly smaller than the one defending Le Havre, Boulogne was attacked not by two divisions, but by two brigade groups at a higher cost in both time—six days—and casualties.[92] The fact that the assault on Boulogne had to be delayed until after the fall of Le Havre so that special armored fighting vehicles could be released from the 1 Corps for use by the 3rd Division also begs the question whether it would have been wiser to have had the 1 Corps execute a second forty-eight-hour operation to reduce Boulogne. This would have released the 2 Canadian Corps for operations along the Scheldt. Moreover, the final attack on Calais, which had to await the fall of Boulogne, may have been unnecessary. It may have sufficed simply to capture Cape Gris Nez and the gun emplacements west of Calais to permit the free use of Boulogne harbor, which was the only reason for seizing Calais in the first place.[93]

Crerar later defended his actions by citing the difficulties of the coastal terrain from a tactical and administrative point of view, but it is also clear, as he informed Montgomery on 13 September, that rather than risk failure at Boulogne after the rapid fall of Le Havre, he wanted Simonds "to button things up properly, taking a little more time, if necessary, in order to ensure a decisive assault."[94] Simonds, on the other hand, had supposedly protested giving priority to the Channel ports and made an earlier suggestion to Crerar that the 2 Canadian Corps instead conduct a relentless pursuit along the coast to Breskens, masking German coastal defenses, and then turn east to cut off the German Fifteenth Army from the Scheldt. To ease transport difficulties, Simonds further proposed provisioning his corps with ammunition, fuel, and bridging by beaching preloaded landing craft at designated intervals during the advance. He was also confident that had he been allowed to explain his concept to Montgomery, it would have been quickly approved.[95] Crerar, in contrast, was less inclined to analyze the intent behind orders received from Montgomery, even when requested to do so. He was also far less healthy than commonly supposed, which allegedly contributed to the impairment of his command ability and powers of decision. A chain-smoker with a persistent cough, he suffered from severe anemia brought on by recurring bouts of dysentery that left him both fatigued and irascible. During the planning stages for the Battle of the Scheldt, a final attack of dysentery that failed to respond to the usual medical treatment necessitated his evacuation to England for tests and treatment on 27 September.[96]

Before his departure, Crerar handed over command to Simonds, whose immediate impact was described as an electrifying breath of fresh air. Whereas Crerar often appeared stymied by the problems facing him and thus relied heavily upon his G (Plans) Section for suggesting operational solutions, Simonds rose to the challenge of personally thinking things through, then giving orders.[97] Even before assuming army command, he had exposed the weaknesses of that section's recommendations related to the opening of the Scheldt Estuary and endorsed by Crerar. In particular, Simonds pointed out that the aim was not simply to capture Walcheren and South Beveland, but to destroy, neutralize, or capture enemy defenses denying free passage through the Scheldt to the port of Antwerp.[98] The critical appreciation that Simonds produced himself was hailed as one of the most striking and original tactical statements of the campaign.[99] In the actual conduct of what must rank among the most arduous and unglamorous of World War II military operations, Simonds distinguished himself as a field army commander. Arguably, in his innovative use of smoke screening, in his flooding of the island of Walcheren, and in his first use of amphibians in Europe, it was his finest hour. Unfortunately for Crerar's reputation, the Battle of the Scheldt was also the most important action fought by the First Canadian Army, for without the port of Antwerp, the broad-front advance of Allied and, most acutely, American divisions into Germany could not have been logistically sustained.

On 22 October, having recovered from his illness, Crerar signaled Simonds that he would be resuming command at the end of the month. Two days later, however, Brooke requested Crerar not to return from sick leave until after Simonds had completed operations in the Scheldt. The reason given was that Montgomery did not want the disruption that would result from a change of command in the midst of a battle, but the evidence also suggests that Montgomery wanted to keep Crerar away so that his more operationally brilliant subordinate could be kept in place.[100] Official historian C. P. Stacey later commented that Lt. Gen. Charles Foulkes, who had taken command of

the 2 Canadian Corps in Simonds's place, recollected that Montgomery told
him that Crerar would not be returning to field army command.[101]

When Crerar did eventually return to First Canadian Army headquarters
on 7 November, he completed a two-day handover before actually taking
charge. On 16 November, he was also promoted to general, a rank never
before held by a Canadian Army officer in the field. By this time, the 2 Canadian Corps had relieved the British 30 Corps in the Nijmegen salient gained
by Market Garden, while the British 1 Corps held the line of the lower Maas
as far eastward as Maren. For the next three months, largely because of the
Battle of the Bulge, the First Canadian Army wintered on the Maas, enjoying
a static period in which it was not involved in any large-scale operations. This
was just as well, because at the end of the Battle of the Scheldt, all formations
of the army—its three Canadian infantry divisions in particular—were thoroughly exhausted.[102]

In the meantime, plans had been laid for the British Second Army to attack
southeast between the Maas and the Rhine, while the U.S. Ninth Army,
also under Montgomery's command, would concurrently make a northerly
converging thrust. The object of this operation, then called Valediction, was to
clear the west bank of the Rhine opposite the Ruhr. Apparently, Montgomery's suspicion of Crerar's abilities contributed to his preference for the
British Second Army to conduct the operation. Stripping the First Canadian
Army of the divisions required by this endeavor, however, would have bordered on being politically unacceptable. In the end, the Second Army, while
holding the Nijmegen salient, was unable to muster sufficient attacking forces
in the Grosbeek area and at the same time defend its long southern front
down to the interarmy boundary, and Montgomery had no option but to
assign the First Canadian Army the task of attacking out of the salient. He
also decided to reinforce Crerar massively with British troops, leaving a trun-
cated British Second Army in static positions for the first time. For his "great
winter offensive effort of the British Empire," Crerar received nearly two-
thirds of the 21st Army Group's entire resources and some 470,000 men,
including Lt. Gen. Sir Brian Horrocks's British 30 Corps of five divisions.[103]
Although Montgomery courteously left the decision to Crerar, the deployment of the 30 Corps on the First Canadian Army's right logically dictated
that it should conduct the offensive. This was duly announced on 7 Decem-

ber during a conference at First Canadian Army headquarters at which the code name Valediction was now changed to Veritable.[104]

Detailed planning for Veritable followed, with a target date of 1 January or as soon thereafter as conditions permitted. As planned, the operation called for the British 1 Corps to deceive the enemy by feigning a northern attack to liberate Holland. The British 30 Corps would initiate the main attack in the opposite direction on a narrow front which the 2 Canadian Corps would subsequently widen with an attack on the left.[105] Possibly because of Simonds's observation that it would be a shame if no Canadian troops participated in the opening stages of this critical battle that was expected to end the war, the 3rd Canadian Infantry Division was placed under the 30 Corps for the main attack. Most likely, Simonds would also have preferred to see his own corps, rather than a British one, play the leading role in Veritable. Indeed, the tacit assumption since the 2 Canadian Corps relieved the British 30 Corps in the Nijmegen salient was that the Canadian corps would undertake the operation. In October, the 30 Corps had outlined a plan, called Wyvern, for just this eventuality and gave it to the Canadians when the 2 Canadian Corps relieved the 30 Corps.

When Montgomery issued what was expected to be his final directive on Veritable on 16 December, however, the U.S. First Army received the full shock of the German offensive that opened the Battle of the Bulge, which postponed Operation Veritable for five weeks. On 19 December, Montgomery instructed Crerar to release the British 30 Corps to the British Second Army so that it could shore up the 21st Army Group's right flank by moving to the area of Hasselt, fifteen miles west of the Meuse. The First Canadian Army's most important responsibility now became the defense and consolidation of the Nijmegen salient. Montgomery indicated that he wished to see Veritable proceed with speed as soon as the situation allowed.[106]

Planning for Veritable thus continued throughout the Battle of the Bulge and intensified with the return of the British 30 Corps on 18 January. Three days later, Montgomery issued a directive expressing his intention to destroy all Germans in the area west of the Rhine between Nijmegen and Julich–Düsseldorf. His plan still called for converging attacks by the First Canadian and U.S. Ninth Armies, but the latter's slow buildup and the threat of the Germans unleashing Roer dam waters prevented the Americans from attacking concurrently. With the target date for Veritable set for 8 February, Montgomery could only urge William Simpson, commander of the Ninth Army,

to make every effort to launch his attack, code-named Grenade, by the fifteenth of the month.

Crerar, in turn, issued his own directive to the 2 Canadian and British 1
and 30 Corps on 25 January. In it, he advocated the technique used at Amiens
in 1918, stressing the need to achieve surprise by eliminating prolonged preliminary bombardment and substituting overwhelming air and ground fire as
the operation commenced or was about to commence. As in Totalize, he also
emphasized keeping the initiative and maintaining the momentum of the
attack by "driving on, and through, the enemy *without let-up*" (emphasis
added). The disposition of enemy defenses in three zones in depth and an initial seven-mile attack frontage that widened to roughly twenty at the final
objective line, Xanten-Geldern, led Crerar to break the operation into three
distinct phases. Specifically, phase 1 called for the 30 Corps to clear the
Reichswald and secure the line Gennep-Asperden-Cleve, after which the
battle would be developed on a two-corps front with the 2 Canadian Corps
operating between the Rhine, including the Cleve-Xanten road. The tasks of
both corps in phase 2 were then to breach the enemy's second defensive system east and southeast of the Reichswald and secure the Weeze-Udem-
Calcar-Emmerich line and the routes between these locations. Finally, in
phase 3, they were to break through the Hochwald "lay-back" defensive lines
and advance to secure the general line Xanten-Geldern.[107] Meanwhile, the
British 1 Corps would conduct a feint attack into Holland.

For the execution of phase 1, the British 30 Corps had been built up to
more than 300,000 troops comprising seven divisions, three independent
armored brigades, eleven regiments of the British 79th Division brigaded,
and five Army Groups Royal Artillery. Faced with three strong German
defense lines and no room for maneuver against them, Horrocks decided that
he had no alternative but to blast his way through. Since the Germans had
flooded the ground on his left flank and continued to dominate the Mook-
Goch road on his right from the Reichswald, the only promising axis of
advance lay north of the forest along the road through Kranenburg, lapped
by the southern edge of the flooded plain. Hoping for favorable going over
frozen ground, Horrocks aimed to break through the Materborn gap
between the Reichswald and Cleve before it could be closed by German
reserves. The corps plan accordingly called for three phases, with the initial
attack to be delivered on the seven-mile front between the Maas and the
Waal by five tank-reinforced infantry divisions: from right to left, the 51st

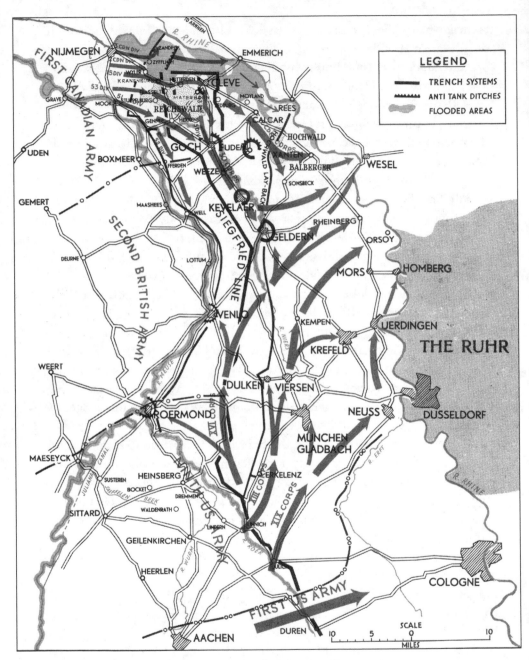

Operations Veritable and Grenade

(Highland), the 53rd (Welsh), the 15th (Scottish), and the 2nd and 3rd Canadian. The first four divisions were to attack simultaneously at 1030 hours and the 3rd Canadian at 1800 hours that evening. After the 15th (Scottish) Division had secured the Materborn feature, Horrocks intended in phase 2 to send the 43rd (Wessex) and Guards Armoured Divisions from corps reserve through the gap to debouch into the open country south of Cleve, with the 43rd driving on Goch and the Guards Armoured on Udem. In phase 3, Walbeck, Geldern, Issum, and Bonning were to be taken.[108]

Since the decision had been made for Veritable to go ahead on 8 February regardless of weather, artillery fire was planned as a major battle-winning factor. Over 1,000 guns, one-third of them mediums, heavies, and superheavies, carried out the bombardment. All told, seven divisional artilleries, five Army Groups Royal Artillery, and two antiaircraft brigades supported the attack by Horrocks's 30 Corps. Contrary to Crerar's original direction to dispense with preliminary bombardment, the 30 Corps' fire plan for Veritable as devised by Horrocks and his artillery commander, Brig. S. B. Rawlins, constituted one of the greatest preliminary bombardments ever. Indeed, the concentration of artillery fire delivered on 8 February was probably not equalled on any front during the entire war in the west. Horrocks accepted the loss of tactical surprise in order to take advantage of the increasingly sophisticated application of artillery firepower that, in this case, proved ingenious as well as flexible, with excellent target discrimination.

The artillery preparation that began at 0500 hours showered enemy headquarters and communications with harassing fire and pounded enemy locations in order to destroy and demoralize as many personnel as possible. At 0740, after a smoke screen had been laid down across the entire front, firing stopped. Thinking the smoke and lull signaled imminent attack, the Germans rushed to their guns to return fire, thereby enabling British survey teams equipped with sound-ranging devices to locate German gun positions. After ten minutes, the bombardment resumed, delivering devastatingly accurate counterbattery and countermortar fire on the located positions. In five bombardments during the day, an average weight of more than nine tons of shells burst on each of 268 targets. The preliminary bombardment also included a "pepper pot" in which all Bofors, tank guns, antitank guns, mortars, and machine guns that could be spared fired on specially selected targets to impede local reinforcement, ammunition supply, and movement. Rocket salvoes from the 1st Canadian Rocket Battery's twelve projectors additionally saturated thirteen targets in German forward positions.[109]

Although air support for Veritable depended on good weather and had been planned as a bonus, plenty had been laid on. Air forces assigned to the operation included heavy bombers of RAF Bomber Command and the U.S. Eighth Air Force; medium bombers of No. 2 Group, 2nd Tactical Air Force; and fighter-bombers of No. 83 and No. 84 RAF Composite Groups and the U.S. Ninth Air Force. To effect close coordination in planning and execution, a representative authorized to make decisions on behalf of Bomber Command was attached to No. 84 Group, while requests to SHAEF for the support of the U.S. Eighth Air Force went through headquarters of the 2nd Tactical Air Force.

The air plan called for both preplanned and impromptu air strikes. Before the attack, railways, bridges, and ferries were to be targeted in order to isolate the battle area without indicating the true direction of the attack. On the night of 7 February, the towns of Cleve and Goch were to be obliterated by Bomber Command, with Horrocks accepting cratering as unavoidable. The main air task on D-Day was to destroy and demoralize the enemy blocking the northern corridor against the 30 Corps. While Horrocks agreed to accept shallow cratering on the Materborn feature, he insisted on airbursts at Nutterden so movement would not be impeded. Responsibility for coordinating close air support over the battlefield rested with No. 84 Group, while No. 83 Group focused on countering the Luftwaffe and maintaining the isolation of the battle area by interdicting enemy rear areas across the Rhine. To ensure effective impromptu air support targets, the 1st Canadian Air Support Signal Unit laid down the procedure for engaging targets of opportunity by wireless and line. At 30 Corps headquarters, a forward control post operated a "cab rank" of fighter-bombers overhead, dispatching them as necessary to strike approved targets. A mobile radar control post capable of directing aircraft in bad weather supplemented this arrangement. Contact cars deployed at divisional headquarters served as mobile wireless links and stood ready to provide visual control of aircraft if authorized by the forward control post.[110]

The attack by Horrocks's 30 Corps began at 1030 hours, covered by a creeping barrage 500 yards deep. The barrage had started slowly on the opening line at 0920 and thickened up to full intensity by 1000, after which it moved forward from 1030 in 300-yard lifts every twelve minutes.[111] A smoke screen blanketed the northwestern edge of the Reichswald, but the enemy, sensing perhaps another ruse, proved reluctant to retaliate. The guns had in fact so surprised and shocked the Germans that the initial attack met only light opposition. The 51st (Highland) Division, which had opted for concentrations and stonks in lieu of barrage support, encountered the stiffest resistance from the southwest corner of the Reichswald. The 3rd Canadian Infantry Division's attack at 1800 also developed into an amphibious effort that saw infantry mounted in Buffaloes fighting their way across the flooded plain on the northern flank.

On the whole, Veritable had gotten off to a good start. On the first day of battle, the 30 Corps broke through the enemy's strong outpost screen and closed to the main Siegfried Line defenses. On 9 February, unfortunately, low-hanging clouds and heavy rain put an end to the air support which to this point had been excellent. With the 2nd Canadian Infantry Division now pinched out of the battle, four divisions continued the advance to crack the Siegfried Line. By the end of the second day, the 53rd (Welsh) Division had reached the northeastern edge of the Reichswald overlooking Materborn. The 51st (Highland) Division had meanwhile fought through the southern half of the forest as far as the Kranenburg-Hekkens road. While the 3rd Canadian Infantry Division seized village after village in its huge flooded sector, the 15th (Scottish) Division achieved even more spectacular progress in the corridor between the Reichswald and the Canadians, taking first Nutterden and then the heights to the west of Cleve. Although divisional reconnaissance reports initially indicated that the enemy in Cleve appeared disorganized and unlikely to offer resistance, patrols seeking an eastern route south of Cleve found their way blocked by a coordinated German defense in Materborn village.[112]

Horrocks's 30 Corps had done well in taking virtually all of its first-phase objectives in two days, but the second-phase task of capturing Goch, Udem, and Calcar proved more difficult. Flooding induced by the rapid thaw that set in at the end of January, in addition to heavy precipitation, turned routes into quagmires. Although planners had taken the possibility of muddy conditions into account, the weather encountered in Veritable set seasonal records for adversity, including the highest flooding in fourteen years and exceptionally bad icing and freezing rain. For a time, nearly fifty engineer, twenty-nine pioneer, and three road construction companies were fully employed in maintaining roads. To make matters worse, on the night of 9–10 February, the Germans opened the sluice gates of the Roer River dams, which caused the river to overflow its banks across the entire U.S.

Ninth Army's front and created a rise along the Maas in the First Canadian Army's sector.

The flood level of the Roer, high enough to prevent a crossing by the Ninth Army, did not recede for two weeks. Operation Grenade, planned for 10 February, had to be postponed, with the dire result that no southern pincer movement would now be launched to draw off enemy opposition facing the Canadian drive from the north. The Germans were thus free to deploy the weight of their reserves against the First Canadian Army without fear of having to contend with the Americans in their rear. On 10 February, having deemed the Canadian offensive to be a strategic move demanding the commitment of all available reserves of men and equipment, the German High Command decided to commit the XXXXVII Panzer Corps in addition to the elite 1st Parachute Division already deployed against the Canadian front. During the night of 11 February, the panzer corps moved into an assembly area at Udem in preparation for a counterattack the next day.[113]

The momentum of the 30 Corps' attack, however, could not to be reversed by the German counterattack. On the evening of 9 February, Horrocks, like Collins in Cobra, had prematurely ordered the reserve 43rd (Wessex) Division to break through the Materborn gap, which he erroneously thought had been seized by the 15th (Scottish). Although this decision produced heavy road congestion all through 10 February, it was clearly not the mistake he later said it was, since the British did manage to secure Materborn and Cleve the next day.[114]

By daybreak on 12 February, the 15th (Scottish) had cut across the Cleve-Goch road to take Hau. The 43rd (Wessex) Division was by 0930 also advancing on Bedburg and southward along the Cleve road to Goch. Resistance began to stiffen, however, as the Germans took up a defensive line running from Hasselt to the west end of the Cleve Forest. Comparatively, operations had gone better on the right and left flanks of the British 30 Corps.

By the night of 14 February, the 51st (Highland) Division had taken Gennep on the Maas and Kessel on the Mook-Goch road, which was slated to become the new main supply route and axis for the 30 Corps. All the while, the 53rd (Welsh) Division continued mopping up pockets of resistance in the Reichswald itself. In the flooded sector on the left flank of the 30 Corps, the "Water Rats" of the 3rd Canadian Infantry had seized Griethausen and Kellen northeast of Cleve without opposition on 12 February. Two days later, they secured the towns of Warbeyen and Hurendeich west of Emmerich across the Rhine. By this time, the left flank of the First Canadian Army had been pushed well ahead of the projected limit of Veritable's first phase as laid down by Crerar. Still, the going had been tough for the 30 Corps, and while it had faced only one division at the start of Veritable, it now faced nine.[115] The chance of achieving an opening through which to launch the Guards Armoured Division, still in reserve, seemed remote even though the front had widened from six to fourteen miles. Veritable had developed into a close-quarter slogging match under the worst possible weather conditions with air support rarely available.

The only way to keep up the momentum in these circumstances, Crerar correctly reasoned, was to add the weight of a fresh corps and stretch the enemy to the breaking point by attacking on a broad front. Although Goch had not been captured or a maintenance route yet established for the 30 Corps south of the Reichswald—both were considered essential preconditions to the commitment of the 2 Canadian Corps—Crerar on 14 February directed Simonds to take over the 30 Corps' left sector the next day. He set the main axis of the 2 Canadian Corps along the road running southeast from Cleve to Udem and that of the 30 British Corps along the line Cleve-Goch-Weeze-Kevelaer.

In taking charge at this point, Crerar reasserted himself in the operational realm that up to now had essentially been Horrocks's show, even in the planning of air support coordinated at army level. Apparently, when Montgomery sat next to Horrocks at 30 Corps tactical headquarters for a few days during Veritable, Crerar merely looked on, playing virtually no direct role in the proceedings.[116] The immensely popular Horrocks nonetheless liked Crerar and later wrote that he was much underrated, noting in particular that he possessed common sense and was always prepared to listen to the views of his subordinate commanders.[117] Yet Horrocks also observed that Crerar operated by very different methods than either he or Dempsey. Whereas Dempsey visited Horrocks fairly frequently during battles, Crerar visited him almost every day. Although Horrocks, like Dempsey, often traveled by light aircraft to make quick personal contacts, he stressed that flying made it difficult to get a feel for the battle in the same way as venturing forward in a jeep. In Horrocks's view, stopping and speaking to people and seeing the looks on their faces better enabled him to "smell the battlefield." Crerar, in contrast with both Dempsey and Horrocks, made a practice of flying over the fighting area almost daily, hoping to gain a clear picture of the front, which may have reflected a highly questionable command approach developed during the long strung-out and largely static operations to clear the Channel ports.[118]

For the most part, Crerar appears to have occupied himself with the enormous administrative and logistical preparations for Veritable and indeed may have relished immersing himself in the details of plans related to food, fuel, and equipment supply; force movement and assembly; ammunition dumping; field engineering tasks; communications; and medical matters. Here he also saw the need to delegate responsibility to his chief of staff, recommending Mann's promotion to major general largely on the grounds that he now commanded a 450,000-man force whose daily maintenance required some 7,250 tons per day and the buildup for the operation an additional 22,200 tons (of which 350 types of ammunition accounted for 16,000 tons).[119] Nearly 2,000 tons of bridging went into the construction of five bridges across the Maas River. During eighteen nights of closely controlled movements, 35,000 wheeled and tracked vehicles traveled an average of 130 miles into concentration and assembly areas along deteriorating routes with many detours. Some 400 miles of road were repaired and 100 miles constructed, widened, and improved.

Meanwhile, the army-wide deception plan—which involved the 1 Corps' feigned attack into Holland, controlled and camouflaged movement, clandestine reconnaissance, and the use of dummy tanks, guns, and positions—proved exceptionally effective and resulted in the complete operational surprise of the Germans. The smoke-screen operations carried out under the auspices of First Canadian Army headquarters were also cleverly implemented on an impressively large scale. To shield the left flank of the 3rd Canadian Division from enemy observation as it advanced along the Rhine, a curtain of dense smoke from zinc chloride and fog oil generators was laid down from the river bend northeast of Nijmegen along the south bank to progressively cover successive divisional forward positions. At its greatest extent, it constituted an almost continuous smoke screen 30,000 yards long.[120]

With the Reichswald cleared, the most immediate operational challenge facing Crerar, who now commanded two corps in the line, was to capture Goch and Calcar, both of which Hitler decreed were to be held at all costs. By this time, it was also becoming clear that although not more than half of Veritable's second phase had been completed, a new offensive would have to be mounted. Heavy fighting continued, however, and on 16 February, the 43rd (Wessex) Division outflanked the Cleve Forest, cut the Goch–Calcar road, and in a brilliant night attack seized the eastern escarpment overlooking Goch. The next night, in his final act of Veritable, Horrocks launched the 15th (Scottish) and 51st (Highland) Divisions against the town in a coordinated corps attack that included elements of the 43rd (Wessex) and 53rd (Welsh). Although the garrison commander surrendered on 19 February, German troops of the II Parachute Corps continued to resist until the evening of 21 February.

On the Canadian corps' front, the German defense of Moyland Wood proved equally tenacious. Only after six days of intense close combat, on 21 February, was the 3rd Canadian Infantry Division able to declare the wood cleared. That afternoon, Crerar also held a conference to outline the details of the new offensive designed to complete the second and third phases of Veritable. Christened Blockbuster, the operation was to be executed by the 2 Canadian Corps, which effectively shifted the weight of the First Canadian Army's effort to the left. The primary responsibility of the British 30 Corps was now to protect the flank of the Canadian corps. In the meantime, preliminary operations called for the 15th (Scottish) Division to capture a wooded area northeast of Weeze on 22 February and the 53rd (Welsh) Division to drive south from Goch to take Weeze and exploit southwest on 24 February. This was to be followed by Blockbuster on the twenty-sixth.[121]

To carry out Blockbuster, Crerar gave Simonds five divisions: the 2nd and 3rd Canadian, the 43rd (Wessex), the 4th Canadian Armoured, and the British 11th Armoured. As briefed to his divisional commanders on 22 February, Simonds's plan highlighted the value of having two fresh armored divisions in reserve and stressed the need to commit them in mass rather than piecemeal. More specifically, the plan called for launching a deliberate attack across the Calcar–Udem ridge, smashing through the enemy's strong Hochwald defenses, and exploiting toward Xanten and Wesel. To make this possible, however, the Calcar–Udem ridge had first to be secured against enemy counterattack from the east in order to provide a firm base from which armor could advance over the open fields leading up to the Hochwald feature.

In Simonds's view, the road-maintenance difficulties that had slowed the initial advance of the 30 Corps in Veritable underscored the need to secure a good main supply route along which to sustain the momentum of the offensive. The embankment of the Goch–Xanten railway line running east-west through the gap between the Hochwald and the smaller Balberger Wald

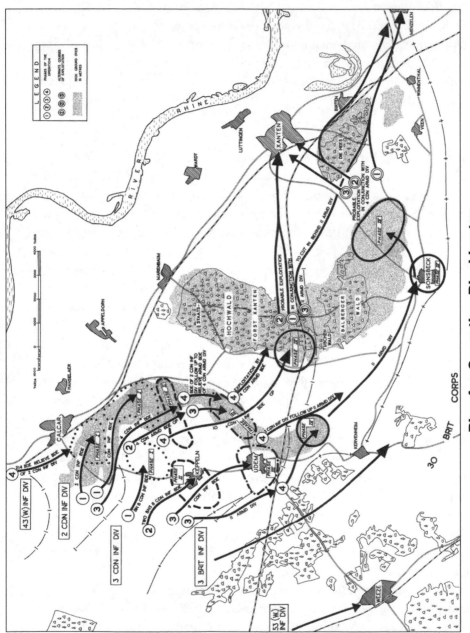

Plan for Operation Blockbuster

struck him as highly suitable for this purpose since the track, reportedly free of mines and demolitions, could be torn up by engineers and developed into a major road as the attack progressed. To get to this point, Simonds gave verbal orders for a continuous operation in four phases. First, at 0430 on 26 February, the 2nd Canadian Infantry Division was to secure the north end of the Calcar-Udem Ridge, hopefully attracting enemy attention and reserves. Then, in the second phase, the 3rd Canadian Infantry Division would seize Keppeln to the west, while the 4th Canadian Armoured Division passed between the two infantry divisions to extend the Canadian hold on the ridge as far as Todtenhugel. In phase three, the 3rd Division was to take Udem, enabling the British 11th Armoured Division to pass south of that town to seize the southern tip of the ridge near Krevenheim. Finally, the 4th Armoured was to seize the railway line in the Hochwald gap while the 11th Armoured captured Sonsbeck and the high ground between it and the Balberger Wald. With the two infantry divisions following to protect their flanks, the armored divisions were then to be prepared to exploit toward Xanten and Wesel.[122]

As plans go, this was not necessarily a bad one, and the proposed end run of the 11th Armoured Division around the Hochwald–Balberger Wald via Sonsbeck looked especially promising. The problem was Simonds's fixation on seizing the Hochwald gap to gain use of the Goch-Xanten railway as a main supply route to sustain operations beyond the Rhine. The so-called Hochwald layback that extended from Rees on the Rhine to Geldern was anchored in the Hochwald and Balberger Wald. Called the Schlieffen position by the Germans—giving some indication of its importance—it was the First Parachute Army's last prepared position on the Rhine's left bank. Constructed to protect the Wesel bridgehead, it was strongest on the northern end where three successive lines roughly 500 yards apart extended from Kehrum along the western front edge of the Hochwald and Balberger Wald to a wooded area one and a half miles west of Sonsbeck. Reinforced with 88-millimeter gun emplacements covering antitank minefields in the north, the Schlieffen position was manned by some of the best troops on the Western Front, including the XXXXVII Panzer Corps in front of Marienbaum and the II Parachute Corps in the Weeze-Udem sector. The 6th Parachute Division defended the Calcar sector and the 116th Panzer Division the Keppeln area. South of Udem, held by the 2nd Parachute Division, the II Parachute Corps retained a hefty reserve comprising the tough 7th Parachute Division, elements of the 8th Parachute Division, and remnants of the 15th

Panzer Grenadier and 84th Infantry Divisions. As might have been expected, the Germans were also able to bring a massive amount of artillery into play from across the Rhine. In fact, fire from German artillery eight miles north behind a river bend on the other side of the Rhine actually landed behind the Canadians. In all, the Germans were able to concentrate 1,054 artillery pieces, 717 mortars, and an unknown number of self-propelled guns, effectively matching Anglo-Canadian numbers.[123]

Crerar must have known that the 2 Canadian Corps would be attacking where the enemy was strongest, which is probably why he warned Simonds and Horrocks on 25 February that if the armored breakthrough on the left had not been achieved by the twenty-seventh, he would transfer the main effort of the First Canadian Army to the British 30 Corps on the right.[124] Since the weakened German LXXXVI Corps held the area from Weeze south to Venlo, this made some sense. The launching of Grenade by the U.S. Ninth Army on 23 February also took some pressure off Blockbuster in this area but made it even more imperative for the Germans to reinforce the northern shoulder of the Wesel bridgehead against a 2 Canadian Corps breakthrough that would have cut off the German line of retreat, which was now bounded by the general line Marienbaum-Kevelaer-Geldern-Kempen-Krefeld.

Crerar's allocation of the main effort to the 2 Canadian Corps may have had less to do with enemy strength, however, than with the fact that British troops had spearheaded Rhineland operations and shed the most blood to this point. Whether for reasons of nationalistic pride, a willingness to share equitable casualties, or both, Crerar and Simonds appear to have deemed it the Canadians' turn. The perception that the Battle of the Rhineland might prove to be the most important terminal action of the war, as earlier suggested by Simonds, may have further disposed Crerar to accept major participation by Canadians, even though it meant committing them against the strongest point in the German defenses. After all, Crerar had been present when Sir Arthur and the Canadian Corps brilliantly broke through five major German defense lines during the Hundred Days of Victory in 1918. While Simonds may also have been aware of the same historical precedent, he was no doubt additionally driven by Crerar's threat to give the main effort to Horrocks.[125]

In certain respects, Blockbuster resembled Totalize, with the 2nd Canadian Infantry Division delivering an all-armored attack at night on a 3,000-yard front behind an artillery barrage. The difference was that whereas Totalize unfolded in oppressive heat with heavy air support, Blockbuster was conducted in miserable conditions of driving rain, icy cold, and sodden fields with no air cover during the critical first two days. A similar artillery program fired by some 700 guns nonetheless commenced at 0345 hours on 26 February, and forty-five minutes later, infantry mounted in Kangaroo armored personnel carriers followed tanks across the start line under the artificial moonlight of searchlights reflecting off low-hanging clouds.

By 1700, the 2nd Canadian Infantry Division had successfully attained the first-phase objectives of Blockbuster. The 3rd Canadian Infantry Division had within the same time frame seized Keppeln, which, with the advance by elements of the 4th Canadian Armoured as far as Todtenhugel that afternoon, marked the completion of the second phase. The assault on Udem, undertaken by the 3rd Canadian Infantry Division at 2100 and completed by the afternoon of the next day, opened the way for the 11th British Armoured Division to advance from Stein to the Gochfortzberg feature a mile northeast of Kervenheim.

Although Blockbuster to this point had cost some 100 tanks and 1,000 casualties, both Simonds and Crerar could look upon the continuous operations of 26 February with some satisfaction. Their hopes for a quick advance through the Hochwald gap in the fourth and final phase were dashed, however, by an unprecedentedly heavy weight of enemy artillery fire and fierce resistance by German parachute forces defending their Wesel bridgehead. The attempt by the 4th Canadian Armoured Division to clear the northwest corner of the Balberger Wald and dash through the gap to the east was bloodily repulsed on 28 February. There was to be no armored breakthrough and the battle quickly devolved into a grim infantry struggle, with the 2nd Division attacking the Hochwald and the 3rd Division the Balberger Wald. Although the weather broke on 28 February to allow the only large-scale close air support received during Blockbuster, it was of little avail in close-quarter fighting in wooded areas. Not until nightfall of 4 March were the Hochwald and Balberger Wald reported to be cleared.[126]

Crerar's failure to switch the main effort of the First Canadian Army away from the bloodletting in the Hochwald gap remains a mystery. During this time, the advance of the British 30 Corps had picked up speed; the British 3rd Division, next to the boundary with the 2 Canadian Corps, pushed forward three miles per day, capturing Kervenheim on 1 March and Winnekendonk the next day. By 3 March, it had reached the deserted Schlieffen Line in front of Kapellen, the same day on which U.S. Ninth Army troops linked up with

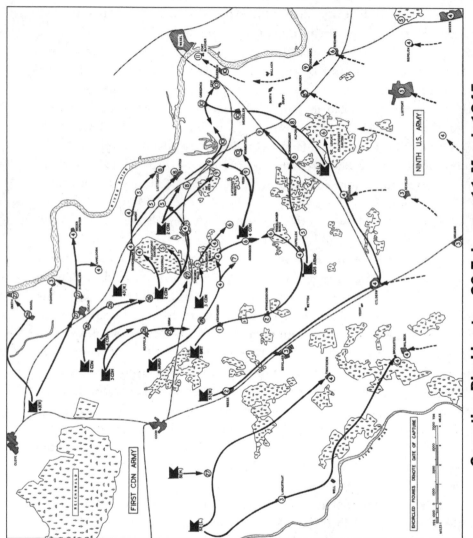

Operation Blockbuster, 26 February–11 March 1945

elements of the 30 Corps at Berendonk, three miles northwest of Geldern. That Crerar should have adhered to his stated intention to intervene in the battle after the failure of the armored breakthrough seems perfectly clear, and it would have prevented Canadian casualties. Again, this would have involved overruling Simonds, this time by stopping him from trying to force the Hochwald gap in a desperate battle of attrition. Here Crerar would have been on operationally firm ground since the bitter experience of Moyland Wood had already indicated just how costly it would be to clear the two larger forests flanking that gap. Crerar did not necessarily have to transfer the main effort to the 30 Corps since he had another option that might have enticed Simonds to outflank the woods from the south and take the gap in the rear. Apparently, Simonds had ruled out using the good road that skirted the woods some three miles south because he feared that it would have to be shared with the 30 Corps and hence become too congested to support all the supplies needed for the forthcoming assault across the Rhine. In fact, the 30 Corps was already looking to fulfill its maintenance requirements by bridging the Maas in the area of Well and Wanssum.[127]

As field army commander, Crerar could have redirected Simonds by placing the British 3rd Division under him and adjusting the intercorps boundary to the Neirs River. This would have had the effect of leaving the main effort with the 2 Canadian Corps while giving Simonds both the space and troop resources of the British 11th Armoured and British 3rd Infantry Divisions to take the gap in the rear by executing a southerly turning movement around the Hochwald and Balberger Wald. As it was, Crerar ended up directing the 30 Corps to attack to the northeast with its right flank on the road from Geldern, through Issum and Alpen to Wesel. Meanwhile, the 2 Canadian Corps drove down the Rhine through Xanten and east from the Balberger Wald through Veen into the heart of the German bridgehead. By 10 March, the Rhineland battles were over and with them Crerar's greatest moment.[128]

The movement of the 1 Canadian Corps from Italy via Marseilles in February saw Canada's overseas army reunited under Crerar beginning on 15 March while Crocker's British 1 Corps reverted to the command of the British Second Army. In the final six weeks of the war, the First Canadian Army experienced more fierce fighting but never on the scale of Veritable and Blockbuster, which had cost 15,634 casualties.[129] The tasks given to the First Canadian Army by Montgomery on 27 March included opening up a major supply route through Arnhem, clearing northeast Holland and the German coastal belt east to the Elbe, and liberating western Holland. During the liberation of Holland, Crerar deliberately attempted to avoid trapping Germans in pockets—which would have risked committing Canadian troops against savage last-ditch stands—and opted instead to sweep northward, forcing the enemy to conduct a general retreat. The First Canadian Army's advance into northern Holland and Germany proceeded rapidly, and by 19 April, offensive operations in western Holland had virtually ceased.

On 22 April, Crerar turned over temporary command of the First Canadian Army to Simonds and returned to Britain for a week of medical checkups and consultations concerning postwar policy. On 4 May, Montgomery ordered all offensive operations to stop at 0800 the next day. Unwilling to exchange formalities with German generals, Crerar left surrender arrangements to his corps commanders. On 21 May, the First Canadian Army's victory parade was held at The Hague, with His Royal Highness Prince Bernhard of the Netherlands taking the salute.

On 21 July, Crerar left for London, and on the thirtieth, the day before his headquarters closed down, he sailed for Canada.[130] Montgomery had tried to get him knighted, but the Canadian government refused, so he was made a Companion of Honour instead.[131] Once home, he received a victory parade and government reception, cross-country tour, and several honorary degrees. Struck off strength on 27 October 1946, he declined to accept the lieutenant governorship of Ontario, which the prime minister offered, and filled instead a few minor diplomatic roles in Czechoslovakia, Holland, and the Far East. All the while, he faded into relative obscurity. On 1 April 1965, he died in Ottawa at the age of seventy-six, largely forgotten, though he had done things that later Canadian army officers could only dream of doing.[132]

CHAPTER TWO

In the Shadow of Montgomery

GEN. MILES C. DEMPSEY, BRITISH SECOND ARMY

Of all the commanders who led field armies on the Western Front in 1944–45, Gen. Miles C. "Bimbo" Dempsey was the youngest and longest serving. Landing in Normandy early on 7 June, he directed the operations of the British Second Army until its headquarters disbanded on 25 June 1945. The Second Army, which traced its lineage back to the World War I formation commanded by the highly competent Gen. Sir Herbert Plumer, was the last great army fielded by Britain and that nation's largest to fight in the most decisive Allied campaign of World War II. Yet the tall, slim, and wiry Dempsey remains an enigmatic figure, forever cast in the shadow of Bernard Montgomery. Surprisingly, he does not even rate a chapter in British military historian John Keegan's book, *Churchill's Generals,* though numerous pages are devoted to three corps commanders who served under him.[1] Although there is at least one fine analytical work on his performance as a field army commander, no biography of Dempsey currently exists.[2]

Part of the problem may have been of Dempsey's own making, as he was a modest man who never sought the limelight. In fact, he shunned publicity and shrank from any form of self-advertisement. In retirement, he resolutely refused to write a book or newspaper article.[3] He not only declined to write his memoirs, but also threatened to burn his diaries to prevent them from being used to foment postwar bickering.[4] Oddly, he may have thought the two-volume *Account of the Operations of Second Army in Europe, 1944–1945,* compiled by headquarters staff under his chief of staff, Brig. H. E. Pyman, constituted a sufficient historical contribution, even though he suggested keeping its contents secret and limiting its distribution to only a few.[5] Dempsey also revealed a defensive side in insisting that only "official" historians be allowed to see his remarks from later interviews with Lt. Col. G. S. Jackson and Capt. Basil H. Liddell Hart.[6]

Of Irish descent, Miles Christopher Dempsey was born in Wallasey, Cheshire, England, on 15 December 1896, the son of a successful marine insurance broker who prospered enough to send his two sons to private school. Educated at Shrewsbury School, where he captained a cricket team for three years, Dempsey went on to take a shortened officer training course at Sandhurst in 1914. Commissioned into the Royal Berkshire Regiment the next year, he trooped to France in 1916 and served in that theater until the end of the war. At the age of nineteen, he commanded a company as an acting captain during the Battle of the Somme and took over as regimental adjutant in February 1917. He survived Passchendaele but was gassed in an enemy mustard barrage at La Vacquerie on 12 March 1918. Evacuated to England for treatment and rest, he thus missed the great German offensive of 1918. On his return to the front on 6 July, he again assumed command of a company. Late in 1918, he was mentioned in dispatches and, shortly thereafter, awarded the Military Cross.

Reappointed adjutant on 5 October, he participated in the occupation of the Rhineland and accompanied his battalion to Iraq and northwest Persia in the campaign of 1919–20. Between 1923 and 1927, he served under Maj. Richard O'Connor at Sandhurst and, in 1930, joined the junior division of the Staff College, Camberley, where he was a student of Montgomery's. On graduation, he assumed a staff captain appointment with the military secretary to the war minister and, in 1937–38, was a general staff officer, grade 2, with Union Defence Forces in South Africa. He returned in February 1938 to take command of the 1st Battalion, Royal Berkshire Regiment, which deployed to France in September 1939 as part of Maj. Gen. Herbert Lloyd's 2nd Division.[7]

Elevated to command the 13th Infantry Brigade in Maj. Gen. H. F. Franklyn's 5th Division in November 1939, he performed well in the three-day defense of the Ypres-Comines Canal, winning the Distinguished Service Order.[8] The 13th Brigade was also on the fringes of the counterattack launched against Erwin Rommel's 7th Panzer Division at Arras. On 29 May, the brigade embarked at Dunkirk and returned to England. Following the establishment of the 7 Corps, comprised of the British 1st Armoured and 1st Canadian Infantry Divisions, Dempsey assumed the position of brigadier, general staff, for the corps commander, Lt. Gen. Andrew McNaughton. Dempsey remained with the corps, which was officially redesignated the Canadian Corps on Christmas Day, 1940, for roughly a year, during which time his quiet competence, notable friendliness, and lack of airs endeared him to the Canadians.

In June 1941, Dempsey assumed command of the 46th (North Midland) Infantry Division and then a new training formation, the 42nd Armoured Division. Shortly after the Battle of Alamein in August 1942, Montgomery asked the War Office to send Dempsey from England to take command of the 13 Corps within the Eighth Army.[9] Since this formation was out of the line on Dempsey's arrival, he was put to work for the next seven months planning the invasion of Sicily. When the Eighth Army landed with little opposition near Syracuse on 10 July 1943, "Lucky" Dempsey's 13 Corps formed the right wing.[10] As the advance up the eastern coast encountered increasing resistance, it also experienced some of the toughest fighting in the thirty-nine-day campaign.

On 3 September, Dempsey's corps, with Simonds's 1st Canadian and the British 5th Divisions under his command, spearheaded the invasion of Italy across the Straits of Messina at Regio. The Eighth Army, with the 13 Corps on the right, then advanced northward along Italy's west coast, covering some 200 miles in thirteen days, to link up with the U.S. Fifth Army at Salerno on 16 September. From there, the Eighth Army's axis of advance shifted to the east coast, where stiffening German resistance and extremely difficult terrain, characterized by steep hills and deep valleys, necessitated heavy fighting between the Biferno and Sangro river lines.

In January 1944, Montgomery selected Dempsey to take command of the British Second Army, which was designated an assault army for the invasion of France.[11] In the five months before D-Day, Lieutenant General Dempsey concentrated on training troops and planning the invasion. By virtue of his experience with landings in Sicily and Italy, he had by this time gained a reputation as an expert in combined operations. Like Montgomery, he worried about the effectiveness of his staff, which possessed little practical experience in running a field army. Dempsey thought it quite clear that his main headquarters would have to hit the ground running in Normandy since big battles were bound to commence at once.[12]

Dempsey also had to deal with corps commanders who had been senior to him and were not necessarily "Monty men" like he was. Of the four corps earmarked for British Second Army, two already had commanders named by the War Office. Lt. Gen. John Crocker, who led the 1 Corps, had enlisted as a private soldier and won the Military Cross and Distinguished Service Order in World War II, finishing as a lieutenant colonel. He distinguished himself in France in 1940 as commander of the 3rd Armoured Brigade and went on to lead the 9 Corps in Tunisia in March–April 1943. A strict disciplinarian, solemn and industrious, he took over the 1 Corps in August 1943 to prepare it for assault landing in France. Crocker's long experience in the Royal Tank Corps made him an excellent choice as the corps commander whose units would spearhead the invasion of Normandy. Like the American Alexander Patch, Crocker would lose his only son in action.[13]

The other confirmed corps commander was Lt. Gen. Neil M. Ritchie, leader of the 12 Corps, who after a fall from grace as the Eighth Army's commander in North Africa had been demoted to major general to command a division and subsequently elevated by Brooke to head a corps. In Brooke's view, Ritchie possessed many admirable qualities.[14] For his part, Montgomery insisted on selecting Lt. Gen. Gerard Bucknall to command the 30 Corps in spite of Brooke's observation that Bucknall was very weak and quite unfit to command a corps. Bucknall had apparently performed well as commander of the 5th Division in Sicily and Italy in 1943.[15]

The appointment of Lt. Gen. Sir Richard O'Connor to command the 8 Corps must have presented a special challenge since he occasionally circumvented Dempsey to deal directly with Montgomery. Allegedly, Montgomery was unhappy with O'Connor's appointment on the grounds of his age (fifty-four in January 1944) and perhaps because he had been quite senior to Dempsey and might resent being commanded by a former subordinate.[16] A highly decorated veteran of World War I, in which he served as a brigade major and battalion commander, O'Connor had been knighted for winning a stunning victory over Marshal Rudolfo Graziani's Italian Tenth Army in Egypt and Libya in 1940–41. As commander of the Western Desert Force, comprising the 7th Armoured and 4th Indian Divisions, he had launched Operation Compass on 9 December 1940 and, in one of the most daring actions of World War II, trapped Graziani's forces at Beda Fomm in Cyrenaica in February 1941. In sixty-two days, a British force that never exceeded two divisions had utterly destroyed ten Italian divisions,

capturing 130,000 prisoners, 380 tanks, and 845 guns in Britain's first victory of the war.

Later that year, O'Connor was captured and interned for more than two
years as a prisoner of war in Italy. After his third escape attempt succeeded, he
arrived back in Britain on Christmas Day, 1943, and following an interview
with Brooke, he assumed command of the 8 Corps on 21 January 1944.
Although O'Connor had survived captivity in unexpectedly good shape,
something of the driving force that inspired his troops in Cyrenaica was lost,
and he had a great deal of catching up to do with respect to waging war.
While his spark of genius may have dimmed, O'Connor remained a good,
sound commander. (The commander of the 49th [West Riding] Division,
Maj. Gen. Evelyn Barker, replaced O'Connor as the 8 Corps commander on
2 December 1944 on the latter's posting to India.[17])

Dempsey was also concerned about the capacity of his staff to cooperate
with No. 83 Group, RAF, commanded by the colorful and popular Air Vice-
Marshal Harry Broadhurst.[18] In 1943, as air officer commanding the Desert
Air Force under Coningham, Broadhurst had established a fine reputation as a
commander of tactical air forces, and Montgomery insisted on having him as
one of his tactical air commanders for Operation Overlord. Broadhurst had
also supported Dempsey's 13 Corps in Italy, and relations there had developed
serious strains as a result of several errors in coordination by Dempsey's staff.
Consequently, Broadhurst was as apprehensive as Dempsey when the former
was posted to be the latter's air opposite number. In the event, after barely
being on speaking terms in Italy, Broadhurst and Dempsey established a lasting
friendship in Normandy. Whatever misunderstandings arose in Italy—which
may have reflected Dempsey's inexperience with air power more than anything else—they were soon forgotten, and neither man made a move without
consulting the other.

Montgomery insisted on close army-air collaboration and decreed that
field army and tactical air force headquarters should always be collocated and
welded together to fight as one inseparable team. On 18 June, he even warned
Dempsey that his then–chief of staff, Brig. Maurice Chilton, knew "nothing
whatever about how to handle air power and the air staff of No. 83 Group
have no confidence in him." As a corrective, Montgomery quickly attached
his brigadier, general staff (BGS), for plans, Brig. Charles Richardson, to Second Army headquarters as a BGS for air since he was a great expert on air
cooperation and could teach Chilton.[19] The excellent relationship that existed

between Broadhurst and Montgomery unfortunately came to be resented by Coningham, who had previously worked harmoniously with Montgomery in the desert campaign. Broadhurst, for his part, disliked being caught in the middle and felt that Coningham's obsessively hostile attitude toward Montgomery adversely affected tactical air operations.[20]

On D-Day, Dempsey's Second Army stormed Sword, Juno, and Gold Beaches and, within two and a half hours, had landed more than 30,000 men, 330 guns, and 700 armored vehicles. While Crocker's 1 Corps assaulted Sword with the British 3rd Infantry Division Group and Juno with the 3rd Canadian Infantry Division Group, Bucknall's 30 Corps assaulted Gold with the 50th (Northumbrian) Division Group. The task of Crocker's corps was to secure a lodgement that included Caen and the important high ground around Carpiquet airfield, while Bucknall's 30 Corps drove seven miles inland to Bayeux. The 2nd Canadian Armoured Brigade was meanwhile to make a rapid fifteen-mile thrust to secure the high ground around Evercy southwest of Caen.

Although the quick capture of Caen and Carpiquet remained a high priority for Crocker, the location of the 21st Panzer Division southeast of Caen meant it was capable of intervening on D-Day. Crocker's plan in the event the enemy forestalled the capture of Caen called for avoiding costly frontal attacks and instead seizing the high ground to Caen's north and masking the city until the 51st (Highland) Division and the 4th Armoured Brigade became available to participate in a concerted attack. In fact, the 21st Panzer did counterattack the British 3rd Division on D-Day and, though staunchly repulsed, managed to delay the advance on Caen. The dash by other 21st Panzer elements to Lion-sur-Mer further exposed a dangerous two-mile gap between the British 3rd and 3rd Canadian Divisions, a vulnerability exacerbated by the continued resistance of German strongpoints near Douvres-la-Deliverande. On the afternoon of 7 June, the 3rd Canadian Division received an additional shock when it was counterattacked and driven back by elements of the 12th SS Panzer Division.

More worrisome still for Dempsey and Crocker, the Germans continued to attack the tough British 6th Airborne Division, which had landed east of the Orne, fighting for ground that, if lost, would have given the Germans fire ascendancy over the Sword area. Since this would have jeopardized the entire Normandy landing, Crocker quite correctly decided to give the highest priority to shoring up the airborne bridgehead east of the Orne. Indeed, without the massed fire support of the 1 Corps' artillery, it is doubtful whether the bridgehead, notwithstanding reinforcement by the 1st Special Service (Commando) Brigade, could have survived. The operations of the British 3rd Infantry Division to take Caen were further constrained by Crocker's decision to divert its reserve 9th Brigade from its original task of helping to take Caen to assisting the beleaguered 6th Airborne by covering the approaches to Pegasus Bridge, the only crossing over the Orne River and Orne Canal north of Caen between Benouville and Ranville. Only by committing the brigade was there any hope for the 3rd to take Caen. The 1 Corps' sector was nonetheless consolidated by the evening of 7 June with the linkup of the 3rd with the 3rd Canadian Division.

As pressure continued to mount on the 6th Airborne on 11 June, Dempsey instructed Crocker to place all his armored reserves on what he called "the heart of the British Empire," the dominating high ground at Columby-sur-Thaon, with orders not to move them without his authorization. As the 6th Airborne withstood repeated panzer and infantry attacks between 10 and 12 June, the 51st (Highland) and 4th Armoured Brigade were also introduced into the Orne bridgehead to outflank Caen from the east. A counterattack by the 21st Panzer on 13 June momentarily blunted the southward movement of the 51st Division.[21]

Dempsey later stated that he never expected the British 3rd Division to capture Caen on D-Day, adding that he had always said if Caen did not fall on the first day, it would take a month to get it afterward.[22] The seizure of the city in a quick stroke, however, was a reasonable objective for attacking troops who were being urged to rapidly establish a viable lodgement. To fall short because of enemy opposition was unfortunate; to fall short because of lack of aggressive action would have been unforgivable. An inland port and distribution center of 54,000 located at the confluence of the Orne and Odon Rivers, Caen commanded the main routes into Normandy and was the linchpin of the German defense there. Since the city and the rivers together constituted serious barriers to movement, the Germans could not afford to let Montgomery capture the city or the important ground surrounding it. To do so would have allowed Allied forces to advance on the Seine and Paris, thus rendering the Germans' position in Normandy untenable and their forces there effectively trapped. Not surprisingly, on the afternoon of D-Day, Obergruppenführer Sepp Dietrich's I SS Panzer Corps assumed responsibility for the Caen sector with orders to hurl the invaders back into the sea.[23] Although not generally emphasized in most historical accounts, the British at this point faced a further geographical reality—that German operations in the Caen area were much easier to sustain logistically than those against the Americans in the western reaches of Normandy. In fact, German supply difficulties more than any other factor determined why the breakout eventually occurred in the west.[24] As the Allies knew from Ultra, the Germans always saw the British as the greater threat and logically hurled their strongest reserves against them.[25]

Significantly, the personal intervention of Dempsey gave his Second Army an early opportunity to envelop Caen from the southwest. When the Panzer Lehr Division's resistance stalled the drive of Bucknall's 30 Corps south of Bayeux, Dempsey went to the headquarters of the 7th Armoured Division on 12 June to see for himself what could be done to regain the initiative. Here he seized upon the suggestion of the commander, Maj. Gen. George Erskine, that it might be possible to outflank the Panzer Lehr by driving on Villers-Bocage from the west and told him and Bucknall to immediately execute the movement with all speed.[26] Dempsey correctly sensed that Erskine had identified a true soft spot in a gap in the German defenses along the Aure River.

That afternoon, the fearless Brig. Robert "Looney" Hinde's 22nd Armoured Brigade spearheaded the drive through the gap and, by late evening, had reached a position five miles west of town. In the early morning of 13 June, a tank-infantry force stormed virtually unopposed into Villers-Bocage. While attempting to secure the high ground northeast of the town, however, Hinde's troops encountered the 501st Heavy (Tiger) Tank Battalion, commanded by the legendary tank ace Michael Wittmann. In short order, Wittmann's five Tigers and a Mark IV Special tank began the systematic destruction of Hinde's lead tank and infantry elements, knocking out some thirty British tanks and armored vehicles. Although Wittmann later lost three Tigers and the Special in attacking Villers-Bocage itself, the arrival of the 2nd Panzer Division forced Hinde to withdraw to tighter positions a mile west near Tracy-Bocage.

That night, after committing his last infantry battalion to Hinde, Erskine warned Bucknall that without additional infantry reinforcement, the 22nd Armoured Brigade could not continue to hang on between the Panzer Lehr in the north and the 2nd Panzer in the south. If Bucknall provided such reinforcement, however, Erskine was confident that Hinde could hold out and continue to threaten the German flank. Instead of reacting quickly to Erskine's request by dispatching an infantry force from the 50th Division through the still-open gap to reinforce the 22nd Armoured Brigade, Bucknall opted to continue the 50th Division's drive south in the hope that it could break through the Panzer Lehr and relieve Hinde. At the time, Hinde's positions astride the Caumont–Villers-Bocage road at Hill 174 were defensible against anything short of a concentrated attack, but by the morning of 14 June, Bucknall recognized that the 50th Division would be unable to break through the Panzer Lehr and provide additional reinforcement. Deciding that the 7th Armoured was now at unacceptable risk, he obtained Dempsey's permission to have it withdraw to new positions east of Caumont. At no time, apparently, had Bucknall ever considered asking Dempsey to divert infantry from the recently landed 49th (West Riding) Division to Erskine. Dempsey, perhaps unfairly, was furious that the 7th Armoured had withdrawn from Villers-Bocage without his permission in the first place. In his view, he had told both Erskine and Bucknall what to do, and they should have finished the job. Although Dempsey can be faulted for not intervening again during the critical moments of 13–14 June, a more competent and forceful corps commander would have obviated any such need. As it was, a fleeting opportunity to turn Caen by rolling up the I SS Panzer Corps' flank from the west was lost.[27]

When Adolf Hitler decreed that Caen be defended unto death, the city became as much a symbol as an operational objective. Montgomery, hounded by detractors and determined to capture Caen, now directed Dempsey to maintain the initiative by launching a series of "colossal cracks"—alternate thrusts in right and left hooks—to shake Caen loose. News that the II SS Panzer Corps had arrived on the front increased the urgency to attack and draw in enemy armor rather than let it be committed at a time and place of the Germans' choosing. The incentive to attract even more massive German armored reserves produced the first major British offensive, Operation Epsom, which saw O'Connor's 8 Corps strike southeast toward the Orne on a four-mile front between Carpiquet and Rauray with three fresh divisions, the 15th (Scottish), 43rd (Wessex), and 11th Armoured.[28] Assisted by supporting attacks from the 30 Corps on the right and the 1 Corps on the left, O'Connor had at his disposal 550 tanks and more than 700 artillery pieces, plus the fire of three Royal Navy cruisers and the 2nd Tactical Air Force.

Preliminary operations commenced on 25 June with a 30 Corps attack by the 49th (West Riding) Division to seize Rauray, the high ground around it, and Noyers on the Caen–Villers-Bocage road. Although the 49th Division, with heavy air support, tore a three-mile-wide gap in the German line, the Panzer Lehr refused to surrender Rauray. On 26 June, when the 8 Corps' attack kicked off, bad weather limited the effectiveness of air support. Spearheaded by the 15th Division, with the 43rd committed on its left, the attack aimed at capturing bridges over the Odon five miles to the south. With the Odon breached, the 11th Armoured Division was then to pass through and drive southeast to seize a bridge over the Orne. Resistance by the 12th SS Panzer Division *(Hitlerjugend)* proved so tough, however, that by noon only modest progress had been made. At this point, O'Connor threw in the 11th Armoured to take the Odon bridges, but it fared little better against the formidable 12th SS.

By the end of the first day of Epsom, the 15th Division had gained only four miles, while the 49th Division in Bucknall's 30 Corps still lay short of Rauray, which did not fall until 27 June. That same day, after decisively repulsing an armored counterattack mounted by Dietrich, the 8 Corps managed to seize a bridge over the Odon. The next morning, the 11th Armoured poured across the bridge and dashed toward the Orne. Dempsey refused to allow the 11th Armoured to cross the Orne for fear of a counterattack by the 9th and 10th Panzer Divisions of the II SS Panzer Corps, which Ultra had identified as being in the vicinity. Alarmed by the development of the British threat to Caen, the Germans strained every sinew to counter it. When the British seized the Odon bridge, the commander of the German Seventh Army, Gen. Friedrich Dollmann, frantically ordered an immediate counterattack by the II SS Panzer Corps and committed suicide several hours later. By the time the counterattack went in on 29 June, the 11th Armoured had captured the commanding Hill 112 on the Caen-Evrecy road. Perhaps because the 15th Division not only stopped the counterattack in its tracks with concentrated artillery fire but also turned it into a rout, Dempsey drew the erroneous conclusion that it was not the main counterattack, which he anticipated would come elsewhere. He therefore ordered O'Connor to pull the 11th Armoured back behind the Odon to meet the expected threat to the 8 Corps, which at that time lacked sufficient depth and striking power to defeat a strong armored counterattack. Dempsey's unfortunate, though understandable, decision proved to be the turning point of Epsom, which Montgomery terminated on 30 June.[29]

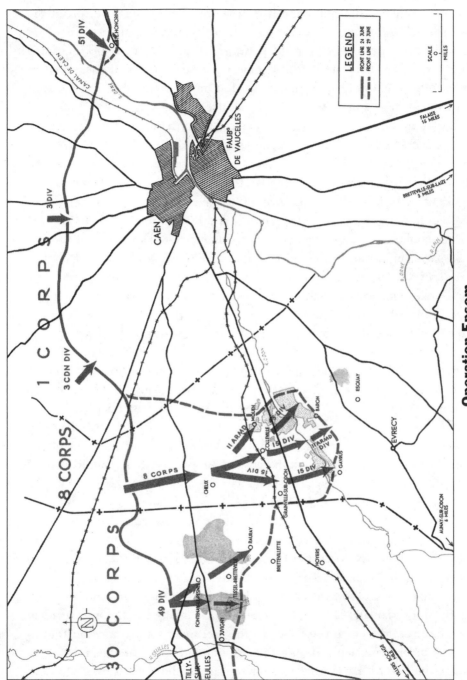

Operation Epsom

While Epsom did not attain its territorial objectives, it had forced the Germans to use all available reserves to stem the onslaught. The hasty and premature commitment of the II SS Panzer Corps, which had been ordered to France from the Eastern Front, proved a costly move that succeeded in pushing back, but not eliminating, the Odon bridgehead.

On 30 June, still determined to capture Caen, Montgomery directed Dempsey to mount a new offensive, Operation Charnwood, to take the city. The plan called for a preliminary operation, Windsor, to be launched on 4 July by the 3rd Canadian Infantry Division. In this operation, the 8th Canadian Infantry Brigade, augmented by the Royal Winnipeg Rifles and supported by the Fort Garry Horse, aimed to secure Carpiquet airport and the approaches to Caen from the west. Fierce resistance by the 12th SS prevented the Canadians from taking more than the village of Carpiquet and a portion of the airfield. Crocker attributed the limited success of Windsor to a lack of control and leadership by the commander of the 3rd Canadian Infantry, Maj. Gen. Rod Keller, who showed signs of fatigue and nervousness bordering on fright. In a 5 July letter to Dempsey, Crocker reported that the division, with the exception of the 7th Brigade, had lapsed into a very nervous and jumpy state that reflected the condition of its commander. Dempsey, who also thought the division was "highly strung," agreed that the operation was not handled well and told Montgomery that it proved quite conclusively that Keller was not fit to command a division. At a time when the situation demanded a clear-cut decision, Dempsey observed, the commander failed to take a grip. Blaming Keller for failing to properly control and inspire his formation, Dempsey remarked that had it been a British division, he would have recommended his removal at once.[30] By this harsh judgment, of course, the modest, but self-assured Dempsey demonstrated that he could be as tough as nails.[31]

The day after the attack on Carpiquet, Crocker issued orders for Operation Charnwood to be carried out on 8 July by the British 3rd Division on the left, the 59th (Staffordshire) Division in the center, and the 3rd Canadian Division on the right. Crocker's plan unfolded in a concentric advance in five phases: first, an assault by the British 3rd and 59th Infantry Divisions from the north in a sustained drive on Caen; second, an attack by the 3rd Canadian Division from the northwest to secure the area as far south as Authie; third, a general push into Caen and onto the line Franqueville-Ardenne; fourth, the final reduction of Carpiquet and mopping up to the River Orne; and fifth, consolidation and further divisional thrusts to obtain bridgeheads over the river. Support for the attack included special armor from the British 79th Division, the firepower of 3 and 4 Army Groups Royal Artillery, and naval gunfire from several ships of the Royal Navy. Charnwood also saw heavy bombers from Bomber Command employed for the first time in a close-support role on the battlefield. Apart from their salutary effect on morale, however, these strategic engines of destruction seem to have yielded less than the expected tactical advantage. Because of a required 6,000-yard troop safety distance, the rectangular target area finally selected (4,000 yards long and 1,500 wide) lay well behind the Germans' forward ring of fortified villages and contained few enemy defensive positions at all. That the ground attack did not commence until 0420 on 8 July—long after 467 bombers dropped 2,562 tons of bombs between 2150 and 2230 the previous evening—further degraded the impact and served to alert the enemy of the imminence of the attack.[32] In a series of nasty close-quarter battles for desperately defended villages and suburbs, Crocker's divisions nonetheless rolled inexorably onward to clear the northern portion of Caen. On 10 July, the 3rd Canadian Division held a ceremonial parade and raised the Dominion flag in the city center. Although the southern suburbs of Caen and the Falaise plain still lay in German hands, the Anglo-Canadians had scored a symbolic victory.[33]

The cost of Epsom and Charnwood had been heavy and was a major reason why Montgomery accepted the cancellation of the former. In the five days of Epsom, O'Connor's 8 Corps incurred some 4,020 casualties, the 15th (Scottish) Division accounting for 2,720 and the 11th Armoured and 43rd (Wessex) Divisions totaling 1,256. The fighting had been exceptionally tough, and in several instances, 12th SS soldiers jumped onto British tanks with explosives strapped around their waists. British infantry casualties in Epsom ran well in excess of 50 percent. When the 43rd Division was given the task of recapturing Hill 112 on 10 July in Operation Jupiter after Charnwood, it precipitated a bloody struggle reminiscent of World War I. The 43rd took Hill 112, lost it to German counterattack, then took it again and held it. In the first two days of the offensive, the 43rd Division and its supporting armor incurred 2,000 casualties. Charnwood cost the 3rd Canadian Infantry Division 1,194 casualties, 330 of them fatal—a heavier loss than on D-Day. The seriousness of the casualty situation prompted Gen. Sir Ronald "Bill" Adam, the adjutant general, to visit Normandy in early July to warn Montgomery and Dempsey that if infantry casualties continued at that rate, it would be possible to replace them only by "cannibalizing" other corps and breaking up

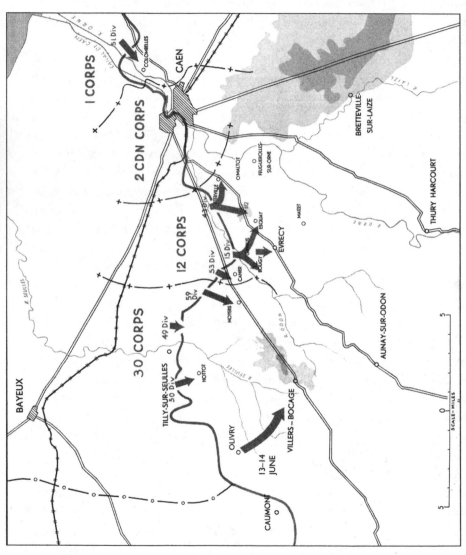

Operations of the British Second Army West of the Orne, 10–18 July 1944

some divisions to maintain the rest. In fact, as casualties continued to rise, the junior 59th (Staffordshire) Infantry Division secretly disappeared in August and the 50th (Northumbrian) Infantry Division in November. Other formations and units that were disbanded included the 27th Armoured Brigade, the 70th Brigade of the 49th Division (replaced by the independent 56th Infantry Brigade), two tank regiments in the 33rd Armoured Brigade, and a regiment each in the 8th and 34th Armoured Brigades.[34]

Recognizing that the British Army had reached its peak, Dempsey took Adam's warning to heart and, having been greatly impressed by the shock effect of the bomber attack at Caen, immediately began devising an offensive plan with casualty conservation in mind.[35] Much like Montgomery and Crerar, Dempsey had always been conscious of casualties as a result of his experience in World War I, but his plan in this case was somewhat radical in that it was essentially technological in nature. Tank reinforcements for the Second Army were pouring into Normandy faster than the rate of tank casualties, so Dempsey planned an operation that utilized the surplus of tanks and economized on infantry. Instead of continuing with infantry attacks in the British sector, he proposed using armored divisions to deliver a smashing blow to the Germans on the eastern flank. To compensate for a critical shortage in 25-pounder ammunition and difficulties in sustaining artillery support, Dempsey looked to the employment of heavy strategic bombers, despite the opposition of the "bomber barons," to blast a swath for the armor.

The primary aim of the operation, called Goodwood, was to destroy the enemy by hitting him hard and wearing down his strength by causing him to either commit reserves or risk a breakthrough. Besides weakening enemy capacity to resist, other goals included completing the capture of Caen and expanding the bridgehead to accommodate reinforcements, supplies, and airfields. As any sensible general would do, Dempsey also privately laid plans for exploitation in the event the German defense collapsed, but he did not disclose these to his subordinates. His ultimate objective was to seize all the crossings over the Orne from Caen to Argentan, thus shutting off the enemy's main force that lay west of the Orne.[36]

Many facets of Operation Goodwood have produced controversy, not least among them its conduct, Dempsey's role in it, and its aims—whether or not it was designed to break out of the Normandy bridgehead. Although Montgomery never favored employing an all-armored corps instead of combined-arms formations, he apparently agreed to Dempsey's proposal because it offered the best chance of gaining a bridgehead opposite Caen "without undue losses," as Montgomery had stipulated after Epsom and Charnwood. As an army group commander, Montgomery was also primarily concerned with coordinating the efforts of Dempsey's Second Army and Bradley's U.S. First Army to gain maximum effect. He originally slated Goodwood for 17 July to coincide with Bradley's Cobra scheduled for 19 July and later postponed. Goodwood ultimately began on 18 July in order to prevent the enemy from concentrating an armored reserve, but Cobra was delayed to 24 July, aborted that day because of bad flying weather, and finally launched on the twenty-fifth. Although reflecting contrasting tactical approaches—Goodwood with its spearhead of three armored divisions and Cobra with its three infantry divisions and reserve of one motorized and two armored divisions ready to exploit—both operations accorded with Montgomery's principal maxims for fighting the Normandy campaign: never lose the initiative and avoid morale-sapping setbacks.[37] In other words, Montgomery regarded ground as something to be fought *over,* not *for,* as did German panzer commanders. Certainly, he needed to expand the bridgehead for airfields, troop buildup, and maneuver room, but in delivering body blow after body blow, alternately west and east of the Orne, he sought first and foremost—as Clausewitz urged—to destroy the enemy's army. In this light, his final direction to Dempsey to "engage German armor in battle and 'write it down' to such an extent that it is of no further value to the Germans as a basis of the battle" made eminently good sense.[38]

That Goodwood was the brainchild of Dempsey lends credence to the later assessment of Montgomery's BGS for plans, Brig. C. L. Richardson, that he was a thinker, the most intellectual general then serving in the field.[39] Dempsey's role in selling the Goodwood concept to Montgomery also stands at variance with Patton's first impression of him as a "yes man."[40] Dempsey was indeed Montgomery's right-hand man, but his contribution as a field army commander has been difficult to assess because of his close and almost symbiotic relationship with Montgomery. Described as loyal but not fawning, his reticent nature and aversion to publicity made him the perfect foil for the flamboyant and egotistical Montgomery. That they had also served together for so long that they thought along similar lines—to the point of often anticipating each other's reactions and decisions—may well have influenced Montgomery's selection of Dempsey for Second Army. Given Montgomery's

Eighth Army practice of working primarily through verbal orders, which he continued in the 21st Army Group, this would have been a particularly desirable command relationship.[41] The very fact that Dempsey owed his advancement to Montgomery would naturally have created some sense of obligation, which would partly explain why Dempsey steadfastly continued to back his boss and refused to be drawn into postwar debates about operations. Montgomery's absorption of most of the flak for Goodwood may have further cemented Dempsey's loyalty. His determination to follow the Montgomery line, however, tended to obscure the depth of his competence as an imperturbable field army commander. Nothing rattled Dempsey, and blessed with an incisive mind, he made decisions promptly and resolutely. He also possessed a prodigious memory, plenty of common sense, and a thorough knowledge of higher staff work. His uncanny ability to visualize ground from reading a map seems to have given him an eye for spotting tactical opportunity, which is doubtless why he insisted on controlling reserves whereby he could influence the battle. It is particularly worth noting that from 11 July, when the 2 Canadian Corps came into line, Dempsey commanded a total of five corps of more than fifteen divisions. Although not as well known to the troops as the charismatic Montgomery, Dempsey was a notably friendly man without airs who inspired confidence wherever he went, particularly among harassed subordinate commanders.[42]

Despite his loyalty to Montgomery, Dempsey may have been frustrated by the latter's often deep involvement in Second Army operations. Whether because of Dempsey's initial inexperience as a field army commander or the restricted nature of the bridgehead, Montgomery allegedly acted more like an army than army group commander in respect to Second Army. Dempsey stoically accepted that the original role of his army, as stated early in 1944, was to protect the flank of the American armies while they captured Cherbourg and the Brittany ports, with no intention of carrying out a major advance until this was done.

On 10 June 1944, Montgomery had confirmed his intent to draw German reserves onto the Second Army's front so that the U.S. First Army could extend and expand.[43] After engaging in this thankless task in Epsom and Charnwood, Dempsey attempted to convert Montgomery to a different theater strategy in which the main breakout role would shift away from the Americans to the British in Operation Goodwood.[44] Although Montgomery refused to accept any fundamental alteration to his broad plan for Normandy, he saw that making the Germans think a British breakout was possible would draw in more of their armored reserves. He therefore acquiesced to Goodwood, but only after expressing doubts about the possibility of breaking through with an all-armored corps. Dempsey's widely distributed operation order of 13 July called for an advance to Falaise, but in a written note on 15 July, Montgomery removed Falaise as an objective and inserted the much closer Bourguebus Ridge overlooking the Caen-Falaise plain.[45] SHAEF never received a copy of the amended order as issued by Second Army on 17 July, and although O'Connor never recalled Dempsey ever mentioning exploitation, it appears that the Second Army commander still stood ready to seize any opportunity that offered a chance of a breakthrough.[46] By deliberately inflating expectations for Goodwood in order to convince the bomber barons that using large numbers of strategic aircraft in a tactical role was vital and would yield worthwhile results, Montgomery also gave the misleading impression that a breakthrough would be achieved.[47] Thus, while Montgomery actually refused to commit himself beyond Bourguebus Ridge, Dempsey saw the chance of a complete breakthrough, and SHAEF expected big results.[48]

The plan devised by Dempsey called for the employment of four corps and a main attack by 750 tanks down a corridor blasted open by 1,600 heavy and 400 medium bombers and fighter-bombers. O'Connor's 8 Corps of three armored divisions was to assemble in the small bridgehead east of the Orne held by the 6th Airborne and 51st (Highland) Divisions and, in the train of massive carpet bombing intended to clear the way, strike south to gain the heights of Bourguebus Ridge, from which further operations into the Caen-Falaise plain could be developed. To fool the enemy about the main effort, Crocker's 1 Corps was to launch a simultaneous supporting attack with infantry and tanks on the left flank, while Simonds's 2 Canadian Corps on the right attacked directly south in Operation Atlantic to secure the southern half of Caen. A diversionary attack was also to be launched from the Odon sector on 15 July by Ritchie's newly arrived 12 Corps, with a view to gaining a firm base for a subsequent advance toward Aunay-sur-Odon or Thury-Harcourt. Farther west, the 30 Corps was to draw enemy reserves into the thick country on its front.

Both Dempsey and Montgomery considered the preliminary aerial bombardment to be critical since there was insufficient space in the bridgehead to deploy enough artillery, which was also short on 25-pounder ammunition, for the delivery of sustained fire. Awesome as the aerial attack was, however, it failed to knock out many of the antitank guns and tanks located in the areas of Emieville, Cagny, and Bourguebus within the 8 Corps' axis of advance down the corridor. German artillery behind Bourguebus Ridge also survived. The German defense was in fact ten miles deep, disposed in five defensive zones based on a grid of interlocking fortified villages and well-dug-in gun positions, backed up by immediate panzer reserves, antitank and flak gun lines, and even stronger mobile armored reserves farther in depth.[49]

Although there is evidence that O'Connor achieved tactical surprise in spite of problems associated with movement into a constricted bridgehead, the 8 Corps' attack foundered largely because he insisted that the spearhead 11th Armoured Division clear the villages of Cuverville and Demouville.[50] The commander of the 11th Armoured, Maj. Gen. George "Pip" Roberts, pointed out to O'Connor that this would tie up his 159th Infantry Brigade when it needed to support the rapid advance of his 29th Armoured Brigade before the Germans could recover from the shock of the bombing. O'Connor rejected Roberts's suggestion to reallocate the task to the 51st (Highland) Division on the right flank of the 2 Canadian Corps, and the 29th Armoured had to carry on with only the support of its integral motor infantry battalion.[51] With insufficient infantry to capture the fortified hamlet of Cagny, which contained 88-millimeter guns and was rapidly reinforced by the Germans, Roberts masked and bypassed what became a key center of resistance that stalled the subsequent advance of the Guards Armoured Division on Vimont-Agences. The accordion-like traffic congestion that developed also held up the 7th Armoured Division, which was earmarked to advance on the left of the 11th Armoured to capture Bourguebus Ridge and St. Aignan de Cramesnil. By noon, with the 29th Armoured Brigade stopped after a 12,000-yard drive and the Guards Armoured stalled by 88-millimeter and Tiger fire from Cagny, the British had lost the initiative.

In the early afternoon, sensing that the British attack aimed at Bourguebus, Sepp Dietrich committed Panthers from the reserve 1st SS Panzer Division to the fray. An uneven shootout followed, between Shermans and Cromwells on one side and Tigers and Panthers on the other; except for repeated attacks by RAF Typhoons, the Germans might have won. O'Connor still hoped to bring the 7th Armoured forward to help the sorely pressed 29th Armoured Brigade, but its movement was so slow that its 22nd Armoured Brigade did not assemble until 1800 for a thrust on La Hogue.

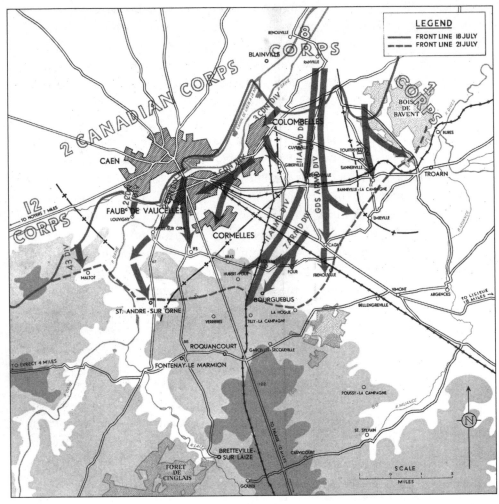

Operations Goodwood and Atlantic, 18–21 July 1944

O'Connor's request for the further saturation bombing of Bourguebus was denied, most likely because all such air assets had been diverted to support Cobra, then planned for 20 July. With the 11th Armoured halted around Hubert Folie—the 7th Armoured sharing Bourguebus with the 1st SS and the Guards barely forward of Frenouville—Goodwood came to an end.[52]

Although the opportunity never arose, Dempsey had been prepared to exploit any situation that might have led to a breakthrough. Indeed, he had collocated his tactical headquarters with the 8 Corps main headquarters on the eve of Goodwood specifically for this purpose. If leading elements reported that no more enemy were in sight, he felt that he should take over and direct the exploitation rather than leave the decision to the corps commander.[53] (One cannot help wondering what might have happened in Totalize had Crerar taken such an approach.) While Goodwood did not succeed tactically, Dempsey considered it a strategic success. The loss of over 400 tanks, many recoverable along with crews, was more affordable than casualties in men, which he claimed to be relatively light. Had Cobra been launched on 19 or 20 July, he could more legitimately have claimed to have tied down four corps of panzers and infantry. If the Germans had moved any of their main forces away to deal with Cobra, moreover, Goodwood would probably have succeeded as Dempsey had originally envisioned.

While casualty figures of 5,537—mostly infantry—do not support Dempsey's contention that they were light, he was certainly correct in asserting that Goodwood was a strategic success. For one thing, the enlargement of the bridgehead virtually eliminated the German threat to the eastern flank, which Montgomery had told O'Connor constituted the bastion on which the whole future of the campaign in northwest Europe turned. With all of Caen and the rivers Odon and Orne now at its back, the Second Army posed a grave threat to the entire German right flank. Given the battering they had taken during Goodwood, the Germans also lacked the strength to take back what they had lost. The fighting capacity of German forces had been stretched to the breaking point, and the new strategic reality rendered their position in the west next to hopeless. Even though the British had suffered heavier casualties than the Germans, the latter were now spread so thinly that it was clear to German field commanders that their forces simply could not continue to absorb punishment of this magnitude. Perhaps equally important, Goodwood forced the German logistical system to concentrate against the British, with the result that fewer supplies reached the Germans in the U.S.

sector in the crucial days before Cobra, causing serious shortages that facilitated the American breakout.[54]

SHAEF's expectation, however questionably assumed, that Goodwood
should have yielded a breakthrough on its own, almost cost Montgomery his job.[55] The recriminations that followed largely overlooked Goodwood's symbiotic connection with Cobra, especially the fact that, as originally
conceived, both operations were to have been launched concurrently for
maximum effect. To Montgomery's credit, he stood by Dempsey and shielded
him from the controversy, but he must have felt justified in his reservations
about the ability of an all-armored corps to force a breakthrough.

Dempsey, on the other hand, must have felt somewhat chastened by the
tactical failure of Goodwood. It is doubtful, therefore, that Operation Bluecoat,
launched on 30 July in support of Cobra, was also Dempsey's creation as some
have alleged, although there is reason to believe that Dempsey still sought to
force a breakthrough. In any case, when Montgomery saw signs that Cobra
could be decisive, he told Dempsey on 28 July to throw caution to the wind
and immediately attack with six divisions from Caumont toward Vire to strike
the flank of the German Seventh Army.[56] Reflecting his approach that it was
more important to kill enemy rather than take ground, Montgomery specified
that Bluecoat would not have a geographical objective; the aim would simply
be to prevent the Germans from redeploying reinforcements against Cobra.
With just forty-eight hours to regroup, Dempsey prepared a two-corps attack
with Bucknall's 30 Corps on the left and O'Connor's 8 Corps on the right.
The main thrust of the 30 Corps, directed on Le Beny-Bocage, aimed at seizing high ground in that vicinity and the area southwest of Villers-Bocage.
O'Connor's 8 Corps was to establish itself on the high ground east of St.-
Martin-des-Besaces with a view to protecting the right flank of the 30 Corps
and subsequently exploiting to Petit Aunay north of the junction of the
Souleuvre and Vire Rivers and northwest of Le Beny-Bocage.[57]

Following an impressive regrouping of fighting elements on short notice,
Bluecoat kicked off on the 30 Corps' front at 0600 on 30 July, supported by
corps and divisional fire plans and 700 heavy bombers.[58] Bucknall directed
the 50th Division on the left to secure the high ground west and northwest
of Villers-Bocage and the 43rd (Wessex) Division to take Point 361 west of
Aunay-sur-Odon. The 7th Armoured Division remained in reserve, ready to
exploit. The attack by the 8 Corps opened an hour later on a two-division

front with the support of 866 medium bomber strikes. The 11th Armoured on the right protected the flank of the 15th (Scottish) Division as it struck out toward Point 309 east of St.-Martin-des-Besaces. As the battle unfolded, the 8 Corps made better progress than the 30 Corps, which Dempsey attributed to Bucknall's poor leadership. Meanwhile, the 11th Armoured had taken Petit Aunay, seized a bridgehead over the Souleuvre River near Le Beny-Bocage by the morning of 31 July, and linked up with the U.S.V Corps. This action threw the Germans into a crisis, penetrating the boundary that separated Panzer Group West from the Seventh Army. Had the British exploited this breakthrough by taking Vire on 2 August, they could possibly have turned the Seventh Army's withdrawal into a rout. As American and British troops were already becoming entangled, however, Montgomery placed Vire within the American sector. Nonetheless, conforming to Montgomery's wishes, the Germans reacted by moving the II SS Panzer Corps, which included the 9th and 10th SS Panzer Divisions, to reinforce the 21st Panzer Division, which was already on the British front. The 30 Corps, meanwhile, continued to flag. When the 7th Armoured, committed to take Aunay-sur-Odon, was forced back on 2 August to the position it had occupied forty-eight hours before, Dempsey lost patience and sacked first Bucknall and his artillery commander, then both Erskine and Hinde. On 4 August, Horrocks replaced Bucknall, and two days later, his 43rd (Wessex) Division captured Mont Pincon in a remarkable feat of arms.[59]

Although Dempsey had failed to effect a breakthrough in the bocage, he had pushed forward twelve to twenty miles on a twelve-mile front, forcing the Germans to commit substantial reserves and holding at least two of their best panzer divisions in place so they could not participate in the Mortain counteroffensive.[60] Montgomery now switched his principal effort to Crerar's First Canadian Army, and the night after the Germans launched their attack on Mortain on 6 August, Simonds's 2 Canadian Corps struck south toward Falaise in Operation Totalize, followed by Operation Tractable on 14 August. Three days later, Canadians entered Falaise, while leading elements of the 53rd (Welsh) Division of Ritchie's 12 Corps passed south of Falaise, advancing on the left flank of the British Second Army as it swung eastward through positions previously occupied by Canadian and American forces involved in closing the gap. Dempsey's task was to advance with all speed to the Seine, cross it, and push on to the Somme. To accomplish this, he directed the 12 Corps to develop a bridgehead over the Seine at Louviers and the 30

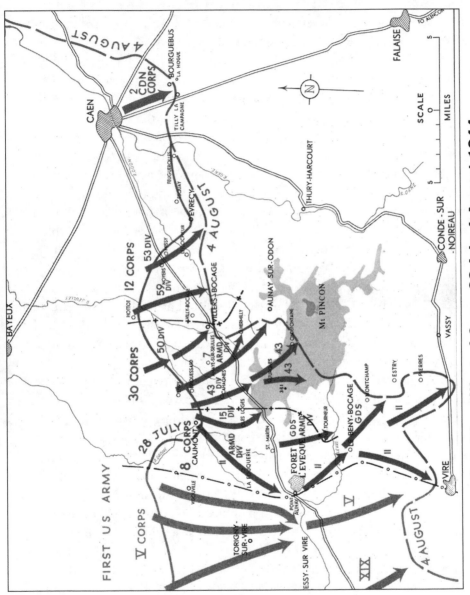

Operations West of Caen, 28 July–4 August 1944

Corps to cross at Vernon north of Mantes-Gassicourt, which the U.S. XV Corps had seized on 18 August.

Since he had anticipated the possibility of a long envelopment at the Seine, Montgomery authorized the Americans to ignore the interarmy boundary and strike down the west bank of the river in front of the British Second and First Canadian Armies. To lend strength to the American maneuver, the U.S. XIX Corps struck north toward Elbeuf and Louviers on 24 August, with the U.S. XV Corps moving on Vernon and Louviers. Two days later, the First Canadian Army established contact with the XIX Corps at Elbeuf, while the British Second Army ran into American elements along the Risle River. While the long envelopment came too late to trap many Germans, it did draw from Dempsey the complaint that American forces across his front delayed his advance from Falaise to the Seine. Unfortunately, his remarks appeared in a British newspaper on 5 September and triggered an angry reaction from Bradley, who saw Dempsey's comment as a direct criticism of U.S. forces. Ironically, Montgomery, who had approved the American maneuver, apologized for Dempsey and lectured him on his lack of tact.[61]

On 23 August 1944, the Second Army began to cross the Seine at Vernon, but not until 29 August did Montgomery commence his pursuit northward. In one week, the Second Army raced 250 miles to the east, demonstrating, as had Patton, that spectacular exploitations resulted mostly from light enemy resistance. Indeed, Dempsey went all out to bring up petrol, oil, and lubricants at the expense of ammunition and other stores.[62] He also employed the 8 Corps' transport to enable Horrocks's 30 Corps to move swiftly in a spearhead role, with Ritchie's 12 Corps close behind. His order to Horrocks was terse: "You will capture (a) Antwerp (b) Brussels."[63]

On 31 August, the 30 Corps arrived in Amiens, having moved so fast that they captured German general Heinrich Eberbach, who commanded Panzer Group West in Goodwood and had just been named Seventh Army commander. By moving through driving rain at night, bypassing enemy pockets, and spearheading a sixty-mile advance in one day, the 30 Corps reached Brussels and Louvain on the evening of 3 September. The following day, the 11th Armoured Division surprised the German defenders of Antwerp who, miraculously, failed to carry out the demolition of port and dock facilities as their comrades had done at Cherbourg and Brest. The continued presence of German troops in the Scheldt Estuary, however, blocked Allied sea access to

Antwerp. For various reasons, control of the estuary was not immediately wrested from the Germans, who used the respite to strengthen their defenses and redeploy most of their Fifteenth Army to the Netherlands via Woensdrecht and Breda.[64]

By the time Roberts's 11th Armoured Division reached Antwerp, it was operating on extremely small-scale maps that had been procured at quick notice. From a practical point of view, this greatly complicated the problem of how a formation with only one armored and one infantry brigade went about seizing a city of 2.5 million people. According to Roberts, "Antwerp was a little red circle with a very thin blue line going through the middle of it." The blue line represented the Albert Canal, along which the Germans were already beginning to defend. Ultimately, with the concurrence of his corps commander, Roberts moved to secure Antwerp's six miles of docks, most of which the Dutch resistance had already seized. This action and the subsequent clearance of the German garrison from the city's central park unfortunately allowed the Germans time to blow the main bridge across the Albert Canal the next day. In the meantime, Dempsey ordered Horrocks's 30 Corps to halt in preparation for a renewed Second Army advance on the Rhine on 6 September. The great pity was that Horrocks, who had not received intelligence on the plight of the German Fifteenth Army, could have driven Roberts another fifteen miles to Woensdrecht, which would have closed off the Beveland peninsula as an exit for that army.[65] (An advance as far as Breda would have cut it off completely.) As it was, the Fifteenth Army withdrew through Woensdrecht and Breda while the Germans stalled the British along the Albert Canal.

Montgomery's focus on seizing the Ruhr and the associated necessity of establishing a bridgehead across the Rhine before the onset of winter remained the major complicating factor affecting the opening of Antwerp. Montgomery correctly recognized that his lightning drive into Belgium had split the German front and opened a yawning gap between the German Seventh Army falling back on the West Wall and the German Fifteenth Army withdrawing along the Channel coast. He decided therefore to exploit this window of opportunity by heading directly for the Ruhr, which by most calculations was still logistically feasible at the time. Intelligence indicated, moreover, that the Germans were not yet organizing the defense of the Ruhr on a comparable scale to that being prepared for Patton.[66] Montgomery had developed a highly imaginative plan to employ the First Allied Airborne

Army in a bold and unorthodox operation, code-named Market Garden, which he hoped would outflank the Siegfried Line and facilitate a rapid breakthrough and penetration deep enough to attain a bridgehead across the Rhine at Arnhem. Although Montgomery has been criticized for this decision, largely because of the outcome, one cannot fault his judgement from an operational art perspective. A successful drive on the Ruhr, the industrial heart of Germany, would doubtless have yielded greater military advantages than a shorter envelopment of the Fifteenth Army through Woensdrecht and Bergen op Zoom. Whether bottling up that army at the mouth of the Scheldt would have hastened the opening of Antwerp is, in any event, debatable.[67] Advancing up the Scheldt to grapple with a cornered enemy, especially on fortified Walcheren, must also have appeared to even the most uninitiated as having the potential to develop into a particularly nasty and protracted struggle. What has also tended to be overlooked in reviewing the Arnhem operation is that success would most likely have yielded Rotterdam, a port more accessible from the sea and as large as Antwerp.[68]

That said, many disagreed with Montgomery's decision, foremost among them Brooke, who recorded in his diary on 5 October that "instead of carrying out the advance on Arnhem he ought to have made certain of Antwerp in the first place."[69] American historian Charles B. MacDonald bluntly called the failure to immediately clear the Scheldt "one of the greatest tactical mistakes of the war."[70] To Basil Liddell Hart, it resulted from a multiple lapse by Montgomery, Dempsey, Horrocks, and Roberts, who were all usually vigorous and careful about important detail.[71] Dempsey later said that his mind was so set on Germany that he forgot about Antwerp, possibly because he had calculated that with Boulogne, Dunkirk, and Dieppe opened, operations could be sustained as far as Münster.[72] The outspoken armored warfare advocate, Maj. Gen. J. F. C. Fuller, defended Montgomery's decision. "The sole limiting factor was that Antwerp was still blocked," he wrote, "yet, in spite of this, Montgomery vigorously urged an all-out advance northwards, and we think that the dictum of history will be that he was right."[73] Like Montgomery, Fuller believed that a single powerful thrust north of the Ardennes would have ended the war in 1944.

There follows the question of whether Dempsey and Montgomery, who was certainly a better quartermaster than many other commanders, could reasonably have been expected to view Antwerp in the same light as the Americans, particularly Eisenhower as Supreme Commander. The British maintained a separate supply system from the Americans, and for the most part, with the exception of pooled items, they exercised a degree of logistical independence.[74] Moreover, as previously mentioned, the First Canadian Army experienced no serious supply problems two weeks after the capture of Dieppe. Clearly, maintaining an Anglo-Canadian army group along the northern seaboard was easier than supplying a larger American army group farther inland. What command level, then, should have been responsible for the supply of army groups?

In any case, during a conference on 10 September, Eisenhower specifically authorized Montgomery to defer clearing the Scheldt until after Operation Market Garden.[75] An expanded version of an earlier one-division airborne operation to gain crossings over the lower Rhine, Market Garden called for the First Allied Airborne Army to lay a "carpet" across rivers and canals in southern Holland along which Horrocks's 30 Corps would sweep sixty-five miles to consolidate a bridgehead at Arnhem.[76] In the airborne phase (Market), the British 1 Airborne Corps, under Lt. Gen. Frederick Browning, was to employ three divisions on 17 September to secure vital bridges across the Maas at Grave, the Waal at Nijmegen, and the Neder Rijn at Arnhem. Specifically, the U.S. 101st Airborne Division was to seize bridges at Eindhoven, Zon, and Veghel, while the U.S. 82nd Airborne Division captured the bridges at Grave and Nijmegen and the British 1st Airborne Division the bridge at Arnhem. In the ground phase (Garden), the Guards Armoured Division was to spearhead the 30 Corps' advance out of a small bridgehead established over the Meuse-Escaut Canal on 8 September. All operations were to be carried out under the overall command of the British Second Army, though Dempsey, like Montgomery in the case of Goodwood, harbored reservations. Indications of increasing German resistance around Arnhem initially prompted him to ask Montgomery to abandon the plan for an airborne attack on the bridge there in favor of seizing a Rhine crossing at Wesel.[77] In his diary on 9 September, he recorded:

> It is clear that the enemy is bringing up all reinforcements he can lay hands on for the defense of the ALBERT Canal, and that he appreciates the importance of the area ARNHEM-NIJMEGEN. It looks as though he is going to do all that he can to hold it. This being the case, any question of a rapid advance to the North-East seems unlikely. Owing to our maintenance situation, we will not be in a position to

fight a real battle for perhaps ten days or a fortnight. Are we right to direct Second Army to ARNHEM, or would it be better to hold a LEFT flank along the ALBERT Canal, and strike due EAST towards COLOGNE in conjunction with First Army?[78]

Montgomery's promise of three airborne divisions appears to have allayed Dempsey's concerns about stiffening German resistance in the Arnhem-Nijmegen area. That Broadhurst's twenty-nine squadrons of No. 83 Group could also strike the Rhine with Spitfires and Typhoons and the Ruhr with Mustangs was likewise heartening. Dempsey's complaints about the inadequacy of his logistical situation seem also to have been addressed by the promise of additional and immediate maintenance to enable him to carry out operations to the north much earlier than would otherwise have been possible. Dempsey later insisted that the plan was his, and he set the start date as 17 September with the operation slated to commence at a time selected by the airborne corps.[79] Dempsey also directed flank protection to be provided by the 8 Corps on the right with the 11th Armoured Division and 3rd Infantry Division and by the 12 Corps on the left with the 7th Armoured Division and 15th (Scottish) and 53rd (Welsh) Infantry Divisions.[80]

Dutch resistance reports, which Dempsey's intelligence staff was not inclined to dispute, painted a picture of growing German strength between Eindhoven and Arnhem. One ominous report hinting of battered panzer formations refitting in the Arnhem area was even sent to Browning's airborne corps, but it disappeared from intelligence summaries because of its vagueness. By the time SHAEF issued Intelligence Summary No. 26 on 16 September, warning that the 9th and 10th SS Panzer Divisions were withdrawing to the area of Arnhem, Second Army headquarters staff had discounted this information.[81] The infectious optimism that characterized planning for Market Garden trumped any such concern. The promise of one bold stroke to turn the northern flank of the West Wall and open the door to the Ruhr was simply too compelling. The need to neutralize V-1 and V-2 rocket sites that increasingly rained death and destruction on Britain added a real sense of urgency to the operation. That the success of Market Garden would likely have led to the attainment of the great port of Rotterdam, sixty miles down river from Arnhem, has also remained an all-too-often overlooked aspect of the operation.

The epic story of Market Garden has been told countless times before, and there is no need to recount it in detail here. Briefly, the airborne landings

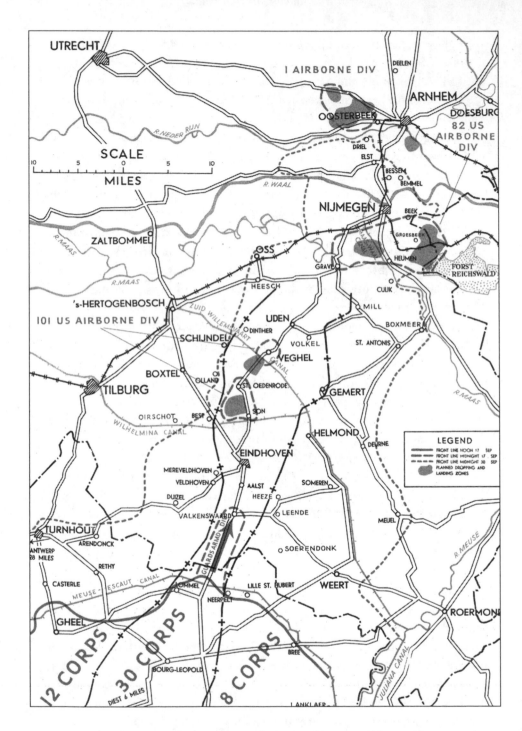

Operation Market Garden, 17 September 1944

on 17 September achieved tactical surprise. The U.S. 101st Airborne Division seized Zon and Veghel on the first day and Eindhoven on the second. The 82nd Airborne quickly grabbed the Grave bridge and another over the Maas-Waal Canal but had to fight hard for Groesbeek Heights overlooking Nijmegen. Meanwhile, because of waterlogged ground restricting tanks to silhouetted movement along roads atop dykes, the Guards Armoured Division proceeded slower than expected and had to throw a Bailey bridge across the Wilhelmina Canal at Zon. Reaching Veghel on 19 September, it also had to support the 82nd in taking the Nijmegen road bridge, which did not fall until the next day. Fortunately, 600 men of the British 2nd Battalion, The Parachute Regiment, had seized the north end of the Arnhem bridge, which effectively prevented German panzers from reinforcing Nijmegen. Unfortunately for the British 1st Airborne Division, which eventually parachuted and air-landed roughly 6,000 soldiers, these were the only troops to gain their objective—and valiant as they were, they were not enough. Arnhem was only nine miles away from the 30 Corps in Nijmegen, but the quick reaction of German panzer formations had sealed off the town. On the morning of 21 September, the isolated and beleaguered paratroopers on the "bridge too far" surrendered, opening the route for German panzers to drive south toward Nijmegen.[82] The remainder of the 1st Airborne Division, which had landed some eight miles west of Arnhem, had meanwhile dug in west of Oosterbeek in a position that the Germans called the "Cauldron." On 22 September, the 1st Polish Parachute Brigade landed south of the Rhine near Driel, but with all crossings now dominated by German fire, it was unable to effectively reinforce the 1st Division. The next day, the 43rd Division of the 30 Corps linked up with the Poles, and Horrocks set about considering how to get two of its brigades across the river. When elements of the 43rd Division and Poles proved unable to force a crossing that may have been possible downstream, Dempsey consulted Montgomery on the morning of 25 September, and both agreed to withdraw the 1st Airborne Division south of the Rhine that night. Final formation casualties totalled more than 8,000 out of roughly 11,000 landed.[83]

It is difficult to dispute that Market Garden was largely a tactical failure. Yet despite counterattacks from west and east on Veghel and Son on 21–25 September, Second Army troops were barely one mile a way from the British 1st Airborne Division, separated only by the 400-yard width of the Rhine. That only 600 men out of roughly 6,000 landed made it to the objective provides evidence that the drop zones in the area northwest of Arnhem were hopelessly far removed from the vital bridge. Had 6,000 men defended the bridge instead of 600, it is unlikely that they would have had to surrender on 21 September. Dempsey quite correctly attributed the failure to gain as good a bridgehead at Arnhem as at Nijmegen to "inept planning by 1 Airborne Division," including selecting their drop zones too far from the objective, poor communications, and subsequent loss of control by divisional headquarters.[84] Although he thought that the troops fought magnificently and could not have done better individually, Dempsey criticized their top command. He rated the 6th Airborne Division in Normandy higher in this regard than the 1st Airborne Division, which he had also commanded in Sicily.[85] To Dempsey, the commander of the 1st Airborne Division, Maj. Gen. Robert "Roy" Urquhart, was "the most vocal, though not the most able, of the divisional commanders."[86] Urquhart's outstanding courage and resolution at Arnhem inspired his 1st Airborne soldiers to hold out against attack after attack, but as a former infantry brigadier, he had no airborne experience or any idea of how an airborne attack should be mounted. Demspey, according to Lewin, would much preferred to have had Maj. Gen. Richard "Windy" Gale of the 6th Airborne, who insisted that one should always aim for a *coup de main* on the objective. Urquhart, on the other hand, accepted at face value the advice of the RAF that flak around Arnhem would render close-in landings impossible.[87]

This pointed to a certain dysfunction in the planning process that neither Montgomery nor Dempsey could overcome. The First Allied Airborne Army, commanded by Lt. Gen. Lewis H. Brereton of the United States, was the SHAEF strategic reserve headquartered at Ascot in England and, as such, orchestrated the intricate air plan related to airfields, aircraft fleets, flying routes, fighter protection, antiaircraft suppression, and resupply. The highly enthusiastic Browning, charged with commanding the Market phase, fleshed out the detailed landing and operational plan at British 1 Airborne Corps headquarters twenty miles away at Rickmansworth outside London. After both agreed on the selection of objectives and airlift allocation, each divisional commander developed his own assault plan. If Dempsey had had only one airborne division under his command, the Second Army and 30 Corps would doubtless have been deeply involved in the detailed planning for its insertion, but with a three-division corps committed, the First Allied Airborne Army and Browning's headquarters took on primary planning responsibility. It was later charged that Montgomery should have sent more senior

staff officers from the 21st Army Group, Second Army, or 30 Corps to participate in the planning in England. As it was, the 30 Corps produced the Garden linkup plan, but the Second Army, with no close contact, had less to say
about the Market airborne dimension.[88] When completed in every interlocking detail by 15 September, the airborne plan was also for all intents and purposes set in stone.[89]

Only after linkup occurred were airborne elements to come under
ground force command. In Gale's view, the airborne divisions should have
been directly linked by efficient radio to the 30 Corps as his 6th Airborne
Division had been to Crocker's British 1 Corps in Normandy. Urquhart did
not recognize communications as the airborne lifeline, however, and failed to
give his signal section the high priority it warranted. Browning's attempt to
control the battle from his corps headquarters on Groesbeek Heights further
complicated matters, since he possessed no real means of influencing operations. Although in contact with the Second Army, his American divisions,
and his commanders in England, he had no communications with the
British 1st Airborne Division. If the airborne corps had simply been fighting
as another ground formation, a corps headquarters would have served a purpose, but here it was more of a nuisance and a drain on sparse airlift that
could have been put to better use elsewhere. Browning's interference further
delayed Gavin's capture of the vital road bridge at Nijmegen. In short, the
30 Corps and Second Army should have planned and controlled the
employment of the airborne divisions from the beginning. Dempsey did not
accept Brereton's view that Market Garden foundered because the 30 Corps
failed to reach Eindhoven within six to eight hours as planned and thereby
caused the delay in taking Nijmegen bridge. The road bridge at Nijmegen
should have been taken by the airborne, in which case the Guards Armoured
Division would merely have dashed across it on arrival instead of having to
help take it.[90]

The failure of Market Garden revealed the essential truth behind the
saying that victory has a hundred fathers, but defeat remains an orphan. As in
Goodwood, Montgomery took much of the blame, but more deservedly
since Market Garden was principally his show. That the First Airborne Corps
was a formation of the SHAEF strategic reserve based in England ensured a
geographical as well as functional separation in planning that limited the
Second Army's influence and control. Dempsey nonetheless demonstrated
that he could get on with the job efficiently without any fuss through daily

visits to division and corps headquarters.[91] Whereas Montgomery focused
on army group–level matters such as airlift, logistic support, and getting the
U.S. First Army to provide protection on his right flank, Dempsey concentrated on maintaining army-level reserves and coordinating the future
actions of the 8 and 12 Corps in support of the 30 Corps. Faced with German counterattacks from both east and west on the waist of the penetration
at Veghel, he placed the 101st Airborne Division under the command of the
8 Corps, which he ordered to clear the main axis from Veghel to Grave. He
also directed the 12 Corps to position one brigade group of the 15th Division at Zon and not to move this reserve without his approval.[92] Confident
of the ability of the Second Army to hold the waist of the penetration,
Dempsey later told his troops that he was "never worried by road cutting."[93]
Like Montgomery, he felt that too much had been said and written about
the "Arnhem disaster" with too little attention paid to the successes of the
101st, 82nd, Guards Armoured, and 43rd (Wessex) Divisions in tearing a
hole through the German defenses with relatively light casualties. Significantly, after the daring river crossing by the 82nd Airborne to capture the
Nijmegen road bridge, Dempsey went so far as to tell Gavin that he was
"proud to meet the Commanding General of the finest division in the
world today."[94] Gavin, for his part, later offered one of the best observations
on Dempsey's character:

> We began talking about a mutual acquaintance, and he observed that
> "he is a decently shy sort of man." This, in fact, was a good descrip-
> tion of General Dempsey himself. He was reticent, almost shy, and
> yet a very hard, demanding taskmaster as an army commander. I was
> to serve under him on the Elbe River later, and I know that when a
> job had to be done, he never hesitated to ask, no matter how
> demanding the circumstances.[95]

Although the only hope of capturing the Ruhr in 1944 evaporated
with the loss of the Arnhem bridgehead, Montgomery persisted in
his attempt to gain a Rhine crossing. Two days after the withdrawal of the
remnants of the 1st Airborne Division, he directed the Second Army to
continue its drive on the Ruhr, this time through Wesel if possible, while
the First Canadian Army opened the port of Antwerp. On 6 October, however, Dempsey advised Montgomery that he did not have enough divisions

"at one and the same time" to successfully defend the Nijmegen bridge-head, eliminate the enemy on his right flank west of the Meuse, and continue to attack southeast between the Rhine and the Meuse.[96] On accepting this judgement, Montgomery informed Eisenhower that while he could possibly carry Antwerp and maintain the Nijmegen bridgehead, he could not do both while dealing with the enemy on his right flank west of the Meuse, which the U.S. First Army, now stalled before Aachen, had been unable to clear.[97] He went on to state his oft-expressed view that the existing system of command was unsatisfactory and that, by implication, the First Army should be placed under his command to force the Rhine crossing that he still thought possible. Eisenhower chose instead to transfer two American divisions to the 21st Army Group, whereupon Montgomery on 9 October directed Dempsey's Second Army to drive the enemy back to the east side of the Meuse and Crerar's First Canadian Army to open the Scheldt as a priority over all other offensive operations. On 13 October, however, Eisenhower stressed to Montgomery the vital importance of opening Antwerp harbor and stated his intention to give Bradley's 12th Army Group primary responsibility for mounting an attack on the Ruhr with the 21st Army Group in support.[98] Montgomery accepted this direction with uncharacteristic good grace and, in a new directive dated 16 October, assigned the opening of Antwerp complete priority over all other operations in the 21st Army Group "without any qualification whatsoever." Recognizing that he was in for a battle of attrition, Montgomery also warned his army commanders to be prepared to accept heavy casualties. Dempsey now closed down all other large-scale offensives and threw the weight of his army northward along the Hertogenbosch-Breda axis to assist the First Canadian Army. By 27 October, both Hertogenbosch and Tilburg had been captured.[99]

The Battle of the Scheldt ended on 8 November 1944, and control of the Nijmegen bridgehead passed to First Canadian Army the following day. On 14 November, Dempsey launched an attack against the German bridgehead west of Venlo on the River Maas. Ritchie's 12 Corps advanced on the southern flank between the Maas and the Noorder Canal, while farther north O'Connor's 8 Corps seized the town of Meijel and crossed the Deurne Canal. In spite of inclement weather and marshy ground conditions, Dempsey's troops managed to eliminate all enemy forces west of the Maas in the Second Army's sector by 3 December, when the town of Blerick, west of the Maas opposite Venlo, fell to deliberate attack. Meanwhile, in conjunction with an American division, Horrock's 30 Corps, operating farther south, had captured Geilenkirchen on 19 November.

On 7 December, Dempsey learned that Montgomery had finally decided to give First Canadian Army the task of conducting the penultimate major Anglo-Canadian offensive, Operation Veritable, with a target date of 1 January 1945. The chief task assumed by the Second Army from this point was to plan the last major offensive of the 21st Army Group, Operation Plunder, the assault crossing of the Rhine to enable a sustained drive deep into the heart of Germany. Initially, the object of Plunder was to isolate the northern and eastern faces of the Ruhr from the rest of Germany, but it was later expanded to include a deeper penetration into Germany. Both Veritable and Plunder were delayed, however, by the surprise German counteroffensive launched against the U.S. First Army on 16 December. Dempsey's involvement during the ensuing Battle of the Bulge focused on defending the line of the Meuse. Crossings at Givet, Dinant, Namur, and Huy were to be held to the end, with Horrock's 30 Corps directed to go straight for any enemy incursion the moment it appeared. On 28 December, the 30 Corps was also committed into the battle area southeast of Namur. It reverted to command of the First Canadian Army on 18 January for participation in Veritable.[100]

Twelve days after the battle for the Rhineland concluded on 11 March 1945, Montgomery launched Plunder. In scale, the 21st Army Group's crossing of the Rhine approximated the magnitude of the Normandy landing and even included two airborne divisions. This reflected to a large degree the truism that "as a war waged by a coalition draws to its end, political aspects have a mounting importance."[101] Worried that the Americans intended to leave Europe within two years after war's end, the British looked to establish a strong presence in northern Germany, liberate Holland and Denmark, and enter important Hanseatic ports before the Russians. In Plunder, Montgomery thus intended not just to get to the other bank of the Rhine, but to do so in such overwhelming force that Britain's greatest army of the war would be poised to follow through with a deep plunge into Germany to seize areas considered politically and militarily vital to Britain's postwar interests.[102] This formidable follow-through far beyond the Rhine would ultimately set Plunder apart from Hodges's U.S. First Army's opportune

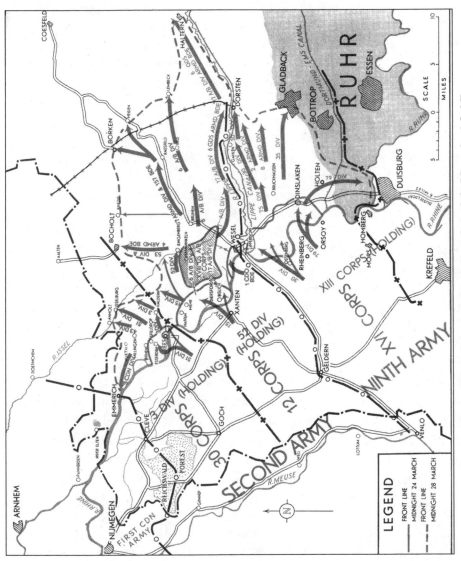

Operations Plunder and Varsity, 24–28 March 1945

seizure of the bridge at Remagen and Patton's Third Army's bounce crossing against light opposition at Oppenheim on 22 March.

Although Plunder was very much Montgomery's show, Dempsey, whom Montgomery slated to command the entire operation, played a critical role in its planning and execution. His headquarters had studied crossing the Rhine as far back as October, and from January 1945, Ritchie's 12 Corps had been placed in reserve near the Maas to undertake detailed planning and rehearsals to develop appropriate assault techniques and the necessary troop-training programs. As in Normandy, oceangoing assault boats and amphibian tanks were employed, in addition to amphibious troop carriers, pontoon bridges, and rafts. The requirement to orchestrate the movement of over 70,000 vehicles and 284 trains (65 for ammunition alone) testified to the immensity of the operation and the competence of the Second Army's staff.[103] Dempsey himself laid down how he intended to employ Maj. Gen. Matthew B. Ridgway's U.S. XVIII Airborne Corps, consisting of the U.S. 17th and British 6th Airborne Divisions, in Operation Varsity, the complementary airborne landing near Wesel.[104] To ensure that linkup occurred quickly, airborne elements well equipped with radios were dropped within Second Army artillery range several hours after the main assault had commenced.

By 23 February, after consulting Broadhurst and the commanders of the First Allied Airborne Army, 12 Corps, and XVIII Airborne Corps, Dempsey settled on his plan. Two days later, he briefed Montgomery, and on 27 February, at his main headquarters, he presented his plan to the air officer commanding No. 84 Group and commanders of the First Allied Airborne Army and 8, 12, and XVIII Corps.[105] In March, Dempsey attended and blessed Ritchie's demonstrations of his assault plan for the 12 Corps, and on 9 March, at Montgomery's tactical headquarters, he reviewed the plan for the Rhine battle with Simpson and Crerar. The 2 Canadian Corps was to come under Dempsey's command for the operation, and on 12 March, Dempsey gave his plan to Simonds, its commander, and left him to study and report back on the problem of taking Emmerich from the east, which would accommodate the eventual crossing of Crerar's First Canadian Army.[106] On 15 March, Dempsey flew to Issum, where on a brilliantly sunny day he studied the Rhine and the country beyond it from Wesel to northwest of Rees. His reconnaissance revealed conditions to be much better than anticipated, with adequate roads and ground on both sides of the river drying out remarkably well. On 22 March, after completing final coordination, Dempsey had the commanders of the 8, 12, 30, XVIII Airborne, and 2 Canadian Corps brief their plans at his main headquarters.[107]

Plunder unfolded according to plan, even though the much greater width of the river and relatively stronger enemy resistance in the north ensured that it would be an opposed crossing.[108] On 23 March, the British Second Army assaulted with massive air and artillery support, with the 12 Corps on the right and the 30 Corps on the left between Wesel and Emmerich, while William Simpson's U.S. Ninth Army provided flank protection on the right by crossing south of Buderich. When elements of the 51st (Highland) Division assaulted at 2100 on 23 March, they reached the far bank west of Rees in six minutes. By first light, all leading assault units were established on the eastern side. Wesel fell to enormous air bombardment and ground attack on 24 March, and the 12 Corps linked up with the XVIII Corps the same day. On 25 March, the 30 Corps captured Rees in hard fighting, and two days later, a bridgehead thirty-five miles wide and twenty miles deep had been created. That night, Dempsey recorded, "It is clear that the enemy is completely beaten and that the opportunity is coming for a very swift advance."[109]

Within a week of the crossing, Dempsey had advanced forty miles with eight infantry, four armored, and two airborne divisions, plus four independent armored brigades. Because of meticulous planning and the application of overwhelming air and artillery firepower, the Second Army's 3,174 casualties between 24 and 31 March were relatively light. Airborne losses of 2,888 over the first three days were comparatively heavier, though perhaps not overly so given Plunder's scope. All things considered, Plunder was an exciting victory and one that Dempsey, who had fought all the way from the dark days of Dunkirk, must personally have relished.

There were no great battles after the crossing of the Rhine, though the advance of the British Second Army to the Baltic involved considerably more fighting. Eisenhower's decision of 28 March to switch the main effort from Berlin to the Leipzig-Dresden line, partly to deal with a rumored Nazi "national redoubt" centered on Berchtesgaden, essentially left the three corps of the Second Army to reduce the seaports of Bremen and Hamburg while fighting their way across the Weser, Leine, and Elbe Rivers in northern Germany to secure the Kiel Canal and cut off the Danish peninsula. Enemy resistance also increased as they encountered SS training schools, German reserve panzer divisions from Denmark, and other German troops crowding into northern Germany. Eisenhower, having detached the Ninth Army from Montgomery on 28 March, now gave him Ridgway's XVIII Airborne Corps again.[110] On 29 April, the Second Army launched an attack across the Elbe in the area of Lauenburg, which was followed by an XVIII Corps crossing at Bleckede. By the evening of 1 May, the British 11th Armoured Division arrived on the outskirts of Lubeck, and the following day, patrols of the British 6th Airborne Division in the XVIII Corps entered Wismar, effectively cutting off the Danish peninsula to Russian intrusion. On 4 May, Montgomery received the surrender of German forces in Holland, northwestern Germany, and Denmark.[111]

The British Second Army ceased to exist as a headquarters in the field on 25 June 1945, and Dempsey began his descent into historical obscurity. His apparent unhappiness on being told that he would succeed Gen. Sir William Slim as commander of the Fourteenth Army in Southeast Asia caused Brooke to record, "I was very much disappointed at his attitude, he is suffering from a swollen head, and I took some pains to deflate it!"[112] Earlier in April, Brooke had also rejected nominating Dempsey for the post of adjutant general with the comment, "I still do not consider Dempsey good enough for it, he requires someone at his elbow to tell him what to do, and as A.G. there is no one at his elbow."[113] As has been shown, however, this stinging indictment of Dempsey is not entirely fair since he had more than enough to do and ample opportunities to make independent decisions as commander of the largest mechanized army ever fielded by Britain.[114] Indeed, Montgomery was well served by having a widely respected field army commander of Dempsey's obvious operational competence; such a division of labor allowed Montgomery to deal with Allied and War Office matters without having to worry about practical aspects at army level. The allegation that Dempsey stoically accepted too much interference from Montgomery in running his army also misses the point. Modern armies run functionally and laterally as well as hierarchically, and in practice as opposed to theory, commanders from platoon to army level must, if the situation warrants, directly order subordinate elements well below them in the chain of command. Of greater significance, perhaps, the unflappable and ever-confident Dempsey appears to have had few enemies. The extreme modesty and almost excessive humility that may have endeared him to Montgomery and others furthermore sets him apart as a most unselfish general.[115]

In the end, Dempsey took over the Fourteenth Army from Slim and followed him as commander in chief of Allied land forces in Southeast Asia in

November 1945. Promoted to the rank of full general in 1946, his last appointment was as commander in chief in the Middle East. Montgomery had begun to groom Dempsey as his eventual successor as chief of the Imperial General Staff, but in early 1947, at age fifty, Dempsey chose to retire to take up the position of chairman of the Racecourse Betting Control Board in July.[116] An exceptionally good horseman who loved hunting and racing, Dempsey held the appointment until 1948. He also served as deputy lieutenant for Berkshire, colonel of the Royal Berkshire Regiment from 1947 to 1956, colonel commandant of the Corps of Royal Military Police from 1947 to 1957, and colonel of 1st Special Air Service Regiment from 1951 to 1960. Although he had remained a confirmed bachelor in his army life, he married Viola O'Reilly in 1948.[117]

In his retirement, Dempsey also struck up a close relationship with the military writer and theorist Basil Liddell Hart, who acclaimed Dempsey as an infantryman who had the gift of handling different types of armor really well.[118] Hart also told Dempsey that "the country is losing more by not having you as the next CIGS."[119] Dempsey, for his part, summarized his service thusly:

> I have gone full circle in my military life. I started as a 2nd Lt. in the Royal Berkshire Regiment in 1915. I have been round the circumference since then, and am back where I began—with the Berkshire soldiers. I am very fortunate that things have worked out the way they have, and I think I am wise to leave it at that.[120]

Dempsey died at the age of seventy-two in his home in Yattendon, Berkshire, on 5 June 1969, a day before the twenty-fifth anniversary of the day his Second Army stormed ashore on the beaches of Normandy.[121]

CHAPTER THREE

In the Shadow of Bradley

GEN. COURTNEY H. HODGES, U.S. FIRST ARMY

O f all the American field armies on the Western Front, the First was the only one to fight continuously from the invasion of France through the conquest of Germany. Ever conscious of its name and precedence, the First Army manifested special pride in having achieved a number of firsts in the European theater of operations. The first American field army to land on the Normandy beaches, it was also the first to break though at St. Lô, the first to liberate Paris, the first to advance into Germany, the first to cross the Rhine, and the first to contact the Russians.[1]

From the time he assumed command of the First Army on 1 August 1944, Gen. Courtney Hicks Hodges never captured the imagination of the American public and remained militarily overshadowed by the larger figure of Omar Bradley, who had led the First throughout the battle of Normandy with Hodges as his deputy commander and understudy.[2] When Bradley moved up to command the 12th Army Group, which included the U.S. First and Third Armies, the First continued to bear the stamp of its D-Day commander. To Gen. George C. Marshall, this was probably not of particular concern; in December 1943, he had messaged Eisenhower that "Hodges is exactly the same class of man as Bradley in practically every respect. Wonderful shot, great hunter, quiet, self-effacing, thorough understanding of ground fighting, DSC [Distinguished Service Cross], etc., etc."[3]

Perhaps not surprisingly, Bradley voiced even greater support for his subordinate, describing Hodges as a spare, soft-voiced Georgian without temper, drama, or visible emotion, a military technician whose faultless techniques and tactical knowledge made him one of the most skilled craftsmen in the entire command. It was only because he was unostentatious and retiring that he occupied an almost anonymous role in the war. In Bradley's view, Hodges successfully blended dexterity and common sense to produce a magnificently balanced command style. Because of his implicit faith in Hodges's judgment, skill, and restraint, Bradley went on to assert that of all his army commanders, Hodges required the least supervision. To Bradley, dubbed the "soldier's general" by the American press, Hodges's epitomized the "general's general" among American commanders, with only William Simpson rivaling his stature.[4] Later in life, Bradley said that he would take Hodges over Patton almost any day, an assessment fully supported in the only published biography of Hodges.[5]

Such glowing assessments of Hodges's generalship, however, have not been universally accepted. American military historian Carlo d'Este found Hodges utterly uninspiring, while Russell Weigley assessed him as prickly and insecure, perhaps even the model of a rumpled, unassertive, small-town banker, the reverse of a strong military commander.[6] Patton, his fellow army commander, certainly did not hold him in high regard, once calling him "apparently . . . less dumb than I considered" and variously a "nothing" and a "moron."[7] A more dispassionate judgment by U.S. military historians Williamson Murray and Alan Millett held that Hodges possessed few operational or tactical abilities despite standing high on Bradley's list.[8]

Specifically, historians have criticized Hodges for his conduct of the Battle of the Huertgen Forest, which D'Este placed foremost among the most ineptly fought actions of the war in the west. The forest became a death trap that consumed soldiers at a shocking rate in futile and costly attacks that gained nothing.[9] To official U.S. historian and decorated infantry company commander Charles B. MacDonald, Hodges fed unit after unit into brutal frontal attacks, with shocking disregard for the tactical realities of the struggle for the Huertgen Forest.[10] Here, in an "American Passchendaele with tree bursts," he persisted in fighting the Germans on ground of their own choosing with a tenacity and tunnel vision reminiscent of the worst of World War I generals.[11] This accorded with Hodges's earlier expressed view that "too many of these battalions and regiments of ours have tried to flank and skirt and never meet the enemy head on"; therefore, it was "safer, sounder, and in the end quicker, to keep smashing ahead, without any tricky, uncertain business of possibly exposing yourself to being cut off."[12] By mid-December, just before a major German onslaught opened the Battle of the Bulge, his First Army had been bled white, with five divisions rendered combat ineffective. Hodges's performance during the Battle of the Bulge has also been criticized, though here his field army did a far better job than commonly supposed. In the eyes of many, the courtly, trimly mustached, gray-haired Hodges appears to have been an unimaginative and colorless leader who lacked Bradley's presence and ability to impress his persona on his army or headquarters staff.[13] "We were a zonal army," he said, "We just slugged. . . . Some people [like Patton] just naturally attract attention, and all my friends tell me that I look more like a school teacher than a general."[14]

Hodges, who rose from the rank of private to full general, was born in the small town of Perry, Georgia, on 5 January 1887, the fourth of eight children. Reflecting Hodges's southern upbringing, a First Army officer later described him as the "Robert E. Lee of World War II" and "every inch the gentleman . . . gracious, understanding, and possessed [of] a keen mind."[15] An accomplished horseman and one of the best shots in Perry, he remained an avid hunter throughout his life. Hodges also held and maintained the not untypical prejudices of his day, having little time for blacks rising above their station in the contemporary social order.[16] The son of a newspaper publisher, he secured an appointment to West Point in 1904, but a failure in mathematics resulted in his dismissal after one year. Unlike his more famous classmate, George S. Patton, who also failed an exam, Hodges did not receive the opportunity to repeat his freshman year. In 1906, he enlisted in the 17th Infantry as a private. After three years of service at Fort McPherson, Georgia, he attained a commission through competitive examination. Following seven more years of service at army posts in the southwestern United States and the Philippines, where he first encountered George Marshall, he obtained a promotion to lieutenant. From March 1916 to February 1917, he accompanied Pershing's Punitive Expedition into Mexico in search of Pancho Villa.[17]

Promoted to captain in May 1917, Hodges went to France in the spring of 1918 with the 6th Infantry Regiment, 5th Division. In the temporary grades of major and lieutenant colonel, he subsequently saw heavy action in Lorraine. As a battalion commander, he earned the Distinguished Service Cross for seizing and holding a bridgehead across the Meuse River. He was also awarded the Silver Star for gallantry in action during the St. Mihiel and Meuse-Argonne offensives. Hodges finished the war as a regimental commander and, after the armistice, participated in the advance of American troops into the Rhineland.

He returned to the United States in the summer of 1919 and remained in the regular army, reverting to the permanent grade of captain. On promotion to major the next year, he completed a course at the Field Artillery School at Fort Sill, Oklahoma. He then received an assignment as an instructor in the Department of Tactics at West Point, where he first met Bradley, who, ironically, taught mathematics. After a four-year tour of duty there, he went on to attend the Command and General Staff School at Fort Leavenworth, from which he graduated in 1925. He subsequently completed tours of duty as an instructor at the Infantry School, Fort Benning, Georgia, and at the Air Corps Tactical School at Langley Field, Virginia. In June 1928, he married the widowed Mildred Buckner in Montgomery, Alabama. Following troop duty with the 38th Infantry at Fort Douglas, Utah, in 1929, he returned to Fort Benning, where he served as a tactics instructor and member of the Infantry Board until 1933. During his time at the Infantry School, Hodges cemented a close friendship with Bradley and won the confidence of Marshall, then assistant commandant. These two contacts would help sustain him through the rest of his career.[18]

In 1933, Hodges and Bradley both attended the Army War College in Washington, D.C. On graduating in 1934, Hodges was promoted to lieutenant colonel and assigned to Vancouver Barracks, Washington, where he served consecutively as the executive officer of the 7th Infantry, and the 5th Infantry Brigade, and the Vancouver District of the Civilian Conservation Corps. In May 1936, Hodges transferred to Manila for tours of headquarters duty with the Philippine Division and the Philippine Department. Here he again served under Gen. Douglas MacArthur, who had been his superintendent at West Point, and made the acquaintance of Dwight Eisenhower. In February 1938, Hodges received orders assigning him to duty at the War College as an instructor, but on repatriation to the United States in August (after an Indochina shooting trip), he was appointed assistant commandant of the Infantry School at Fort Benning in the rank of colonel.[19] In April 1940, he received his promotion to brigadier general, which drew a congratulatory letter from Eisenhower.[20] In October, Hodges became commandant of the Infantry School, but with war looming, Marshall called him to Washington in February 1941 to assume the position of acting chief of infantry. Within three months he was promoted to major general and appointed chief of infantry.[21]

Hodges's replacement at the Infantry School was his good friend Bradley, six years his junior. From 25 to 29 November, Hodges attended the Carolina maneuvers as an observer and rendered a critical report that noted frontages were excessive and that the desire for speed too often resulted in haste.[22]

In 1942, after the reorganization of the army on the entrance of the United States into World War II, Hodges was named commanding general of the Replacement and School Command, Army Ground Forces, at Birmingham, Alabama, but the need for experienced senior commanders was so great that Hodges shortly received orders to proceed to Texas to activate the X Corps as part of the U.S. Third Army under Gen. Walter Krueger. In February 1943, he was promoted to lieutenant general and succeeded Krueger upon his reassignment to command the Sixth Army in Australia. On Marshall's order, from 28 October to 23 November 1943, Hodges visited Allied field formations and installations in French North Africa and Italy and, once again, submitted a detailed and critical report on what he saw.[23]

Hodges retained command of the Third Army until he turned it over to Patton and went overseas to become deputy commander to Bradley in the U.S. First Army.[24] According to Patton loyalist Col. Robert S. Allen, Hodges may have been removed for failure to demonstrate strong command ability. Allen described Hodges as shy, quiet, and inarticulate and observed that because of his inability to talk on his feet or his disapproval of Krueger's "bare-knuckle frankness," Hodges abolished Krueger's critique system for maneuvers. Instead of conducting the critiques himself, Hodges turned them over to corps and divisions, which had little experience and less time to prepare comprehensive observations. The results were thus very spotty and had limited value. In contrast with Krueger, who kept a firm hand on policies and decisions while leaving details to his chief of staff, Hodges let his chief of staff run the entire show, to the point that he, rather than Hodges, appeared to command the army.[25]

Whatever the case, Eisenhower intentionally slotted Hodges as deputy commander of the First Army in anticipation that he might take over the field army on Bradley's elevation to command of the 12th Army Group.[26] At one point, he even seriously considered having Hodges replace Patton as head of the Third Army.[27] Apparently, Hodges believed he should have taken command of the First Army on his arrival in Britain in February 1944, but this would have meant elevating Bradley, who had not yet commanded a field army, over Patton, who had. In fact, the succession arrangement was not offi-

cially approved until 18 May 1944, and since the position of deputy commander was not an authorized appointment at the time, Hodges was left
largely supernumerary to establishment. He nonetheless served as a training
assistant and alter ego to Bradley for invasion planning. In Normandy, he acted
as an observer while entertaining visitors, awarding medals, and attending conferences between visits to corps and divisions.[28]

When Hodges took command of the U.S. First Army, it was the largest
and most experienced American field army on the Western Front. Consisting
of the V, VII, and XIX Corps and controlling nine divisions, it had approximately 250,000 men.[29] To assist him in directing this formation, Hodges had
a 759-man headquarters establishment with four general staff (G) sections
and fourteen special staff sections (such as artillery, engineer, antiaircraft,
chemical, ordnance, signal, medical, supply, finance, personnel, legal, and chaplain).[30] The four general staff sections—personnel (G1), intelligence (G2),
operations, including movement and liaison (G3), and supply and technical
services (G4)—constituted a collective headquarters brain that advised the
commander and acted in his name to coordinate and supervise the execution
of his plans. A chief of staff controlled the working of the staff through a
deputy chief of staff for operations to whom the G2, G3, and G4 sections
reported and a deputy chief of staff for administration who supervised
administrative special staff and G1. The headquarters was divided into a main
echelon of command and supply elements headed by the deputy chief of
staff for operations and a base echelon, often a hundred miles in the rear,
headed by the deputy chief of staff for administration.[31]

Hodges inherited Bradley's staff, most key members of which had served
with the latter's II Corps headquarters under Patton's Seventh Army in Sicily.
Significantly, Patton was extremely unpopular in the headquarters, which
punctured the "legend from Sicily" by displaying a picture of him that closely
resembled photos of Benito Mussolini.[32] Collectively, the staff regarded
Patton as a loud-mouthed, vulgar showman who paid scant attention to
important detail. His headquarters, in their view, neglected supply and communications with forward units. They carried this attitude toward Patton into
Normandy, where, conscious of their veteran status in the American order of
battle, they also looked down on Bradley's less-tested staff at 12th Army
Group headquarters. Frequently, U.S. First Army staff officers would bypass
their counterparts at the 12th Army Group to deal directly with their former
commander, Bradley. Relations between the two staffs were consequently

often cool. Indeed, because of connections during the Tunisian campaign, relations between First Army headquarters and British 21st Army Group staff were in many ways warmer. When Hodges took over this irascible and touchy organization, he did not change much, but his method of command significantly altered the headquarters' working atmosphere and operational tone.[33]

Unlike the more outgoing Bradley, the shy and taciturn Hodges did not enjoy a close relationship with his extended staff. At 5 feet, 9 inches, ramrod straight in his carriage, and fastidious in his dress, he appeared stiff and aloof.[34] He struck Bradley's aide, Maj. Chester B. Hansen, as "essentially a brittle, impersonal general to the bulk of his staff."[35] He did not eat his meals with the full headquarters as did his predecessor. Nor did he like to call large staff conferences to explain his intentions, which he left to his chief of staff and G3. Hodges preferred instead to confide in and rely on an inner circle of upper staff officers with whom he informally dined, occasionally drank, and spent hours poring over the situation map at his command post.[36] The overall effect was to make him more remote and less accessible as a commander. One consequence was that lower staff echelons often felt excluded from the team. Another was that it enhanced the position and power of the chief of staff, who arguably assumed the role of deputy commander despite the disappearance of that position on the elevation of Hodges to army command. In addition to increasing the tensions that already existed between the chief of staff or G3 and the G2—largely a result of personality conflict—the wide latitude that Hodges gave the chief of staff left many observers with the impression that it was the chief of staff, not Hodges, who ran the U.S. First Army.[37]

Hodges inherited his chief of staff, Maj. Gen. William Kean, from Bradley. Although Hodges enjoyed a reputation for being a reserved and soft-spoken gentleman who cared for his men and treated people with respect, Bill "Captain Bligh" Kean was a ruthless taskmaster and perfectionist who drove himself and his subordinates relentlessly. Described as methodical and unemotional, he wielded the whip hand over the army's staff.[38] In this respect, he complemented Hodges's command style, handling the mundane paperwork that Hodges apparently hated and generally running the day-to-day operation of the First Army headquarters. Without question, Kean's dominance within the First Army's command structure greatly increased under Hodges, but allowing his abrasive character and intimidating approach to run unchecked did not produce a calm and happy working environment. One admired, feared, or hated Kean with a passion. Yet while the staff may have suffered a loss of cohesion with the departure of Bradley, Hodges retained supreme confidence in Kean and gave his staff substantial latitude in the implementation of his orders.[39]

The great confidence that Hodges placed in his chief of staff was not universally transferred to his corps commanders. His relationship with Maj. Gen. Charles H. Corlett, commander of the XIX Corps, can be described only as one of mutual distrust. Corlett had come from the Pacific theater, where he had directed operations in the Aleutian and Gilbert Islands. Tough and outspoken, he had experience with amphibious operations, but Normandy invasion plans were so well advanced by the time of his arrival in mid-March that few cared to listen.[40] In early July, because of corps command inexperience, ill health, or both, he had managed to tangle up two divisions in a crossing of the Vire River, which may have prompted Hodges to observe that he had "that hospital look" of commanders who drove themselves to exhaustion. For his part, Corlett later claimed that Hodges and his headquarters issued orders covering tactical details that were more properly within the purview of corps command.[41]

What galled Corlett the most about Hodges was the comparatively greater faith he placed in the commander of the VII Corps, Maj. Gen. J. Lawton Collins, who had also come to Europe from the Pacific. At forty-eight, Collins was the youngest corps commander in the U.S. Army. He had commanded the 25th (Tropical Lightning) Infantry Division at Guadalcanal with distinction under Patch and became Bradley's favorite early in the Normandy campaign. Responsible for the reduction of Cherbourg, he went on to design and execute the VII Corps' breakthrough in Operation Cobra. Given Collins's record of successful field command, Hodges and his staff essentially let the VII Corps do as it wished. To ensure his own success, Hodges also tended to give the aggressive and self-confident Collins the leading role in important operations.[42] Significantly, Eisenhower and Bradley would also have preferred "Lightning Joe" Collins over Simpson as the next field army commander within the 12th Army Group after Hodges and Patton.[43]

Compared to Collins, the other corps commanders within the U.S. First Army did not enjoy much of Hodges's confidence. He even exploded in the presence of Collins, bawling out Maj. Gen. Leonard T. Gerow, the V Corps' commander, for his failure to press an attack into the Huertgen Forest.[44] Gerow, a graduate of the Virginia Military Institute, was a World War I veteran and had headed the War Plans Division in Washington before Eisenhower, with whom he had attended staff school at Leavenworth. Fortunately for him, and notwithstanding the fact that his corps plan had completely broken down on Omaha Beach, he retained the confidence of his former classmate Omar Bradley. Eventually, in January 1945, he took command of the semi-occupation U.S. Fifteenth Army.

In contrast, the commander of the III Corps, Maj. Gen. John Millikin, was less fortunate. Transferred from Patton's Third Army to Hodges's First in February 1945, he was sacked by Hodges on 17 March for his slow buildup of the Remagen bridgehead. Hodges's lack of confidence in Corlett, Gerow, and Millikin translated into increased army interference in corps operations, unrelenting pressure to speed up advances, and incessant demands for detailed reports. Hodges's whiplash method of command, painstaking attention to detail, and deeply developed interest in low-level tactics seem also to have driven him to micromanagement, away from the broad perspective of an army commander. According to the G3 of the V Corps, situation reports submitted to the First Army had to show positions of platoons, whereas the Third Army demanded only positions of regiments.[45]

Hodges followed a daily routine that saw him rise about 0630 hours and, after breakfast, hold a meeting with his inner circle of staff officers. Here he received briefings on the current situation and discussed future plans. The daily meeting usually finished by 0900 hours, after which Hodges often conferred with individual staff members before giving orders for the day to his chief of staff. He then left by jeep or plane to visit subordinate formations. At first, he made daily trips to corps, division, and the occasional lower-level headquarters, but such visits declined over time, with the result that he never became well known to his troops. During the crucial period from September 1944 to February 1945, Hodges rarely visited the front. When he did not visit his units, he spent the day in his war room, often meeting with the chief of staff, G2, G3, and other leading staff officers. He seldom drafted orders himself, leaving them to be prepared by the different sections, which would ultimately result in the submission of a consolidated draft for his approval.[46] If he left the headquarters to visit subordinate commands, he usually returned about 1500 hours and received an update from his chief of staff on daily developments. At this time, he also frequently discussed press briefings with his publicity officer. Around 1830 hours, Hodges dined with his inner staff, often holding meetings with them until he retired around 2200.[47]

Headquarters routine changed somewhat after the breakout from Operation Cobra. By this time, the command echelon had grown so large that it required five days' notice to move. Since it could not move more than a hundred miles in a single jump, neither could it keep up the pace of advance. To rectify this situation, on 5 August, Hodges ordered the formation of a small tactical headquarters to maintain control over corps and divisions in the rapidly expanding front. The concept of a tactical headquarters was not a new idea, but Hodges was the first to introduce it within the First Army. Initially, the tactical headquarters included Hodges, his chief of staff, and key personnel from the G2, G3, artillery, engineer, and signal sections. Later, cells from the G4 section and IX Tactical Air Command headquarters joined the group.[48] Commanded by Maj. Gen. Elwood R. "Pete" Quesada, the IX Tactical Air Command had been collocated with First Army headquarters since Normandy. It commonly controlled six fighter-bomber groups, each group with three squadrons of twenty-five planes each—P-38 Lightnings, P-47 Thunderbolts, or P-51 Mustangs. Requests for air support usually came from frontline divisional air-ground cooperation parties staffed by a tactical air party officer and the division G3 for air. These were sent directly to the First Army's G3 at the combined operations center with information copies to the corps G3 for air so that corps-level air-ground cooperation parties could monitor or intervene as necessary. Since air targets could not always be predicted, however, a fighter group was often assigned to a specific corps or division for an entire day to engage targets of opportunity.[49]

Hodges assumed command of the U.S. First Army at 1025 hours on 1 August 1944 after its successful breakthrough in Operation Cobra enabled Patton's Third Army to break out at Avranches. Unfortunately for the First Army's reputation, Eisenhower noted, a mistaken notion grew up that the Third Army made the breakthrough when, in fact, it was achieved by Bradley and Collins. Although Bradley authorized Patton to take immediate control of the VIII Corps on 27 July, Third Army headquarters was not activated until the day Hodges took command.[50] By that time, the First Army, with three corps and nine divisions, was centered between Patton's VIII Corps driving south from Avranches and Dempsey's British Second Army advancing on Caumont. Cobra had been conducted between 24 and 30 July by Maj. Gen. J. Lawton Collins's VII Corps, with the 1st, 4th, 9th, and 30th Infantry and the 2nd and 3rd Armored Divisions under his command. Hodges, who had played no significant role in planning or executing Cobra, immediately faced the challenge of wheeling the VII Corps from the southwest toward the east and the Seine.[51] As a first step, he ordered Collins's VII Corps to seize Mortain, twenty miles east of Avranches, while Patton's VIII Corps, under Maj. Gen. Troy Middleton, struck westward into Brittany to secure ports. Through the gap that developed between these two formations, Patton hurled Maj. Gen. Wade Haislip's XV Corps, with orders, from 2 August, to exploit to the east toward Le Mans.[52]

On the same day, Hitler ordered Field Marshal Günther von Kluge to launch a strong counterattack along the Mortain-Avranches axis to cut the American forces in two. This was the first test of Hodges as a field army commander. The German attack, directed by SS Col. Gen. Paul Hausser's Seventh Army, commenced in the early hours of 7 August when four armored divisions of the XXXXVII Panzer Corps slammed into and flowed around the U.S. 30th Infantry Division on Hill 317 east of Mortain.[53] Hodges reacted by reinforcing Collins's VII Corps to seven divisions and increasing its artillery allocation. His staff coordinated with the IX Tactical Air Command the provision of close air support and resupply for the beleaguered division, which suffered 1,000 casualties a day. Fortunately, the Americans managed to hold Hill 317, which gave them a commanding view of the German axis of attack. The Americans subsequently launched counterattacks against both flanks of the enemy penetration.

On the same day that the Germans struck at Mortain, the First Canadian Army had also launched a major armored night attack toward Falaise in the enemy's rear. By 0800 hours on 8 August, it had broken open the northern flank of the base of the German salient. This compelled German logistical units to withdraw southward, leaving the German Seventh Army without rear installations. At this point, Kluge knew that his head was in a noose. To exploit this development, Bradley ordered Patton's Third Army to turn Haislip's XV Corps from Le Mans toward Alençon-Argentan to effect a short encirclement at Falaise.[54] On 11 August, Hitler agreed to let Kluge call off his attack and begin preliminary withdrawal.[55]

Although Allied success hinged on the First Army's stalwart defense at Mortain, Patton's Third Army had claimed more of the limelight than Hodges's First in the closure of the Falaise gap. Hodges had ordered his army to resume the offensive as early as 9 August, but his corps commanders could not deploy their forces to do so until after the German Seventh Army broke off its action at Mortain. Beginning on 12 August, the V Corps and XIX Corps mounted converging attacks from the northwest, which ultimately squeezed the Germans out, but the VII Corps' attack from the southwest did

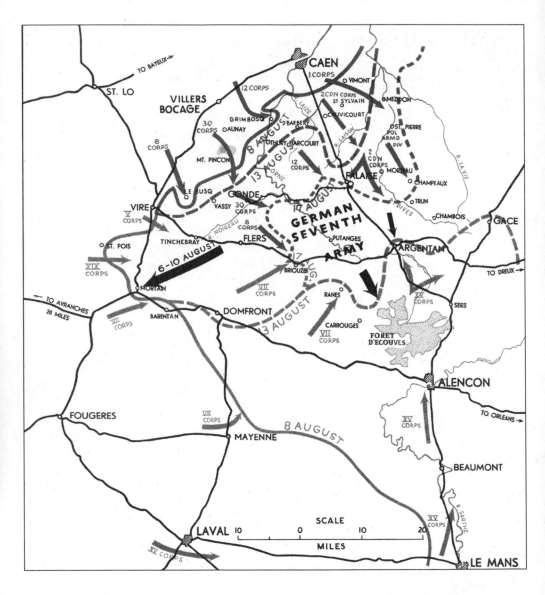

**Closing the Falaise Pocket and the German Counterattack
on Mortain, August 1944**

not really get underway until 13 August. In this fluid situation, Bradley made an extraordinary intervention. In consultation with Kean at First Army headquarters while Hodges was absent visiting divisions on 16 August, Bradley decided to have Gerow and his V Corps headquarters take charge of three divisions—two of them left behind by Haislip's XV Corps[56]—holding the Argentan shoulder. When Gerow reported to Hodges, he was told to proceed with these divisions and close the Falaise gap from the south. The First Army's staff, however, did not know the locations of the divisions, so in the middle of the rainy night of 16 August, Gerow and ten officers, traveling in three jeeps with one broken down radio, had to find the three divisions in unfamiliar countryside. Early on the morning of 18 August, after bringing up his corps artillery and making a hurried plan, Gerow nonetheless had the 90th Division attack. The next day, the V Corps linked up with the 1st Polish Armoured Division of the First Canadian Army at Chambois.[57]

Preoccupation with the task of reducing the Falaise pocket ensured that the First Army was in no position to drive on the Seine before 17 August. On 16 August, the day the Canadians entered Falaise, Bradley sent the Third Army racing toward the Seine to effect a longer envelopment, leaving the First Army to help reduce the pocket. By the time of the final closure of the gap along the Trun-Chambois line on 21 August, Patton's Third Army was already on the Seine. By 20 August, the Third had a bridgehead northwest of Paris at Mantes-Gassicourt and, by 24 August, another south of Paris at Melun. Meanwhile, the U.S. First Army did manage to execute a comparatively impressive maneuver. When Hodges received orders on 17 August to assume a sixty-four-mile front between Argentan and Dreux, with a view to striking north from west of Mantes-Gassicourt toward Rouen, he assigned Corlett's XIX Corps to man that front. Like Gerow's V Corps, the XIX Corps had also been squeezed out in the reduction of the Falaise pocket. To move it ninety miles east from the Domfront area required coordinated leapfrogging through both the VII Corps' and the V Corps' sectors—a difficult task accomplished through the use of truck transport from the VII Corps and, in the case of moving the 2nd Armored Division assigned to XIX Corps, from the V Corps. As the XIX Corps completed its movement on 19 August, Hodges received approval to have Corlett strike north toward Rouen across the front of the advancing British Second Army to cut off the retreating Germans. On 20 August, the XIX Corps attacked in support of Haislip's XV Corps, which struck out from Mantes-Gassicourt toward Louviers along the west bank of the Seine. On 24 August, the XV Corps passed from Patton to Hodges, and the next day, XIX Corps seized the river town of Elbeuf in front of the First Canadian Army.[58]

The long envelopment at the Seine came too late to prevent the escape of substantial numbers of Germans. It also sparked a comment from Dempsey that the American thrust across his front had delayed his advance. Bradley, who considered the statement to be a direct criticism of American forces, angrily took the matter up with Eisenhower. Disentangling the two armies nonetheless took some time. After linking up with the Anglo-Canadians on 26 August, the American corps began to withdraw south. To coordinate the complex road movement of two British corps through the XIX Corps, Hodges met with Dempsey on five separate occasions between 22 and 27 August.[59] Although the successful shift of the XIX Corps to the east and north and back to the south had been a remarkable feat by the First Army—especially as compared to the ramshackle redeployment of V Corps headquarters—popular attention continued to be showered on the U.S. Third Army. At this point, Hodges's army was twice as large as Patton's and had more armor. Following Eisenhower's decision on 23 August to turn the U.S. First Army northeast to support the main Allied drive by the 21st Army Group, however, Bradley ordered the XV Corps to revert to Patton. In the regrouping that followed, the XIX Corps assumed responsibility for the Mantes-Gassicourt bridgehead with the 2nd Armored and 30th and 79th Infantry Divisions under its command. Farther south, Collins's VII Corps, comprising the 3rd Armored and 1st and 9th Infantry Divisions, took over the Melun bridgehead. Between the bridgeheads, the V Corps deployed the 5th Armored and 4th and 28th Infantry Divisions.[60]

On 23 August, a boundary adjustment between the First and Third Armies brought Paris within Hodges's zone of advance. The French 2nd Armored Division, which had been intentionally placed in the Allied order of battle from D-Day to participate in the liberation of France, spearheaded the occupation of Paris on 25 August.[61] When Maj. Gen. Jacques Philippe Leclerc first asked Hodges on 20 August for permission to drive on Paris, however, Hodges curtly rebuffed him. In response, the determined Leclerc sent a reconnaissance in force toward the city, which then drew the ire of his corps commander, Gerow. In the meantime, mounting pressure from Charles de Gaulle and reports of an uprising in Paris had persuaded Eisenhower and Bradley to send a liberating force to the French capital.[62] Bradley personally

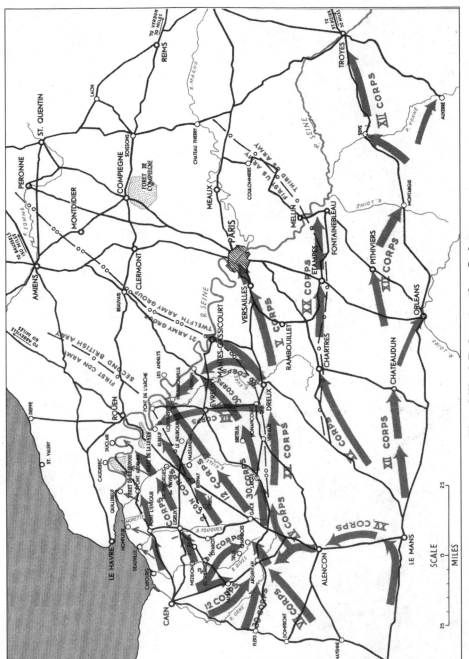

The Allied Drive to the Seine

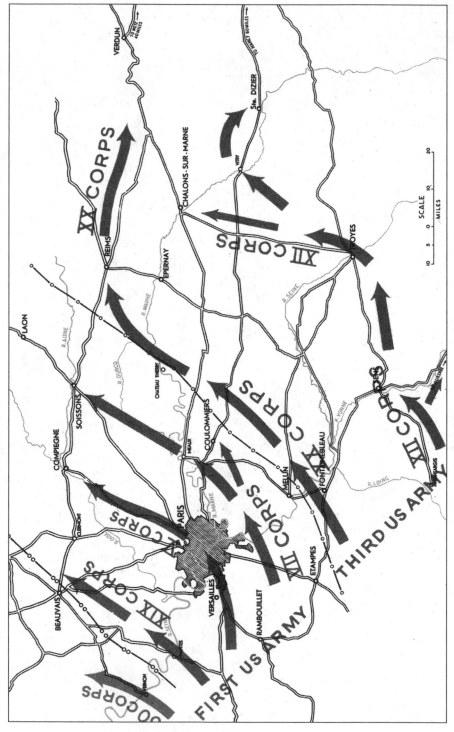

The 12th Army Group Crosses the Seine

delivered an order to Hodges to turn Gerow's V Corps in that direction and, on encountering Leclerc, ordered him to drive on Paris. Neither Hodges, who disliked what he perceived to be Leclerc's insolence, nor Gerow, who repeatedly complained about the drunken abandon and lax discipline of French troops during the advance, manifested such sensitivity. In any event, the French 2nd Armored Division beat the U.S. 4th Infantry Division into the city to take the formal surrender of the German garrison commander in the name of the provisional government of France. There followed a brief dispute between Gerow, who considered himself the authorized Allied commander, and the already effectively functioning Free French military governor, Gen. Pierre J. Koenig. On 28 August, First Army headquarters transferred its authority to the Free French, leaving the French 2nd Armored Division in place to maintain public order.[63] The Paris altercation would not be the last Franco-American misunderstanding of the war.

By the end of August 1944, Hodges's First Army was well on its way toward the Belgian frontier, advancing rapidly on a seventy-eight-mile front with the XIX Corps, V Corps, and VII Corps abreast from left to right. The First Army's advance protected the southern flank of Montgomery's 21st Army Group, but on Bradley's insistence, it remained under the command of his 12th Army Group. Given the speed of the advance because of light German resistance, Hodges experienced difficulty in maintaining effective communications with his wide-ranging corps. This was especially true in the case of Corlett's XIX Corps, which effected liaison directly with Horrocks's British 30 Corps. On 31 August, when Bradley ordered Hodges to again turn north to cut off escaping Germans, Hodges sent his G3 to direct Corlett to drive on Tournai, a critical crossroads forty-five miles west of Brussels. The trouble was that Tournai lay within the 21st Army Group's sector, and when the XIX Corps reached it on 2 September, Montgomery protested that it was blocking the British advance on Brussels. At the time, Hodges was apparently under the misconception that Bradley had turned him north in order to link up with a planned but never executed parachute assault in the area of Tournai. Shortly thereafter, the Americans withdrew. Meanwhile, in response to Hodges's earlier direction, Collins's easternmost VII Corps had also turned north in time to arrive in Mons, just twenty-seven miles southeast of Tournai, on 2 September. By doing so, the VII Corps cut off the Mons pocket, forcing the surrender of more than 25,000 men of the German Seventh Army and clearing the path to the German border. A jubilant Hodges, pleased with his performance announced to his staff on 6 September that with ten more days of good weather, the war would be over.[64]

By this juncture, however, supply shortages within the U.S. First Army had reached alarming proportions, the most critical being fuel. Most of the V Corps had run out of gas on 2 September. To enable the V Corps, now on the right, and VII Corps, on the left, to continue the advance, Hodges had halted his weaker XIX Corps—which had lost its 79th Division to the Third Army—short of Tournai for several days after the battle for the Mons pocket. On 4 September, Eisenhower reversed his decision of 23 August to allocate priority of supply to the First Army over the Third, further exacerbating the situation for Hodges. In accordance with this reversal, Bradley revoked Hodges's supply priority and announced an equal split in daily tonnage between the First and Third Armies. On 27 August, Hodges placed priority on combat supplies over combat forces. Despite the grounding of the XIX Corps, the 5th Armored Division in the V Corps ran out of gas on 7 September. Refueled again, it was the first to enter Germany on 10 September. The heavily fortified Siegfried Line still lay before the First Army, however, and Hodges was told that he would not have sufficient ammunition for five days of hard fighting before 15 September. He nonetheless deferred to Collins's suggestion for a reconnaissance in force to induce a quick and easy breach of the line and ordered both the V Corps and VII Corps to attempt rapid penetrations of the German defenses, which included belts of bunkers, antitank dragon's teeth, and pillboxes.[65]

A breakthrough by the V Corps and VII Corps offered the possibility of a quick advance to the Rhine and then to Cologne, Bonn, and Koblenz. On 12 September, however, Collins's reconnaissance in force encountered stiffening resistance. A stronger attack the following day nonetheless attained two thin penetrations of the Siegfried Line in the Stolberg corridor between Aachen and the Huertgen Forest, which formed the northernmost tip of the Belgian Ardennes and the German Eifel region. The 9th Infantry Division's attempt to sweep through the Huertgen's dense woods, gorges, and ridges to protect Collins's right flank on 15 September precipitated one of the bloodiest struggles of the war. Within a month, the overextended division incurred roughly 5,500 casualties.

The widely dispersed V Corps under Gerow had meanwhile launched a secondary attack against the heavily wooded German Eifel on 14 September, but the combination of poor weather (which negated close air support), logistical shortages, thickly wooded hills, and the tenacity of German defenses made the going extremely tough. On 16 September, Gerow called off the offensive. Two days later, Collins ordered his troops to hold and consolidate their positions. After consulting his corps commanders on 22 September, Hodges indefinitely postponed the entire offensive, which Montgomery had hoped would help support Market Garden, which had started on 17 September, by at least fixing German reserves in place. Hodges and his staff continued to believe, nonetheless, that the Germans were beaten and that the end of the war was in sight. They were thus eager to resume the advance to the Rhine along the Aachen-Cologne axis as soon as logistics permitted. Although Hodges claimed a severe cold kept him confined to headquarters during this time, except for an occasional trip to see Bradley, his isolation may also have stemmed from the "tempestuous discussion" he had had with Gerow on 11 September over what Gerow considered to be the overly dispersed deployment of the V Corps. In the main, however, Hodges performance to this point appears to have been generally satisfactory.[66]

With Market Garden having fallen short and Patton stopped dead in his tracks before Metz, Eisenhower finally placed priority on opening Antwerp to ameliorate the American supply situation. In order to assist the 21st Army Group with this task, on 25 September, Bradley directed Hodges to extend his front forty miles northward to include the Peel Marshes and reduce the German salient that had developed there west of the Meuse between the U.S. First and British Second Armies. Hodges was then to drive on the Rhine between Düsseldorf and Bonn. To strengthen Hodges, Bradley transferred the 7th Armored and 29th Infantry Divisions to the First Army and ordered Simpson's U.S. Ninth Army to take over the inactive Ardennes-Eifel sector from Gerow's V Corps. This allowed the V Corps to take over fifteen miles of the VII Corps' front around Monschau, which reduced Collins's frontage from thirty-five to twenty miles. On the northernmost flank, from the Peel Marshes south, the XIX Corps assumed responsibility for a front of sixty-five miles, which confirmed in Corlett's mind his inferior status. Granted, Hodges had given him two armored and two infantry divisions, as compared to one armored and two infantry divisions each for the V Corps and VII Corps, but he also expected Corlett to clear the Peel Marshes and help Collins execute the main effort. As set forth on 29

September, Hodges's plan called for the V Corps to advance on Bonn while the VII Corps cleared the Huertgen Forest and circled Aachen from the south to link up with the XIX Corps, which was to bypass the city to the north. Once east of Aachen, Collins's VII Corps, supported by the XIX Corps on its northern flank, was to establish a bridgehead over the Roer and drive toward the Rhine at Cologne.[67]

Shortly after the XIX Corps commenced its drive north around Aachen on 2 October, the First Army discovered that its ammunition requisitions had not been filled by the notoriously inefficient U.S. Communications Zone (COMZ) logistics support command. The 12th Army Group, which had instituted ammunition rationing on 2 October, now stopped the further supply of ammunition to field armies until COMZ built up stocks in its depots, which was not expected to happen before 7 November. The opposition encountered by Corlett's XIX Corps in the Peel Marshes had meanwhile proven far stronger than expected, with the result that Bradley, on Eisenhower's direction, ordered the First Army to turn over the Meuse salient to the British Second Army. Hodges was then assigned the more limited task of expanding his penetration of the Siegfried Line. At this point, over the objections of Collins and Corlett, Hodges ordered Aachen to be captured rather than bypassed. During the two weeks of close combat that ensued, relations between Hodges and Corlett irrevocably soured. Corlett considered the orders he received to be "generally oral and pretty sketchy" and found Hodges highly resentful of any suggestions to the contrary. Matters went from bad to worse when, in Bradley's presence, Hodges reprimanded Corlett for exceeding his 2,000-round artillery ammunition allotment. Corlett, who was tired, run down, and perhaps even sick, lashed back in the harsh and forceful tones of one who understood the actual situation at the front.[68] From there on, the slow progress of the XIX Corps and the unrelenting badgering of it by an unsympathetic Hodges ensured the complete deterioration of their relationship. Three days before Aachen fell on 21 October, Bradley, at Hodges insistence, relieved Corlett for reasons of health and transferred the XIX Corps, now under the command of Maj. Gen. Raymond S. McLain, to the U.S. Ninth Army.[69]

The transfer was convenient, for Bradley had just decided to shift the newly arrived Ninth Army from the Ardennes-Eifel area to the sector between the U.S. First and British Second Armies. The Ninth simply took over the XIX Corps while the First took over the VIII Corps—heretofore under the Ninth in the Ardennes—avoiding a mass movement of troops.

Bradley later stated that he made this change to prevent his most experienced army and its temperamental staff from falling under British control in the event that Montgomery persuaded Eisenhower to give the 21st Army Group an American field army.

To adjust to this latest redeployment, on 25 October, Hodges's headquarters moved from Verviers to the old Belgian resort city of Spa, where it occupied the stately Hotel Britannique. There, having received earlier direction from Bradley to attack east on 5 November and seize a bridgehead over the Rhine in the Cologne-Bonn area, Hodges issued a field order that bordered on micromanagement. Once again, he assigned the main effort to Collins's VII Corps, but with a shift of the intercorps boundary, the plan hinged on Gerow's V Corps capturing Schmidt, a key crossroads village overlooking the Roer headwaters on the southeastern fringes of the Huertgen Forest. With this preliminary attack, to be launched through the woods rather than up the more open Monschau corridor, Hodges hoped to gain maneuver room for the VII Corps, protect its southern flank, and divert enemy reserves from the main effort. To accomplish this, he gave Gerow four divisions, but one was to be earmarked for possible use in the main attack by Collins, who had been asked to prepare two attack plans, one with three divisions for 5 November and one with four divisions for 10–15 November. Since the V Corps still had twenty-seven miles of front to cover, Gerow felt he could spare only the 28th Division for the Schmidt attack.[70]

On 1 November, because of the delay of the 21st Army Group's operations and the arrival of reinforcements, Bradley postponed the U.S. First Army's main offensive until 10 November. At this point, Collins's VII Corps—with one armored and three infantry divisions, sixteen field artillery battalions, an infantry regiment, an armored combat command, and a cavalry group—stood ready to deliver the principal thrust. Gerow's V Corps comprised one armored and three infantry divisions, thirteen field artillery battalions, and a cavalry group, while Hodges retained control of one armored and one infantry division as his army reserve. Farther to the south, Middleton's VIII Corps deployed one armored and three infantry divisions, thirteen field artillery battalions, and two cavalry groups. For the attack on Schmidt, which was not postponed, Gerow's V Corps had priority for artillery ammunition. The experience of the 9th Infantry Division in its second attempt to penetrate the Huertgen on 6 October—in which two regiments lost 4,500 casualties for an advance of less than two miles in ten days—also prompted Gerow to place eight battalions of artillery in direct support of the 28th Infantry Division. The division, reinforced with three combat engineer battalions, a chemical mortar battalion, and tank and antitank attachments, also had call on another six artillery battalions for preparatory fire.

On 2 November, the 28th Infantry Division passed through the wreckage of the 9th into the attack with three regiments abreast in a plan that Hodges had considered excellent.[71] Initially, the 28th, commanded by D-Day hero Maj. Gen. Norman Cota, made good progress, taking Kommerscheidt and advancing into Schmidt by the evening of 3 November. The Germans concentrated their reserves against this single thrust and, the next morning, counterattacked with tanks and infantry, overrunning Schmidt and threatening Cota's right flank in the area of Monschau. Driven back on Kommerscheidt northwest of Schmidt, the Americans tried desperately to hold on while divisional reserves were committed elsewhere. This might have resulted from Gerow's alleged insistence on having Cota disperse his forces in pursuit of other objectives rather than concentrating them against Schmidt. Allegedly, too, Cota never ventured out in the forest to see the situation firsthand and thus lost control of the battle.

On 5 November, Hodges visited the 28th Division's command post to vent his personal displeasure. Two days later, Cota recommended withdrawing from the Kommerscheidt salient. When Hodges visited the 28th Division with Eisenhower and Bradley on the eighth, he reprimanded Cota for not knowing the dispositions of his units. Over the next few days, he continued to criticize Cota for not properly deploying his troops to withstand artillery bursting in trees and assigned him a number of new tasks that were clearly beyond the capability of the now-decimated division.[72] If units were properly deployed and dug in, Hodges insisted, "no matter how heavy enemy artillery was, casualties would not be high nor would ground be lost."[73] By the time Hodges agreed to its relief on 13 November, the 28th Division had incurred 6,184 casualties.

Meanwhile, the plan to launch a major offensive toward the Roer by the U.S. First and Ninth Armies, Operation Queen, had been approved on 7 November. Since the two field armies deployed only fourteen divisions on a fifty-six-mile front, Bradley had included an air program that dwarfed Cobra. If weather permitted, Queen would open with attacks by 4,500 airplanes, almost half of them heavy bombers. On the First Army's front, more than 1,000 B-17s and B-24s were slated to bomb personnel and field installations in the Eschweiler-Weisweiler and Langerwehe-Jungersdorf urban industrial areas, while mediums engaged closer targets near the villages of Luchem, Echtz, and Mariaweiler. Much farther out, 1,000 more heavies of RAF Bomber Command were to attack the towns of Düren, Jülich, and Heinsberg. Nearly 750 fighter-bombers were also to be available on call for close air support. To avoid the short bombings that plagued Cobra, planners took elaborate safety precautions and placed the bomb line about 3,600 meters beyond the line of departure.

The First Army's offensive launched on the afternoon of 16 November constituted the Allies' principal thrust on the Western Front, and Bradley believed it would be decisive in the defeat of Germany. Hodges, possibly influenced by his experience of bitter fighting in the Argonne Woods during World War I, remained unshaken in his belief that the Huertgen Forest had to be secured. As in the case of Aachen, he thought that bypassing the forest simply posed too great a risk, a view shared by Collins. Thus, Hodges called for Collins's VII Corps to deliver the main thrust through the Stolberg corridor while continuing to clear the edge of the Huertgen Forest on his right flank. Gerow's V Corps, as usual, received a supporting role. Collins, for his part, assigned the central thrust from Schevenhutte through Gressenich and Hamich to the 1st Infantry Division, which also had responsibility for shoring up the high ground on the fringe of the Huertgen Forest. Once it took Hamich Ridge, the 3rd Armored Division on the left of the 1st was to exploit rapidly into the Roer plain. Meanwhile, on the VII Corps' extreme left, the 104th Infantry Division was to seize the commanding Donnerberg Ridge, the industrial outskirts of Stolberg, and the town of Eschweiler. At the same time, on the VII Corps' right flank, the 4th Infantry Division was to clear the area between Schevenhutte and the village of Huertgen.

Despite the elaborate planning and preparation that went into Operation Queen, however, the VII Corps managed to advance only two miles in four days.[74] Neither the air nor artillery programs produced the expected effect on the enemy. Pushing the bomb line so far forward to protect American troop concentrations left German frontline troops essentially unharmed. Düren, Jülich, and Heinsberg were devastated, and one German division detraining in Jülich was hit particularly hard, but apart from some disruption to communications and rear artillery emplacements, the fortified German defensive barrier remained intact. The bombardment had not blown a hole through which ground forces could dash.[75]

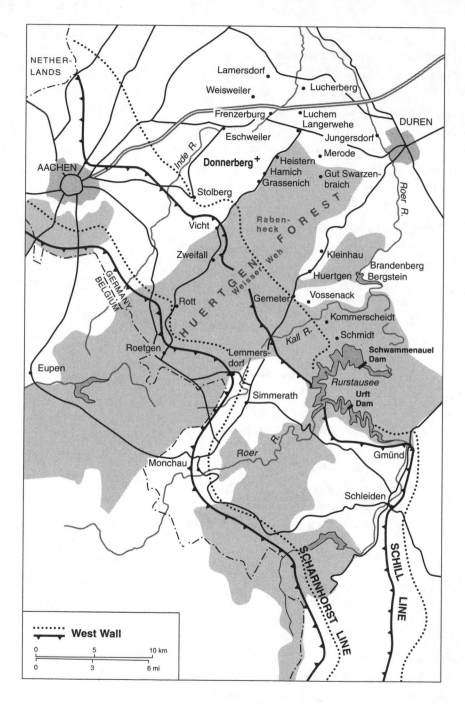

NETHER-
LANDS

Lamersdorf

Weisweiler

Lucherberg

Frenzerburg

Luchem
Langerwehe

DUREN

Eschweiler

Jungersdorf

Donnerberg +

Heistern
Hamich
Grassenich

Merode

Gut Swarzen-
braich

AACHEN

Stolberg

Roer R.

Vicht

Raben-
heck

F O R E S T

Zweifall

Kleinhau

Brandenberg
Bergstein

Huertgen

Rott

H U E R T G E N

Weisser Weh

Gemeter

Vossenack

GERMANY
BELGIUM

Kommerscheidt

Roetgen

Kall R.

Schmidt

Schwammenauel
Dam

Eupen

Lemmers-
dorf

Rurstausee

Urft
Dam

Simmerath

Roer
R.

Monchau

Roer

Gmünd

Schleiden

SCHARNHORST LINE

SCHILL
LINE

········· **West Wall**

━━━━━━━ **West Wall**

0   5   10 km

0   3   6 mi

The Huertgen Forest

Against the Donnerberg Ridge, the 104th Division made no headway, which left the 3rd Armored Division's line of advance exposed to crossfire from that position and the Hamich Ridge on the right. In the 1st Infantry Division's sector, the attached 47th Infantry Regiment became locked in house-to-house fighting in Gressenich while the 16th Infantry Regiment's advance on Hamich encountered stiff resistance from the fringes of the Huertgen Forest. Meanwhile, the 26th Infantry Regiment on the division's right gained only a few hundred yards as fighting in the forest degraded the value of supporting tanks and artillery but greatly increased the shower of steel from enemy mortar and artillery shells that burst on contact with tree tops. Deeper in the woods and aggressively counterattacked from the start of its silent attack, the 4th Infantry Division got nowhere. On its left, the 8th Infantry Regiment stalled before Gut Schwarzenbroich while in the center the 22nd Infantry Regiment struggled to capture the heights at Rabenheck. Farther to the right and out of contact with the 22nd, the 12th Infantry Regiment doggedly clung to a defensive position between the Weisser Weh and Germeter-Huertgen road that had previously been occupied by the now decimated 28th Division.[76]

Hodges was not pleased with the slow progress of the painstakingly pre-pared attack, which he expected to be "the last big offensive necessary to bring Germany to her knees."[77] He criticized the tactics of the 104th Divi-sion, which to his mind "still had much to learn," and complained about the 4th Division "going about the attack in the wrong way—running down roads as far as they could instead of advancing through woods tightly buttoned up yard by yard."[78] In light of the excessively wide regimental dispositions of the 4th Division at the time, such criticism appears unduly severe—fighting in the Huertgen could resemble fighting in the night. On 19 November, Hodges wisely reduced the 4th Division's front by moving the intercorps boundary northward. He then ordered both the V Corps and the VII Corps to plan renewed attacks for 21 November, with Gerow's V Corps assaulting on the immediate right of the VII Corps, along with the fresh 8th Division from the VIII Corps that had assumed responsibility for the 28th Division's sector. The 8th, supported by Combat Command Reserve of the 5th Armored Division, was to take the key crossroads of Huertgen just inside the eastern fringe of the forest. Hopes ran high because by 20 November the VII Corps' situation looked more promising. Although the 4th Division remained stalled, the 1st Division had made some gains, and the 104th Division, after clearing Stolberg, had reached the outskirts of Eschweiler. In the afternoon, Hodges motored to see the 8th Division commander, Maj. Gen. Donald A. Stroh, and returned to his headquarters "exceedingly well pleased with the tactical planning which had been evolved."[79] Indeed, he was so upbeat that after two weeks of routinely working sixteen-hour days from 0800 to midnight, he admitted he needed some rest and left his office at 2230.

Gerow's V Corps launched its new attack on 21 November with heavy artillery preparation—in contrast to the VII Corps, which had used almost no artillery to support the 4th Division on 16 November.[80] Still, the 8th Division made slow progress. Since Hodges had personally instructed Stroh "to go slowly, buttoned up, and to avoid if possible mine casualties," he was not initially disappointed. He was also busily preoccupied in working out with his artillery adviser, Brig. Gen. Charles E. Hart, a deliberate fire plan that targeted enemy rear areas and gradually shifted artillery fire forward to deal with potentially deadly German mortar nests. On 23 November, however, Hodges visited Stroh and, in the presence of Gerow and Collins, told him in no uncertain terms that he was not satisfied with the progress being made. Minefields had not proven to be as formidable as feared, and Hodges expressed the view that the 8th's lack of progress reflected a "lack of confidence and drive." He made it quite clear to Stroh that he expected better results the next day.[81] Unfortunately, because of poor weather, enemy fortifications, rugged and forested terrain, and ferocious German opposition, Stroh could not deliver. The village of Huertgen was not cleared of Germans until noon on 28 November. Stroh, worn out from two years of steady combat and saddened by the death of his only son, a bomber pilot shot down over Brest, had requested leave the day before. Gerow, considering him unable in the circumstances to lead the division, immediately approved. Hodges concurred and arranged for his relief the same day.[82]

By 5 December, the V Corps and VII Corps had narrow spearheads inching out of the Huertgen toward the Roer River. With elements of the 5th Armored Division, the 8th Infantry Division, now commanded by Brig. Gen. William G. Weaver, had captured Kleinhau, Huertgen, Brandenberg, and Bergstein. Within the VII Corps, the battered 4th Infantry Division, also supported by armor, had taken Grosshau and advanced to Gey. Farther to the left, the 1st Infantry Division had seized Frenzerburg, Langerwehe, and Jungersdorf northwest of Düren, while the 104th Infantry Division had reached the vicinity of Lamersdorf and Lucherberg beyond Eschweiler. To the 5,500 and 6,184 casualties incurred by the 9th and 28th in the Huertgen Forest were now added 6,053 from the 4th Division (including 2,000 to trench foot, respiratory disease, and battle exhaustion), 5,200 from the 8th Division and CCR of the 5th Armored (including 1,200 to the noncombat perils of the grim forest), and 1,479 from the 1st Division elements that fought there. All told, the struggle for the Huertgen Forest claimed an estimated 24,000 Americans killed, wounded, and missing and up to 9,000 victims of trench foot, respiratory disease, and battle exhaustion. By this time, the shortage of replacements, especially for trained riflemen and combat officers, had reached crisis proportions.[83] When asked by Kean whether American divisions would be expected to fight at half-strength like the Germans, Bradley replied, "Yes, I am afraid that is so."[84]

Hodges can be rightly faulted for his conduct of the Huertgen Forest battle. Never visiting below divisional level, he failed to gain a true feel for what was happening in the appalling conditions in which his troops struggled. Thus, he expected too much of tired, understrength, overstretched divisions that were left in the line too long. Introduced piecemeal and unable to generate or obtain reserves, they were never able to concentrate sufficient combat power to deal with German infiltration and reserves. As a field army commander supposed to think days ahead, Hodges should also probably have earlier recognized the importance of the Roer dams—that as long as the Germans controlled them, their waters could be released to flood the valley and trap Americans who had crossed the Roer.[85] With the dams in American hands, however, the Germans would have been forced to withdraw or run the risk of having a flooded Roer at their backs.[86] If Hodges had had a "plans" subsection within his G3 headquarters staff section, his preoccupation with the tactical details of operations in progress might have been supplanted by a greater appreciation of longer-range problems, such as those associated with the dams—problems that were properly the responsibility of a field army commander.[87] Moreover, if Hodges had focused on the capture of the dams, he might have avoided the bitter battle for the Huertgen Forest since the best route to the dams lay south of the forest through the Monschau corridor. By this route, the Americans could also have outflanked the defenses of the forest instead of taking them head on. This would have been all the more desirable because the makeshift assemblage of German troops hiding within the forest, while capable of defending their own ground, possessed little capacity to mount offensive operations from the woods. In other words, the most certain way to make the Huertgen Forest a menace was for the U.S. to choose to fight there.[88] In insisting on doing just this, Hodges essentially accepted battle on the Germans' terms in difficult, unfamiliar terrain that neutralized U.S. advantages in tank mobility, artillery, and air power in support of foot soldiers. To Charles B. MacDonald, who fought there, the real tragedy was that it was a misconceived and basically fruitless battle that could have, and should have, been avoided.[89]

Although Hodges had by 11 November recognized the significance of the dams, and accordingly directed that no troops were to advance beyond the Roer except on his orders, he did not switch his main effort from the Stolberg corridor that drew him into the Huertgen. He instead expressed the hope that the dams could be destroyed by air attack to release an uncontrolled but brief tide, thus obviating any need for his First Army to take them. After several bomber strikes failed to destroy the dams, however, all air effort ceased, much to the disappointment of Hodges, who continued to advocate air action in his unshaken belief that a 1,000-plane raid could do the job. The plan that Hodges worked out for the capture of the dams called for the VII Corps to attack on 10 December toward the Roer, where it would wait until the V Corps jumped off on 13 December to seize the Schwammenauel and Urfttalsperre dams. Following this, the 8th Division would deliver a third attack southward. Hodges, who had predicted on 27 November that the war would be over in two months, ventured that the VII Corps would have no difficulty in reaching Düren and that, while the going might at first be slow in the V Corps' sector, "the Boche simply has not the reserves to meet this 1-2-3 punch."[90]

The initial progress of the VII Corps on 10 December appeared to confirm as much. So did the attack of Gerow's V Corps up the Monschau corridor on the thirteenth. Having been allotted the major share of artillery ammunition, Gerow called for the new 78th Division to strike through the Monschau corridor to Schmidt, driving on the dams from the north, while the 2nd Division moved through the Monschau Forest to envelop the dams from the south. Meanwhile, the tired 8th Division remained engaged on the eastern edge of the Huertgen Forest to the north of the Monschau corridor while the 99th Division provided flank protection to the south. On the beautiful day of 14 December, both the 78th and 2nd were stopped cold by increasingly stiff opposition and, in the Monschau Forest, on rugged terrain eerily reminiscent of the Huertgen.[91]

During the foggy morning of 16 December, numerous reports of enemy attacks began to emanate from Middleton's VIII Corps in the Ardennes. Deployed along a relatively quiet seventy-five-mile front no longer viewed as a likely German counterattack approach, the VIII Corps served as a formation in which to acclimatize new divisions and rest and refit shattered veteran ones.[92] With three times the normal corps frontage, it also took up the slack for the concentration of the V Corps and the VII Corps to deal with the dams and advance on the Roer farther to the north. Hodges initially considered the German actions to be "spoiling attacks" designed to take the pressure off the V Corps' drive on the Roer dams.[93] When Gerow asked for permission to suspend the V Corps' drive and organize a defense of the northern shoulder on Elsenborn Ridge, he was refused since no one thought the situation to be critical. By late morning, however, it became more evident that the enemy was making a concerted thrust along the general area of the boundary between the V Corps and the VIII Corps. In fact, what was unfolding was an all-out offensive by eight panzer and seventeen infantry divisions of the Germans' Sixth SS, Fifth, and Seventh Armies that aimed at producing a second Dunkirk. Hodges immediately placed the 1st Infantry Division, resting in Aubel, on a six-hour alert, and not long after a call to Bradley, he was given the 7th Armored Division from Simpson's Ninth Army and the 10th Armored Division from Patton's Third. Still, within the totally surprised First Army headquarters, debate raged all day and into the evening between the G2 and G3 sections over the nature and scope of the offensive. Early on 17 December, Hodges agreed to let Gerow do as he saw fit. When German forces broke through the Losheim gap that morning, he also sensed that his field army was in deep trouble.[94]

At this point, Hodges's grip on the situation appears to have failed. Indeed, the overwhelming evidence indicates that he was incapacitated for at least two days and that effective command of the First Army devolved on Kean, his chief of staff. Even before the German onslaught, Hodges had shown signs of fatigue, and on 15 December, he had retired early with a cold. Arguably, he had driven himself to exhaustion by a punishing schedule that allowed him only one hour of sleep a night during the drive on the Roer— the very same shortcoming he had observed in Corlett. On 17 December, he spent almost the entire morning in the G3 section. The First Army's deputy chief of staff for operations, Col. S. L. Myers, later recounted that Hodges had the flu and, though feeling bad because of what had happened, still man-

aged to maintain sufficient presence of mind, to provide general overall guidance, "except for very, very brief interludes." According to a later interview
with Kean, however, Hodges had been bedridden, barely conscious with viral
pneumonia. Kean's military aide further recalled finding Hodges sitting in his
office with his head in his arms on his desk and Kean ordering that hence-
forth he himself would receive all calls and visitors.[95] Significantly, when Maj.
Gen. James Gavin reported to Hodges in person at 0900 on 18 December, he
described the First Army commander as "a bit weary—he had been through
a trying forty-eight hours," but Kean was "very much on top of the situation."[96] With the concurrence of Hodges, Kean directed the deployment of
one of Gavin's airborne divisions to Bastogne under the VIII Corps' command.[97] There is good reason to believe, therefore, that Kean had managed to
minimize the effect of his commander's lack of vigor, a task made easier by
Hodges's long-established practice of working through a small inner group
of staff officers.[98]

By midnight on 17 December, First Army headquarters, at Kean's direction, had started the countermoves of 60,000 troops and 11,000 vehicles that
included two infantry divisions, two armored divisions, an infantry regiment,
and one each of infantry, artillery, tank, and tank destroyer battalions. Simultaneously, the displacement of logistical installations commenced. Since the
Germans intended to use captured gasoline to maintain their offensive, two
fuel dumps with roughly three million gallons of gasoline were moved by
road and rail from the area of Malmedy. After three days, only 124,000 gallons remained, and these were ignited; the Germans managed to seize only
50,000–60,000 gallons. Four thousand tons of supplies in the First Army's
depot at Eupen and the ration depot at Welkenraedt were moved to safer
areas. Since ordnance depots were kept open as long as possible, the Germans
overran two ammunition points, but even here much was saved. While the
medical section successfully moved its evacuation hospitals from Malmedy to
Verviers, the map depot at Stavelot was lost. By 22 December, most ordnance
service installations had been shifted behind the Meuse. In the end, the First
Army saved the bulk of it supplies, about 45,000 tons in all. Between 17 and
26 December, more than 48,000 vehicles and 248,000 personnel were also
moved and regrouped.[99]

The deteriorating situation on 18 December had forced the First Army's
headquarters to move hurriedly that evening from Spa to Chaudfontaine,
which further confused a confusing situation.[100] The loss of most of the G4

traffic control section to a V-1 missile deepened the gloom that descended on the headquarters during its relocation. Faced with disorder in the rear area and lacking reliable information about the situation on the front, neither Hodges nor his headquarters possessed a clear grasp of how the battle was unfolding. Part of the problem reflected the inadequate information–gathering capabilities prescribed for a field army commander by doctrine. The First Army never devised an efficient system like that of Montgomery's Phantom service and his team of bright young liaison officers dispatched to lower formations and units with the express purpose of reporting developing situations to him in a timely manner.[101] Most First Army liaison officers were still assigned to corps, adjacent armies, and higher headquarters mainly to convey Hodges's intentions. Keeping him informed was secondary to briefing G3 routinely in the afternoon. Hodges attended only half of these briefings. Although this left First Army headquarters out of touch with events at the front and unable to adequately assist forward units, it did manage to shore up the northern shoulder holding out against the German penetration by rushing reinforcements there. In addition to saving the great bulk of its supplies, it also rounded up substantial replacement equipment. For this and much of the direction forthcoming from headquarters, Kean deserved most of the credit. According to Bradley's aide, he had in the moment of crisis proven to be a "Rock of Gibraltar."[102]

With the German penetration now ballooning between Chaudfontaine and Bradley's mispositioned 12th Army Group headquarters in Luxembourg, Eisenhower on 20 December placed both Hodges's First and Simpson's Ninth Armies under the operational control of Montgomery's 21st Army Group. Simultaneously, the British 2nd Tactical Air Force assumed control of the First's and Ninth's respective IX and XXIX Tactical Air Commands, giving Quesada overall responsibility for both. Middleton's VIII Corps had meanwhile been transferred to Patton's Third Army, which remained under Bradley. This was a sound arrangement, and many in Hodges's beleaguered staff, to whom the 12th Army Group appeared remote and even uncaring, saw benefits in the change.[103] When Montgomery first arrived at Hodges's headquarters on 20 December, he provided a degree of direction and support that had not been forthcoming from Luxembourg. The British 30 Corps had already taken up a position on the northern bank of the Meuse near Liege, and a brigade later assumed responsibility for defending Meuse bridges.[104] Eventually, the British provided the First Army with 200 medium tank replacements,

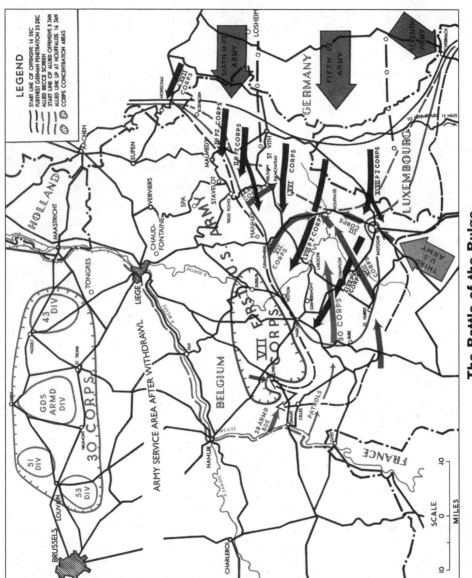

The Battle of the Bulge

enough 25-pounder guns and ammunition to equip four artillery battalions, and thirty 6-pounder antitank guns to replace American 57-millimeter models lost in combat. Throughout the battle, Montgomery visited Hodges's headquarters daily in the afternoon to talk over the situation and lend support.[105]

At 0230 on the morning of 20 December, a major from Montgomery's staff had a bedside conference with Hodges and Kean.[106] Montgomery followed in the afternoon, and during his first meeting with Hodges, he agreed that it was imperative for the V Corps to hold the northern shoulder at all costs. On the whole, Montgomery approved of most of the First Army's dispositions, including the proposed drive to link up with the 7th Armored Division at the road junction at St. Vith. He then requested that the U.S. Ninth Army take over the VII Corps' front to enable Collins to assemble a counterattack force of at least three new divisions in the area of Durbuy and Marche behind the Ourthe River.[107] Montgomery retained personal control of this force to prevent a Liege–Namur crossing, since he did not think that Hodges had an adequate grip on the situation.[108] He recorded that he dealt mainly with Kean and that Hodges looked worn and anxious.[109] Montgomery's intelligence chief was less kind and remarked that Hodges looked as if he had been poleaxed. When Montgomery later hinted that he might have to remove Hodges, Eisenhower defended his subordinate but essentially gave permission to do so.[110] Eisenhower's deputy G2, Brig. Gen. Thomas J. Betts, went to investigate conditions at First Army headquarters on 21 December and reported the place a mass of confusion and recommended that Hodges be relieved.[111] Ultimately, Montgomery did not relieve Hodges but exercised much closer supervision over the First Army than he had in the past. Through his Phantom service and liaison officer "gallopers," he was also able to offer information on low-level developments that Hodges's system was unable to acquire. At the same time, American corps commanders were informed of Montgomery's intentions long before written orders could be passed down the chain of command.[112] Montgomery further supplemented his Phantom and liaison reports with numerous personal visits to divisions and corps, the only senior commander to do so.[113]

By 21 December, Hodges was on the mend, and the next day, his headquarters moved to the "peace and quiet" of Tongres. Here Hodges took up residence in a private home where, "with a chance for rest, and with good food again provided, he . . . [began] feeling fitter and better able to cope with the constant pressure of . . . work and strain."[114] Indeed, he felt well enough to travel in the bitter cold of 23 December to discuss counterattack planning with Collins at Marche. The gravest threat at this juncture appeared to be a German thrust in the vicinity of Manhay between the VII Corps and Matthew Ridgway's XVIII Corps fighting in the center to the right of the V Corps, which held the northern shoulder. In the face of mounting enemy pressure, Montgomery had granted permission for the beleaguered 7th Armored and 106th Infantry to withdraw from St. Vith, where their vigorous six-day defense had helped the 101st Airborne hold out at Bastogne. By Christmas Eve, the situation grew bleaker since German penetrations as far west as Celles—but still four miles from Dinant on the Meuse—compelled the VII Corps to sidestep and, although designated a reserve, blunt the enemy spearhead. At this point, in response to Hodges's request for more 21st Army Group troops to back up his line, Montgomery gave him the 51st (Highland) Division as a reserve while reconstituting Collins as an uncommitted reserve.[115] Meanwhile, on the southern flank of the German salient, Patton's Third Army had launched a drive to relieve Bastogne.

In retrospect, it can be seen that the German offensive approached its high water mark late on Christmas Day, but it was not clear at the time that the Germans had no reserve capacity to continue attacking. In fact, the Germans did manage to mount one last offensive on the Western Front, but this came in the form of Operation *Nordwind* on 31 December against the 6th Army Group in Alsace. After *Nordwind,* which aimed partly at easing American pressure on the left flank of the Germans' Ardennes drive, much of the concern about German reserves dissolved. Up to this point, however, the First Army's G2 worried that the Germans had seventeen uncommitted divisions, eleven near Aachen and six facing the northern shoulder held by the V Corps.[116] All of this naturally affected Allied counterattack planning related to the reduction of the German salient. Classically, the best way to reduce a salient was to trap the enemy inside by slashing through its base on both sides from strongly held shoulders, and the best way to defend against such an attack was to employ reserves to strike along the salient's outer edges through the flanks of those forces attacking inward from the shoulders. For this reason, as the Germans had learned through painful experience in Russia, it was often more sensible to tackle a salient midway between its base and tip.[117] In the case of the Battle of the Bulge, planners also generally agreed that the road network at the base of the salient was incapable of supporting any attack in that area.[118]

After Christmas Day, Hodges and most of his staff concluded—correctly, as things turned out—that the German offensive had run its course and that the First Army could now transition to the counteroffensive. To a certain extent, this represented the triumph of the G3 section, which had dismissed the pessimistic estimates of the G2 by arguing, as far back as 21 December, that the German attack had been blunted. Even as early as 19 December, Hodges and his staff had wanted to counterattack, but Montgomery believed in rolling with the punches. He saw ground as "something to be fought over, not for" and insisted that the main German effort be allowed to run its course, ideally past its culminating point—that juncture in every attack where the defensive must be assumed in order to be viable—when a counterattack would have maximum effect.[119] The most critical actions, in the meantime, were to shore up the northern shoulder and channel the enemy penetration to prevent the Germans from crossing the Meuse and advancing on Liege and Antwerp, Hitler's actual objective. Obviously, the Allied stakes were highest on the northern side of the salient, although its ultimate reduction depended on Bradley's coordinated action from the south. To ensure this, on 19 December, Eisenhower had instructed Jacob Devers's 6th Army Group to assume the defensive and take over twenty-five miles of Patton's southern front, which, in turn, enabled Patton to attack northward. When Patton's 4th Armored Division in Millikin's III Corps broke through to besieged Bastogne in the south and middle of the salient on 26 December, counterattack planning within the First Army intensified.[120]

On 27 December, Collins presented Hodges with three counterattack plans, two aimed at Bastogne and one at St. Vith, which would have invited a classic salient defense by the Germans. The plan finally approved by Hodges called for Collins's VII Corps to attack midway between the base and tip of the salient toward Houffalize, where it would link up with Patton's Third Army breaking out of Bastogne. The thrust was at first to be made along the west bank of the Ourthe River, but when Montgomery deployed the British 30 Corps to take over the VII Corps' sector west of the river, Hodges shifted Collins's attack east of the Ourthe. On 3 January, the VII Corps attacked with two armored divisions: the 3rd Armored backed up by the 83rd Infantry Division on the left, and the 2nd Armored backed up by the 84th Infantry on the right. Ridgway's XVIII Corps of one infantry, one airborne, and two armored divisions was at the same time charged with protecting the left flank of the VII Corps and attacking toward St. Vith. Unfortunately, the good flying weather that had prevailed since 23 December turned for the worse, bringing freezing rain and heavy snow. Marshy terrain and a dearth of good roads east of the Ourthe, coupled with intense German efforts to seize Bastogne, further impeded the rapid advance of the VII Corps.[121]

Hodges, plagued with a cold since 30 December, exercised little influence over the slugging match that developed. Unlike Montgomery, who went forward to visit Collins and Ridgway, he remained for the most part at Tongres, receiving few visitors while recuperating.[122] After meeting with Montgomery on the afternoon of 4 January, the day before his fifty-eighth birthday, he went straight to bed with a slight temperature. Not until five days later did he feel good enough to visit Ridgway to discuss the plan of attack using the 7th Armored and 30th and 75th Infantry Divisions. By the time the attack jumped off on 13 January, however, he was back in his old form, making known his impatient displeasure with the slow progress of the 30th and 75th. Following Ridgway's recommendation, Hodges later relieved the commander of the 75th Division. On 15 January, the V Corps joined in the attack, and that evening, Hodges learned that Collins's troops had entered Houffalize.[123] There, the next day, the U.S. First and Third Armies linked up, and Montgomery called for a farewell chat. On 17 January, Hodges's army reverted to Bradley's command, and the next day, he returned to his old headquarters at Spa. With the recapture of St. Vith on 23 January, the Ardennes salient was practically erased. Five days later, American lines were restored to what they had been before the morning of 16 December.[124]

The Battle of the Bulge constituted Hodges's greatest test of the entire European campaign. Thanks to the resourcefulness and often magnificent performance of the individual American fighting man and the sound direction of lower-ranking commanders and staff officers, the U.S. First Army survived its ordeal and went on to achieve glory. Gerow's performance—probably his best—in conducting the V Corps' defense of the northern shoulder unquestionably saved the whole show. The leadership of Ridgway in the operations of the XVIII Airborne Corps was of similarly high quality.[125] Collins's VII Corps counterattack, beginning on 3 January under the most appalling conditions, was as inspired as—and doubtlessly facilitated—Patton's later breakout from Bastogne toward Houffalize on 9 January.[126] Unfortunately for the First Army, Patton's dash to the relief of Bastogne during 22–26 December had captured the imagination of the press and public while the efforts of Hodges's long-suffering army had not.[127] Bastogne and its relief came to symbolize the entire Battle of the Bulge.[128] With good reason, many First Army officers expressed resentment at what they perceived to be the self-glorification of Patton and the Third Army's role in the reduction of the Ardennes salient. Indeed, it is difficult to escape the conclusion that while it was primarily the First Army's doggedness and redeployment that won the day, Patton and his Third Army stole the show. Some of the blame for this can no doubt be attributed to Hodges's shot nerves and failure of leadership because of fatigue and illness. In the opinion of one American military historian, "If not for considerations of coalition politics and concern for the impact his dismissal might have [had] at a critical moment of the battle, he probably would have—and should have—been relieved during the Battle of the Bulge."[129]

Although Hodges may have failed as a field army commander, the performance of his staff and troops ensured his survival. He was never again seriously challenged as an army commander. He also turned out to be lucky. On 7 March, after having finally captured the Roer dams[130] and cleared the enemy from the west bank of the Roer, the First Army, in a stroke of good fortune, seized the still-intact Ludendorff railway bridge across the Rhine at Remagen. Remagen was clearly a windfall, generating sensational headlines in the American press. At the time, the First Army formed the northern pincer of Bradley's Operation Lumberjack, which, with the Third Army as its southern pincer, aimed at clearing German forces west of the Rhine between Cologne and Coblenz on the Moselle. In this operation, Collins's VII Corps was charged with capturing the prize city of Cologne while Maj. Gen. John Millikin's III Corps—which had replaced the XVIII Airborne Corps which had reverted to SHAEF reserve—advanced to the Rhine to link up with the Third Army on the Ahr River south of Remagen. Huebner's V Corps was responsible for covering the III Corps' right flank. Although the VII Corps occupied Cologne on 6 March and a jubilant Hodges visited the city the next day, the capture of the bridge at Remagen focused all attention on the activities of Millikin's III Corps. The enthusiastic rush to exploit the bridgehead, however, created a chaotic entanglement of men, weapons, vehicles, and equipment not entirely of the III Corps' making. Since intelligence indicated that the Germans were frantically assembling forces to destroy the bridgehead, the First Army poured more resources into the area than the ground and road infrastructure could bear, and it fell to Millikin to sort the congestion out.[131]

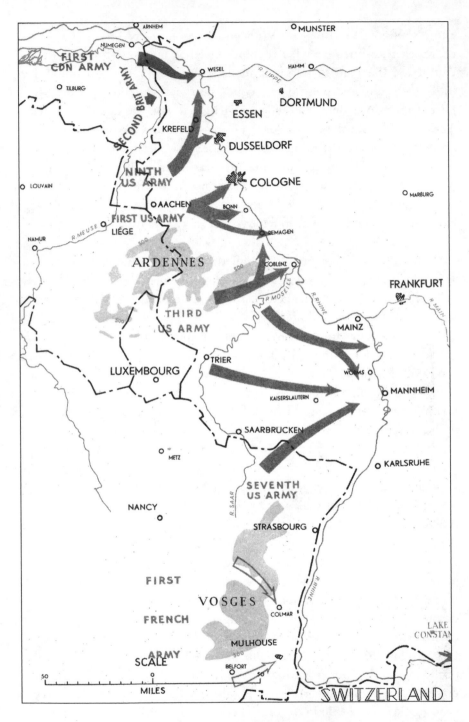

The Allied Drive to the Rhine

Unfortunately for Millikin, the impatient Hodges considered the pace of development of the first Allied bridgehead across the Rhine to be too slow. He showed little sympathy for his subordinate's predicament, and his headquarters offered less help. Hodges simply thought that Millikin lacked sufficient control over the situation, especially in regard to the deployment of troops on the eastern bank and the elimination of German indirect fire. He complained, as well, about the III Corps' failure to forward correct and speedy information on the disposition of troops that had crossed and those that had not. Hodges was particularly irritated by the failure of the III Corps to drive north along the Rhine's east bank to open a crossing for the VII Corps, which he wished to feed into the bridgehead. As usual in tight situations, Hodges preferred to rely on Collins, who on 12 March had openly remarked, "What a shame it was that VII Corps had not been the people to establish the bridgehead," adding that "at the end of the first day, he would have been out at the Autobahn."[132] Three days later, Hodges asked Bradley about the possibility of replacing Millikin; both agreed that while Millikin was a good officer, he was not too good in a pinch.[133] On 17 March, in the middle of the battle for the bridgehead, Hodges fired Millikin. How he did this was revealing. He first welcomed Millikin's replacement, Maj. Gen. James A. Van Fleet, to his headquarters and then called Millikin to say, "I have some bad news for you." Hodges thereupon told Millikin that he was relieved and that, if he wished, he could drop by First Army headquarters the next day. Millikin retorted, "Sir, I have some bad news for you too. The railroad bridge has just collapsed."[134]

On 19 March, Bradley told Hodges to build up his forces in the Remagen bridgehead to nine divisions and prepare for a breakout. Six days later, the First Army attacked out of the bridgehead with Collins's VII Corps on the left striking eastward toward the Dill River more than forty-three miles distant. Van Fleet's III Corps in the center and Huebner's V Corps on the right meanwhile drove southeastward to link up with the Third Army along the Lahn River. After establishing contact around Limburg, both armies then wheeled northeastward, with the First Army's advance centering roughly on Geissen, then north through Marburg toward Paderborn in a wide encircling movement. Not surprisingly, given the fast pace of divisional advances, Hodges was compelled to trust the discretion of his corps commanders because communication was often difficult. By 1 April, with the linkup of the First and Ninth Armies at Lippstadt, ninety-five miles east of the Rhine, the encirclement of the Ruhr was completed. In accordance with Bradley's controversial decision to clear the pocket rather than fling his full force eastward against a collapsing

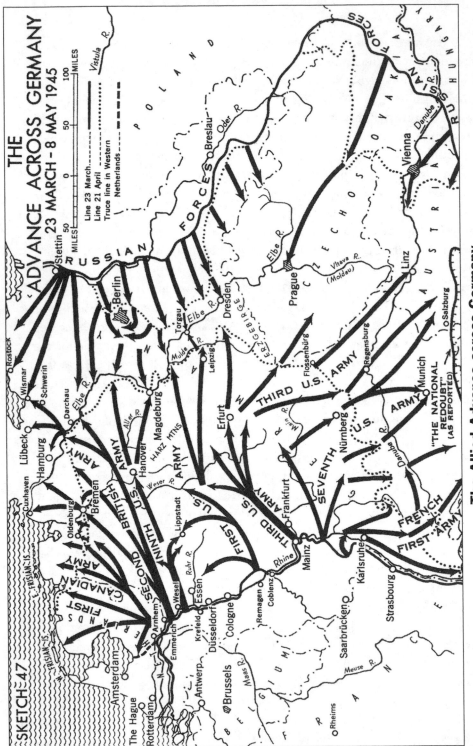

The Allied Advance across Germany

enemy, Hodges now directed the III Corps and the newly regained XVIII Corps to commence mopping-up operations. The combination of heavily forested and urban terrain and stiff resistance by the Germans' Fifth Panzer Army and elements of the First Parachute and Fifteenth Armies—which together disposed twice the estimated 150,000—dashed hopes for a quick reduction. Once again, Hodges displayed his impatience with the slow rate of the III Corps' progress, personally berating Van Fleet and threatening to relieve one of his assistant divisional commanders. Not until 14 April did the First and Ninth Armies meet within the Ruhr, and not until the eighteenth did the remaining 317,000 Germans surrender.[135]

With the reduction of the Ruhr pocket, attention focused on capturing Berlin and meeting up with the Russians. The spectacular gains of the Russian winter offensive in January had brought the Red Army to the gates of Berlin. Whereas western forces were still more than 200 miles away, the Russian bridgehead over the Oder River at Lubin was only thirty-five miles from the German capital and backed up by over a million men. At the Yalta Conference, the Allies had decided to divide Germany into Russian, British, and American occupation zones, the boundaries of which had previously been agreed. For better or for worse, Eisenhower now reversed his earlier decision to advance on Berlin. On 28 March, he decided instead to send the First and Ninth Armies toward Leipzig, southwest of Berlin, in order to adopt strong defensive positions in the area of the Mulde and Elbe Rivers. By this time, Eisenhower considered the reduction of a rumored Nazi "redoubt" in the Alps to be vastly more important than the capture of Berlin. The effect of this decision on the First Army was that while eight divisions of the III and XVIII Corps mopped up the Ruhr pocket, six divisions of the V and VII Corps swept south of the Harz Mountains, driving toward Leipzig and Dessau. By 16 April, both corps had closed to the Elbe-Mulde river line, and three days later, Leipzig fell to the V Corps. On 25 April, troops from the same corps established the first Allied contact with the Russians at Torgau on the Elbe.[136]

The next day, Hodges learned that he and his headquarters had been selected to command a field army in the invasion of Japan. That Marshall recommended Hodges to MacArthur for service in the Pacific was not surprising since both Bradley and Eisenhower retained an unshakeable faith in his command ability. In a promotion list prepared at Eisenhower's request in December 1944, Bradley had ranked Hodges third behind Bedell Smith and Spaatz, but ahead of Patton in sixth place. Significantly, he rated Collins

seventh, Gerow eighth, and Kean twelfth, all well ahead of field army commanders Patch and Simpson, whom he listed as fifteenth and sixteenth,
respectively.[137] Eisenhower later told Marshall that "it would be difficult
indeed to chose between [Patton], Hodges and Simpson for army command,
while Patch is little, if any, behind."[138] He had nonetheless taken precautions
to protect Hodges's reputation. "Bradley and I believe that our successful
Army commanders should eventually be promoted to four-star rank," he
wrote to Marshall on 12 March, "but I would consider it unwise at this time
to imply a comparison to the discredit of Hodges, Patch and Simpson by
making Patton on a separate list ahead of them."[139] In a later message, Eisenhower described Hodges as a "scintillating star."[140] As a result, Hodges was
promoted to the rank of full general on 15 April 1945, one day after Patton.[141] Almost to the end, Bradley insisted that it was only because he was
unostentatious and retiring that Hodges was left behind in the European
headlines sweepstakes and approached anonymity in the war.[142] Ironically, the
most ruthless senior American commander in the European theater, Bradley,
did not fire the second most ruthless, his protégé Hodges, for making mistakes that would have cost others their heads.[143]

Arguably, just as Bastogne allowed Patton to escape the mire of Lorraine,
so Remagen enabled Hodges to salvage a reputation tarnished by the Huertgen and the Battle of the Bulge.[144] The headlines generated by Remagen
were laudatory indeed, and Hodges later insisted it was "the bridge that
changed the war." In his view, its seizure and exploitation saved thousands of
soldiers' lives, paved the way for the spectacular encirclement of the Ruhr,
and shortened the war.[145] Without question, Remagen also secured Hodges
in his position as a field army commander. Accordingly, shortly after the German surrender on 8 May 1945, he and his advanced planning staff left for
New York en route to the Philippines to plan the role of the First Army in
the projected invasion of the Japanese home islands. With the capitulation of
Japan, however, Hodges and Kean were left only to witness the surrender ceremony aboard the USS *Missouri* in Tokyo Bay. Thereafter, they returned to
the United States to join the rear echelon of the First Army's headquarters in
Fort Bragg, North Carolina. Here the First Army took command of ground
force troops along the eastern seaboard, absorbing the Eastern Defense Command. Following the reorganization of the nation into six army areas, the
First Army under Hodges moved on 11 June 1946 to Governors Island, New
York, and assumed responsibility for an area encompassing the states of New

England as well as New York, New Jersey, and Delaware. Hodges remained in command of the First Army until the prospect of being reverted in rank on the army peacetime establishment prompted him to retire to San Antonio, Texas, in 1949.[146] He died on 16 January 1966, eleven days after his seventy-ninth birthday. He is buried with his wife in Arlington Cemetery.

CHAPTER FOUR

In the Shadow of Britannia

GEN. WILLIAM H. SIMPSON, U.S. NINTH ARMY

Gen. William H. "Big Simp" Simpson commanded the U.S. Ninth Army throughout operations conducted from Brittany to the Elbe River between 5 September 1944 and the end of the war. The Ninth Army was the last American field army to be continuously deployed against the Germans on the Western Front and the first to reach the Elbe.[1] Unique among the four American field armies on this front, the Ninth passed under the operational control of the 21st Army Group from 20 December 1944 during the Battle of the Bulge and remained under Montgomery's direction until 4 April 1945, after the encirclement of the Ruhr Pocket. No other American army served so long or closely with the British as the Ninth, and Simpson remained under Montgomery's command longer than any other American general. Married to an English woman, he appears to have gotten along well with the British and often spoke highly of Montgomery, more than once holding him up as a shining example of professional military excellence.[2]

For the good of his reputation among Americans, however, Simpson may have gotten along too well with Montgomery, and the British connection surely accounted for the lack of recognition accorded him during and after the war as compared to Patton, Hodges, and even Patch. He was confirmed as a lieutenant general only on 6 February 1945 and was not promoted to full general until 1954, and then only on the retired list. Although Simpson had graduated with Patton from West Point in 1909 and ended up commanding more tanks than, and a field army as large as, Patton's Third, he remains an almost completely unknown figure. His name cannot even be found listed in the *Dictionary of American Military Biography* edited by Roger J. Spiller, Joseph G. Dawson III, and T. Harry Williams.[3] Although he has been the subject of several articles and an unpublished dissertation, no biography of Simpson has yet appeared.[4]

If Simpson got along well with the British, he also got along well with others. He seems to have been a good-natured and affable leader who enjoyed the confidence of officers and enlisted soldiers alike. The highly regarded commander of the XIX Corps' 2nd Armored Division, Maj. Gen. Ernest N. Harmon, called Simpson one of the truly great leaders of the European theater, a real "general's general," under whom it was a pleasure to fight. Unimpressed by Hodges, Harmon considered it a rich reward to get Simpson as his superior on the transfer of the XIX Corps from the First to the Ninth Army.[5] Possessing a good sense of humor and quick wit, Simpson was a notably sincere and friendly person with a knack for making others feel comfortable.

Variously described as lanky and broad-shouldered, tall and raw-boned, he stood six feet, two inches, and weighed 170 pounds at age fifty-six.[6] Always immaculately dressed, he had an arrestingly remarkable bald head, which a *Life* magazine article said reminded people of biblical prophets, medieval ascetics, and ancient Egyptian kings.[7] Reportedly, Patton first introduced his old classmate to his headquarters staff by saying, "Gentlemen, this is General Simpson. When he isn't commanding Ninth Army, he acts as an advertisement for hair tonic."[8]

Although the unassuming and soft-spoken Simpson presented a contrast with the colorful and outspoken Patton, he regretted his lack of contact with Americans and felt that his career advancement suffered because of it. "You probably noticed that I didn't get my fourth star over there," he later told an interviewer.[9] Yet while he could never forget the disappointment over not receiving promotion to four-star rank while he was in active command of the Ninth Army, he still felt grateful for the recognition even if it did come late.[10] Simpson nonetheless considered it a blessing to be sent to the British as the Ninth Army was then built up to twelve full divisions and stayed that way to the end of the war.[11]

The son of a Confederate veteran of the Tennessee Cavalry, William Hood Simpson was born on 19 May 1888 in the town of Weatherhead, Texas, about thirty miles west of Fort Worth. He attended school there and reportedly starred on the high school football team. At age seventeen, he received an appointment to West Point, graduating 101st out of 103 in the class of 1909 that included Devers as well as Patton.[12] Commissioned a second lieutenant of infantry after graduation, Simpson joined the 6th Infantry Regiment at Fort Lincoln, North Dakota, and trooped with it to the Philippines that fall. In July 1912, the 6th Infantry transferred to a new duty station at the Presidio of San Francisco, where he served for two years. Subsequently ordered to Texas on a border patrol assignment, Simpson returned to San Francisco for duty with the Panama Pacific Exposition in 1915. The following year, he rejoined his regiment in Texas and participated in Pershing's expedition into Mexico.

After promotion to first lieutenant, Simpson served as an aide to Maj. Gen. George Bell Jr., who from 25 August 1917 commanded the 33rd Division stationed at Fort Logan, Texas. In the same year, Simpson accompanied Bell on a tour of observation with the French, British, and American armies in France. Promoted to captain in May 1917, he became the assistant chief of staff in the 33rd Division, which embarked for France in April 1918. While overseas, Simpson attended the American Expeditionary Force General Staff School at Langres and saw action with the 33rd Division in the Saint-Mihiel offensive on 12–16 September and the Meuse-Argonne campaign on September 26–11 November. He received the Distinguished Service Medal for staff service and the Silver Star for personal gallantry. At the end of the war, he was appointed divisional chief of staff with the temporary rank of lieutenant colonel.[13]

After occupation duty, Simpson returned to the United States in June 1919 to assume the position of chief of staff of the 6th Division at Camp Grant in Rockford, Illinois. On 30 June 1920, he reverted to his permanent rank of captain but received a promotion to major the next day. Early in 1921, he reported for duty with the Office of the Chief of Infantry in Washington. The following December in El Paso, he married Ruth (Webber) Krakauer, a London-born widow whom Simpson had first met at West Point. After two years in Washington, he took the Infantry School Advanced Course at Fort Benning, Georgia, from which he graduated in 1924. He then went on to the Command and General Staff School at Fort Leavenworth, Kansas, completing the course as a distinguished graduate on 19 June 1925.

From 1925 to 1927, Simpson commanded the 3rd Battalion, 12th Infantry Regiment, in Maryland. In August 1927, he entered the Army War College, where he headed a committee on medals and decorations that persuaded Marshall to introduce a liberal system of awards. Following graduation in 1928, Simpson joined the General Staff in the War Department, where he worked in the military intelligence section. From 1932 to 1936, he served with the Reserve Officer Training Corps at Pomona College, Claremont, California, teaching military science and tactics. Promoted to lieutenant colonel in October 1934, he returned to the War College as an instructor in 1936.

In September 1938, Simpson received a promotion to full colonel and, on leaving the War College in 1940, assumed command of the 9th Infantry Regiment at Fort Sam Houston, Texas. On promotion to the temporary rank of brigadier general on 1 October 1940, he took over as assistant division commander of the 2nd Division. Following an assignment to command the Infantry Replacement Center at Camp Wolters, Mineral Wells, Texas, he was promoted to temporary major general in September 1941. That October, he assumed command of the 35th Infantry Division at Camp Robinson, Arkansas, taking it to California shortly before the U.S. entered the war. Transferred to Fort Jackson, South Carolina, in May 1942 to lead the 30th Infantry Division, he subsequently took command of the XII Corps, which was activated in September. In October 1943, Simpson was appointed commander of the Fourth Army at San Jose, California, in the grade of temporary lieutenant general.[14]

In January 1944, Simpson took the Fourth Army headquarters to Fort Sam Houston, Texas, where it assumed the training mission of the Third Army, which was slated to move to Europe. There he received instructions to raise another army headquarters to execute the training mission while he took his own headquarters, redesignated the Eighth Army, overseas. On 6 May 1944, Simpson flew with his advance party to Britain, where on 15 May he attended the final SHAEF briefing for the Nomandy invasion at St. Paul's School in London. The next day, he reported to Eisenhower, a War College classmate, who informed him that his Eighth Army would become the Ninth to avoid duplicating the British Eighth. Later in the month, Simpson met with Patton and Bradley, with whom he had never served before, and began to play a part in the Operation Fortitude deception measures for Overlord. With the arrival of the main headquarters body at the end of June, Simpson established his command post in Clifton College in Bristol and assumed responsibility for receiving, training, and equipping incoming units for movement to France. On 18 July, Simpson and key members of his staff flew to France for a familiarization visit. There he met with Hodges, who accompanied him on a tour of combat units and formations. The following day, he sat in on Bradley's Cobra planning conference attended by Collins, Gerow, Quesada, Middleton, and Hodges. Over the next few days, he visited Cherbourg and called on Collins, Gerow, and Corlett at their corps headquarters. On 24 July, he narrowly avoided becoming a casualty of short bombing by the U.S. Eighth Air Force. Fortunately, he did not accept Lesley McNair's invitation to go with him to observe the opening of Cobra the next day—when McNair perished in a short bombing—and returned instead to Bristol.[15]

In the second half of August, Bradley directed Simpson to deploy to France, but there is reason to believe that his ascendancy to field army command was not yet entirely assured at this time. As Eisenhower explained to Marshall in a letter on 31 August, he and Bradley had originally planned to deploy four armies commanded by Hodges, Patton, Simpson, and probably Gerow. Eisenhower suggested that if Patch's army of three divisions were to be separated from the French and placed on the northern flank of the Dragoon operation, it could conceivably be reinforced to become the fourth American army. Eisenhower then went on to propose that if the formation of an additional army were put off, Bradley might prefer to step up an experienced corps commander ahead of Simpson. While stressing that no one objected to Simpson, Eisenhower pointed out that some corps commanders, notably Gerow and Corlett, had actually demonstrated a capacity for handling large formations and were better bets for taking over a new field army command than one who had not actually demonstrated such capacity.[16] Although Eisenhower specifically mentioned Gerow and Corlett for possible army command, military historian Russell Weigley has asserted that while Eisenhower and Bradley would have preferred Collins as the next field army commander in the 12th Army Group after Hodges and Patton; they got Simpson instead because Marshall wanted to assure generals who had trained large formations in the U.S. that they would not be excluded from leading them in action overseas.[17] On 1 October, Eisenhower advised Marshall that Simpson would be kept in command of the Ninth Army but added, "If I had been able to foresee two or three months ago the actual development in command arrangements, I would probably have advanced a corps commander to take over this army." Simpson remained in command by default mainly because arrangements had "gone so far" that Eisenhower thought "it best to follow through."[18]

Unaware of these discussions, Simpson and his headquarters eagerly assumed responsibility for operations in Brittany and covering the 12th Army

Group's southern flank. As Patton had raced east with his main body while dispatching Middleton's VIII Corps to deal with Brittany, it had become progressively more difficult for him to support operations there. Bradley's solution was to have Simpson's Ninth Army take the VIII Corps from Patton's Third, thereby enabling Patton to concentrate on operations in eastern France. Accordingly, the Ninth Army's headquarters moved to France, becoming operational at Rennes on 5 September, and assuming command of the VIII Corps with its one armored and four infantry divisions. By this time, Middleton was twelve days into the siege of Brest—which Patton had prematurely reported as captured on 6 August—where he was complaining about ammunition shortages, lack of aggression in his infantry, and neglect by his army. To enable Middleton to focus entirely on the speedy reduction of Brest, Simpson relieved him of the task of containing enemy garrisons at Lorient and St. Nazaire and took direct command of the 6th Armored and 83rd Infantry Divisions, which were deployed, respectively, at Lorient and St. Nazaire and along the Loire River as flank protection.[19] Simpson also assisted Middleton with ammunition supply, which eventually improved to the point of becoming a deluge. On 8 September, Middleton launched a full-scale coordinated attack on Brest with the 29th, 8th, and 2nd Infantry Divisions, supported by artillery, tanks, and air strikes. In the ensuing close-quarter battle, the Germans fought ferociously, and resistance did not cease until 20 September, six days after SHAEF had decided that Brest was no longer needed as a port. In any case, the port was utterly destroyed, and Simpson considered it a hollow victory.[20]

On 14 September, the XXIX Tactical Air Command (TAC) under Brig. Gen. Richard E. Nugent was activated with four fighter-bomber groups to provide air support for Simpson's Ninth Army. Initially formed by the merger of the 84th and 303rd Fighter Wings under one headquarters, the XXIX TAC developed by 1 October into a full-fledged separate TAC composed of the 36th, 48th, 373rd, and 404th Fighter-Bomber Groups and the 363rd Tactical Reconnaissance Group. Nugent had been assistant chief of staff for operations in the Ninth Air Force. A 1924 graduate of West Point, he had started his career in the infantry but later joined the Air Corps. Following tours as a bomber pilot and assistant military attaché to London in 1940, he received promotions to colonel in March 1942 and brigadier general in June 1943. Prior to joining the Ninth Air Force, he had commanded a fighter wing. Although the XXIX TAC collocated with the Ninth Army and

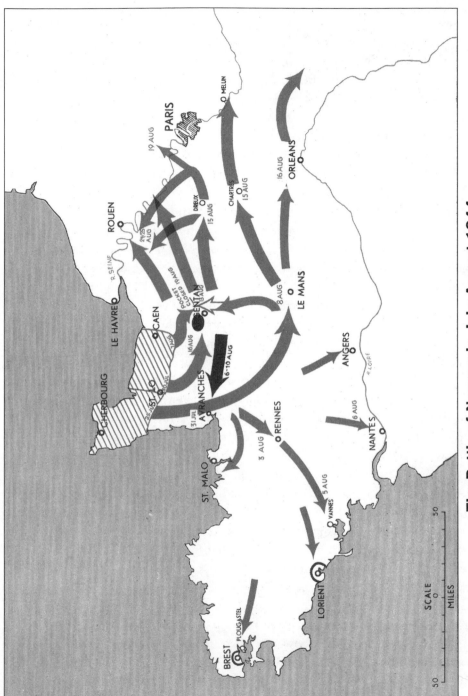

The Battle of Normandy, July–August 1944

deployed air-ground cooperation parties to corps, divisions, and, in certain cases, combat commands and regiments, Nugent adhered to three precepts of tactical air power: maintain air superiority, isolate the battlefield (thought to be the most difficult), and attack targets in close cooperation with ground forces.[21] According to the recollection of one corps commander, the standard operating procedures of the Ninth Army made no provision for the forwarding of immediate-request air missions.[22]

During the siege of Brest, the Ninth Army's long-range planning had focused on occupying a sector on the southern right flank of Patton's Third Army and possibly crossing the Rhine at Karlsruhe, Wiesbaden, or Mannheim. Following the Allied landing in southern France, however, Eisenhower gave priority to strengthening Patch's Seventh Army over building up Simpson's Ninth.[23] In discussing future operations with Bradley on 20 September, Simpson learned that plans had changed. The Ninth Army, now including Middleton's VIII Corps, would be inserted between the First and Third Armies on a quiet sector of the Ardennes currently being held by Gerow's V Corps in the First Army. To enable his army to take over roughly 100 miles of front between the city of Luxembourg and St. Vith, Simpson was also to receive Maj. Gen. Alvan C. Gillem's three-division XIII Corps by 15 October.

On 29 September, the Ninth Army's forward command post opened at Arlon, fifteen miles west of Luxembourg, and the early days of October passed with Middleton's VIII Corps relieving First Army elements in the front line.[24] By now reduced to two infantry divisions, the VIII Corps commenced intensive patrolling, small-scale raiding, and artillery dueling. Simpson was surprised to learn on 9 October, that the Ninth Army was once again to be relocated, this time to a sector north of Aachen on the left flank of Hodges's First Army. What prompted this switch was Bradley's premonition that Eisenhower was going to reinforce Montgomery's 21st Army Group with an American formation for operations north of the Ardennes. Since Simpson's army was the greenest, Bradley reasoned that he could spare it the easiest. In the redeployment, Simpson turned over the VIII Corps to Hodges and moved his headquarters from southern Belgium to southern Holland, taking over the First Army's XIX Corps, now commanded by Maj. Gen. Raymond S. McLain.[25]

In discussions with Eisenhower in May 1944 about who his three corps commanders should be, Simpson selected Gillem as his first choice among ten or eleven names.[26] Gillem was born in 1888 and had enlisted as a private in the 17th Infantry in Georgia in 1910. Soon commissioned, he served in

Mexico and with the American Expeditionary Force in Siberia. A 1923 graduate of the Command and General Staff School at Fort Leavenworth, he attended the War College in 1926. Prior to World War II, he commanded an infantry battalion for two years, an infantry regiment for ten months, an armored brigade in 1941, and an armored division for ten months before and after Pearl Harbor. In December 1943, he took command of the XIII Corps. Unlike Gillem, Raymond McLain was a National Guard artillery officer, a banker from Oklahoma City, and the sole non-regular among American corps commanders. Although he had attended only a three-month National Guard staff course at Leavenworth, McLain had distinguished himself in command of the 90th Infantry Division and, after Hodges fired Corlett, had taken over the XIX Corps in November 1944. The last corps to come under Simpson was the XVI Corps, headed by fifty-three-year-old Maj. Gen. John B. Anderson. One year younger than McLain, Anderson was a graduate of Leavenworth and the War College, where he also served on the faculty from 1934 to 1938. He assumed command of the XVI Corps in January 1944.[27]

Simpson's headquarters opened at Maastricht on 22 October and began the process of building up the Ninth Army to six divisions in preparation for Operation Queen, the main Allied effort by Bradley's 12th Army Group to cross the Rhine and capture Cologne. On 8 November, Gillem's XIII Corps of three divisions assumed responsibility for a sector north of the XIX Corps. The role of the Ninth Army in this general offensive was to clear the west bank of the Rhine within its limited zone while protecting the left flank of the First Army, which spearheaded the operation. Queen commenced shortly after noon on 16 November with a heavy air strike by over 3,000 bombers and an artillery bombardment to cover the assault of the First and Ninth. Because of the narrow twelve-mile frontage of the Ninth Army, McLain's XIX Corps delivered the weight of the offensive for the first few days, with the 2nd Armored Division attacking in the north, the 29th Infantry Division in the center, and the 30th Infantry Division in the south. Gillem's XIII Corps on the northern flank of the XIX Corps meanwhile assisted Horrocks's British 30 Corps in the capture of Geilenkirchen on 19 November.[28] The elimination of the Geilenkirchen salient enabled the XIII Corps to deploy adjacent to the already committed XIX Corps, with the 84th Division north, the 102nd Division south, and the 7th Armored Division in reserve. Although the ground stretching to the Roer River was flat and open, the numerous small towns and villages dotting the area enabled the Germans to develop a

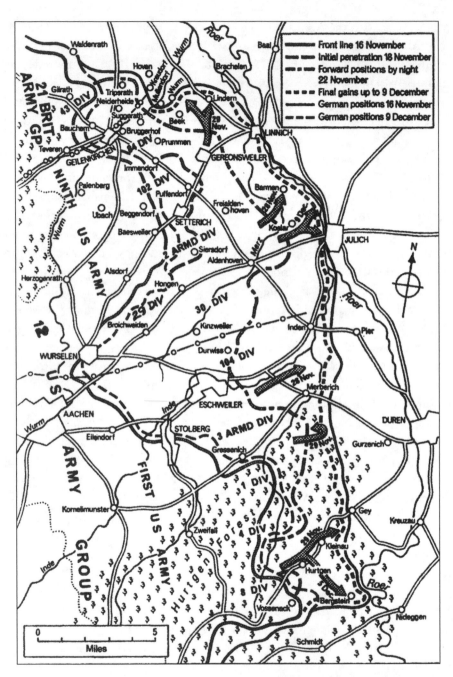

12th Army Group Operations, November 1944

defensive network of mutually supporting positions. Fierce enemy resistance, combined with foul weather, heavy rain, and record flooding, ensured that the battle devolved into one of attrition. In twenty-three days, the Ninth Army incurred 10,256 casualties for an advance of only six to twelve miles. By 9 December, Simpson's army had nonetheless cleared the west bank of the Roer throughout its sector.[29]

Although Queen had fallen well short of attaining its objectives, Simpson could take some satisfaction in knowing that his Ninth Army had advanced more rapidly than the First, possibly because of superior concentration of force rather than better terrain. The Ninth made no major mistakes, and its principal headquarters appeared to perform with quiet efficiency. Unlike the noisy and bumptious Third Army and temperamental First, observed Bradley, the Ninth remained uncommonly normal and the most congenial.[30] Simpson himself relied heavily upon his staff, with whom he enjoyed especially cordial relations. He had an extremely close relationship with his chief of staff, Brig. Gen. James E. Moore, and gave him a great deal of latitude. As Moore later revealed, Simpson was not "his own G3" like Patton and Montgomery, who personally outlined operational concepts. When Simpson received an assigned mission, he usually called in his G2, G3, and G4 and, after providing only general guidance, asked them to develop and present three plans, complete with maps and overlays.[31] After hearing these, he would then choose the plan he liked best and request that it be rewritten to include aspects from the other plans that appealed to him. As Moore stated, "He didn't have to scratch his head about schemes and things, we put staff studies together for him so that he could go out and be seen by the troops." Moore admitted that this system would not have suited Bradley and definitely not Patton or the "the kind of guy that dreams up things in his sleep and wants somebody to work it out for him the next day." He also ventured that the system worked only because of Simpson's supreme confidence in him as chief of staff. Moore could even commit the army reserve, telling Simpson after the fact.[32] Their professional relationship was so close that some called them "the Hindenburg and Ludendorff of the American Army."[33]

Once satisfied with a plan of operations, Simpson told the G2 and G3 to sort out staff details and write up the order. This done, he called a conference of concerned subordinate commanders and staff officers to whom the G1, G2, G3, and G4 outlined their respective sections of the operations order.[34]

Since corps commanders conducted the tactical battle, Simpson always explained the concept to them, frequently orally, and solicited their views before issuing the final order. During the corps planning process, consultations between corps and army staffs continued. Once all corps plans were prepared and submitted to army headquarters, Simpson convened a larger conference at which he and his corps commanders discussed and modified plans as necessary. Meanwhile, Simpson's daily routine carried on, starting with a morning conference during which he and his key officers received updates on the military situation.[35] Following the meeting, he gave appropriate guidance and often met with Nugent and his G3 to discuss air support plans and, if required, with his artillery adviser. He also adjusted his daily visit schedule as necessary to deal with serious matters. Each evening around 1800, Moore assembled his G staff and deputy chief of staff, Col. George A. Millener, for an informal review of the most important staff decisions that had been made during the day and the plans for the next. Later, the senior staff members joined Simpson at the evening meal, after which another officer gave an update on the operational situation. Simpson then telephoned each of his corps commanders to see how things were going and ask them how they felt about plans for the next day. Once finished, he generally discussed the calls informally with a small group, usually the chief of staff, G2, G3, G4, and sometimes the deputy chief of staff. After this, Simpson relaxed by watching a movie or receiving a visitor and taking a brief walk before retiring for the night.[36]

Patton thought Simpson relied too heavily on his staff. Unlike Simpson, he personally provided the guidance by which his G3 developed operational plans for the Third Army, and he was not content simply to rule on proposals produced by the staff.[37] Montgomery was equally adamant that the commander had to make the plan, that "nobody else can make it and it must not be forced on him by the staff, by circumstances, by the enemy."[38] In his view, the commander himself had to be involved from the beginning, thinking his way through the operational challenge by personally assessing the situation to determine the best course of action and outline a plan. The responsibility of the staff was to provide factual information and advice to enable the commander to do this. The commander's guidance helped to optimize staff efficiency by eliminating the wasted effort that the staff would put into plans that stood little chance of ever being adopted. Giving the chief of staff the necessary authority to make all decisions in implementing the commander's plan and to coordinate the work of the staff further enabled the commander to devote himself to the prosecution of future operations.[39] That Simpson did not operate in the manner of Patton or Montgomery may well have prompted Col. Robert S. Allen to charge that the Ninth Army had a generally mediocre staff not held in high regard by other American headquarters. Allen noted the relief of the Ninth Army's G2, Col. Charles P. Bixel, in the middle of the Ruhr offensive and suggested that other members of Simpson's staff should have been removed as well.[40] Simpson later admitted that all was not well within his G2 section, accepting SHAEF's observations that the Ninth Army's G2 reports and returns were below standard compared to the submissions of other armies. He subsequently determined Bixel's mental state to be so poor that he had no choice but to relieve him.[41]

Simpson was apparently deeply influenced by British general Archibald Wavell's biography of Field Marshal Edmund Allenby, a British commander in World War I. Wavell noted that Allenby did not "devil his staff to death." He laid down his general policy and let his staff get on with their assigned tasks without checking on them at every turn and trying to do everything himself. Like Allenby, Simpson sought to avoid getting immersed in detail. At his command post, he passed his guidance and questions through his chief of staff, which also had the effect of enhancing Moore's position among the staff. Simpson does not appear to have isolated himself from his staff as Hodges did, however, and he encouraged them in their briefings with a warm smile and soft-spoken, friendly demeanor. He seldom raised his voice, even in the rare moments he got angry.[42] Although he also encouraged army staff officers to visit their counterparts at corps and division, Simpson himself did not feel the need to visit every division and relied instead on conferences and telephone calls to make contact. Once combat commenced, he closely monitored the situation but generally refrained from interfering with a subordinate commander's conduct of operations. He was nonetheless prepared to modify plans or influence the battle by employing army-level resources. Although he tended not to bypass a corps commander to give orders to a division, there is some evidence to suggest that he was ready to allow staff officers lower in rank than the chief of staff to assume responsibility for ordering divisions around if they thought the situation warranted such action. For the most part, Simpson's visits to subordinate units were inspirational in nature, focusing on morale and the welfare of the troops. Yet on occasion, when Moore and the G3 concluded that a certain division was moving sluggishly, they would suggest that Simpson drop in for a motivational visit. Though the even-tempered Simpson usually just made an appearance in such cases, in at least one instance, he uncharacteristically pounded a table and furiously ordered a divisional commander to get off his tail and take his objective by nightfall.[43]

One can only wonder how Simpson and his staff would have coped had they remained in the line in the Ardennes sector up to 16 December. As it turned out, the Ninth Army, relocated to the north, sat out the Battle of the Bulge, furnishing forces to reinforce Hodges's First Army in the south. As Simpson recalled, Hodges was nearly all in and called him on 17 December to ask for reinforcements.[44] The same day, Simpson dispatched the 7th Armored and 30th Infantry Divisions to St. Vith and Malmedy. Three days later, the 84th Infantry Division moved south, followed by the 2nd Armored and the newly arrived 75th Infantry on 21 December. Anderson's newly arrived, but not yet activated, XVI Corps headquarters also vacated Tongres, Belgium, to allow Hodges's headquarters to redeploy there.

Under Montgomery's operational control beginning on 20 December, the Ninth Army took over the VII Corps' sector of the First Army's front with orders to defeat any enemy attack. Following regrouping, three more divisions passed to Hodges: the 5th Armored and 83rd Infantry Divisions left behind by the VII Corps and the 51st (Highland) Division sent to Simpson as a reserve by Montgomery. This left Simpson's Ninth Army defending a thirty-eight-mile front along the Roer River from north of Monschau to north of Linnich, with the XIII Corps (the 29th and 102nd Infantry Divisions) deployed in the north and the XIX Corps (the 8th, 78th, and 104th Infantry Divisions) in the south. To alleviate a starvation diet of ammunition, one American artillery battalion received German 105-millimeter howitzers while another two were equipped with British 25-pounder gun-howitzers.

For two months, the Ninth Army held a thinly defended line with limited air support, gradually improving its defensive posture, preparing counterattack plans, and carrying out an intensive patrolling and ground reconnaissance program. All this time, the possibility of concurrent German drives from the south and north remained a serious concern. Since the northern flank appeared particularly vulnerable to further attack because of a road network that favored the Germans, plans were also laid to displace or destroy supply depots positioned east of the Maas River.[45]

During this time, planning continued for the crossing of the Roer, which remained an extremely effective barrier for the Germans as long as they possessed the Roer dams, now opposite the Ninth Army's front. All the Germans had to do to trap the Ninth Army if it crossed the river was open the flood-gates of the dams to widen the river. Detailed planning for the Roer crossing had commenced in early December when the Ninth Army first reached the river, but everything then hinged on the First Army's securing the dams. The delay gave the Ninth Army time to build up supplies and organize river-crossing schools on the Maas and Inde Rivers where infantry could train with engineers. It also developed its own plans to take the dams if required, though this remained the First Army's responsibility after the post-Bulge readjustment of its boundary to north of Duren.

Two days after the First and Third Armies linked up at Houffalize on 16 January, Montgomery gave Simpson his orders for assaulting across the Roer in Operation Grenade, the southern pincer of a two-pronged attack on the Rhineland. Tentatively set for 10 February, Grenade was to coincide with Operation Veritable, the northern pincer, to be launched by the First Cana-dian Army on 8 February. Before the U.S. First Army finally captured the Roer dams on 9 February, however, the Germans jammed open the discharge valves instead of blowing them out completely. This produced a sustained overflow of the Roer throughout its length and prolonged the flood period to the greatest possible extent, rendering the Roer impassable to the Ninth Army.[46] As Simpson waited impotently for the waters of the Roer to subside, the First Canadian Army was left to fight alone.[47]

Simpson described his relations with Montgomery at this point as very cordial. Montgomery was polite but aloof and had found numerous excuses beforehand to visit Simpson, seeming to sense that the Ninth Army would eventually come under the 21st Army Group. Simpson correctly noted that Montgomery was skeptical of him at first, which accorded with Mont-gomery's initial assessment of Simpson as extremely easy to work with and a much more delightful personality than Hodges, but not up to the standard of an army commander.[48] Simpson, on the other hand, thought that Mont-gomery had shown great calm during the Battle of Bulge and conducted preparations to meet the Germans with complete self-possession.[49] What Simpson particularly liked was that Montgomery left him alone and "didn't bother him a bit," which permitted substantial freedom of action in planning and execution.[50] The result was that both Simpson and Moore, his chief of staff, got on remarkably well with Montgomery.[51] To a large degree, Simpson also shared some of Montgomery's ideas, among them an affinity for meticulous planning and keeping the battlefield orderly, and passed them along to his corps commanders.[52] Like Montgomery, Simpson was also casualty conscious, and his guiding principle seemed to be never to send an infantrymen where a shell would work just as well.[53] Apparently, American ammunition stocks were so low during Operation Queen that Simpson had personally approved allocations as far down as artillery brigades and continued the use of captured German munitions.[54] Significantly, when Montgomery visited Ninth Army headquarters on 13 November, he predicted that Simpson's offensive would not get very far for lack of ammunition.[55]

This was not to happen in Grenade despite Bradley's announcement to a startled Montgomery on 19 January that the U.S. ration of 105-millimeter artillery ammunition was limited to twenty-seven rounds per gun per day. As recorded in Simpson's personal calendar, this shortage was expected to last until the following November, which meant supplies had to be "massed for a drive of any size, as opposed to the British system of shooting hundreds of rounds."[56] Apparently, British divisional artillery ammunition expenditures were more than double those of American divisional artillery, often averaging more than sixty rounds per gun per day. This scale could not be matched across the U.S. front, and ammunition allocation had to be carefully controlled. Simpson gave the matter his personal attention, setting up a program of rationing and stockpiling to ensure an ample ammunition supply for Grenade. The results were relatively impressive, with the XIII Corps, XIX Corps, and 34th Field Artillery Brigade receiving three "units of fire" for the first day, two for the second, one each for third, fourth, and fifth days, and half a unit per day thereafter.[57] The XVI Corps' allocation comprised one unit of fire for each of the first three days, a half unit for the fourth and fifth days, and one-quarter of a unit per day thereafter.[58] All told, Simpson started Grenade with nearly 46,000 tons of ammunition on hand, enough for twenty days' firing at normal rates of expenditure. In deploying over 2,000 guns—roughly one for every ten yards of front—Simpson also effected the largest concentration of firepower any American field army had yet gathered for an attack on the Western Front. Much of the credit for encouraging such weight, according to Russell Weigley, went to Montgomery, who insisted that the Ninth Army, once committed to the 21st Army Group's offensive, had to be able to deliver the massive power punch that had become his own offensive trademark.[59]

For Grenade, Simpson's Ninth Army had been built up to a strength of more than 300,000 men and 1,000 tanks in three corps totaling eleven divisions, one of them British. Gillem's XIII Corps included the 5th Armored and 84th and 102nd Infantry Divisions; McLain's XIX Corps, the 2nd Armored and 29th, 30th, and 83rd Infantry Divisions; and Maj. Gen. John B. Anderson's recently activated XVI Corps, the 8th Armored, British 7th Armoured, and 35th Infantry Divisions. Simpson retained the 95th Infantry Division in reserve, believing one of his primary functions to be the commitment and then immediate reconstitution of army reserves.[60] The plan of attack called for a night crossing on a narrow front with Gillem's XIII Corps assaulting with the 84th Division on the left and the 102nd Division on the right on a two-mile front at Linnich. McLain's XIX Corps was to assault with the 29th Division on the left at Jülich and the 30th Division on the right at Krauthausen on a three-mile front. To the north of the XIII Corps, Anderson's XVI Corps had the task of simulating a crossing to draw enemy from the left flank of the assault before crossing unopposed into a bridgehead secured by the XIII Corps. Simpson was pleased that his army was to deliver the main effort, with the U.S. First Army providing right-flank protection by having Collins's VII Corps force a crossing at Düren.[61]

Since the ground assault was to be launched under cover of darkness, no heavy bombing strikes were planned. Nugent's XXIX Tactical Air Command, with the assistance of medium bombers from the 9th Bombardment Division, was thus left to soften up and isolate the target area beforehand. The XXIX Tactical Air Command was also increased from three to five fighter-bomber groups, with one group assigned to each of the three attacking Ninth Army corps and two reserved to support each of the armored divisions assigned to exploit success. Although the U.S. Ninth Air Force turned down Nugent's request for more groups, largely because he was under the operational control of the British 2nd Tactical Air Force, he was told he could get more help from Quesada's XIX Tactical Air Force.[62]

The Ninth Army assaulted across the Roer on a fourteen-mile front at 0330 on 23 February after a forty-five-minute artillery bombardment reinforced by mortars, antiaircraft guns, infantry cannon, and tank destroyers that smothered German defenses.[63] Because of elaborate security precautions, including the massing of supplies and troops at night, the Germans were caught by surprise and never able to mount a major counterattack. By the end of the first day, the bulk of the infantry of the Ninth's four assault divisions had crossed the river. Despite considerable interference from enemy artillery and aircraft, the construction of heavy bridging was completed the next day. On 25 February, the Ninth Army made junction with the U.S. First Army to form a bridgehead twenty-five miles long from north of Baal to south of Düren.

By this time, it was clear to Simpson that the Ninth faced no firm enemy resistance. Having prepared two plans, one for rapid advance and one for a more methodical pace, he now initiated the former, giving free rein to his corps commanders. In short order, Gillem's XIII Corps committed its armor in a northward drive to cut off Erkelenz, the capture of which on 26 February rendered the Siegfried defenses opposite Anderson's XVI Corps untenable. This action also opened up the wide open spaces of the Cologne plain into which the XIII Corps poured, passing west and north of Munchen-Gladbach to reach Kreveld and the Rhine on 3 March. Meanwhile, Anderson's XVI Corps crossed the Roer at Hilfarth on 26 February and raced east to Rheinberg and north through Venlo to link up with the First Canadian Army at Geldern on 3 March. At the same time, McLain's XIX Corps advanced east to the Erft Canal, where on 28 February it wheeled northeast past Munchen-Gladbach in an armored drive to the Rhine near Uerdingen, clearing the western bank down to Nuess by 3 March. For all practical purposes, Grenade ended on 5 March, ten days after its launch across the Roer.[64]

Simpson was justifiably proud of the performance of his army in Grenade, citing the operation as a classic example of skill in maneuver. In his view, the operation succeeded, with relatively light losses in men and equipment, in striking the Germans in extremely vulnerable spots on his flank and rear. He particularly noted the examples of the sudden swing to the north following the Roer River crossing, which forced the Germans out of strongly prepared positions in the Siegfried Line, and the bypassing of Munchen-Gladbach, which left it isolated and vulnerable to mopping up later. The steady progress of the attack was further facilitated by good tank-infantry cooperation, air support from Nugent's XXIX Tactical Air Command, and the retention of a reserve that enabled Simpson to rotate weary formations with fresh ones to maintain the momentum of the attack throughout the entire operation. While admitting that the terrain had been highly conducive to the effective conduct of such an operation, Simpson highlighted the importance of the painstaking effort that had been put into the preparation and perfection of plans at all levels. He found it especially gratifying to watch his "preconceived build-up" take shape as the operation progressed; except for minor deviations, the general plan had unfolded very much as had been intended.[65]

Arguably the Ninth Army's most brilliant contribution to Allied victory in Europe, Grenade unquestionably vaulted Simpson into the first rank of American field army commanders.[66] The river crossing cost just over 1,400 casualties while total losses to 10 March numbered some 7,300—less than half the 15,634 incurred by Anglo-Canadian forces in Veritable. As pointed out by Canadian official historian Col. C. P. Stacey, however, "It is no disparagement of the splendid effort of Simpson's soldiers to say that First Canadian Army had somewhat the harder task of the two."[67] In concentrating eleven divisions against Crerar's forces, the Germans left only 30,000 and seventy tanks to face the Americans. Only four weakened divisions faced the Ninth Army when it finally attacked across the Roer. Reserves previously held back to counter the American thrust had also been sucked north into the Reichswald battle.[68] Given his reluctance to intervene in the Hochwald gap bloodbath, this may have been exactly what Montgomery desired, for Crerar drew the Germans onto him just as Dempsey had done at Caen, leaving Simpson to break through on the right as Bradley had done in Cobra.[69]

As the first American field army to reach the Rhine in the north, the Ninth was eager to be the first to cross. Montgomery, however, had assigned the planning and execution of the Rhine crossing, Operation Plunder, to the British Second Army, having given Veritable to the First Canadian Army and Grenade to the Ninth. For Veritable, Montgomery had given Crerar's First Canadian Army a British corps, and he now wished to augment Dempsey's British Second Army with an American corps, telling Crerar on 16 January that he thought the Rhine crossing would be better handled by one rather than two army commanders.[70]

Simpson, who had initiated planning as far back as November for the Ninth Army to cross the Rhine, was taken aback on learning of this proposal. In the exhilarating atmosphere of Grenade, he and his ambitious staff and corps commanders had planned to take the Rhine on the run south of Uerdingen and turn north to clear the east bank for further crossings. Montgomery aimed not just to cross the river but to unleash a massive, sustainable, and unstoppable drive into the heart of Germany, and he feared that a bounce crossing by Simpson south of the Ruhr would turn the Ninth Army into a liability, entangling it in the industrial jungle fronting the Rhine northeast of Uerdingen. Montgomery also wanted an ammunition supply of 600 rounds per gun, which the Ninth Army would have to build up. He therefore refused to authorize a crossing but relented in the face of Simpson's nationalistic objection to the Ninth's being left out of a historic operation—an objection supported by Dempsey as well—to allow the Ninth to participate in Plunder.[71] Although Montgomery's stance triggered widespread suspicion within the ranks of the Ninth Army that he intended to steal the glory for the British, Simpson did consider it plausible that Montgomery may have made the decision primarily because one army headquarters could more easily control the operation.[72] In any case, the fact that the Ninth was not the first, but the second-to-last American army to cross the Rhine continued to rankle.

In Plunder, the Ninth Army crossed north of the Ruhr on a ten-mile stretch between the river's densely populated northern face and Wesel. Anderson's XVI Corps made the crossing, code-named Flashpoint, at 0200 on 24 March, with the 30th and 79th Infantry Divisions assaulting north and east of Rheinberg. For the crossing, Simpson had built the XVI Corps up to 120,000 men in five divisions (the 8th Armored and the 30th, 35th, 75th, and 79th Infantry). Anderson also had the 34th Artillery Brigade of thirteen battalions, two antiaircraft artillery groups, a six-battalion tank destroyer group, three engineer combat groups, a naval unit with landing craft, a heavy mortar battalion, a smoke-generating battalion, and the entire XIX Corps artillery of eleven battalions. Additionally authorized was a British-scale daily ammunition expenditure of eight units of fire for all calibers of XVI Corps divisional artilleries (1,000 rounds per 105-millimeter gun) and nine units for the 34th Artillery Brigade.

The XVI Corps' attack opened with an hour-long bombardment by over 2,000 guns supplemented by 1,406 Eighth Air Force heavy bombers striking Luftwaffe bases farther to the east. In short order, assaulting elements had crossed at a cost of only thirty-one casualties, which prompted Eisenhower, who witnessed the Ninth Army's attack, to remark that "Simpson performed in his usual outstanding style," placing him in Patton's league.[73] By the end of the day, both divisions had all of their infantry battalions and considerable numbers of support troops on the other side, covered by fighter-bombers of the XXIX Tactical Air Command. On the second day, three heavy floating bridges were in operation, and by 26 March, three more opened at Wesel for initial use by the British. As was expected, southern and southeastern thrusts into densely populated areas encountered stiff resistance, but heavy fighting eventually produced a bridgehead roughly ten miles wide and twelve miles deep by 27 March. Because the British Second Army retained the use of routes through Wesel to deliver the main effort, Simpson had to build up his bridgehead through tactical bridges near Rheinberg. Although this allowed him to get the 2nd Armored and 83rd Infantry Divisions across, the larger problem was not solved until Montgomery gave the Ninth Army control of the Wesel routes and bridges from 30 to 31 March. Meanwhile, Simpson had pushed the 2nd Armored Division on through Haltern to the Dortmund-Ems Canal by daylight on the thirtieth, beginning what Simpson called "the breathless race" to the Elbe.[74]

By 1 April, leading elements of Gillem's XIII Corps reached the out-skirts of Münster. On the same day, the 2nd Armored Division of McLain's XIX Corps made contact with forward units of the 3rd Armored Division of the U.S. First Army at Lippstadt, thus completing the encirclement of the Ruhr. Three days later, the Ninth Army reverted to the command of Bradley's 12th Army Group and received orders to reduce, rather than con-tain, the Ruhr pocket in conjunction with the First Army. The Ninth's share of this questionable undertaking lay north of the Ruhr River, includ-ing the bulk of the densely populated urban area of the pocket. This pro-duced an undesirable two-front battle that became more widely separated as Ninth Army formations also continued to advance toward Berlin. McLain's XIX Corps, advancing eastward with the 2nd Armored and 30th and 83rd Infantry Divisions, had to simultaneously coordinate the actions of the 8th Armored and 95th Infantry Divisions in the Ruhr battle. To alleviate this problem, Simpson transferred the 8th and 95th to Anderson's XVI Corps, which went on to eliminate the last German resistance in the Ninth Army's zone in the Ruhr.

Meanwhile, the XIII Corps and XIX Corps, each with one armored and two infantry divisions, continued to advance rapidly against crumbling Ger-man defenses. Enemy attempts to make stands on the Weser River and around Bielefeld proved feeble, and the Ninth Army rolled on, often down highways, to take Hanover, Hildesheim, and Brunswick in quick succession. On 11 April, the 2nd Armored Division raced fifty-two miles to gain a bridgehead over the Elbe River near Magdeburg but had to abandon it in the face of heavy German resistance on the fourteenth. The XIX Corps' 83rd Infantry Division had meanwhile captured Barby on the Elbe around noon on 12 April and immediately established a secure bridgehead over the river. On the same day, the 5th Armored Division of Gillem's XIII Corps reached the Elbe at Tangermuende, and following in the rear, the 84th Infantry closed on the

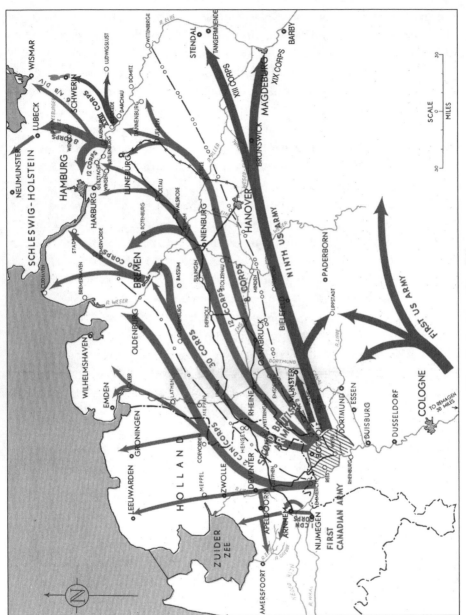

The Drive to the Elbe

river on the fifteenth. Although Berlin was only fifty miles away, Simpson was now told to stand fast along the Elbe.[75]

Simpson appears to have been unaware at the time that on 28 March, Eisenhower had decided not to go to Berlin and cabled Stalin to suggest a junction with Soviet forces along the Erfurt-Leipzig-Dresden line.[76] This was the day after Montgomery issued orders to Simpson and Dempsey to drive hard to the Elbe, with the right of the Ninth Army directed on Magdeburg and the left of the British Second Army on Hamburg. In placing priority on this drive and stressing that its ultimate objective would be Berlin, Montgomery's instruction contradicted Eisenhower's earlier direction that the Ruhr was to be mopped up before any eastward advance took place. More than anything else, this aspect may have prompted Eisenhower to strip the Ninth Army from Montgomery and redirect Bradley along the Erfurt-Leipzig-Dresden axis.[77] The wisdom of driving on Berlin seems to have been firmly implanted in Simpson's mind, nonetheless, and he contended to the end of his life that the Ninth Army could have captured Berlin well ahead of the Russians had he not been stopped on the Elbe.

On 15 April, the day Simpson received the halt order, both the XIX and XIII Corps were closed up to the Elbe. In the XIX Corps' sector, the 83rd Division, with elements of the 2nd Armored, held a secure bridgehead at Barby, fifteen miles south of Magdeburg. A pontoon bridge that could carry all division loads was in operation, and preparations were being made to construct a second bridge after nightfall. Attacks launched that same day had expanded the bridgehead to thirty square miles. The remainder of the 2nd Armored and a second infantry division occupied positions near Magdeburg, and a third infantry division held the western bank of the Elbe up to Tanger-muende, thirty miles north of Magdeburg. A regiment of the 83rd Division, with tanks from the 8th Armored, provided right-flank protection. From Tangermuende north, just fifty-three miles from Berlin, Gillem's XIII Corps of one armored and two infantry divisions held the western bank of the Elbe, ready to execute an assault crossing. Meanwhile, Anderson's XVI Corps, having completed operations in the Ruhr pocket, which was finally liquidated by 17 April, was regrouping and preparing to release forces for the Elbe front.[78]

Simpson stressed that on 15 April, the Ninth Army comprised over 330,000 men and three corps totaling thirteen divisions—three armored, one airborne, and nine infantry. Of these, two armored and five infantry divisions occupied positions on the Elbe River from Barby northward, and the 8th

Armored Division in army reserve could have been assembled near Barby by daylight on the sixteenth to raise the total divisions immediately available for assault to eight. Since the Ninth Army had advanced 226 miles from the Rhine to the Elbe in nineteen days, Simpson confidently assumed that an additional fifty to sixty miles could be covered to reach Berlin well before the Russians, though they were massed less than fifty miles distant in bridgeheads on the Oder.[79] At the time, the Ninth Army's morale was high, buoyed by the goal of reaching Berlin that Simpson and his staff set before they left Fort Sam Houston. They had also welcomed the shift of the Ninth Army to the northern flank of the 12th Army Group since it aimed the Ninth directly at the German capital.[80] According to Simpson's G4, the supply situation was also good, with no logistical problems that could have prevented or seriously hampered the advance of the Ninth Army on Berlin. Specifically, the Ninth had enough vehicle lift and ammunition on hand, backed up by an adequate resupply chain, and all units possessed sufficient rations for four days and more than enough fuel to support the advance. Although Simpson expected to encounter pockets of enemy resistance on the drive to Berlin, he thought that these could be bypassed in light of the fact that the Germans' western defense, now largely based on scratch units, had generally lost cohesion and the troops in pockets had nowhere to go.[81] On 15 April, when Simpson presented Bradley with his plan to enlarge the Elbe River bridgehead "to include Potsdam," Eisenhower turned it down.[82]

Before replying to Eisenhower's request for the junction of Soviet and Allied forces, Stalin called Marshals G. K. Zhukov and I. S. Konev to Moscow and directed them to devise a plan for launching an offensive on 16 April to capture Berlin and carry the Red Army to the Elbe. This done, he replied to Eisenhower that Berlin was no longer important and promised that the main thrust of the Soviet offensive, beginning about the middle of May, would be along the Dresden-Leipzig axis to make junction with western forces. Stalin apparently feared that the British might yet force Eisenhower to take Berlin. This fear was not entirely groundless. Churchill increasingly advocated abrogating the Yalta agreement on national zones of occupation because of Soviet refusal to allow free elections in Romania and Poland as agreed at Yalta. Although it is doubtful that Churchill could have challenged the Yalta settlement for Germany without destroying his coalition government with the Labour Party, he nonetheless continued to personally push for the Allies to hold territories seized and occupied by their armies.

The day after Simpson received his stop order, in keeping with Stalin's direction, the First Byelorussian and First Ukranian Fronts attacked Berlin before dawn. Although the initial assault failed, the Russians pressed on in spite of heavy casualties. By 20 April, Soviet soldiers had entered the city and commenced to fight their way block-by-block to the center of Berlin's almost 350 square miles. On 25 April, the spearheads of Zhukov's and Konev's forces met west of the city, the same day that Konev's troops also established contact with American elements. Altogether, the Soviets had swiftly deployed an awesome force of 2,500,000 men in 20 armies and 150 divisions with 6,000 tanks, 7,500 aircraft, 41,000 artillery pieces and mortars, 3,000 rocket launchers, and nearly 100,000 motor vehicles to take Berlin. At dawn on 2 May, the surviving German garrison of roughly 100,000 men formally surrendered. The cost to the Soviets was 360,000 dead, missing, and wounded—more than the total strength of Simpson's Ninth Army.[83]

In light of the horrific casualties incurred by the Soviets, it is perhaps too easy to dismiss Simpson's rather British fixation on pressing on to Berlin.[84] It is conceivable that a rapid drive by Simpson might have gained an American-controlled land route to supply the already agreed-to Allied occupation of Berlin, thus ending its landlocked isolation in the Soviet zone. For a disappointed Simpson, the last two weeks of the war were something of an anticlimax, with active operations focused primarily on mopping up remaining enemy pockets of resistance. After establishing contact with Soviet forces near Zerbst on 30 April and relinquishing its Elbe bridgehead on 6 May, the Ninth Army assumed occupational duties such as establishing military government, evacuating prisoners of war, and sorting out displaced persons.[85]

On 15 June, all Ninth Army forces were transferred to the Seventh Army, and Simpson returned to the United States to undertake a mission to China in July. After homecomings in Fort Worth and Weatherhead, he flew to China, where he was earmarked to become commanding general of field forces and deputy commander under Lt. Gen. Albert C. Wedemeyer, commander of American forces in the China theater.[86] Simpson was to command two armies, one north of the Yangtze River under Lt. Gen. Lucian K. Truscott and one south of the Yangtze under Maj. Gen. Robert B. McClure, who already commanded a Chinese combat formation in that area. Indirectly, Simpson was also to control some 270 Chinese divisions. While in the process of arranging for his Ninth Army headquarters to join up with him, the war with Japan ended, and Simpson again returned to the United States.

On the deactivation of the Ninth Army at Fort Bragg on 10 October 1945, he assumed command of the Second Army at Memphis, with Moore still his chief of staff.[87] Simpson remained in command of the Second Army through its transfer to Baltimore in June 1946 until his retirement on 30 November 1946. From December 1947, he resided in San Antonio, Texas, where he finally received presidential advancement to full general on the retired list in 1954.[88] Simpson died at the age of ninety-two in Brooke Army Hospital on 15 August 1980.[89] He is buried with his wife in Arlington Cemetery.

Generals of the First Canadian Army. Crerar is seated at center. Guy Simonds, commander of the 2 Corps, is on his right. LIBRARY AND ARCHIVES CANADA/PA134281

Harry Crerar, commander of the First Canadian Army.

Seated, from left to right: Bernard Montgomery, Dwight Eisenhower, and Omar Bradley.
Standing, from left to right: Crerar, William Simpson, and Miles Dempsey. LIBRARY AND
ARCHIVES CANADA/PA136327

Miles Dempsey, commander of
the British Second Army.

Dempsey, Montgomery, and Simonds. LIBRARY AND ARCHIVES CANADA/PA142101

Dempsey with John Crocker, commander of the British 1 Corps, and Gerard Bucknall, commander of the 30 Corps.

Left to right: Bradley, Montgomery, and Dempsey.

Left to right: Pete Quesada, commander of the U.S. IX Tactical Air Command; Bradley; and William Kean, Bradley's—and later Hodges's—chief of staff.

Left to right: Hodges, Bradley, and Patton. U.S. ARMY

Left to right: Eisenhower, Patton, Bradley, and Hodges. LIBRARY OF CONGRESS

Courtney Hodges, commander of the U.S. First Army.

Simpson (third from left) surveys the ruins of Jülich, along with Montgomery and others.
U.S. ARMY

William Simpson, commander of the U.S. Ninth Army.

Simpson (left) and Charles Gerhardt, commander of the 29th Infantry Division, prepare for the assault on the Roer. U.S. ARMY

Patch shakes hands with Patton. U.S. MILITARY ACADEMY

Alexander Patch, commander of the U.S. Seventh Army.

De Lattre greets a crowd in Dijon in September 1944.

Jean de Lattre de Tassigny, commander of the French First Army.

Left to right: de Lattre; Jacob Devers, commander of the 6th Army Group; Marie Emile Béthouart, commander of the French I Corps; and Joseph de Goislard de Monsabert, commander of the French II Corps, at the Franco-Prussian War memorial in Belfort, France, in November 1944. U.S. ARMY

De Lattre makes a point using a map while Devers (left) and Eisenhower (right) look on.

French colonial troops. LIBRARY AND ARCHIVES CANADA/PA143831

A Canadian Ram tank converted to an armored personnel carrier. BRITISH ARMY TANK MUSEUM

U.S. infantry troops in an M3 half-track. U.S. NATIONAL ARCHIVES

American soldiers in the Huertgen Forest, scene of brutal fighting in the fall of 1944.

The bridge at Remagen, seized by soldiers of Hodges's First Army in March 1945.

A column of American infantry trudges to the front during the Battle of the Bulge.

Canadian Shermans at Sonsbeck, March 1945. LIBRARY AND ARCHIVES CANADA/PA113682

Canadian troops in Xanten after the success of Operation Veritable in March 1945.
LIBRARY AND ARCHIVES CANADA/PA137461

In the Shadow of Patton

LT. GEN. ALEXANDER M. PATCH, U.S. SEVENTH ARMY

L t. Gen. Alexander M. "Sandy" Patch Jr. followed in the footsteps of Patton in commanding the U.S. Seventh Army from 1 March 1944 to 29 May 1945. The Seventh was the third American field army to be deployed in France, and Patch was the only Allied army commander to have directed a major formation in Pacific combat. While he headed the same army as his celebrated predecessor, however, Patch never attained anything near Patton's fame. Indeed, though he conducted an almost perfect amphibious assault after the disasters of Salerno and Anzio and defeated the last big German offensive on the Western Front, he may well be the most underrated general of World War II.[1] Promoted to lieutenant general only on 7 August 1944, he was the last Allied field army commander to achieve that rank. Also the first of his peers to die, Patch remains among the least well known of the Allied field army commanders and has been dismissively described as "sturdy, dependable, workmanlike, accomplished."[2] Depicted as highly able rather than brilliant and careful without being timid, he has been the subject of only one biography— by a loyal former staff officer.[3] In a 1 February 1945 ranking, Eisenhower placed Patch tenth, Hodges eleventh, and Simpson twelfth.[4] Comparing Patton to the other American field army commanders a month later, Eisenhower wrote that "it would be difficult indeed to choose between him, Hodges and Simpson for Army command, while Patch is little, if any, behind the others."[5] On his October 1945 list for promotion to the permanent grade of brigadier general, Marshall rated Patch first and Simpson fourth.[6]

Arguably, Patch's lack of renown owed something to the fact that he worked for a Marshall man, Jacob Devers, not an Eisenhower man like Bradley. This left Patch out of the Overlord inner circle, which, coupled with Eisenhower's uncertainty about how best to handle the 6th Army Group, ensured that the Seventh Army received only a secondary supporting role after its successful assault landing in southern France. That invasion, code-named Dragoon (originally Anvil), was more the brainchild of Marshall than Eisenhower, who never really viewed it as critical to operations in northwest Europe. As late as 31 August, Eisenhower even told Marshall that he and Bradley planned to have four armies going in "through our own ports" and if Patch's force were switched to the left flank of the Dragoon operation, it could be built up to become the fourth American army in their region.[7] That Operation Dragoon unfolded not under Eisenhower, but under the British commander of the Allied Mediterranean theater, Gen. Sir Henry Maitland "Jumbo" Wilson, further detracted from the accomplishment of Patch at a time when Patton was rampaging across France.

To his considerable discredit, Eisenhower also harbored a personal animosity toward Wilson's deputy, Lt. Gen. Jacob L. Devers, whom Marshall on 16 July had appointed to head the 6th Army Group, slated to become operational when SHAEF assumed control of all Allied forces in southern France. Devers had been responsible for the Overlord buildup as commander of the U.S. Army's European theater of operations, and Marshall had apparently been surprised that Eisenhower, on being named Supreme Commander, had not given Devers an Overlord command. Eisenhower had instead recommended that Devers take his place as commander of the North African theater and be appointed Wilson's deputy in the Mediterranean theater. Although Marshall accepted Eisenhower's right to pick his own team and acted on his recommendation, he suspected that Eisenhower had sent Devers to the Mediterranean merely to get rid of a potential rival.[8] The disappointed Devers now inherited responsibility for overseeing the Anvil buildup. In the process, he urged the formation of the 6th Army Group to control the U.S. Seventh and French First Armies and, at Wilson's suggestion, asked for and received Marshall's authorization to command the formation.[9]

Marshall thought highly of Devers and, despite his low twenty-fourth ranking on Eisenhower's 1 February list, ultimately promoted him to full general on 8 March 1945, ahead of Bradley (12 March), Patton (14 April), and Hodges (15 April).[10] A Pennsylvanian born in 1887, Devers had graduated from West Point with Patton and Simpson in 1909 and joined the field artillery. Having spent most of his career in the artillery, on 1 October 1940, he assumed command of the 9th Division at Fort Bragg, North Carolina, with Patch commanding his 47th Infantry Regiment. In August 1941, Devers took over the post of chief of the Armored Force at Fort Knox, Kentucky, and in September 1942, he received a promotion to temporary lieutenant general. In May 1943, Marshall sent him to replace Eisenhower as European theater commander.[11]

Eisenhower and Devers apparently had a falling out over the allocation of resources between Europe and North Africa when Eisenhower commanded the latter. Devers had blocked the release of heavy bombers for use in Italy as requested by Eisenhower and had received the backing of the Combined Chiefs of Staff, infuriating Eisenhower.[12] That Eisenhower held a low opinion of Devers was confirmed by his comment to Patton that Devers was "22-caliber."[13] Patton had also observed earlier that "Ike hates him" and later recorded that Eisenhower felt personally handicapped by having to keep Devers under his command when he did not trust him.[14] Like Eisenhower, Bradley had no use for the athletic and youthful-looking 6th Army Group commander who had been an instructor at West Point when he was a cadet. In Bradley's opinion, Devers talked too much and said nothing. He later called him egotistical, shallow, intolerant, not very smart, and much too inclined to rush off half-cocked.[15]

George Marshall clearly did not share this view. Congratulating Devers on his 1940 promotion to major general, Marshall said, "You can have the satisfaction that you were promoted solely on your own performance of duty and it was in no way affected by influence or propinquity."[16] Devers performed well at the head of the Seventh Army and the largest French force ever commanded by a non-Frenchmen, and Marshall's confidence in him appears to have been well placed. Devers was also smart enough to run his headquarters with 311 officers, compared to over 900 in the headquarters of the 12th Army Group.[17] It further looks as though Devers could have done Eisenhower's job.[18] In the view of one supporter, "There was a deliberate effort by Eisenhower and Omar Bradley to sidetrack Devers and to belittle his accomplishments."[19] Practical, dependable, and capable, the cheerful and good-looking Devers has been even more underrated than Patch.[20]

Patch remained grateful to Devers for giving him command of the Seventh Army and felt that without his strong and forceful backing, he would never have had the opportunity.[21] Although raised in Pennsylvania like Devers, Patch was born on 23 November 1889 in Arizona at Fort Huachuca, one of a number of strongpoints raised to defend settlers against the Chiricahua Apaches. His father, Capt. Alexander M. Patch, was the post quartermaster, an 1877 West Point graduate who had lost his right leg in cavalry operations in 1879. Following his retirement from the army, the elder Patch moved his family to Lebanon, Pennsylvania. Here Sandy Patch grew up, acquiring a reputation as a pugnacious youth with a quick temper. After attending Lehigh University for a year, he accepted an appointment to West Point in 1909, apparently on his father's insistence. His older brother, Joseph, enlisted as a private the same year and eventually rose to command the 80th Infantry Division. Although Patch excelled in track events at West Point and appears to have been a popular cadet, his overall performance was less than stellar, and he graduated seventy-fifth out of a class of ninety-three in 1913. On commissioning, he joined the 18th Infantry Regiment at Texas City and served with that unit in Texas and Arizona on Mexican border duty. In 1916, he received a promotion to first lieutenant and participated in operations against Pancho Villa. In November of the same year, he married a general's daughter, Julia Littell, whom he had met as a cadet.

On promotion to captain in June 1917, Patch trooped with the 18th Infantry to France, where he served until November. After attending the British Machine Gun School in England, he commanded the Machine Gun Battalion of the 1st Division until April 1918 and directed the American Machine Gun School until October 1918. Patch participated in the Aisne-Marne, St. Mihiel, and Meuse-Argonne campaigns, receiving temporary promotions to major in January 1918 and lieutenant colonel in October. He concluded his service with the 18th Infantry in France and Germany in February 1919 and filled staff positions at American Expeditionary Force headquarters and the headquarters of the District of Paris. He returned to the United States in May 1919 and reverted to captain.[22]

From roughly 1920 to 1924, after brief stints in Fort Benning, Georgia, and Washington, Patch served as a professor of military science and tactics in the rank of major at Staunton Military Academy, a private secondary school in the Shenandoah Valley of Virginia. Although considered a dead end by many, Patch enjoyed this duty, serving two additional tours there in 1925–28 and 1932–36. In 1922, he also took the Field Officer's Course at the Infantry School, Fort Benning, and during 1924–25, he attended the Command and

General Staff School, Fort Leavenworth, Kansas, where he achieved distinguished graduate status. In 1928–31, he served with the 3rd Battalion, 12th Infantry Regiment, at Fort Washington, Maryland, after which he attended the Army War College in 1931–32. Following a tour as a member of the Infantry Board at Fort Benning as lieutenant colonel in 1936–39, Patch served as a senior instructor of the state National Guard in Montgomery, Alabama. On promotion to colonel, he assumed command of the 47th Infantry Regiment in Devers's 9th Infantry Division in November 1940 and on promotion to brigadier general in August 1941 took charge of the Infantry Replacement Center at Camp Croft, South Carolina.

Summoned to Washington in mid-January 1942, Patch received a promotion to major general and an assignment to take "Poppy" Task Force 6814 to the South Pacific to defend New Caledonia and the outlying New Hebrides against Japanese attack. A French possession, New Caledonia had been offered to the United Sates as an advanced Pacific base by the French government in exile headed by Gen. Charles de Gaulle. From his arrival in New Caledonia in March 1942, Patch faced myriad problems, not the least of which was keeping the peace between local supporters of de Gaulle and those loyal to the Vichy government in France. Fortunately, Patch got along well with the French, learned to appreciate their sensitivities, and, through common sense, patience, and diplomacy, discharged his responsibilities in a way that earned the respect of all parties.[23]

While in New Caledonia, Patch melded together three National Guard infantry regiments with supporting arms and services to form the Americal (America-Caledonia) 23rd Infantry Division. In October, the 164th Regimental Combat Team of the Americal reinforced Maj. Gen. Alexander M. Vandegrift's sorely pressed 1st Marine Division Group that had assaulted Guadalcanal on 7 August. On 19 November, Patch arrived on Guadacanal with orders to take over from Vandegrift and his exhausted Marines and eliminate all Japanese forces from the island. On 9 December, Patch's force assumed control of a bridgehead not much larger than what the Marines had initially gained on landing in August. Although the Marines felt that they had won the ground battle and that all the army had to do was mop up, 21,000 Japanese continued to control most of the island, including the heights overlooking the bridgehead. Initially, Patch mustered only 20,000 troops, including two regiments of the 2nd Marine Division, but after the arrival of the remainder of the Americal and Maj. Gen. J. Lawton Collins's 25th Infantry

Division, he was able to plan a major offensive. On 2 January 1943, Patch took control all 43,000 of these troops as the commander of the XIV Corps; by 9 February, they had secured Guadalcanal.

Described by Collins as a tall (6 feet), sparse, attractive man full of nervous energy and drive, Patch proved remarkably cool under fire and did not spare himself during the final push. In forming a composite division from 2nd Marine, Americal, and other army elements in order to relieve worn-out regiments, he also displayed considerable higher-command acumen. One gains the impression, however, that Patch may have thought he was left to do the dirty work after the Marines gained the glory. That Vandegrift received a tumultuous homecoming and the Medal of Honor on 4 February for his Guadalcanal service may also reinforce the thought. In any case, Patch later told Marshall that the army made the larger contribution to operations on Guadalcanal. Significantly, too, he apparently considered Collins too aggressive and the Marines not aggressive enough.[24]

Concern over the state of Patch's health prompted Marshall to order his recall to the United States, ostensibly to make use of his combat experience in training. Patch had a history of lung ailments and suffered bouts of influenza and pneumonia in World War I. He succumbed to pneumonia again en route to New Caledonia and endured tropical dysentry and malaria on Guadalcanal, where the pressures of command left him vulnerable to burnout. After reporting to Marshall, Patch assumed command of the IV Corps at Fort Lewis, Washington, on 25 May and once more came down with pneumonia. His return was further marred by his alleged indiscretion in making public remarks about the shooting down of Japanese admiral Isoroku Yamamoto by American aircraft, which the navy feared might have compromised radio intelligence intercepts of Japanese security codes. Fortunately for Patch, Marshall decided to take no action since disciplinary proceedings against a corps commander would have involved publicity that could have made matters worse. At the end of 1943, the IV Corps moved to Camp Young, California, and Patch assumed command of the California-Arizona Maneuver Area. In the new year, the IV Corps entrained for Norfolk for transit to Casablanca. Early in March 1944, Patch arrived in Algiers and reported to "Jumbo" Wilson and his deputy, Devers. There Patch learned that he would take command of the U.S. Seventh Army in preparation for the invasion of southern France.[25]

The Seventh, said to have been "born at sea, baptized in blood," was the first American field army to be deployed in Europe during World War II. Led by Patton in Operation Husky, it had landed in Sicily in July 1943 and fought its way to Messina, the capture of which on 17 August ended the Sicilian campaign. The next few months saw the Seventh Army reduced from a formation of six divisions to a skeleton headquarters bivouacked in the area of Palermo completing historical reports and conducting command post training. On 19 December, it received the primary task of planning an amphibious assault similar in size to Husky to be launched against the southern coast of France.[26] When Patton left the Seventh Army on 1 January 1944, Lt. Gen. Mark W. Clark, commander of the Fifth Army, assumed responsibility for planning the invasion of southern France. The same month, a Seventh Army headquarters staff cell, called Force 163, proceeded to Algiers to begin work on the operation. Although Clark had been nominated by Eisenhower and Devers to lead the Seventh Army in Anvil, the operational situation in Italy and Clark's personal inclination to remain in that theater precluded his transfer from the Fifth Army.[27] The choice of Patch to replace Clark was anything but preordained. In earlier discussions of American senior appointments for European and Mediterranean operations, neither Marshall nor Eisenhower mentioned Patch; Marshall had even agreed to reappointing Patton as the Seventh Army commander for Anvil.[28] Conceivably, Patch received command of the Seventh Army largely because his close friend Gen. Walter Bedell Smith urged Eisenhower to ask for him.[29] On the other hand, just as Patch thought, Devers may have made the choice; in a cable on 18 February 1944, Marshall told him that he had no objections to the appointment of Patch if Devers wished to make it.[30] The outspoken Devers held Patch in high esteem, later describing him as a frank and fearless fighter who said what he thought.[31]

Whatever the case, Anvil had been the subject of much rancorous debate between the Americans and the British, and it was not clear at the time that the invasion of southern France would even take place. First broached by the Americans at the Quebec Quadrant Conference in August 1943, it reflected Marshall's determination to concentrate American forces on one decisive front, thereby ensuring the preeminence of the U.S. in the fight against Germany. Marshall, who pushed for the invasion of France as early as 1942—however unrealistically—had never been entirely happy with the decision to invade the Italian mainland. At the Washington Trident Conference in May 1943, Marshall had nonetheless accepted the British argument that knocking Italy out of the war would force the Germans to redeploy substantial troops to replace thirty-five Italian divisions and shore up their southern flank. The

Allied invasion of Italy also promised to free up Sardinia, Corsica, and air bases from which to launch strategic bombers on Germany.[32] By the time of Quadrant, however, the Americans had begun to envision employing the newly reconstituted French North African Army in an invasion of southern France. They therefore proposed mounting operations against Sardinia, Corsica, and southern France after Italy had been knocked out and cleared as far north as Rome. The trouble was that the three-division assault envisioned for Anvil competed with Overlord for amphibious resources, especially for landing ships, tank (LSTs), of which there were only 300 in total inventory. According to Eisenhower, who had been directed to prepare a plan for Anvil by November, this factor simply ruled out any possibility of launching two simultaneous amphibious operations in the spring of 1944. Since the Germans had sent twenty-five divisions to fight in Italy by October 1943, he also concluded that supporting the Italian campaign with all resources available in the Mediterranean might be the best way to draw German forces away from Normandy. At the Cairo Sextant Conference on 22–26 November, he nevertheless suggested moving the French army into southern France after Allied forces reached the Po Valley in Italy.[33]

During the Tehran Eureka Conference that followed from 28 November to 1 December 1943, the Russians vehemently opposed further Allied operations in the Mediterranean and Balkans that might detract from Overlord. While calling for a halt to advances in Italy beyond the Allied line already attained, Stalin also floated the idea of sending all troops from Italy to southern France. The thought of effecting a giant pincer movement over 500 miles between Provence and Normandy, however unrealistic for the Allies, surely appealed to his Eastern Front soul. He went on to stress, nonetheless, that not even Anvil should be allowed to interfere with Overlord. In the end, Roosevelt and Churchill promised Stalin that they would launch Overlord in May in conjunction with a supporting operation against the south of France on the largest scale permitted by landing craft available at the time.[34] They also agreed to advance no farther than the Pisa-Rimini line in Italy. Eisenhower and his Mediterranean Allied Forces Headquarters (AFHQ), in turn, produced a second outline plan that proposed a two- to three-division amphibious assault east of Toulon by a force of three or four American and six or seven French divisions. With Eisenhower's assignment as Supreme Commander for Overlord, the task of invading southern France fell to Wilson, who took over as commander in chief (later Supreme Allied Commander) in the Mediterranean theater on 8 January 1944. Anvil nonetheless remained tied to Overlord since the Combined Chiefs of Staff had agreed that both operations would take precedence over all others in 1944.[35]

At this point, Anvil again came under threat. When Eisenhower arrived in London, he found that Montgomery had expanded the size of Overlord from three to five ground divisions, which reduced the amphibious lift for Anvil to one division. Eisenhower judged this to be insufficient and again began to harbor doubts about the value of the operation. Meanwhile, the Anzio landing on 22 January 1944 had stalled, prompting calls for the rein-forcement of the Italian theater as opposed to pulling troops from Italy for Anvil. Within a month, support for another amphibious operation faded among Allied planners in both Britain and the Mediterranean. Although Eisenhower continued to stress that Anvil had been promised to Stalin and would make the best use of the French Army, he obviously did not consider the operation as essential to Overlord from a logistical perspective. He there-fore concluded that he had no choice but to cancel Anvil.[36]

The Combined Chiefs of Staff concurred on 24 March, but not before Marshall had accused Eisenhower of "localitis," of having being taken in by the British. Ever the advocate for Anvil for political as well as military reasons, Marshall wanted to see U.S. forces concentrated in France, not Italy. Indeed, Devers may have reflected more than reinforced Marshall's view in recom-mending that all U.S. forces be withdrawn from Italy, including the Fifth Army and Twelfth Air Force.[37] With the bulk of American forces deployed in France, there would be absolutely no doubt that the U.S. would exercise pre-ponderant power on the Western Front and no way that the U.S. would play a secondary role to the British and French as in World War I. Since the Americans controlled the bulk of Allied amphibious lift, Marshall would ulti-mately have his way.[38] The great Channel storm of 19 June, plus notoriously poor logistical planning on the part of SHAEF, further enabled him to argue that Anvil would provide vital port facilities.[39] Feeling Marshall's pressure and fearing that stalemate might develop in Normandy, Eisenhower urged on 23 June that Anvil be launched in August, preferably in the middle of the month. Despite an eleventh-hour effort by Churchill to torpedo the operation, the British ultimately acquiesced. Accordingly, on 2 July, the Combined Chiefs of Staff directed Wilson to conduct the operation on 15 August.[40]

On assuming command of the Seventh Army on 2 March, Patch consol-idated his headquarters in Naples. There, from March to July 1944, he planned Anvil in conjunction with American vice admiral Henry K. Hewitt, commander of the Western Naval Task Force, and Brig. Gen. Gordon P. Saville, commander of the XII Tactical Air Command, dedicated to support the Seventh Army.[41] Patch's own staff consisted of Col. Arthur A. White, chief of staff; Lt. Col. William H. Craig, G1; Col. William W. Quinn, G2; Col. John Guthrie, G3—all West Pointers—and Lt. Col. Oliver C. Harvey, G4. Col. William C. Baxter held the G3 (Air) post.[42] The civil-affairs post (later G5) was held first by Col. Harvey S. Gerry and later Col. Joseph L. Canby, who had served with Patch in World War I. Col. Leo V. Warner, a West Pointer, joined the staff in July 1944 as deputy chief of staff; he had won the Distinguished Service Cross in World War I and, because he spoke French fluently, usually greeted French officers visiting Patch's headquarters.[43] White graduated only two years after Patch at West Point and had been an assistant professor of military science and tactics at Harvard for six years. A stocky, beetle-browed introvert with a penetrating gaze, he was a highly intelligent and exacting chief of staff. Patch considered the staff to be White's preserve, but his cardinal rule was that any staff officer could say yes to a subordinate commander's request, but only he could say no. To Patch, the primary role of the staff was to assist combat commanders and their troops; he tended to side with commanders over staff. From all indications, he had no real feel for, or understanding of, staff work and evinced scant sympathy for staff concerns. During visits to subordinate commanders, often over lunch and several drinks, he approved courses of action that the staff had rejected. This practice—which may explain why Haislip, the XV Corps' commander, was not an admirer of the Seventh Army's staff—obviously increased White's problems, and he expressed some bitterness about it after the war.[44]

Although the staff felt they received blame for what they considered to be command errors, White knew that Patch had brought him from Guadalcanal and trusted his principal staff officers. Patch did not give White the latitude that Hodges gave Kean in the First Army. The no-nonsense Patch thought a good leader should always have a plan, and he seemed to expect his staff to implement his directions rather than formulate options for him to consider. As a group, the unpretentious Seventh Army staff appear to have gotten along well with each other, often playing cards in the evening after supper when all the work was done. From most accounts, Patch encouraged the development of this camaraderie through his humility and good sense of humor.[45]

Though a believer in strong discipline and capable of being stern and forthright, Patch was not a stickler. Personally, he took pains with his dress, commonly appearing in breeches and riding boots with a silk scarf around his neck. Modest and quiet, he frowned on the use of profanity and did not rant or rave, having learned to control his terrible temper by the time he was a brigadier general—though his piercing gray-blue eyes could twinkle as well as turn cold. He also liked to recite Kipling and enjoyed socializing and having a drink (or more) with good friends, though not with his soldiers.[46] A smoker who often rolled his own cigarettes with one hand, he nonetheless mixed easily with enlisted men and wanted the publicity to go to those who did the fighting, not to him. Patch was also concerned about casualties, morale, and the welfare of his troops, which may have been reflected in the Seventh Army's frostbite and trench foot casualties, which were almost always substantially less than those of the Third Army.[47]

The painstaking planning involved in Anvil—which, for security reasons, became Dragoon on 1 August—naturally drew Patch and his staff closer together. On the repeated urgings of Devers, who pointed out that French forces would be commanded by a full general, Patch was also finally promoted to lieutenant general on 7 August.[48] While overall control of the landing remained with Wilson at Allied Force Headquarters, which coordinated heavier air support from other agencies, the detailed assault plan had to be worked out by Patch and his team. As commander of the Western Naval Task Force, Hewitt controlled all ground and naval forces from the moment the Seventh Army embarked up to the time Patch established his headquarters ashore on 16 August.[49] In all, Dragoon called for the commitment of some 150,000 men (about 60,000 in the initial assault), supported by 885 ships (including five battleships and nine escort carriers, seven of which were British), 1,375 smaller landing craft, and more than 4,000 strike and transport aircraft. As finally outlined, the landing plan incorporated three phases: first, a covering operation carried out the night before by American, French, British, and Canadian commandos and paratroops; second, a main assault delivered by three divisions of the U.S. VI Corps, supported by a combat command of the French 1st Armored Division; and third, a follow-up attack by four divisions of French Army B to capture the ports of Toulon and Marseilles.[50]

Complicating matters, Maj. Gen. Lucian K. Truscott, the experienced commander of the VI Corps, requested that he command all elements involved in the initial assault to avoid what happened at Salerno. Patch refused on the grounds that the Seventh Army, XII Tactical Air Command, and Western Naval Task Force had already completed much of the detailed planning and that creating corps-level air and naval planning staffs at a late date risked

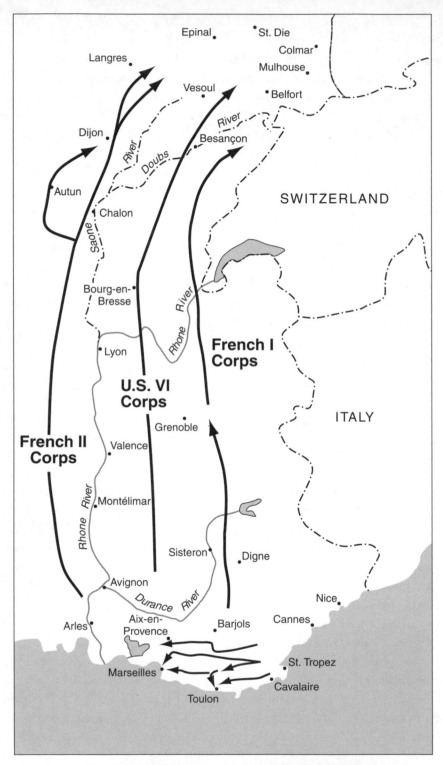

Operation Dragoon and the Drive North

sowing confusion. Patch also felt that the VI Corps' staff could not effectively control airborne and commando operations while directing three divisions in the assault. He decided instead that Truscott should assume command of airborne and commando forces only when they physically joined the VI Corps on the mainland (or as otherwise ordered by Seventh Army).[51] Before the invasion, Patch assured Truscott that he would not interfere with his tactical handling of the battle. This was probably wise, since Truscott had completed his fourth amphibious assault at Anzio, where he had replaced the fired commander of the VI Corps, Maj. Gen. John P. Lucas.[52]

On 15 August, the birthday of Napoleon, Truscott's VI Corps hit nine assault beaches on the French Riviera between Cape Cavalaire and Antheor Cove, roughly centering on St. Tropez, with John O'Daniel's 3rd Infantry Division on the left, William Eagles's 45th Infantry Division in the middle, and John Dahlquist's 36th Infantry Division on the right. They were flanked by French commando units and the U.S.-Canadian 1st Special Service Force, which seized the Hyeres islands of Port Gros and Levant to the southwest.[53] The landing followed a four-phase air campaign that started on 5 August to neutralize the Luftwaffe, coastal defenses, lines of communication, and enemy artillery. In the wake of one last concentrated air strike and with naval gunfire drenching the beaches, the main assault force went ashore at 0800 hours. Only the 36th Division encountered serious resistance, and by the end of the day, some 86,000 troops and 12,000 vehicles had been disembarked. By nightfall, some units had also advanced as far as ten miles inland. Compared with the Normandy landings, there was no contest, and total American casualties were less than 600. Although German resistance stiffened on 16 August, casualties remained low, and by that evening, twenty-four to forty-eight hours earlier than expected, Truscott's forces had attained their initial objectives. Meanwhile, leading elements of the main body of French Army B had commenced landing in anticipation of attacking Toulon and Marseilles.

Dragoon coincided with the closure of the Falaise gap, which drew many German troops away from southern France, and on 17 August, Hitler ordered Col. Gen. Johannes Blaskowitz to pull back the bulk of his diminished Army Group G into the Vosges Mountains. Only garrisons dedicated to destroying and denying port facilities to the Allies were to be left behind.[54] Patch learned about this from Ultra intercepts. He also knew that the Germans were not going to shift divisions from Italy to threaten his eastern flank.

With Patch's concurrence, Truscott was eager to push out beyond the bridgehead line to avoid another Anzio. To that end, Combat Command 1 (CC1) of the French 1st Armored Division had spearheaded a drive by the 3rd Infantry Division to Trets just short of Aix-en-Provence. In the meantime, the 45th Division had cleared out Barjols and reached the Durance River farther to the north. At this point, Patch ordered Truscott to return CC1 to the French as had been promised. Truscott disputed this decision on the grounds that CC1 constituted his most powerful striking force and that countermarching it east would cause major traffic problems that would inhibit his westward advance.[55] Patch remained unmoved; already experiencing gasoline and vehicles shortages, he considered the capture of Toulon and Marseilles critical to the success of the invasion, and de Lattre had planned to use CC1 to seize the ports. In the event, a traffic jam did ensue, but the French also moved on the ports six days earlier than planned.

At the same time that he accelerated de Lattre's assault, Patch ordered Truscott to occupy positions around Aix-en-Provence to protect the French northern flank. He further charged Truscott with securing crossings over the Durance River, capturing Sisteron, and preparing Dahlquist's 36th Division to drive on Grenoble. Reports of the arrival of the 11th Panzer Division in the Aix-en-Provence area, however, caused Truscott to keep his main body facing west. Coupled with the limited westward advance of the VI Corps, this may have cost Truscott an opportunity to cut off the German withdrawal up the Rhone Valley.[56] The loss of CC1 had compelled Truscott to activate a mobile force under his deputy corps commander, Brig. Gen. Frederick B. Butler, whom he directed to strike northwest along the Route Napoleon with the 36th Infantry following in train. By 19 August, Task Force Butler—including thirty medium tanks, twelve tank destroyers, twelve self-propelled artillery pieces, a motorized infantry battalion, and engineer elements—had crossed the Durance River and entered Sisteron.

Following Patch's order the next day to send a division north to Grenoble, Truscott assigned the task to the 36th Division and obtained Patch's approval to send Task Force Butler on a western drive toward Montélimar to cut off the withdrawing Germans. Convinced that this would be the main German axis, Truscott hoped to establish a blocking position on the high ground north of Montélimar. Not surprisingly, Task Force Butler's arrival in this area on 21 August drew a strong response from the Germans and precipitated an eight-day running battle. Unfortunately, neither Truscott nor Patch immediately designated Montélimar as the major effort, and Dahlquist's 36th Division remained largely focused on driving north toward Grenoble. The situation was further exacerbated by transport shortages and logistical problems related to the rapid advances from the invasion beaches. The inability of the American forces to concentrate on a single blocking point on the Rhone made it extremely difficult to close the German escape route. Much to the disappointment of Truscott, the German Nineteenth Army managed to get away, albeit with heavy losses in manpower and equipment.[57]

By 28 August, in the only serious fighting of the landing's initial stages, both Toulon and Marseilles had fallen to the French, prompting Wilson to remark to Devers that Patch was far superior to his other army commander in the theater.[58] Three days later, the struggle for southern France had ended, and the race for the German border had begun. Issued six days earlier, Patch's orders called for Truscott's VI Corps to push rapidly to Lyon, seventy-five miles north of Montélimar, then to Dijon to link up with Patton's Third Army and, subject to Eisenhower's concurrence, eventually to Strasbourg on the Rhine. The tasks Patch assigned to de Lattre left French forces widely dispersed and straddling the VI Corps. While screening the area west of Avignon and pushing reconnaissance elements north along the west bank of the Rhone, the French were also to advance on the VI Corps' right along a north-northeasterly axis through Grenoble and the Belfort gap roughly ninety miles east of Dijon. French forces were also to assist the 1st Airborne Task Force in screening the Franco-Italian border. When Patch issued more specific orders on 28 August, de Lattre objected strongly to this proposed dispersal of his forces. Screening the extreme western and eastern flanks of the Seventh Army in addition to providing protection for both sides of the VI Corps' advance, de Lattre pointed out, would prevent him from concentrating sufficient combat power to force the Belfort gap. Sensibly, Patch conceded the point and reduced de Lattre's screening tasks both west of the Rhone and along the Franco-Italian frontier. In the compromise reached, de Lattre agreed to send the French 1st Armored and the French 1st Infantry Divisions up the west bank of the Rhone, while his main body protected the VI Corps' right flank east of the river. Following the fall of Lyon, however, the two French divisions west of the river were to join de Lattre's main body east of the VI Corps for a stronger drive on Belfort.[59]

At this point, Truscott urged a change in plans. Noting that the French were well north of Lyon and that de Lattre would need at least a week to concentrate his forces in the Bourg-en-Bresse area, he suggested on 2 September that his VI Corps, with three mobile infantry divisions already massed east of Lyon, was better placed to take on the task of forcing the Belfort gap. Adding that the French were better positioned to pursue the bulk of the retreating German forces in a drive through Dijon and the Vosges passes to Strasbourg, Truscott convinced Patch to agree to his proposal.[60] Again, de Lattre objected, more than a little irritated that the two Americans had made decisions affecting French troop deployments without consulting him. Knowing that he would shortly command more than twice as many divisions as Patch and Truscott, he also felt he had a good case for uniting his army on the right of the line. Although de Lattre admitted that it would take several days to regroup his 1st Armored and 1st Infantry Divisions with his main force, he quickly pointed out that the 3rd Algerian Division east of the VI Corps had already commenced significant reconnaissance and armored deployments toward Belfort. On 3 September, underscoring the point that he would soon be commanding an independent army, de Lattre announced the formation of two French corps: I Corps, under Lt. Gen. Emile Bethouart, controlling the 3rd Algerian, 9th Colonial, and later 2nd Moroccan Divisions; and II Corps, under Maj. Gen. Joseph de Goislard de Monsabert, controlling the 1st Armored and 1st Infantry Divisions west of the Rhone. In compliance with the plan advocated by Truscott, de Lattre directed Bethouart's I Corps to operate on the right of the VI Corps in support of its drive on Belfort. Meanwhile, de Monsabert's II Corps was to push north toward Dijon and then swing east toward Strasbourg. For his part, Patch issued supplemental orders incorporating de Lattre's changes on 4 September.[61]

Because of the disarray of German defensive deployments, the northward advance of Patch's Seventh Army proceeded at a rapid pace in the early days of September. Within the VI Corps, O'Daniel's 3rd Division initially led off, with Dahlquist's 36th Division on the left and Eagles's 45th Division in the rear. On the VI Corps' right flank, the 3rd Algerian Division kept pace, while to the west the French II Corps' drive on Dijon quickly pierced the receding German line. By 9 September, the VI Corps had advanced 300 miles from the Dragoon beaches in just twenty-six days, straining the support capability of the XII Tactical Air Command. The same day, Truscott directed his three divisions to wheel to the east, pivoting on the 45th Division in the Isle-sur-le-Doubs region, with the 3rd in the center aiming for Vesoul and the 36th on the left heading toward the Vosges foothills. Vesoul fell on 12 September, and two days later, Truscott's three divisions closed up to Luxeuil and the entrance to the Belfort gap. To the north, elements of the French II Corps from Dijon began to arrive above the 36th Division, while in the south leading elements of the French I Corps occupied the sector between the 3rd Division and the Swiss border. Convinced that the German Nineteenth Army was close to collapse, Truscott now planned to launch what he expected to be a final push into the Belfort gap. Early on 14 September, however, he received new orders from Patch canceling currently planned operations in anticipation of the Seventh Army's transfer from the Mediterranean to the European theater. Since the original deployment plan calling for the French to push through the Belfort gap to the Alsatian plains had recently been reaffirmed by Eisenhower and Devers during SHAEF coordinating conferences between 4 and 6 September, Patch had little option but to comply.[62]

On 15 September, following the junction of Anvil and Overlord, Eisenhower assumed operational control of Allied forces in southern France. Since SHAEF faced considerable logistical difficulties at the time, the 6th Army Group, created the same day under Devers, retained responsibility for administering its own semi-independent supply chain through Mediterranean ports. The XII Tactical Air Command headed by Saville, with whom Patch worked closely, simultaneously transferred from the Twelfth to the Ninth Air Force while French Army B became the French First Army.[63] This left the Seventh Army with little more to control than Truscott's VI Corps, although Devers decided that Patch would continue to direct the French First Army until its redeployment to the right of the line was completed.

While this arrangement satisfied de Lattre, Truscott saw that it would leave his VI Corps facing the rugged Vosges Mountains. In a strongly worded letter, he reminded Patch of his recent approval of the VI Corps' operations against the Belfort gap to take advantage of a fleeting opportunity. Asserting that fighting through the Vosges would simply be a waste of veteran divisions, Truscott suggested that his VI Corps should either assist in breaching the gap or be used more productively to capture Genoa and assist in the destruction of enemy forces in Italy. He further requested that Devers be shown his proposal.[64] In the circumstances, Patch could only hold his temper and placate Truscott as best he could, relaying the good news that his promotion to the rank of lieutenant general had been confirmed on 2 September.[65] The fact of the matter was that Eisenhower wanted the Seventh on the right of the Third Army so that he could concentrate American forces in a central mass, and he probably would have preferred to have it under Bradley's 12th Army Group. This would have left de Lattre on his own and encouraged French demands for an army group with a Gaullist equivalent of Montgomery. Having an American 6th Army Group exercise command over a large and growing French Army, on the other hand, greatly enhanced the perception and reality of American power in the European theater.

The trouble was that beyond promising Bradley on 15 September that the Seventh Army would always be maneuvered to support the 12th Army Group, Eisenhower had given little serious thought to the employment of the 6th Army Group, and his personal dislike of Devers did not dispose him to do so either.[66] Eisenhower initially assigned Devers three general tasks: destroy the German forces opposing him, secure crossings over the Rhine, and breach the Seigfried Line just inside the German frontier. The northern boundary established for the 6th Army Group ran northeast from Langres past Epinal, forty miles north of Vesoul, to Strasbourg on the Rhine. While the southern boundary technically ran along the Swiss border, the army group also inherited responsibility for sealing off the Franco-Italian border farther south. Within this sector, Devers deployed de Lattre's French First Army opposite the Belfort gap, with de Monsabert's II Corps north and Bethouart's I Corps south, with orders to drive through the gap and then head north to clear the Alsatian plains. Patch's Seventh Army, with one corps of three divisions, meanwhile moved into position opposite the rugged Vosges Mountains with orders to advance northeast across the mountains along the Vesoul–St. Die axis to Strasbourg.

On 20 September, the day before the French First Army completed its redeployment, Truscott's VI Corps attacked across the Moselle River with three divisions abreast on a thirty-mile front. Because of the speed of the attack—which caught the enemy in hastily prepared forward positions rather than more defensible, developed ones on the Moselle itself—the VI Corps managed to push bridgeheads across the river by 25 September. Notwithstanding this success, however, the Seventh Army had only just begun to scale the formidable High Vosges, which could be circumvented only by the Saverne gap in the north and the Belfort gap in the south. Since the Saverne gap lay in the operational zone of Haislip's XV Corps of the Third Army immediately to the north of Truscott's VI Corps, Devers asked Eisenhower on 22 September to transfer the XV Corps to Patch's Seventh Army, pointing out that the 6th Army Group could easily support the two-division XV Corps

The Vosges

plus an extra third division and that such a transfer would also alleviate supply problems in the 12th Army Group. Devers's proposal particularly appealed to SHAEF logistical planners, and on 26 September, Eisenhower agreed to the transfer of Haislip's XV Corps. He further decided to give a third division to Haislip in October and divert three more divisions bound for the 12th Army Group through northern ports to Marseilles to join the 6th Army Group.[67]

When Haislip's XV Corps joined the Seventh Army on 29 September, it retained responsibility for clearing the area east of Luneville. Patch further directed Haislip to seize Sarrebourg, some twenty-seven miles beyond Luneville and ten miles short of the Saverne gap, and to assist the VI Corps in capturing Rambervillers on the southern intercorps boundary running roughly east to Baccarat. The XV Corps' northern boundary along the Rhine-Marne Canal to Sarrebourg remained unchanged, except that it now reminded Patch of his responsibility to protect Patton's southern flank. By this time, the Third Army, with nine divisions spread across an eighty-four-mile front, had ground to a halt before the imposing defenses of Metz. As might be expected, Patton's spectacular drive after his breakout from Avranches in August had compelled the Germans to concentrate powerful reserves against the Third Army. In front of Metz, the heavily reinforced German First Army stopped Patton cold, keeping him at bay for the entire month of October and well into November. Even after the city fell on 22 November, the surrounding forts continued to hold out—Driant until 6 December and, the last, Jeanne d'Arc, until 13 December.

Similarly, Patch's advance on the Vosges encountered growing resistance among increasingly formidable woods and hills. As attacks by Truscott's VI Corps during 26–30 September revealed, any quick thrust over the Vosges appeared unlikely. Both Patch and Devers thus gave major attention to forcing the Saverne gap north of the High Vosges. Clearing the six-by-four-mile Parroy Forest, which commanded the main road leading to Sarrebourg and the Saverne gap, took the 79th Infantry Division of the XV Corps until 12 October.

Tragically for Patch, a subsequent 79th Division advance also claimed the life of his only son, Capt. Alexander M. Patch III, killed by enemy mortar fire on 22 October while leading Company C of the 315th Infantry Regiment.[68] This enormously personal blow raised concerns about his capacity to continue to command the Seventh Army. Bradley later asserted that the psychological effect on Patch had been so devastating as to impair his effectiveness as an army commander. To ensure that no such emotional burden was laid upon the Supreme Commander, Bradley shortly thereafter posted Eisenhower's son to a special communications unit to keep him out of combat.[69] In the postwar years, Haislip's nephew also emphatically stated that Patch was nearly incapacitated by the death of his son and would have been relieved had he not been shielded by a "West Point Protective Society."[70] Since Bradley was not close to Patch in any personal or military sense and Haislip provided no sources for his allegation, the charge that the death of his son rendered Patch ineffective as an army commander is questionable. That Patch came from a military family and was married to the daughter of a general would seem to indicate otherwise, that he considered it his duty to carry on. Unlike Stroh, Patch never asked to be relieved, but rather opted to stay the course just as O'Daniel of the 3rd Infantry Division and Crocker of the British 1 Corps did after the deaths of their only sons.[71] In a letter to his wife, Patch wrote that their son gave "his noble young life to the service of his country in as gallant a manner as ever we could hope for" and that he "died as a complete, loyal, exemplification of his Alma Mater—West Point."[72] Patch also insisted that nothing special be done for his son since it was a time of dying and death recognized neither rank nor family. As for being protected by West Point solidarity, the acrimony between the Eisenhower-Bradley team and Devers—all graduates—belied the very conception. That many of Patch's principal staff officers happened to be West Pointers was of far less significance than the fact that his chief of staff quite properly took it upon himself to run the whole show during Patch's period of grieving.[73] No doubt Patch reeled from the blow, but his command performance by 1 November was apparently good enough that Devers observed that "Patch is a great army leader."[74]

At the beginning of October, the major formation commanders of the 6th Army Group had realized that personnel and supply problems ruled out any hope of mounting a general offensive. Despite the capture of Marseilles, Toulon, and minor Riviera ports, the best efforts of Communication Zone logisticians could not overcome the tyranny of geography that left the 6th Army Group overextended. The tenacious German defense of the Parroy Forest further convinced both Patch and Truscott that the cessation of all offensive operations would only give the enemy time to rest and dig in even deeper. To keep the pressure on the Germans, they decided to launch the VI Corps in a limited attack on St. Die, a communications center that would in any case have to be taken in a northeast drive across the Vosges to

Strasbourg. In accordance with Truscott's plan, Eagles's 45th Division attacked from Rambervillers, which had been seized in late September, toward Brouvelieures and Bruyeres, but a German counterattack on 6 October stopped it halfway. Dahlquist's 36th Division, charged with undertaking a supporting attack in the VI Corps' center, found the going equally tough and measured its daily progress in yards between 4 and 14 October. In the south, the attack of the 3rd Division, arguably Truscott's best and most experienced, ran into trouble almost immediately and took until mid-October to reach the area of Le Tholy. With rain and fog limiting visibility and mined and muddy back roads impeding movement, the infantry was for the most part compelled to slog forward without effective armor, artillery, or air support. The result, as several formation commanders duly noted, was a significant decline in fighting aggressiveness and an alarming rise in line company desertions that numbered between fifty and sixty cases per division. Sharp exchanges between Patch and Truscott over troop relief operations in an interarmy boundary adjustment may also have reflected the pressures and tensions of the fighting. Devers's official movement of the interarmy boundary north of Le Tholy on 14 October, sought by the French to gain more maneuver room for their drive on the Belfort gap, allowed Truscott to redirect the 3rd Division from what he considered a dead end to spearhead a renewed attack on St. Die.[75]

The renewed VI Corps attack, aptly called Operation Dogface, aimed to seize the high ground north of St. Die overlooking a ten-mile stretch of the Meurthe River Valley. As originally planned, Dogface was to be a prelude to a much larger offensive scheduled by Devers to hurl the entire 6th Army Group across the Vosges and through the Belfort gap. Although Dogface initially called for limited diversionary attacks by Haislip's U.S. XV Corps on the northern flank and de Monsabert's French II Corps in the south, the general exhaustion of these formations, coupled with supply shortages, precluded them from playing more than deception roles. Worried about the state of his infantry, Truscott would nevertheless go it alone. Following preliminary operations by the 45th and 36th Divisions to secure Bruyeres and Brouvelieures on 15–23 October, Truscott intended to launch a three-division attack on St. Die on 23 October. O'Daniel's 3rd Division, having been rested and secretly deployed behind the northernmost 45th Division, was to strike through the 45th to spearhead the attack. On 20 October, Truscott accelerated the 3rd Division's attack through a dangerous gap that had opened between the two forward divisions. Although the 3rd made rapid progress, advancing halfway to St. Die, German resistance did not abate in the battle of attrition that ensued. Indeed, hope of further rapid progress gradually began to fade with Truscott's departure to take command of the Fifth Army in Italy on 25 October, the same day he handed over the VI Corps to Maj. Gen. Edward H. Brooks. By the end of October, the VI Corps' attack, so promising at first, appeared to have stalled.[76]

At this point, Patch and Devers decided to launch the U.S. XV Corps' and French II Corps' supporting attacks. On 31 October, Leclerc's French 2nd Armored Division of the XV Corps drove on Baccarat, catching the Germans by surprise and occupying the town by 1 November. Two days later, de Monsabert's French II Corps unleashed a reinforced 3rd Algerian Division in a limited attack immediately south of the VI Corps. Although the Germans were again surprised, the 3rd Algerian Division gained only a mile in three days of fighting in the densely wooded area around Le Tholy. Meanwhile, Brooks's VI Corps continued to push on, relieving the French 2nd Armored in the Baccarat area and advancing almost to Raon l'Etape, which the Germans considered to be the major VI Corps objective. By this point of the Vosges campaign, extreme fatigue had afflicted both sides, but the arrival of the additional divisions promised by Eisenhower gave the Americans some respite. On 9 November, the fresh 100th Infantry Division under Maj. Gen. Withers A. Burress, relieved Eagles's 45th Infantry Division and, two days later, seized positions on either side of Raon l'Etape on the high ground overlooking the Meurthe River Valley. On 12 November, the second of Eisenhower's three promised divisions, the 103rd Infantry under Maj. Gen. Charles C. Haffner Jr., assumed responsibility for O'Daniel's weary 3rd Division in the central sector. Although the 3rd had not managed to secure St. Die, it had, at high cost, reached the west bank of the Meurthe. Unfortunately for the 36th Division in the south, it was not similarly relieved, and by the end of Dogface, it remained well short of the Meurthe and its final objective. By 7 November, its 442nd Regiment was down to thirty effectives in each rifle company. Two days later, one company mustered only seventeen riflemen fit for duty while another had only four.[77]

Dogface left all three of the VI Corps' veteran divisions at the point of exhaustion. Pushing ten miles through the Vosges on a fifteen-mile front had been slow and costly. Neither had the XV Corps, after the clearance of the Parroy Forest, made much progress at all. This relatively lackluster performance by Patch's Seventh Army in October appears to have convinced Eisenhower that Devers's 6th Army Group was unlikely to make much of a contribution to any Allied advance in November. When Eisenhower asked on 16 October whether the 6th Army Group's line of communication from the Mediterranean could be used to increase the flow of supplies to Patton's Third Army, Devers replied that he could provide Patton with 1,000 tons of supplies a day, but only after 15 November.[78] This seems merely to have confirmed in Eisenhower's mind the critical need to open Antwerp for the supply of his northern Allied armies. Consequently, his directive of 28 October gave priority to clearing the Scheldt Estuary and called for the main Allied thrust to be delivered north of the Ardennes. South of the Ardennes, the bulk of Hodges's First Army and all of Patton's Third were to seize the Saar basin and advance generally northeast to the Rhine, securing bridgeheads over the river near Frankfurt. Eisenhower further directed Devers's 6th Army Group to protect Patton's right flank, clear the west bank of the Rhine in its sector, and ultimately seize crossings over the river between Karlsruhe and Mannheim. Patton's Third Army was to launch its attack against the Saar as soon as logistics permitted, but no later than five days after Bradley's 12th Army Group commenced its offensive in the north. The initial selection of 10 November as Patton's target date led Devers, in turn, to choose 15 November for the start his own offensive.[79]

As worked out by Devers's staff, that was the earliest date by which the 6th Army Group's logistical system could support a sustained offensive to carry the U.S. Seventh and French First Armies to the Rhine. It also nicely accorded with a staff study of enemy counterattacks which concluded that the Germans usually started moving their general reserves either on the evening of the second day or morning of the third day of a strong Allied offensive. Thus, if Patton attacked on 10 November, Patch's Seventh Army should not strike before 13 November, the date by which German reserves would begin their deployments against Patton. By echeloning their attacks in this manner, the Allies could conceivably disrupt the Germans' reserves and force them to abandon their previously rehearsed counterattack routes, leaving them to react only in an unplanned and uncoordinated manner. In keeping with this general pattern, the Seventh Army's plan called for Haislip's XV Corps to attack on 15 November, with Brooks's VI Corps jumping off two days later. The XV Corps was first to drive on Sarrebourg and then to swing east to force the Saverne gap. From there, the corps would strike northeastward astride the Lower Vosges in a corridor some twenty miles wide, with the Third Army's XII Corps on the left and the VI Corps on the right. Meanwhile, the VI Corps was to advance through the Hantz and Saales passes northeast of St. Die and break out onto the Alsatian plains to seize Strasbourg. Between 10 and 15 November, the French II Corps was also to launch a three-day, limited-objective attack to support the VI Corps and divert attention from the French I Corps' attack on the Belfort gap, which was planned for 15 November as the main effort of the French First Army.[80]

Patton attacked on the Lorraine front on the morning of 8 November, two days early. Fortunately, the logistical state of the 6th Army Group enabled Devers, who learned of the advance in timing only the day before, to launch his armies on 13 November. The XV Corps' attack began on that date along with the French II Corps' supporting attack and the main French drive on the Belfort gap by the French I Corps. The VI Corps' attack followed on 15 November after preliminary assaults to secure better start positions along the west bank of the Meurthe. After initial difficulty all along the line, the 100th Division managed by 18 November to clear Raon l'Etape, and two days later, the 3rd Division crossed the Meurthe in the St. Michel area. On 21 November, both divisions began to make substantial progress, and that evening, Brooks, sensing that the Germans were withdrawing across his front, ordered a pursuit. From north to south, the 100th, 3rd, 103rd, and 36th Divisions raced northeastward toward Strasbourg and onto the Alsatian plains. On breaking out of the Vosges on 26 November, however, the VI Corps found that Strasbourg, fifteen miles distant, was already in the hands of the XV Corps.

Strasbourg had originally been a VI Corps objective, but the progress of the XV Corps had been such that on 21 November, Patch ordered Haislip to take it. Although the earlier attack by the XV Corps in the wet snow and flood had started off slowly, with the 44th Division inching forward in the north and the 79th Division in the south, the German defense started to unravel around 15 November. Haislip's commitment of elements of the French 2nd Armored Division the next day further enhanced the momentum of the attack. By 19 November, the XV Corps' left flank was more than ten miles beyond the right wing of the Third Army's XII Corps. That afternoon, Haislip initiated the exploitation phase of his attack by unleashing the rest of Leclerc's 2nd Armored Division in a risky deep penetration. In a series of spectacular maneuvers, the 2nd Armored ran circles around the Germans and effected, by 22 November, the complete penetration of the Vosges. To show his appreciation as well as sensitivity in dealing with an ally, Haislip gave Leclerc the well-deserved honor of liberating Strasbourg the next day.[81]

Devers's offensive, launched in a snowstorm and conducted under the most arduous weather conditions, had shattered the German Nineteenth Army in a series of blows. Even allowing for the relatively depleted state of the Germans, this accomplishment was nothing short of remarkable. To de Lattre's great credit, the French I Corps achieved a rapid rupture of the German front and drove through the Belfort gap on 16 November. Three days later, elements of the French 1st Armored Division reached the Rhine at Rosenau. The French I Corps' threat to the Germans' rearward communication and withdrawal routes farther north also directly contributed to the collapse of German resistance in front of the French II, U.S. VI, and U.S. XV Corps. On 20 November, aware that the French First Army had been the first to reach the Rhine, with the Seventh Army a close second, Patton wrote his wife, "The Seventh Army and the First French Army seem to have made a monkey out of me this morning."[82]

Eager to capitalize on the advantageous situation that had developed, Devers and Patch now prepared to carry out plans for a Rhine crossing that envisioned the VI Corps exploiting through a XV Corps bridgehead. Since the densely wooded Black Forest escarpment that dominated the east bank of the Rhine opposite the Vosges appeared to be a strategic dead end, the 6th Army Group focused on Rastatt, twenty-eight miles north of Strasbourg, as the southernmost crossing area with good avenues of approach up the Rhine Valley toward Karlsruhe. In Devers's view, launching the Seventh Army immediately into Germany at Rastatt was likely to yield better operational results than sending it south to help reduce the German Nineteenth Army's salient that remained sandwiched between the First French and U.S. Seventh Armies west of the Rhine. In fact, crossing the Rhine offered the possibility of threatening or taking the salient in the rear. The reduction of the 850-square-mile Colmar pocket, as the salient came to be called, was thus to be left to de Lattre's French First Army. The movement of river-crossing units and equipment was accordingly set in train by 24 November on orders from Devers and Patch.[83]

On 24 November, Eisenhower and Bradley began a tour of the southern front. Stopping first at Patton's headquarters in Nancy, they found that the Third Army's attacking forces had been nearly halted. Here a frustrated Patton requested that they assign Devers a portion of his seventy-five-mile front or, alternatively, return Haislip's XV Corp to the Third Army. Bradley, eager to get the main effort against the Saar basin going but afraid that a corps transfer would prove too time-consuming, supported the idea of assigning the southern portion of Patton's zone to Patch's Seventh Army. Eisenhower seems also to have made up his mind that something had to be done to assist Patton. After traveling to meet Devers and Patch at Luneville, Eisenhower and Bradley went on to Haislip's headquarters at Sarrebourg and Brooks's command post at St. Die only to find their staffs busily planning to grab bridgeheads over the Rhine and strike into Germany itself. Eisenhower was still concerned about Patton's flagging offensive, and he quickly stopped all preparations for a Rhine crossing, even issuing verbal orders to Haislip to change direction immediately and advance generally northward astride the Low Vosges in close support of Patton. In effect, he reoriented the Seventh Army's axis of advance from east to north against the West Wall and southern flank of the German First Army that was stalling Patton. Stunned by the new orders, Devers protested that it made more operational sense to reinforce and strengthen the successful Seventh rather than the stalled Third. A Seventh Army crossing at Rastatt, followed by a drive north to envelop the Saar basin, was, in his view, the best way of assisting Patton. Against Bradley's objections that it would be foolhardy to try to crack the prepared defenses of the West Wall there, Devers countered that reconnaissance had found many of these defenses unmanned and that the Germans currently had few troops in front of the Seventh Army. After a bitter and heated argument that saw an angry Eisenhower and equally angry Devers storm out of the conference, the Seventh Army turned away from Rhine to support Patton.[84]

The decision to relieve Patton rather than cross the Rhine was a blow to Devers and Patch.[85] Between 25 and 26 November, Patch and his disappointed Seventh Army headquarters drew up new plans based on Eisenhower's instructions. With Brooks's VI Corps still engaged in clearing the area between the Vosges and the Rhine down to the northern edge of the Colmar pocket, however, it was difficult for Patch to push both his corps northward at once. The initial reorientation of the Seventh Army thus left the XV Corps driving north while the VI Corps continued east. Since advancing in two different directions on two widely separated fronts dissipated the combat power of the Seventh Army, there was little hope that Patch could launch a major northern offensive before 5 December. This delay in turn allowed the German First and Nineteenth Armies time to rest and refit. As the First German Army withdrew north, it also established a substantial defensive line based in front of the German border running from Haguenau, roughly along the Moder River, to Sarre-Union. In preparation for a drive against this line, Patch transferred the 100th Infantry Division to Haislip on 27 November, which enabled the XV Corps to deploy the 44th, 100th, 45th, and 79th Divisions west to east from the Third Army boundary. To compensate for the loss of the 100th Division, Patch at the same time gave Brooks's VI Corps the French 2nd Armored Division in Strasbourg. Brooks then directed the 3rd Infantry Division to take over responsibility for Strasbourg and launched the French 2nd Armored Division on a southern drive toward the Colmar pocket to complement the advance of the 36th and 103rd from the west. Following the clearance of Selestat on 4 December, the VI Corps was able to turn north, but because of stiffening German resistance in the Colmar pocket, Patch decided to leave the 36th to help the French 2nd make the final push south to Colmar.[86]

Meanwhile, Haislip's northern advance proceeded so slowly that at one point the Third Army's XII Corps had to wait for the XV Corps to come up on its right before continuing to advance northward. On 2 December, Devers, increasingly concerned about the slow progress of the Seventh Army's northern drive, directed that both the VI and XV Corps immediately support Patton's Saar offensive. Patch responded quickly, ordering Brooks's VI Corps to swing north and take up a position on the right of Haislip's XV Corps, which, reduced to the 44th and 100th Divisions, was to attack north on a narrower front ten to fifteen miles wide, while the VI Corps (the 45th, 79th, and 103rd Divisions) would push forward on a broader front of some thirty miles. To increase striking power, Patch assigned the 14th Armored Division, under Brig. Gen. Albert C. Smith, to the VI Corps and the recently arrived 12th Armored Division, under Maj. Gen. Roderick R. Allen, to the XV Corps. Devers also ordered elements of the 42nd, 63rd, and 70th Divisions, scheduled to arrive at Marseilles in December, to be sent north as quickly as possible to relieve the 3rd Division at Strasbourg.

The XV Corps initially encountered little German resistance when it attacked on 5 December, but it increased substantially two days later. As had almost become the norm for the Seventh Army, the XII Tactical Air Command was able to provide significant air support for only four days between 5 and 20 December, and on three of those days, limited visibility curtailed the planned missions. By 20 December, the XV Corps had nonetheless battled its way through Hottviller on to the fortified Maginot works around Bitche still held by the Germans.

In the meantime, preliminary operations by the VI Corps' 45th Division on the left and the 79th Division on the extreme right commenced on 5 and 7 December.[87] Main attacks by the 79th Division to attract German attention began on 9 December, followed by the 45th and 103rd Divisions a day later. During 11 December, all three of the VI Corps' attacking divisions made considerable progress. Soon convinced that the Germans were conducting only delaying operations, Brooks unleashed the 14th Armored Division in a general pursuit on 13 December. On the morning of 15 December, the VI Corps stood ready to move across the German border in strength and, by evening, had made incursions in several areas. By 18 December, however, increasing enemy artillery fire and counterattacks signaled that a major German offensive was underway in the area of the Ardennes.[88]

For the second time now, Eisenhower directed Devers's 6th Army Group to suspend all offensive operations. To Devers, this was a particularly bitter pill to swallow since a Seventh Army attack across the Rhine in November could have spoiled Hitler's Ardennes offensive and certainly precluded the reinforcement of the Colmar pocket. Having rescued the Third Army on 24 November, he noted, he had to turn this time to rescue the 12th Army Group.[89] To enable Patton's forces to counterattack into the Ardennes, Patch's Seventh Army once more assumed responsibility for a large portion of the Third Army's front. Carried out between 19 and 26 December, this action left the Seventh holding an extended front 126 miles long with only six infantry divisions forward and two armored divisions in reserve. Making matters worse, in response to SHAEF direction, Patch nominated the 36th Infantry and 12th Armored Divisions to pass from the Seventh Army into Eisenhower's reserve. To compensate, Devers brought the French 2nd Armored Division back and rushed elements of the newly arrived 42nd, 63rd, and 70th Divisions forward. Since Eisenhower deemed Brooks's VI Corps to be dangerously exposed in the newly gained Lauterbourg salient, he also ordered Devers to leave Strasbourg and withdraw to the line of the Vosges, abandoning the Alsatian plain. When Devers flew to Paris on 27 December to ask him to reconsider, Eisenhower remained adamant, telling him that he would get no more replacements, ammunition, or help and that resources would be taken from him. Devers realized that the weaker he got, the more likely the Germans were to attack, but both he and Patch felt confident that the VI Corps could withstand any German attack. Since Devers was also convinced that the position he was giving up was stronger than the one to which he was going, he instructed Patch to have Brooks prepare three intermediate withdrawal positions and a final line on the Vosges in the event of heavy attack.[90] The Seventh Army was to conduct a fighting withdrawal.

Part of Devers's reluctance may have reflected his sympathy with the French, who insisted on holding Strasbourg for its symbolic value alone. Patch had also raised this point and agreed that withdrawal was not warranted. De Lattre was of the same view and issued orders to defend the city. On learning of the withdrawal order on 28 December, de Gaulle made clear French intentions to defend Strasbourg—on their own if necessary. The next day, Devers and Patch deduced that they would be subjected to German attack all along the front within the next forty-eight hours. When Eisenhower read Devers's report on 31 December, however, he questioned why his orders had not been carried out, blaming it on disloyalty and even trickery. On 1 January, Devers received an angry call from Eisenhower's chief of staff ordering him to direct the Seventh Army to withdraw to the line of the Vosges immediately. Devers replied that he had prepared to withdraw by stages since Eisenhower had not stipulated any need for immediate withdrawal. At the same, he informed the chief of staff that the Germans had launched heavy attacks against Patch on New Year's Eve. A still-rankled Eisenhower ordered Devers to keep two divisions in SHAEF reserve and confirmed that his withdrawal order still stood. While Devers assured Eisenhower's chief of staff that he would give up Strasbourg and retire to the line of the Vosges by 5 January, the intransigent stance of the French now delayed this redeployment. Shocked that Alsace and part of Lorraine would also be deliberately evacuated without combat, de Gaulle threatened to remove the French First Army from SHAEF's control if Strasbourg were abandoned. In the face of such resistance, Eisenhower finally relented, revoking his withdrawal order and releasing the SHAEF reserve to Devers, but only after a stormy conference with de Gaulle on 3 January. Three days after this meeting, Eisenhower expressed his desire to replace Devers with Patch; apparently, only his uncertainty about de Lattre's reaction stopped him.[91]

To ensure the success of their Ardennes offensive, the Germans had meanwhile started to consider secondary attacks against Allied counterattacks in the Bulge. Noting that Patch's army had been greatly overextended in order to let Patton drive north, the Germans decided to launch Operation *Nordwind* ("North Wind") to break through the northern sector of the Seventh Army and Operation *Zahnartz* ("Dentist") in the rear of Patton's Third Army. While the main object of *Nordwind* was to destroy Allied forces, it also aimed to split the Seventh Army and bring the northern portion of Alsace back into the German fold as Hitler fervently desired. In brief, the German plan for *Nordwind* called for a two-division attack down the Sarre River Valley against the XV Corps and a four-division attack through the heavily wooded area east of Bitche against the VI Corps. The equivalent of two panzer divisions were kept in reserve to exploit any breakthrough that developed.

Although Allied intelligence indicated that German forces were building up between Saarbrücken and the Colmar pocket, specific enemy intentions remained unclear. In Patch's estimation, however, the Sarre River Valley constituted the most dangerous approach since a penetration there threatened to split his army and leave the VI Corps stranded on the Alsatian plains. Devers agreed and on 30 December authorized Patch to position elements of the SHAEF reserve to establish a secondary line of defense behind the XV Corps. Locating his own headquarters at Saverne, Patch concentrated the bulk of his strength in Haislip's XV Corps, which deployed the 103rd, 44th, and 100th Divisions west to east on a thirty-five-mile front. East of the Vosges in the salient from Bitche to Lauterbourg, with orders to fall back at the first sign of a major German attack, Brooks's VI Corps deployed the 45th, 79th, and 36th Divisions from left to right. The 36th covered the Rhine River front from Lauterbourg south to Strasbourg, and the 14th Armored Division waited in reserve. Since infantry elements of the green 42nd, 63rd, and 70th Divisions arrived before their organic armor, artillery, and supporting attachments, Patch ushered them into line under their assistant division commanders as Task Forces Linden, Harris, and Herren, respectively. While Patch initially sent all three to Brooks to defend the Rhine River front, he later transferred two regiments of Task Force Herren, along with the French 2nd Armored Division, to bolster Haislip's XV Corps. To cover the ground between the Third Army and the XV Corps and between the XV and VI Corps, Patch deployed small mechanized screening forces.[92]

On 31 December, air reconnaissance reported German troop movements all across the northern front, and Patch warned his two corps commanders to expect a major enemy attack—with the XV Corps likely to bear the brunt—during the early hours of New Year's Day. Leading German elements struck

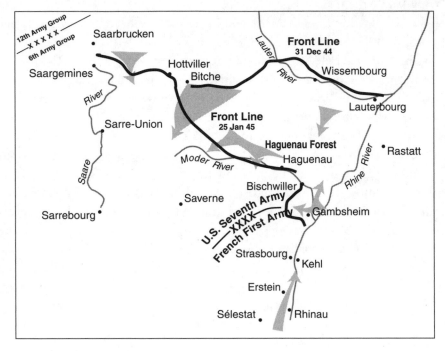

German Offensives, 31 December 1944–25 January 1945

American front lines around midnight but barely made a dent in the XV Corps' sector, where the 44th and 100th Divisions were entrenched in depth. Although the Germans eventually managed to make a narrow penetration on the 44th Division's right wing, the 100th held firm. Over the next few days, repeated counterattacks by the 44th and 100th and Task Force Harris, supported by elements of the French 2nd Armored Division, eroded whatever small gains the Germans made in the XV Corps' sector.

On the western wing of the VI Corps, the Germans made better progress, having surprised the Americans by mounting their main attack silently through difficult terrain and dense woods that concealed movement. Within four days, the attacking enemy divisions had broken through on a ten-mile front east of Bitche and pushed another ten miles south through the Vosges. To stem the German tide, Brooks redeployed the 45th Division, with Task Force Herren from the Rhine front and a regiment of the 49th Division under its command, across the VI Corps' sector to block the eastern exits of the Vosges and the approaches to Saverne. Although this redeployment exacerbated command and control problems by completely entangling elements of Task Force Herren and the 45th and 79th Divisions, Brooks's hasty reaction temporarily contained the German onslaught. In the ensuing muddle, the fighting quickly devolved into a bitter infantry seesaw around numerous Alsatian mountain hamlets and villages. Harsh subzero weather and rough terrain negated Allied armor, artillery, and air superiority in what was essentially a battle of attrition. To break the impasse and reinvigorate the drive south, the Germans on 2 January introduced the fresh, full-strength, and winter-trained 6th SS "Nord" Mountain Division into the fray. Patch now decided to redeploy the entire 103rd Division from the left wing of the XV Corps to the eastern shoulder of the major German penetration. While the Germans countered with further redeployments of their own, they remained hemmed in on three sides, unable to make any further progress. By 5 January, *Nordwind* had blown out.[93]

Strictly speaking, Operation *Nordwind* was only the first in a series of German attacks against the 6th Army Group. From 5 to 25 January, Patch's Seventh Army, greatly weakened by the massive diversion of supplies and replacements for the Battle of the Bulge, withstood several more multidivision attacks. On 5 January, Heinrich Himmler's Army Group *Oberhein* attacked across the Rhine at Gambsheim north of Strasbourg into the eastern flank of Brooks's VI Corps. At the same time, the 6th SS Mountain Division smashed through 45th Division's defenses in the western sector of the VI

Corps. Two days later, the German First Army launched its reserve panzer corps (the 21st Panzer, 25th Panzergrenadier, and 245th Volksgrenadier Divisions) against the northern portion of the Lauterbourg salient in the VI Corps' eastern sector. By 9 January, German panzers had pierced the VI Corps' center and forced it back to the Haguenau Forest. When Brooks committed his final reserve, the 14th Armored Division, the Germans responded by feeding in parachute and infantry reinforcements piecemeal. The ensuing struggle, which saw the VI Corps fighting on three sides, now devolved into a chaotic close-quarter conflict waged by small tactical units. At this point, SHAEF promised to make the 101st Airborne Division available to Devers, and Patch transferred both the 36th Infantry and 12th Armored Divisions to Brooks. A German drive from Lauterbourg down the west bank of the Rhine on 16 January and its subsequent linkup with the Gambsheim bridgehead left Brooks outflanked. His decision to rapidly withdraw below the Haguenau Forest on the night of 20–21 January nonetheless bought him time to organize a shortened line of resistance behind the Moder River. By 24 January, he had the 45th, 103rd, 79th, and 36th Infantry Divisions deployed in a cohesive defense from west to east, with the 12th and 14th Armored Divisions and Task Force Linden in reserve. This was narrowly enough to withstand the last series of German attacks undertaken on the night of 24–25 January in a driving snowstorm. The following day, Patch's Seventh Army counterattacked on a two-corps front, and on 26 January, the Germans called a halt to their last major offensive of the war.[94]

Meanwhile, Devers had finally committed a heavily reinforced French First Army to reduce the Colmar pocket on 20 January. Just as Bradley had unjustifiably described the Seventh Army's defensive efforts as poorly handled, Eisenhower unfairly blamed Devers for the continued existence of the Colmar pocket. In fact, the pocket's survival resulted as much from Eisenhower's decision to turn the Seventh Army north to support Patton as from the inability of the French First Army to reduce what Hitler fanatically chose to defend as an ancient part of Germany. Had the Seventh Army been allowed to cross the Rhine, it would have made the French task easier by threatening to take the pocket in the rear. Reinforcing de Lattre with the VI Corps as Eisenhower suggested at the time would also have left Patch's Seventh Army less able to support Patton. In the end, Eisenhower agreed to send additional troops to Devers, but only in order to free the Seventh Army for defensive operations.[95] De Lattre thus received Maj. Gen. Frank W. Milburn's newly arrived XXI Corps (the 3rd, 28th, and 75th Infantry and 12th Armored Divisions) for the final clearance of the Colmar pocket. Once this was accomplished in the first week of February, Milburn's XXI Corps reverted to the Seventh Army, which had in the meantime carried out limited attacks to gain improved positions for launching future offensive operations into Germany. By early March, following rest, replenishment, and regrouping, the Seventh Army now deployed, from north to south, the XXI Corps (the 70th and 63rd Infantry Divisions), the XV Corps (the 44th, 100th, and 79th Infantry Divisions), and the VI Corps (the 14th Armored and 42nd, 103rd, and 3rd Algerian Infantry Divisions). The 3rd, 36th, and 45th Infantry Divisions remained in reserve. Patch now commanded twelve divisions and three corps.[96]

By this time, all three of his corps commanders had proven their worth in action. Haislip, who had graduated from West Point a year before Patch, was by far the most experienced, having commanded the XV Corps since February 1943. He had also graduated from the Command and General Staff School with Patch in 1925, served on the faculty of the school in 1932–36, and attended the Army War College. A graduate of the *Ecole Supérieure de Guerre* (1925–27), he had developed a close working relationship with Leclerc of the French 2nd Armored Division. As part of the Third Army, Haislip had raced across France and would probably have preferred to stay with Patton. He was not close to Patch and had disagreed with his order to take Bitche on the grounds that it was a diversion on the way to the Siegfried Line. He nonetheless complied, and Patch appreciated his fighting ability. Unlike Haislip, Brooks of the VI Corps was not a West Pointer, but a graduate of Norwich University (The Military College of New England). A World War I veteran the same age as Bradley, he had spent most of the interwar years in the classroom. He instructed at the Artillery School for four years, graduated from the Command and General Staff School in 1934, taught military science and tactics at Harvard for two years, attended the Army War College, and instructed at the Command and General Staff School for two years. Over a period of eighteen years, he spent only about six commanding batteries in the Philippines and at Fort Riley, Kansas. A protégé of Devers, he had bypassed the rank of colonel and distinguished himself as commander of the 2nd Armored Division. Brooks was one year younger than Milburn, who had commanded the XXI Corps since December 1943. A 1914 West Pointer, Milburn had graduated from the Command and General Staff School with Collins in 1933. Although he did not attend the Army War College, he had served on the faculty of the

Command and General Staff School in 1934–38. A favorite of Patch, Milburn came late to the Seventh Army after helping de Lattre close the Colmar pocket with the XXI Corps.[97]

In early March, Devers approved and forwarded to SHAEF a proposed plan for the Seventh Army, called Operation Undertone, for attacking northeast through the part of the West Wall that defended the Saar and onto the Rhine through a set-piece attack by the XXI, XV, and VI Corps abreast. Given the breadth of the assault against the imposing depth of the West Wall in heavily wooded, hilly terrain, Patch and his planners expected a hard fight. At this point, Bradley and Patton put forth a plan to have the Third Army cross the Moselle River and assail the West Wall from the rear, thereby easing the Seventh Army's task. The concept called for the nine divisions of the Third Army's XX and XII Corps to wheel southeastward across the Moselle to roll up the Saar and cut off the Germans behind the fortifications that faced Patch's Seventh Army. Both corps would trap what remained of the German Seventh Army and squeeze the German First Army between the U.S. Third and Seventh Armies. While Devers expressed concern about a possible collision of armies, he saw the advantages of taking the Germans in the rear, which was exactly what he could have done earlier against the Colmar pocket had the Seventh Army been allowed to cross the Rhine.

Patch, while appreciative of Patton's support, saw that, once again, Patton would cruise on the hard fighting of another army. Whereas Patch selected 15 March for the start of Undertone, Patton jumped off two days before, purportedly because he feared the Seventh Army might beat the Third to the Rhine. In the event, the Seventh met less resistance than it would have without the threat to the Germans' rear, but still more than that encountered by the Third Army. This situation compelled Eisenhower to ask Patch if he had any objections to Patton's cutting across his front to trap as many Germans as possible. When Patch replied that he had none because "we are all in the same army," Eisenhower suggested shifting the interarmy boundary to run just north of Kaiserslautern to the Rhine at Worms. Patton thereupon proposed that he penetrate Patch's zone still deeper to encircle the entire West Wall opposite the Seventh Army and meet the Seventh's right flank, the VI Corps, on the Rhine. Patch agreed, and on 24 March, armored elements of the Seventh and Third Armies linked up south of Speyer at Germersheim, where the Germans blew the bridge.[98]

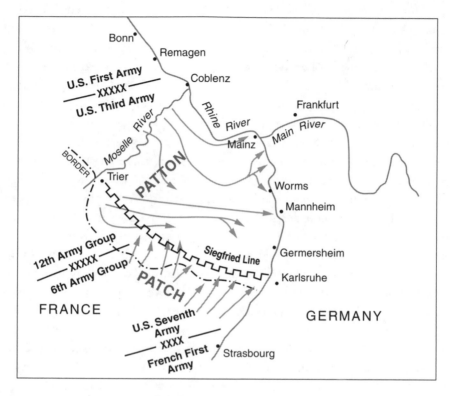

Operation Undertone

Two days later, Patch's Seventh Army finally crossed the Rhine at Worms, with the XXI and VI Corps passing through the XV Corps' bridgehead. By 28 March, all corps were advancing—Haislip's XV on the left heading toward Lohr beyond the loop of the Main River, Milburn's XII in the center striking toward Wurzburg, and Brooks's VI on the right making for Mannheim and Heilbronn. In keeping with Eisenhower's cable of the same day promising Stalin that the main Allied effort would be directed on Leipzig rather than Berlin, the final objective of the Seventh Army was decreed to be the Nürnberg area. Since Eisenhower and especially Bradley tended to believe rumors of fanatical Nazis making a last-ditch stand in a "national redoubt" centered on Berchtesgaden, the Seventh Army received the additional task of attacking from Nürnberg down the Danube Valley to Linz in Austria to prevent any consolidation of German resistance in the south. To Eisenhower, this was "vastly more important than the capture of Berlin."[99] Yet while the threat of the national redoubt conveniently justified the redirection of the main Allied effort away from Berlin toward the German south, as Eisenhower implied in his Stalin cable, it was not enough to enhance the role of the 6th Army Group. SHAEF simply rejected Devers's suggested plan to have his army group deal with the possibility and directed Bradley's more favored 12th Army Group to deliver the final thrust into Germany, with the 21st Army Group providing flank protection in the north and the 6th Army Group doing the same in the south. In its advance on Nürnberg, Patch's Seventh Army thus inherited the secondary task of guarding the 12th Army Group's right flank as it swept across Germany. It was also given a 118-mile front—more than twice that of any of Bradley's armies.[100]

Fortunately, except for certain pockets, cohesive German resistance was generally waning. By 3 April, elements of Haislip's XV Corps had fought their way through Aschaffenburg to Lohr and pushed on to clear Bamberg north of Nürnberg ten days later. In the Seventh Army's center, Milburn's XXI Corps secured Würzburg after a three-day battle, and the 42nd Division went on to seize Schweinfurt on 11 April. Farther south on the army's right flank, Brooks's VI Corps took Mannheim and captured Heidelberg without a struggle but encountered determined enemy resistance in Heilbronn that lasted until 12 April, when the city was finally cleared. By 16 April, elements of the XV Corps closed on Nürnberg from the north while the XXI Corps approached from the west. Supported by artillery and a constant stream of aircraft from Barcus's XII Tactical Air Command, Patch's soldiers relentlessly fought their way forward to secure the symbolic prize of the city that had hosted so many Nazi rallies. The battle for Nürnberg was bloody and difficult, but after a grim five-day struggle, the city fell to American arms on 20 April, the fifty-sixth birthday of Adolf Hitler. Two days later, the 12th Armored Division of the XXI Corps crossed the Danube at Dillingen; not far behind, the XV Corps reached the river on the twenty-fifth.

Meanwhile, bordering on favoritism for Patton, SHAEF on 15 April had issued another directive reassigning responsibility for attacking the national redoubt from the 6th Army Group to the 12th. The Third Army was to deliver the last great offensive of the war, and to accommodate the major right wheel that this required, the inter–army group boundary was redrawn along a southeast line running from Würzburg toward Austria midway between Munich and Salzburg. This not only shortened the 6th Army Group's frontage by fifty miles, but also entailed the transfer of the 14th Armored Division from Patch to Patton since Nürnberg now lay in his zone (which fed the myth that the Third Army captured it).[101]

The 6th Army Group also had to make boundary adjustments within its zone since the new axis cut off the route of the French, who—still following earlier direction and pursuing their own purposes—crossed into the Seventh Army's zone to capture Tübingen south of Stuttgart on 16 April. Devers had originally assigned the capture of Stuttgart to de Lattre's French First Army but had since cautioned the French commander that Brooks's VI Corps had been directed to bypass Stuttgart and advance south through Tübingen to Lake Constance and the Swiss border. Devers also wanted the VI Corps to be able to move rapidly and unimpeded so that an accompanying scientific intelligence unit, code-named ALSOS, could investigate reported German nuclear experiments at Hechingen south of Tübingen (and keep any nuclear information out of the hands of the French). Although annoyed by the French incursion, Devers accepted the *fait accompli,* and impressed by de Lattre's capture of Stuttgart on 22 April, he shifted the interarmy boundary to legitimize his movements. To ensure the Seventh Army running rights over main routes, however, he transferred Stuttgart to Patch's control the next day, precipitating another political clash between de Gaulle and SHAEF related to French efforts to secure their own occupation zone in Germany. (The alleged misconduct of French troops in Stuttgart further complicated matters for Devers and Patch.[102]) In the end, the French stayed in Stuttgart, which possibly encouraged de Lattre to authorize an armored dash forty miles inside the

**The U.S. Seventh Army's Drive into Germany,
5 April–7 May 1945**

Seventh Army's zone to Ulm, where on 24 April the French flag was raised to commemorate Napoleon's great victory of 1805. Although Devers considered this intolerable and ordered de Lattre out immediately, Patch allowed the French to maintain an honor guard in Ulm for a time after its capture.[103] Luckily, the 10th Armored Division of the VI Corps, which reached the Danube just west of Ulm at Ehingen on 22 April, recognized the French as allies and did not fire upon them. By this time, the Seventh Army occupied a front of some eighty miles along the river from Ehingen to Neuburg, west of Ingolstadt, with the VI Corps on the right, the XXI Corps in the center, and XV Corps on the left poised to attack Munich.[104]

Only shattered German formations now faced the Seventh Army, which, according to the VI Corps' Brooks, pursued instead of attacked. Augsburg fell to the XXI Corps on 28 April and Landsberg shortly thereafter. By 29 April, after clearing Oberammergau and Garmisch-Partenkirchen, the VI Corps had captured Fussen and crossed into Austria. The same day, elements of the XV Corps overran Dachau, where alleged shootings of SS guards by American troops prompted Patch to convene an inquiry since he was not prepared to countenance any illegal treatment of prisoners of war no matter who they were. Also on the twenty-ninth, XV Corps troops entered the outskirts of Munich, fighting their way to the city on 3 May. That same day, Brooks's VI Corps seized Innsbrück and went on the secure the Brenner Pass the next day. Because of a boundary change that transferred responsibility from Patton to Patch, Salzburg capitulated to the XV Corps on 4 May. The seizure of Berchtesgaden the same day finally exposed the myth of the national redoubt. Of equal significance, on 4 May, reconnaissance elements of the VI Corps linked up with their counterparts in Truscott's U.S. Fifth Army at Vipiteno south of the Brenner Pass. On the fifth, the Germans on the Seventh Army's front surrendered unconditionally in a meeting between Brooks and Lt. Gen. Erich Brandenberg of the German Nineteenth Army. That afternoon, Lt. Gen. Hermann Foertsch, representing Army Group G, surrendered to Devers in the presence of Patch and Haislip. This brought the Seventh Army's combat operations in the European theater to an end.[105]

A s a field army commander, Patch generally refrained from interfering in corps battles. Yet it was Patch, not Truscott, his corps commander, who had made most of the critical planning decisions for Dragoon. He also kept a tight grip on the VI Corps to ensure the success of de Lattre's attacks on

Toulon and Marseilles and thereafter focused on replacements, equipment, and supplies to facilitate the advance of his Franco-American army up to Lyon and beyond. He further worked closely with Saville to produce the air plan for interdicting the withdrawing Germans. In the foul weather and close-quarter fighting in the Vosges, there was little opportunity for an army commander to influence the battle. During *Nordwind*, however, Patch played a key, if nondramatic, role in the original disposition of his forces and the later creation and commitment of reserves; to Patch, a commander's skill hinged on his ability to decide whether, when, and where to commit his reserves. In monitoring the course of the battle, he closely tracked current intelligence on German locations and intentions as well as the status and plans of his own forces. At the same time, while standing ready to offer advice and assistance, he let his corps commanders conduct their own operations. On the whole, Patch's relationship with his corps commanders appears to have been a healthy one marked by give-and-take on complicated matters of high command that were not always easily resolved by the simple method of giving an order and demanding that it be carried out. Patch did not always see eye to eye with Truscott, de Lattre, and Haislip, but he was confident enough to accept their ideas when they made sense.[106]

In May, Patch turned the Seventh Army over to Haislip and returned to the United States. While Marshall apparently intimated to him that he would be participating in the attack on Japan, he was instead posted to Fort Sam Houston near San Antonio to take command of the Fourth Army. At the end of August, he went on temporary duty to head the War Department Reorganization Board examining postwar military structure. In October, he submitted a report recommending a separate air force, a single armed forces department, combining coastal and antiaircraft artillery with the field artillery, and eliminating the horse cavalry. On a file copy of the report, he also penned a personal recommendation to abolish the Marine Corps, which he still did not hold in high regard. In November, after returning to San Antonio, Patch fell ill with pneumonia for the last time. He died on 21 November 1945, two days short of his fifty-sixth birthday. His ashes were buried at West Point three days later. In keeping with his wishes, no cadet formation paraded at his funeral. He did not want to impose.[107]

CHAPTER SIX

In the Shadow of Napoleon

GEN. JEAN DE LATTRE DE TASSIGNY, FRENCH FIRST ARMY

O f all Allied officers who led field armies on the Western Front in 1944–45, Gen. Jean Joseph Marie Gabriel de Lattre de Tassigny attained the highest national distinction. On the eve of his state funeral in January 1952, the president of the French Republic placed a baton on his casket beneath the Arc de Triomphe, making him a Marshal of France. While de Lattre has been lionized in several French biographies,[1] however, he has often been maligned in English accounts for his overweening Gallic pride and misunderstood antics. Although unpredictably explosive and more theatrical than even Patton, he remains relatively unknown among Allied field army commanders. Even so, aside from Patton, he has been the subject of more biographical works in English than any of his fellow army commanders, and his own commendable history of the French First Army has also been translated, prefaced by Eisenhower.[2] Yet few in the English-speaking world are even aware that the French deployed a field army on the Western Front in 1944, let alone that it was larger than the First Canadian Army at war's end. At the time of the German surrender, nine divisions of French troops stood in control of a considerable area of German territory, leaving the president of the Provisional Government of the French Republic, Gen. Charles de Gaulle, in a strong negotiating position to gain a zone of occupation.[3]

Throughout his life, de Lattre appears to have been driven by the glory that was France, and after personally experiencing the humiliation of 1940, he passionately strove to resurrect her greatness. Born in the Vendée in the

little village of Mouilleron-en-Pareds—also the birthplace of the great
French premier and war leader, Georges Clemenceau—on 2 February 1889,
he received a strict Catholic-school education and upbringing in a family of
minor gentry. From 1898 to 1904, he attended the College of Saint-Joseph at
Poitiers, a Jesuit institution that stressed religion, duty, honor, and country.
Like Napoleon, whom he forever venerated, de Lattre sought first to go into
the navy, spending 1904–06 on a preparatory program at the Vaugirard Naval
School in Paris. For various reasons, however, he decided to join the army
instead, completing the Saint-Cyr preparatory year at Sainte-Genevieve in
Paris in 1907–08 and joining the 29th Dragoons for the one year of troop
service required of entrants at the time. He entered Saint-Cyr in 1909, but
disenchanted by the discipline and what he considered mediocre teaching, he
graduated close to the bottom of his class in 1911. Blessed with a splendid
physique and skilled as a horseman, de Lattre nonetheless went on to do well
at the Cavalry School at Saumur. He joined the 12th Dragoons in September
1912 and went off to war with them two years later.[4]

In World War I, de Lattre was wounded four times, the second time in
the chest during a cavalry skirmish in which he killed two Germans with his
sword. He took the full force of a German cavalry lance, which broke off,
leaving him vomiting blood and close to death. Fortunately, his troop sergeant
later managed to extract the broken lance by placing his boot on de Lattre's
neck. Partly as a result of his returning to action too soon, de Lattre's dam-
aged right lung never fully recovered; it bothered him for the rest of his life.
After another wound, tired of waiting for the cavalry to see more action, he
volunteered for the infantry in 1915 in response to an army-wide appeal.
On joining the 93rd Infantry Regiment, he took command of a company in
the rank of captain and eventually rose to command its 3rd Battalion. During this time, he fought in the bloody 1916 Battle of Verdun, where he was
wounded again, and managed to survive Gen. Robert Nivelle's disastrous
1917 Aisne offensive. After more than two years of frontline fighting as a
company and battalion commander, de Lattre became the intelligence officer
on the staff of the 21st Division. In this capacity, he weathered the final German offensives of May 1918, which decimated his old regiment. By war's
end, de Lattre had been riddled with wounds, decorated twice, and mentioned in dispatches eight times.[5]

After the war, de Lattre joined the staff of the 18th Military Region at
Bordeaux and subsequently served with the 49th Infantry Regiment at

Bayonne. At the end of October 1920, he departed for Morocco, where he joined the staff of the Meknes Region. Later appointed chief of staff of the Taza Region, he was again seriously wounded in August 1925 while leading an attack in the Rif campaign. Returning to France in 1926, he briefly served with the 4th Infantry Regiment at Auxerre. In 1927, he entered the *Ecole de guerre* and passed out two years later with distinction. During this time, he married nineteen-year-old Simonne Calary de Lamaziere. In July 1929, he assumed battalion command in the 5th Infantry Regiment. Posted to the 4th Bureau of the army staff in the Ministry of War in February 1931, he received his promotion to lieutenant colonel in March 1932 and shortly thereafter became *chef de cabinet* to the commander in chief, Gen. Maxime Weygand. Subsequently promoted to colonel, he took command of the 151st Regiment at Metz in 1935. Two years later, he attended the *Centre des hautes études militaires*, graduating with distinction.

In 1938, de Lattre assumed the appointment of chief of staff of the French Fifth Army deployed along the Maginot Line north of the Swiss border on the Rhine, and in March 1939, he received a promotion to brigadier general. Although only a brigadier general—the youngest in the army—he was given command of the 14th Infantry Division in February 1940. During the German invasion of France, de Lattre's division performed well in defensive actions at Rethel and on the Aisne River from 15 May to 11 June. Ordered to withdraw to the Marne, it doggedly held the enemy at bay for a day at Mourmelon. Falling back on the Loire River on 18 June, it again put up a heroic resistance at Nevers. On hearing news of an imminent armistice, de Lattre personally appealed to the French High Command to send the 14th Division to either England or North Africa since it still possessed a capability to fight.[6]

After the 22 June armistice, de Lattre assumed command of the Clermont-Ferrand area in what was left of France, an unoccupied neutral southern zone governed from Vichy. As a newly promoted major general, he focused on training and modernizing the 100,000-man metropolitan army allowed under armistice terms. In September 1941, at the request of Weygand, who had been appointed delegate general of the Vichy government in North Africa, he transferred to command French forces in Tunisia. By agreement with Weygand, who was also commander in chief in French North Africa, de Lattre worked to ensure that any Axis attempt to enter Tunisia would be resisted with force. Since the Germans suspected Weygand of harboring pro-Allied and anti-German sympathies, they forced his removal in

November 1941. In January 1942, the Vichy government recalled de Lattre and placed him in command of the military district of Montpelier. While in that position, encouraged by the Allied landing in North Africa in November, de Lattre schemed to produce active military resistance to the anticipated German occupation of Vichy France. His efforts proved futile, however, as Vichy loyalists took immediate steps to foil his plans. Subsequently arrested and jailed, he was sentenced by special state tribunal on 9 January 1943 to ten years' imprisonment at Riom.[7] With much preparation and the assistance of his son, he engineered his escape on the night of 2 September and was whisked from France to Britain.[8]

The French Army, traditionally composed of metropolitan, African, and colonial components, rose phoenix-like from the ashes of 1940.[9] Under the terms of the Franco-German armistice of 22 June 1940, the Germans re-annexed Alsace and Lorraine and occupied northern France. They also restricted the Vichy army to 100,000 men but allowed another 100,000 soldiers for French North Africa to ensure its continued neutrality. Meanwhile, Brig. Gen. Charles de Gaulle issued a radio appeal from London urging the people of France to fight on with the British Empire. On 7 August, Churchill recognized him as head of all Free Frenchmen and concluded a formal agreement that constituted the Charter of Free France. One year later, on 24 September 1941, a French National Committee was established in London under the presidency of de Gaulle, who was fast becoming the symbol of the resurrection of France. By the end of 1942, he exerted control over French Equatorial Africa, the Cameroons, Syria, Madagascar, Djibouti, and the island of Réunion. The potential manpower of these areas, when added to Frenchmen who had already escaped to Britain, offered the prospect of producing an army of roughly 100,000 men. In late 1940, de Gaulle had started working toward this end, creating staffs as well as ground, naval, and air forces. Known as Free French Forces (*Forces françaises libres*), these had grown to 35,000 by October 1942. Like the French Forces of the Interior (FFI) resistance groups within occupied France, Free French Forces operated under the control of the British, who also assumed responsibility for subsidizing, arming, and equipping them.[10]

The first Free French ground formation fielded was L Force, named for its aristocratic commander, Col. Jacques Philippe Leclerc, the *nom de guerre* of Vicomte Philippe François Marie de Hauteclocque, a 1924 Saint-Cyr graduate who had commanded a battalion in the French 4th Infantry Division. Following his escape from France in 1940, he assumed the name of a workman, Jacques Leclerc, to protect his wife and family from German reprisal.[11] After winning the first Free French victory of the war at Kufra in the Libyan Desert in March 1941, L Force, also known as Leclerc Column, went on to distinguish itself in support of the British Eighth Army in Tunisia. Reconstituted as the 2nd Free French Division with British rates of pay, Leclerc's command later moved to Morocco, where it was eventually kitted out with the full weaponry and equipment of a U.S. armored division and redesignated the French 2nd Armored Division for the invasion of Normandy. Two other formations, the 1st and 2nd Free French Brigades, also fought gallantly under the Eighth Army. The 1st Brigade performed heroically in the critical Battle of Bir Hakim in Libya under the command of Brig. Gen. Pierre Koenig, whom de Gaulle later appointed to head the FFI. In February 1943, both brigades combined to form the 1st Free French Division that fought alongside L Force in southern Tunisia.[12]

Not all French overseas possessions, however, rallied to de Gaulle. In French North Africa (Tunisia, Algeria, and French Morocco) and French West Africa, military authorities opted instead to sustain the territorial integrity and sovereignty of the French empire through the Vichy regime. There is some evidence to suggest that they fully intended to take up arms against the Axis after biding their time, a possibility rendered more likely by a German occupation of Vichy France. Their first step was to reorganize, reequip, and train the forces authorized under the terms of the Franco-German armistice. Under the guise of providing for the defense of North Africa against any invader, including the British in the Western Desert, they further managed to obtain German agreement to increase the strength of the Army of Africa from its original ceiling of 100,000 to 120,000 and, by 1942, to 137,000. Individual staffs and other groups of officers set up a secret program to increase army strength above authorized levels. Unlike the Metropolitan Armistice Army in France, the Army of Africa escaped the close scrutiny of Axis armistice commissions that might have prevented it from secretly hiding an extra 60,000 active soldiers and formulating plans to mobilize another 109,000 in the event of hostilities. By November 1942, there were nearly twice the number of troops allowed by armistice terms in North Africa. The French could also field one light mechanized brigade and five mobile divisions, three in Algeria and two in Morocco.[13]

   The Allied decision to invade North Africa on 8 November 1942 in
Operation Torch elevated the importance of the Army of Africa over Free
French Forces. In secret negotiations conducted earlier that year, the Americans had extracted a promise of support from French war hero and escaped
prisoner of war Gen. Henri Giraud, whom they considered the most likely to
succeed in leading French North and West Africa into the war on the Allies'
side. In October, acting on the instructions of President Roosevelt, Maj. Gen.
Mark W. Clark landed by submarine at Cherchel, Algeria, to assure Giraud's
representative, Maj. Gen. Charles Mast, that the U.S. would equip French
North African forces for operations against the Axis. In marked contrast, Free
French requests for American materiel support had been refused on the
grounds that de Gaulle's forces offered comparatively limited striking power,
and security concerns prevented the Free French from participating in Operation Torch. Unfortunately, Giraud did not arrive in North Africa until 9
November, too late to ensure that the Torch landings took place entirely
unopposed. At Oran and especially Casablanca, the Allies met with strong and
often bitter French resistance, which ceased only on 10 November as a result
of a contentious agreement between Clark and the Vichy minister of
national defense, Adm. Jean François Darlan, who happened to be in Algiers
visiting his sick son. Darlan had initially ordered desultory resistance to the
Allies but consented to an armistice in exchange for being recognized as
Vichy High Commissioner for North Africa. On 14 November, he appointed
Giraud commander in chief of all French ground and air forces in the
region. An agreement between Darlan and Clark on 22 November further
stipulated that command of French forces in the Allied cause was to remain
"under French direction." The Army of Africa, with more than 300,000 men,
had joined the Allies.[14]
   The need for modern equipment had been highlighted by French losses
in the Tunisian campaign, during which 45,000 North African troops thrown
into battle had incurred 24 percent casualties, largely because of the inadequacy of their weapons and equipment. The French rearmament program
proposed in Maj. Gen. Charles Mast's plan called for fielding eight infantry
and two armored divisions and an associated number of tanks, artillery pieces,
air assets, and service elements. Equipping such a force would have required
stripping twelve U.S. divisions and delayed the overseas shipment of 250,000
American troops, and the U.S. reassessed the plan. At the Casablanca Conference, held in the suburb of Anfa on 14–26 January 1943, Roosevelt person-

ally approved a memorandum prepared by Giraud that called for the U.S. to equip a sizeable French force of three armored and eight motorized infantry divisions, as well as an air force of 500 fighters, 300 bombers, and 200 transport planes. Since Roosevelt made this arrangement without consulting Churchill or Marshall, the so-called Anfa Plan produced some misunderstandings with respect to implementation. To Marshall, who first learned of the plan from the French, it seemed as though Giraud had intentionally misrepresented the details. Giraud, on the other hand, thought the Americans were refusing to honor their full commitments. Roosevelt finally clarified the issue by explaining that he had agreed only in principle to French rearmament, not to specific details or dates regarding the equipment of French divisions. In any case, Marshall firmly backed the program for French rearmament and insisted on giving them the best equipment available. On 12 July 1943, he advised Eisenhower to use French troops wherever possible instead of bringing in more troops from the U.S.[15]

The Anfa Plan provided the spark that led to the reforging of the French field army. By mid-April 1943, with a parade strength of about 16,000 officers and 317,000 men, Giraud had already activated most of the eleven divisions included in the plan.[16] By 12 August 1943, a total of four infantry and two armored divisions and two corps headquarters had been equipped. At the Quebec Quadrant Conference on 11–24 August 1943, the Combined Chiefs of Staff approved the 15 August Plan, which called for the equipping of two additional corps headquarters, three infantry and two armored divisions, and associated combat support and service elements. Problems related to the provision of French service support troops showed these targets to be overly ambitious, and a new plan, approved by SHAEF and the French National Defense Committee on 23 January 1944 and the CCS on 2 March, consequently called for equipping only five infantry and three armored divisions and ancillary troops. All of these formations were structured along American lines and, with the exception of Leclerc's 2nd Armored Division, earmarked for Operation Anvil.[17]

Of all the factors that affected French rearmament arrangements, none caused greater difficulty than the fractious French political environment. The assassination of Darlan on 24 December 1942 allowed Giraud to assume supreme civil and military authority in French North and West Africa. Meanwhile, de Gaulle continued to head the French National Committee and the British-armed Free French Forces. The polyglot French National Council of the Resistance, meeting secretly in Paris, endorsed de Gaulle as political leader and Giraud as military commander in chief in May 1943. Although the Free French had been outraged by Allied collaboration with the Vichyite Darlan in Torch, they had agreed prior to Anfa on the desirability of uniting all French forces. Accordingly, in Algiers on 3 June 1943, the *Comité français de libération nationale* (CFLN) was established, with Giraud and de Gaulle as copresidents. On 26 August 1943, the British, Canadian, and American governments extended limited recognition to the CFLN as the representative of all Frenchmen fighting the Axis, pending the establishment of a government by the liberated people of France. Buoyed by this recognition, in October 1943, the CFLN eliminated the dual-head arrangement and elected de Gaulle sole president. It then moved to establish a National Defense Committee with the president, a commissioner of national defense, and the commander in chief sharing responsibility for French forces. This effectively stripped Giraud of much of his power to deal singlehandedly with the Allies, as Devers duly noted.[18] Another decree in December empowered the National Defense Committee to make all decisions related to the deployment, armament, and organization of French forces. Finally, on 4 April 1944, the CFLN issued an ordinance making the president of the CFLN the titular head of the armed forces. It further established a General Staff of National Defense that rendered the post of commander in chief irrelevant. On 15 April 1944, the politically outmaneuvered Giraud bade farewell to the French forces.[19]

Although de Gaulle was more amenable than Giraud to the downward adjustment of the eleven French divisions called for by the Anfa Plan, Roosevelt remained suspicious of his political machinations.[20] Backing de Gaulle also risked losing the chance of persuading Vichy to turn more powerful forces against the Germans in the future. Roosevelt and his anti-Gaullist administration preferred Giraud to the end, possibly because the British Foreign Office backed de Gaulle, but also because Roosevelt believed only a government chosen by the liberated people of France in free elections could be considered sovereign. In December 1943, he told the State Department that French military authorities were to be dealt with only through Eisenhower, the newly appointed Supreme Allied Commander, and not on a government-to-government basis. Having refused to recognize the legitimacy of the CFLN, he reiterated to Marshall on 28 April 1944 that military questions involving French forces should be discussed directly between the Supreme Allied Commander and the French military authorities, "not as between one

sovereign government in full possession of its sovereignty and another government which has no de facto sovereignty."[21] This meant that the French
Army, with no staff representation in either the Combined Chiefs of Staff or
SHAEF, was to be—somewhat like the Canadian Army—little more than an
alliance force subject to the higher strategic direction of imperial powers.

On the other hand, de Gaulle's CFLN clearly considered itself a *de jure*
government in full possession of its sovereignty. De Gaulle was also determined that France would have a political voice. On 27 December 1943, following the Cairo Conference decision that the bulk of the French Army
would participate in Operation Anvil with a token force for Overlord, he met
with Gen. Walter Bedell Smith, Eisenhower's chief of staff; Minister Edwin
Wilson of the United States; and Minister Harold Macmillan of the United
Kingdom to set forth the conditions under which French forces would operate under Allied command. Specifically, they were to be placed at the disposal
of the Combined Chiefs of Staff and employed by the Supreme Allied Commander in consultation with the French High Command. The CFLN reserved
the right to appeal to the British and American governments, and the French
High Command reserved the right to appeal to the Allied High Command.
When the Combined Chiefs of Staff attempted to stipulate on 11 March
1944 that the disposal of French forces equipped by the U.S. and Britain was
"a matter for agreement between the CCS and the CFLN," the CFLN
insisted that the agreement should be between it and the two Allied governments, not with the Combined Chiefs. The question of the control of French
forces was thus not resolved before Overlord or Anvil; indeed, it was not until
23 October 1944 that a reluctant Washington, joined by London and Moscow,
formally recognized the legitimacy of de Gaulle's provisional government.[22]

D e Lattre landed in England in October 1943 and sent a telegram to de
Gaulle pledging his complete loyalty. Expressing the hope that he
would soon be able to serve usefully in General Giraud's army in North
Africa, he at once began lobbying. While in England, he made an excellent
impression on the Canadian Minister to Allied Governments in London, Maj.
Gen. Georges Vanier, who described de Lattre as dynamic, intelligent, well-
mannered, good-looking, and debonair. In further contacts, however, Vanier
was struck by the contradictions in de Lattre's impulsive temperament, how at
one moment he could be absolutely charming and at another time use language more appropriate to the barrack room. On one occasion in particular,

Vanier concluded that de Lattre was ripe for a mental home. According to Vanier, de Lattre arrived at a dinner engagement shouting, much to the embarrassment of his hosts, about Brooke's declining to meet with him. De Lattre went on to boast of his seven wounds and fifteen citations, making clear that he felt he had earned the right to lead a French Force into northwestern France and that, unless he did, there would be a bloody revolution and civil war. Apparently unaware that Leclerc's division had already been selected to participate in the Normandy invasion as a token French force, de Lattre said that he was not interested in marching into France through the southern "back door." Delivering the weight of the French Army through Anvil, as favored by Giraud, was too far from Paris in de Lattre's view, leading him to believe that the Americans wanted to avoid the embarrassment of having French troops rescue their own capital. While Vanier was left to wonder whether de Lattre's outbursts were deliberate exercises in histrionics or indications of more serious shortcomings, he continued to regard him as one of the two or three most interesting men he had ever met.[23]

On his arrival in Algiers on 20 December 1943, de Lattre immediately paid his respects to de Gaulle and then called on Giraud, who on 26 December placed him in command of the French Second Army, which was renamed Army B on 23 January to designate a headquarters specifically slated for Anvil. To de Lattre, now *general d'armee,* it was clearly in the French national interest to raise a large army to spearhead Allied liberation efforts. Only by spilling the blood of her men in conquering Germany, de Lattre told Devers, could France regain her prestige.[24] Over the next seven months, he fashioned the body and soul of Army B, responding in turn to direction from Giraud and then de Gaulle after he became *chef des armees.* Throughout this period, de Lattre also liaised with Allied Forces Headquarters, Mediterranean theater,[25] which in an internal report assessed him as temperamental, inclined to be theatrical, and quick to take offense where none is intended. The report also stressed that he was frank and easy to deal with once his confidence had been gained.[26] Although Devers at the time assessed de Lattre as a brilliant person who made a favorable first impression on most people, he and his staff marked him as a difficult personality and dangerous man.[27] De Gaulle was also apparently wary of the ambitious nature of de Lattre, and perhaps with good reason.[28] On one occasion over dinner, de Lattre reportedly complained about the shoddy treatment accorded him by Lt. Col. L. E. Dostert of the French subsection of Allied Force Headquarters, who appeared to favor Giraud. Referring to Dostert as "Giraud's nurse," de Lattre said that he, de Lattre, was a full five-star general commanding an army, that he had been wounded fifteen times, and that he was the most popular general in all France, behind not even de Gaulle.[29]

De Lattre's appointment occurred during a period in which French political and military relations were at their stormiest. The Gaullist Free French, who had kept the tricolour flying high since June 1940, considered themselves morally superior to those who had opted to support the Vichy regime. The Army of Africa, on the other hand, resented being branded collaborationists and plainly envied the greater fame of Koenig's 1st Free French Division and Leclerc's Column. Nowhere was this acrimony more evident than at the Tunis victory parade on 20 May 1943, where the Free French preferred to march with the British rather than the Army of Africa. The jealousy of Giraud and his military establishment, as much as the aggressive animosity of the Free French, explains why Free French formations were banished from North Africa for two months. This situation began to improve only with the ascendancy of de Gaulle in Algiers and the subsequent performance of Army of Africa commanders like Gen. Alphonse Juin, who in January 1943 had undertaken active operations against the Axis in support of British and American forces. While Juin incurred the wrath of Giraud in proposing that his troops be placed under the British First Army, he instructed the French commander in southeast Algeria that Free French forces serving with the British Eighth Army were to be accepted as fellow French soldiers by the Army of Africa. Having earned the respect of such Allied commanders as Clark, Patton, Eisenhower, and Alexander for his field performance, Juin was subsequently promoted to full general and named to command the *Corps expeditionnaire français* (CEF) for operations in Europe.[30]

According to Vanier, de Lattre and Juin had hated each other ever since they left Saint-Cyr on the same day, and it was probably fortunate for French internal relations that de Lattre arrived in North Africa only in December 1943, after Juin's CEF deployed to Italy in November and remained in that theater for nine months with the U.S. Fifth Army.[31] Initially planned as an entirely Army of Africa formation of one armored and two infantry divisions, the CEF eventually comprised over 100,000 men and four infantry divisions. The first to see action were the 2nd Moroccan Infantry Division, the 3rd Algerian Infantry Division, and the 4th Group of Tabors.[32] In February 1944, they were joined by the 4th Moroccan Mountain Division and the 1st

Motorized "Free French" Infantry Division.[33] Since Army of Africa infantry
divisions were adept at hill and mountain fighting, they performed superbly in
the Italian terrain and completely confuted contemptuously low American
estimates of French fighting efficiency. That Juin knew a great deal about
mountain artillery, understood logistics (especially the value of mules), and
appreciated the power of foot maneuver placed him foremost among corps
commanders in Italy. Devers considered Juin's troops magnificent and attributed their performance ·to his leadership. In fact, Devers, Wilson, Alexander,
and Clark all rated him the outstanding corps commander in the theater.[34]

De Gaulle had no interest in keeping French troops in Italy. Since the
U.S. could not equip French forces for both Italy and southern France, the
liberation of France had to take priority. At the Cairo Conference on 3
December 1943, the Combined Chiefs of Staff had already decided that the
rearmed French Army would ultimately participate in the liberation of
France. The Italian interlude, also approved at Cairo, aimed mainly at providing French troops with battle experience before they were committed to
operations in their own country. In keeping with the decision at Cairo to
launch both Overlord and Anvil simultaneously, the bulk of the French forces
were to participate in Anvil, with only a token force in Overlord. De Gaulle,
having been assured by Eisenhower on 30 December 1943 that he would
"not enter Paris without the French at my side," was also secretly determined
that a Free French division should be the first to enter Paris. The most obvious choice was Leclerc's 2nd Armored Division, which had been refitting and
training in Rabat, Morocco, since August 1943. In April 1944, over the objections of de Lattre, who wanted this formation for his own army, the 2nd
Armored shipped to England to become part of Patton's Third Army.[35] This
turned out to be fortuitous since the Free French Leclerc hated the Vichyite
de Lattre with a passion.[36]

In April 1944, de Lattre received formal notification that his Army B
would be participating in Operation Anvil as a follow-on force. On the seven-
teenth, French headquarters informed Allied Force Headquarters that de
Gaulle had officially appointed de Lattre to command French forces for the
invasion of southern France.[37] In the view of some, de Gaulle selected de Lattre as army commander only because he preferred to have two successful
commanders rather than a single very famous one, like Juin, who could conceivably challenge his authority. Although the Allies would have preferred Juin,
he was appointed chief of the Defense Staff, with his CEF now falling under

de Lattre's command.[38] De Lattre retained Juin's chief of staff, Brig. Gen. Marcel Carpentier. At this point, Army B had approximately 256,000 troops distributed among two armored and five infantry divisions, sixteen groups of artillery (three of them heavy), six regiments of tank destroyers, two armored reconnaissance regiments, four engineer and three pioneer regiments, and twelve antiaircraft artillery groups. Fighting elements included three groups of Moroccan Tabors (the 1st, 2nd, and 3rd), "Africa" and "France" commando groups, and a shock battalion roughly akin to a U.S. Ranger battalion.[39]

De Lattre's idiosyncratic command style, characterized by passion and drama, taxed his staff beyond what was required to serve frontline troops. Devers, who found him difficult to handle for more than just his limited knowledge of English, ventured that de Lattre caused more trouble with his own staff and troops than he did with the Allies.[40] Certainly, few commanders could have been more difficult to serve than the energetic, notoriously unpunctual, and ruthlessly authoritarian de Lattre—which may partly explain why he had four chiefs of staff in succession.[41] De Lattre's unpredictable temperament and his refusal to make early decisions on future operations meant that his principal staff officers were forever saddled with having to anticipate his fast-changing moods and plans. These exertions, not to mention middle-of-the-night summons imposed an almost intolerable strain upon his staff and ensured that the working environment of his headquarters was always one of tension. Seldom in his headquarters, de Lattre's routine exacerbated this since he intimately controlled operations by radio or telephone, giving detailed tactical directions to subordinates and bouncing decisions on his staff at very short notice. Daily operations orders would typically be redrafted three or four times by his staff, with each draft often prompting de Lattre to think of some new move. His orders for April were redrafted seventeen times and, not surprisingly, were detailed, precise, and clear.[42]

For the invasion, de Lattre established a "think tank" of five officers with whom he spent a great deal of time discussing major problems. While such a group would have equated to the normal war plans section of any field army, de Lattre, for reasons perhaps related to French national considerations and civil affairs, added an overarching "brain trust." Headed by an inspector of finance and later by a lawyer, it included men and women from all walks of life, among them a councilor of state, a biologist, de Lattre's brother-in-law, and a journalist. The enigmatic William Bullitt, former U.S. ambassador to France and the Soviet Union, was one of the more prized members, and de

Lattre also accepted on staff an American G5 civil affairs officer, Col. Harvey S. Gerry, who spoke perfect French.[43] Besides providing de Lattre with the intellectual stimulation he craved, the brain trust advised on matters pertaining to welfare and morale, escorted an unending stream of visitors to headquarters, and looked after the press and publicity. The ladies visited the sick and wounded. As members belonged to every extreme of the French political spectrum, they also formed an invaluable link with the heterogeneous elements of the French First Army.[44] Like the rest of de Lattre's staff, they endured endless tirades that, according to Devers, occurred at least twice a week to the point where de Lattre seemed to lose balance.[45] At other times, the staff received de Lattre's cloying ingratiations while standing ready at all times of the day or night to accompany him forward. From Besancon to Montbeliard to Guebwiler, de Lattre's headquarters came to resemble the domain of a *grand seigneur.* Small wonder that he acquired the sobriquet "Le roi Jean"—"Jean the king."

The first operational task assigned to de Lattre was not Anvil, but rather the capture of the island of Elba. Code-named Brassard, Giraud originally conceived this operation as a sequel to the almost exclusively French liberation of Corsica by 15,000 troops under Lt. Gen. Henry Martin between 13 September and 4 October 1943. Brassard was to have been mounted from Corsica by Martin, the French I Corps' commander, working in concert with Wilson's Allied Force Headquarters, but de Gaulle pushed for greater French involvement and made de Lattre French High Command representative for Brassard as well as Anvil. In the event, an exclusively French ground force— including elements of the 9th Colonial Infantry Division of mainly black African troops, the 2nd Group of Tabors, the Shock Battalion, and the "Africa" Commando Group—attacked and secured Elba between 17 and 19 June 1944.[46] The French preferred such an all-French operation since they deeply resented American and British staff discussing the employment of their forces without French consultation.[47]

The sheer number of French forces earmarked for Anvil, along with growing confidence in their battlefield performance, not surprisingly led the French to demand a greater operational voice. Pointing out that the planned American contribution was less than the equivalent of four divisions and that the people of France were more likely to rally to French leadership than American, they proposed the appointment of a French ground commander.[48] On 27 December 1943, Eisenhower's chief of staff,

Bedell Smith, had confirmed the use of French forces "in the form of a French army" and intimated in January 1944 that a southern army group of a French and an American army might be headed by a French general.[49] When Wilson pointed out that lack of experience in amphibious warfare would limit the French role in the initial assault, however, de Gaulle accepted that the landings should be conducted under American command. As a quid pro quo, he wanted an independent French field army to be established after the amphibious phase. Devers warned Marshall in March that the French were pushing for an army commander and staff, adding that he believed it would be necessary to accommodate them for reasons of prestige and the fact they would field two corps of seven divisions.[50] Although Wilson and Devers appeared to have been ready to accept a French deputy commander and integrated staff if pushed, de Gaulle and his generals signaled their willingness to have the French army serve under an American army group headquarters.[51] As finally agreed between Wilson and de Gaulle, de Lattre would temporarily assume command of the first French corps ashore, taking orders from the commander of the U.S. Seventh Army, and when the second French corps landed, he would assume full command of Army B under the continued direction of Patch.[52]

Operation Dragoon, as Anvil was renamed on 1 August 1944, unfolded with covering operations by French and Allied commandos and paratroopers. Next followed the main assault by three divisions of the U.S. VI Corps, supported by Combat Command 1 (CC1) of the French 1st Armored Division, which disembarked on the night of 15–16 August. Finally, Army B landed in two echelons with a view to capturing the ports of Toulon and Marseilles. The first echelon, a 37,000-man force, followed twenty-four hours after the VI Corps' "assault convoy" and comprised the 1st Free French Division, the 3rd Algerian Division, CC2 of the French 1st Armored Division, a Spahi (Algerian cavalry) reconnaissance regiment, two regiments of tank destroyers, and two heavy artillery groups. The second echelon, a 28,000-man force, disembarked between 21 and 25 August and comprised the 9th Colonial Infantry Division, three Groups of Tabors, the Shock Battalion, a regiment of tank destroyers, and various artillery formations and support elements.

De Lattre and his staff landed on the night of 16 August along with the 1st Free French Division, the 3rd Algerian Division, and CC2 of the 1st Armored Division. Since the invasion was now progressing beyond expectations, de Lattre decided not to wait until 25 August for the rest of his vehicles and equipment, but to attack immediately before the Germans could react more strongly. Assured by Patch that CC1 would revert to French command on 19 August and that the Seventh Army's artillery ammunition stocks would be available for his use, de Lattre ordered the 1st Free French Division to attack Toulon from the east and the 3rd Algerian to encircle it from the north and west. He directed CC1 to protect the maneuver on Toulon and prepare the axis of advance toward Marseilles. When elements of the 9th Colonial Infantry Division arrived ahead of schedule, de Lattre placed them on the right of the 1st Free French and charged his deputy, Lt. Gen. Rene Marie Edgard de Larminat, to coordinate the eastern operation against Toulon.[53] The French began their attack on Toulon on 20 August and completely invested the city by the next day, with troops fighting house-to-house. By 26 August, the 9th Colonial Infantry Division had completed the final reduction of all organized resistance, and the Germans surrendered just before midnight.

Meanwhile, elements of Maj. Gen. Joseph de Goislard de Monsabert's 3rd Algerian Division—buttressed by CC1, Tabors, commandos, and other troops progressively released from Toulon by de Lattre—had reached the outskirts of Marseilles by 22 August. At this point, on learning that the 11th Panzer Division had arrived in the area of Aix-en-Provence, de Lattre ordered de Monsabert to hold in the suburbs until reinforcements came up. Choosing instead to exploit an FFI uprising in the city rather than strictly obey de Lattre, de Monsbert fed his troops forward through enthusiastic civilian crowds to reach the center of the city on 23 August. This unplanned drive—subsequently supported by de Lattre, who hoped to take Toulon and Marseilles simultaneously rather than consecutively as originally planned—triggered an intense urban battle for the center of Marseilles. After a dogged fight, the Germans surrendered on 28 August. The capture of Toulon and Marseilles a full week earlier than expected confirmed the success of Dragoon.[54]

By any measure, Army B had performed well in its first actions under de Lattre. Though risky, his decision to attack early proved sound since it denied the Germans time to prepare better defenses. Yet when de Lattre ordered de Monsabert to hold in the suburbs of Marseilles because of a possible threat from the 11th Panzer Division in the Aix–Provence area, he as much as admitted that Army B was overextended. Moreover, de Larminat, who led the attack on Toulon, was dissatisfied with de Lattre's coordination of operations—possibly because de Monsabert, despite de Lattre's direction to the contrary, placed greater priority on the capture of Marseilles while de Larminat was concerned only with Toulon. De Lattre's pulling troops from de Larminat to reinforce de Monsabert may also have created more friction. In a heated argument with de Lattre, de Larminat strongly urged that one commander take charge of both Toulon and Marseilles. Although it may well have been better if one dedicated headquarters (de Larminat's) coordinated the movements of all troops converging on Toulon until its capture was complete, de Lattre sacked de Larminat on the spot.[55] From Dever's observations, the suspicion lingers that de Larminat's Free French roots may also have had something to do with his removal. A 1914 Saint-Cyr graduate, de Larminat had fought throughout World War I and subsequently served in Morocco and Indochina. During 1933–35, he attended the *Ecole de guerre* and was later chief of staff to Weygand. In 1940, he attempted to continue the resistance in Syria but was forced to flee to Chad, where he joined Free French forces. Promoted to brigade and division command by de Gaulle, he later commanded two divisions in Italy. Devers greatly admired the quiet and thorough de Larminat, who went on to command the Detachment of the Atlantic in the Gironde Estuary.[56]

At the height of the fighting for Toulon and Marseilles, Patch issued instructions for the next phase of operations. On 25 August, he directed the U.S. VI Corps to advance along the Lyon-Dijon-Strasbourg axis and Army B to move into Alsace and the Upper Rhone valley through the Belfort gap. He also assigned the French the tasks of screening west of the Rhone River and providing right-flank protection for the VI Corps. When Patch confirmed these orders three days later, he directed Army B to take over responsibility for the Franco-Italian border from Allied special service and airborne forces. De Lattre understandably objected to these instructions since they threatened to divide the French forces under his command and permanently impede his drive on Belfort. The two commanders subsequently reached a compromise whereby the French 1st Armored and 1st Free French Divisions would advance up the west bank of the Rhone while the rest of Army B secured the VI Corps' flank east of the Rhone and assumed partial responsibility for the Franco-Italian border. Once Lyon fell, the French divisions west of the Rhone were to be reunited with the main body of Army B for a concentrated drive on Belfort. On 2 September, however, Truscott suggested that his VI Corps massed east of Lyons, was better positioned than the French to drive on Belfort. Pointing out that de Lattre would require at least a week to concentrate his forces and that western French elements were in any case

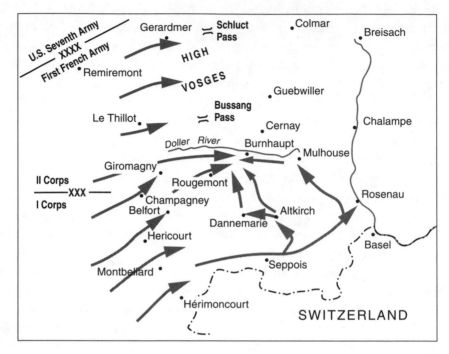

Forcing the Belfort Gap

already well north of Lyon, he recommended to Patch that they be redirected on Strasbourg, leaving Belfort to him.[57] Patch formally agreed to this proposal on 3 September.

De Lattre once more objected since it looked as if American commanders were making decisions without consulting the French, whose 200,000 men now comprised two-thirds of the Seventh Army. Worse yet, such a change in plan left French forces split, delaying their unification as an independent army on the right of the Seventh Army. Although de Lattre again complied, directing his forces to advance right and left of the VI Corps on Belfort and Dijon, respectively, he privately raged to Devers's senior liaison officer that he was through with the Seventh Army, which he thought had idiots on its staff who hated France. Charging that Patch was not up to the rapidly changing situation, he further expressed his wish to be under Devers as soon as possible with his own separate French army zone.[58]

De Lattre got his wish on 15 September, when, coincident with the transfer of the Seventh Army from Allied Force Headquarters to SHAEF, the 6th Army Group and French First Army both came into being. Devers now halted Truscott's drive on Belfort and issued new orders that fully united de Lattre's forces on the southern right flank. Since Eisenhower had long believed that U.S. forces should occupy the center of a broad advance into Germany, it naturally followed that French field forces should operate on their right. Although he would have preferred to place the Seventh Army under Bradley's 12th Army Group, Eisenhower apparently feared that the French First Army was not fully capable of assuming responsibility for the Allied right wing. His greater fear, however, may have been that de Gaulle would most likely have pressed for French command of the 6th Army Group had it included only a French army. This would have forced Eisenhower to deal with two national commanders, possibly de Lattre as well as Montgomery.[59] Keeping a French field army under an American army group commander, on the other hand, assured overall U.S. control and enhanced perceptions of American power.

French forces established first contact between SHAEF and Allied Force Headquarters on 11 September, when elements of the French 2nd Armored Division of the Third Army's XV Corps linked up west of Dijon with the Seventh Army's French 1st Infantry Division of the French II Corps.[60] By this time, de Lattre had established two French corps in anticipation of the junction with SHAEF, triggering the formation of the 6th Army Group with the French First Army under its command. Lt. Gen. Marie Emile Bethouart commanded the French I Corps (the 3rd Algerian, 9th Colonial, and later 2nd Moroccan Divisions). Born in 1889, Bethouart entered Saint-Cyr in 1909 and finished World War I thrice wounded as a battalion commander. After the war, he trained for mountain warfare, attended the *Ecole de guerre,* and served on the General Staff in Paris. In April 1940, he led a light Franco-Polish division in the capture of Narvik, but after the fall of France, he preferred to wait to resume the fight from North Africa rather than join de Gaulle. Bethouart, known as the "Black Beast," aided the Allies in Operation Torch and was temporarily stripped of his rank and jailed for his efforts. On his release, Giraud appointed him chief of the French Military Mission in Washington. On returning to North Africa in December 1943, he assumed command of a corps, and from April to August 1944, he served as chief of staff of the National Defense Committee.[61] Devers considered Bethouart an outstanding and thoroughly reliable commander.[62] He also thought de Monsabert, commander of the French II Corps (the 1st Armored and 1st Infantry Divisions), to be a fine officer and a bold and aggressive fighter. A 1911 Saint-Cyr graduate and battalion commander in World War I, de Monsabert had attended the *Ecole de guerre* in 1920–22 and distinguished himself in operations in Tunisia and Italy.[63] That both he and Bethouart had Vichy, rather than Free French, backgrounds surely suited de Lattre. In contrast to Devers, who exercised loose control over his army commanders and Patch, who gave wide latitude to Truscott, de Lattre kept both corps commanders on a tight rein whenever distance allowed.[64] This may have reflected de Lattre's penchant for effecting advances and encirclements through daring Napoleonic maneuver, which itself may have reflected his inability to influence the course of battle through the employment of artillery assets or air strikes.

The French may have fielded more artillery pieces than the opposing enemy, but all too often, they experienced serious ammunition shortages. For example, de Lattre complained that, between 1 and 10 December, the 6th Army Group allowed his army only forty-five rounds per gun per day for 105-millimeter howitzers and, between 10 and 20 December, only thirty rounds. Since the II Corps actually consumed forty-three rounds daily from 7 to 14 December, total army stocks for 15 December numbered only 400 rounds, not counting the 10–20 December allocation. By way of comparison, on 29 January, the U.S. 3rd Infantry Division fired a barrage of 16,438 rounds while the 2nd Moroccan and 9th Colonial Divisions had allocations of 4,000 and 1,500 rounds.[65]

The French First Army also appears to have suffered from a comparative lack of air support. The fledgling French tactical air force of twelve squadrons originally represented only one-twentieth of Allied air strength in the XII Tactical Air Command. On 1 September, Saville established a French air section within the XII Tactical Air Command, followed a month later by the 1st French Air Corps under General Gerardot. Coincidentally, the First Tactical Air Force under Maj. Gen. Ralph Royce assumed responsibility for coordinating XII Tactical Air Command and 1st French Air Corps within the 6th Army Group. Although the small but good 1st French Air Corps received additional U.S. air support, it appears to have been unable—possibly because of its lack of assets or undeveloped intercommunication procedures—to provide the French First Army with the air support it needed.[66] On 22 December, in response to de Lattre's complaints, Devers said he would talk to Royce about having the French First Army deal directly with him and have Royce, in turn, give direction to the 1st French Air Corps.[67] On 30 January, Devers also spoke with Saville in the hope that he could "remove the mental hazards" afflicting de Lattre with respect to air support.[68]

The concentration of the French First Army on the right of the line, with French II Corps in the north and I Corps in the south, entirely satisfied the independent-minded de Lattre. In keeping with Devers's direction for his army to drive through the Belfort gap and head north to clear the Alsatian plain, he planned to have the II Corps outflank the gap to the north and the I Corps fight directly through it to Mulhouse twenty-three miles away. De Lattre hoped to launch his attack around 27 September, but only three of seven French divisions had been deployed forward in line by mid-September. Logistical and redeployment problems further delayed the start date to after 20 October. De Monsabert's II Corps was nonetheless drawn into action in the southern Vosges by Truscott's request for an attack to support his VI Corps in the area of Le Thillot. De Lattre approved this action, which began on 25 September. He also chose to reinforce de Monsabert when it began to fail, sending him the 3rd Algerian Division, the 3rd Tabors, and eventually the 2nd Tabors, the Shock Battalion, the "Africa" Commando Group, and the French parachute regiment of two battalions. He further extended the frontage of Bethouart's I Corps northward and accepted Devers's northward movement of the French First Army's boundary to Gerardmer, almost due west of Colmar. De Monsabart, having failed to take Le Thillot and deducing that he lacked the strength to take Gerardmer and force the Schlucht Pass to the east, now decided to launch his main thrust through the High Vosges between Gerardmer and Le Thillot toward Guebwiller, thirteen miles south of Colmar. He intended to hinge this maneuver on the 1st Free French Division, which he hoped would be able to advance eastward just north of Belfort. When the offensive commenced on 4 October, however, few significant gains were made. Close, indecisive forest combat conducted under arduous conditions had exhausted the soldiers of the French II Corps. By 17 October, de Lattre finally decided that enveloping the Belfort gap through a deep northern drive across the High Vosges was not worth the cost, and he brought the operation to a halt.[69]

Given the state of his troops and the increased precipitation and freezing temperatures expected in the mountains, de Lattre decided to shift his point of main effort back to the more open terrain of the Belfort gap area. Frustrated at having been drawn into an indecisive battle in the High Vosges, he also faced serious logistical problems. In discussions with both Patch and Devers, he complained that his formation had been shortchanged in supply and equipment. Devers's French-speaking senior liaison officer, former U.S. senator Lt. Col. Henry C. Lodge Jr., reported that he had never seen de Lattre more excited or irate over his discovery that the Seventh Army had received twenty-one trains while the French First Army had gotten only six.[70] Lack of fuel, de Lattre charged, had prevented him from bringing up enough troops and ammunition for de Monsabert to sustain his thrust. De Lattre also produced figures to show that whereas his army, with five reinforced divisions, had received only 8,715 tons of supplies during 20–28 September, the Seventh Army, with three divisions, had received 18,900 tons. Although Devers recognized that there was some truth to de Lattre's contention that the French First Army received less favorable logistics treatment, the situation was not quite so stark as this in reality. The training and doctrinal inadequacy of the French support system, as well as language problems, also contributed to de Lattre's difficulties. Base 901, the logistic support agency for the French First Army, never exceeded 29,000 men when, by U.S. calculations, it should have had 112,000 to support an eight-division army. Such logistical limitations not surprisingly meant that the French First Army's offensive operations could not normally be sustained for more than ten to fourteen days.[71]

Another major problem faced by de Lattre was that of manpower. The French First Army was basically a colonial army of Algerians, Moroccans, and Senegalese that had started to run out of trained replacements from Africa before the end of October. Many of those who had fought from Italy to France were also beginning to feel that they were bearing a heavier burden than the metropolitan French, who, in turn, did not necessarily identify with the darker-skinned French First Army. With winter coming on and the harsher cold of France already affecting the performance of some colonial troops, de Lattre instituted a policy of *blanchissement,* or "whitening," aimed at replacing over 15,000 black troops from tropical and subtropical Africa, most of them in the 1st Free French and the 9th Colonial Divisions.[72] Before Dragoon, plans were made to tap the manpower resources of continental France, and by the end of November, some 75,000 FFI troops had swelled de Lattre's ranks. Care had to be taken in the training and integration of these troops, however, since many FFI had different political persuasions—including communists—than the conservative regulars of the North African army. Luckily, de Lattre enjoyed some favor with the left, having won the confidence of militant communist miners while commanding at Montpelier.[73] For the most part they were kept together as battalions or regrouped as regiments to fill out divisions or replace troops within them. In other cases, separate units beyond those approved for the French rearmament program were created, leaving de Lattre to scrounge for equipment. The training problem remained immense, but eventually, 137,000 FFI troops amalgamated with 250,000 soldiers of the French empire to sustain the French First Army as a national instrument.[74] Much of the credit for this belonged to de Lattre's inspired leadership.

Although de Lattre had largely managed to sort out his logistical and manpower problems before his attack on the Belfort gap, he now received orders for additional deployments that threatened to dissipate his army and disrupt his plans. In October, Devers warned him to be ready to assume responsibility, starting on 11 November, for the entire Franco-Italian border between Switzerland and the Mediterranean (it was already two-thirds manned by the 4th Moroccan Division and the FFI units being formed into the 27th Alpine Division).[75] When de Lattre pleaded that his Belfort attack should take precedence, Devers agreed to delay the relief. Around the same time, however, de Gaulle advised de Lattre that the French 1st Armored Division would be required to liberate the area of Bordeaux. On 2 November, in response to de Gaulle's agitation, SHAEF further directed the 6th Army Group to assume responsibility for Operation Independence, the clearance of the Gironde Estuary, still held by Germans to block any opening of the port of Bordeaux. Devers, in turn, called on de Lattre to provide 60,000 troops for this task, which was to commence on 10 December and be completed by 1 January 1945. The 1st Armored was slated to move on 11 November and the 1st Free French on 27 November. Although postponements delayed the westward movement of these formations—indeed, the 1st Armored never went—planning for this operation constantly frustrated de Lattre's preparations for battle.[76]

Notwithstanding this shadow hanging over him, de Lattre persevered in planning to seize the Belfort gap. In fact, he had been considering a southern attack on the gap since early October. After a personal reconnaissance of the Hericourt-Montbeliard-Herimoncourt front, he put an initial concept of operations to his I Corps commander, Bethouart, who, with his staff and de Lattre's 3e Bureau (G3), began to work out the possible actions his corps might take within the general framework outlined by de Lattre. On 16 October, following further studies by his division commanders and their staffs, Bethouart presented de Lattre with a comprehensive plan for an offensive. The next day, de Lattre decided to seek a decision on the I Corps' front, and sensing that de Monsabert's activities in the High Vosges had drawn in German reserves, he terminated the II Corps' attack. From north to south, de Lattre deployed the II Corps, whose 3rd Algerian and 1st Free French Divisions were reinforced by a few regular and FFI units. Next came the I Corps, with Group Molle (a reinforced brigade consisting mainly of FFI units) on the left, the reinforced 2nd Moroccan Division in the center, and the reinforced 9th Colonial Infantry Division on the right. De Lattre further strengthened the I Corps with the 5th Armored Division, CC2 of the 1st Armored, a 4th Moroccan Mountain Division regimental combat team, two tank destroyer battalions, light infantry, and numerous other minor units. First priority for units in the army general reserve went to the I Corps, which was allocated more than a dozen groups of artillery. To ensure that the Germans continued to think that the main French thrust was coming through the Vosges, de Lattre set in train a number of practical deception measures. Again in response to a Seventh Army request, the II Corps launched a limited-objective supporting attack to the west of Gerardmer between 3 and 5 November. De Lattre ordered further diversionary attacks for 13–14 November, while all troops earmarked for the I Corps' offensive moved in great secrecy to their attack positions southwest of Belfort.[77]

When the I Corps attacked through the snow at noon on 14 November, it achieved complete surprise. Because the 9th Colonial Division in the south assaulted two hours earlier, however, the 2nd Moroccan encountered an alert enemy. Nonetheless, by nightfall, the Moroccans had penetrated the German front to a depth of three miles. The following day, de Lattre released his armor to Bethouart, retaining only CC1 as his reserve, and the 2nd Moroccan, with CC4 and CC5, and the 9th Colonial, with CC2, continued to make reasonable progress (Bethouart retained CC3 and CC6 as his reserve[78]). On 16 November, expecting a breach, de Lattre released CC1 to the 1st Armored Division for exploitation tasks. The next day, the German front began to fall apart, and by evening, Bethouart's I Corps had reached beyond the Hericourt-Montbeliard-Herimoncourt line to attain the French First Army's first objective.[79] At this point, de Lattre approved Bethouart's plan to push the 1st Armored Division through the breach opened by the 9th Colonial Infantry Division. He also framed a general order for exploitation that set the line Rougemont-Dannemarie-Seppois as a first-phase objective to be attained by the I Corps. The second-phase objective, the line Ribeauville–Colmar–the Rhine from Brisach to Switzerland, was thereafter to be gained by de Lattre himself, directing the I Corps east toward the Rhine, II Corps toward Colmar, and the 5th Armored Division toward Cernay.

On 19 November, de Lattre appeared at his most Napoleonic as he busied himself with personally pushing forward the command posts of both the I Corps and the 9th Colonial Division. That evening, CC3 of the 1st Armored Division raced to Rosenau, making the French First Army the first of all Allied armies to reach the Rhine. In the center of the chaotic struggle, however, the Germans defended Dannemarie doggedly, and the 5th Armored Division, largely because of poor road movement and traffic control planning by corps and division staffs, could not mount any viable thrust on Cernay. Despite de Lattre's personal interventions, the 1st Armored, fighting hard to gain Mulhouse, was not able to muster sufficient force to exploit northward along the Rhine.[80]

On 20 November, de Lattre took direct control of the reinforced 2nd Moroccan Division and, two days later, issued new instructions for the I Corps to exploit north toward Colmar and eventually Strasbourg, with a view to crossing the Rhine in the area of Brisach. At the same time, he ordered the II Corps to advance east through the Schlucht and Bussang Passes. Because the 1st Free French Division had also seized Giromagny the same day and started to outflank Belfort in the north, he assigned the 2nd Moroccan Division and CC6 to de Monsabert to effect better coordination among these formations. Apparently, de Lattre hoped that the French 2nd Armored Division, then with the U.S. Seventh Army, might have been turned south to attack the

Germans from the north. Since Patch's army had been directed to move north to support Patton's Third, however, de Lattre soon realized that the 6th Army Group would not conduct any kind of pincer movement with its two armies. With the French First Army left alone to face the German Nineteenth Army, he concluded that the most he could do was bottle it up in a pocket. On 23 November, he accordingly modified his aims, ordering both his corps to drive toward Burnhaupt on the Doller River below Cernay to effect a rather risky double encirclement and annihilate German elements from the Belfort gap. Bethouart's I Corps, now reinforced by the 4th Moroccan Division, was to capture Dannemarie and move on Burnhaupt from the east while de Monsabert's II Corps advanced from the west. Following the final clearance of Mulhouse and Belfort on 25 November and the seizure of Dannemarie on the twenty-seventh, the French pincers closed at Burnhaupt the next day, bringing the Belfort offensive to an end.

It was a huge achievement since the seizure of both Belfort and Mulhouse completely outflanked German defenses in the Vosges Mountains.[81] In this operation, de Lattre demonstrated that he was a maneuverist par excellence as well as an inspirational leader. As Vanier observed, he showed no consideration for his men (who adored him nonetheless).[82] De Lattre drove his troops relentlessly and was prepared to take casualties—more than 10,000 in this case.

The astonishing success of the French First Army in the Belfort gap and the U.S. Seventh Army in capturing Strasbourg left the German Nineteenth Army holding an 850-square-mile salient west of the Rhine. Jutting out thirty miles west from the Rhine just below Neuf-Brisach, it formed a half-circle from Rhinau in the north to Kembs in the south. As a result of Eisenhower's decision on 24 November to turn the Seventh Army north to support the Third Army, Devers had little choice but to assign primary responsibility for the reduction of the Colmar pocket to the French First Army. To assist de Lattre in accomplishing this task, Devers placed the U.S. 36th Infantry and French 2nd Armored Divisions under his operational control on 5 December. He also moved the French First Army's northern boundary to seven miles below Strasbourg in order to accommodate the northward shift of the Seventh Army to assist Patton.[83]

When de Lattre tried to pinch off the salient by launching the I Corps toward Cernay on 13 December and the II Corps toward Colmar two days

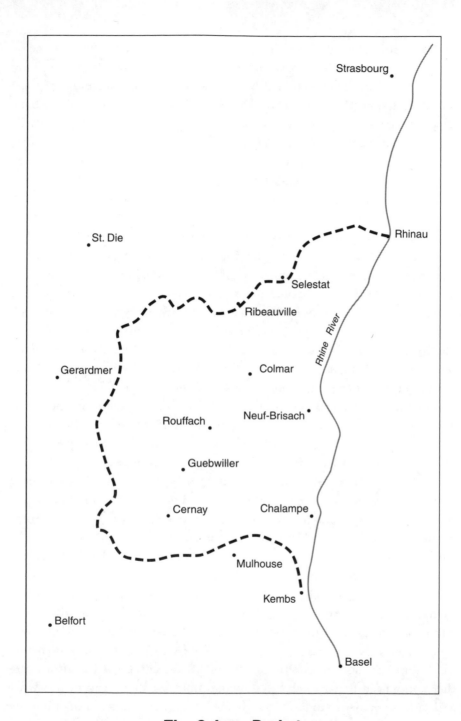

The Colmar Pocket

later, he made little progress. A disappointed Devers, convinced that a force of eight Allied divisions faced only 16,000 Germans, attributed this to attacking piecemeal.[84] But the French First Army's weak logistics chain and its critical shortage of trained infantry replacements and line officers capable of handling African colonial troops combined to degrade the army's effectiveness. To make matters worse, the 1st Free French Division, finally dispatched to participate in Operation Independence, could not be turned around in time to take part in the Colmar struggle after SHAEF again decided to postpone the operation at the eleventh hour. The U.S. 36th Division had also been so taxed in previous actions that it had to be taken out of the line and replaced by the U.S. 3rd Division on 15 December. Meanwhile, Leclerc of the French 2nd Armored Division bitterly hated serving under de Monsabert and de Lattre and strongly argued for the return of his formation to the U.S. Army.[85] For these reasons and others related to the increasingly inclement weather and sheer exhaustion of many French First Army formations, more than a week of attacks on the Colmar pocket ultimately proved fruitless.[86] On 22 December, in response to developments wrought by the Germans' Ardennes offensive, Devers called a halt to operations, but he warned the French First Army to be ready to resume the offensive no later than 5 January.[87]

The Battle of the Bulge greatly affected the development of operations in the 6th Army Group's sector. At Verdun on 19 December, Eisenhower ordered Devers to cease all offensive operations and take over twenty-five miles of front from Patton's Third Army, which was now directed to attack north. Worried that the Germans might choose to unleash a second thrust against the Seventh Army, Eisenhower further directed Devers on 26 December to pull his main line of resistance back to the slopes of the Vosges. Since this retirement called for Alsace and part of Lorraine to be deliberately evacuated, it drew violent objections from de Gaulle, who had learned of the plan on the twenty-eighth. In particular, he could not accept recently recaptured Strasbourg being abandoned without a fight because it symbolized the resurrected greatness of France.[88] Since the evacuation of the city also risked condemning more than 300,000 French citizens to vengeful German reprisals, de Gaulle sent a strong protest to SHAEF and offered three newly formed FFI divisions to assist in the defense of the city. On 1 January, he further announced that French forces would hold Strasbourg no matter what and ordered de Lattre to look to its defense.[89] In a stormy confrontation the next night, Juin conveyed to Eisenhower's chief of staff, Bedell Smith, de

Gaulle's threat to withdraw the French First Army from SHAEF's control if Strasbourg were abandoned.[90]

The issue was finally resolved on 3 January during a SHAEF conference between Eisenhower and de Gaulle with Churchill in attendance. At this contentious meeting, Eisenhower's explanation of the military necessity for the withdrawal failed to convince de Gaulle, who insisted that the abandonment of Alsace-Lorraine would be a national disaster. When Eisenhower declared that his order would stand despite French objections, de Gaulle again threatened to withdraw the French First Army from SHAEF. At this point, Eisenhower lost his temper and told de Gaulle that the crisis would not have arisen had the French First Army done its job in liquidating the Colmar pocket.[91] He also criticized the French for not keeping their divisions up to strength and added that if the French pulled out of SHAEF, the Allies would provide no further fuel, ammunition, or other logistical support. Unfazed, de Gaulle retorted that he could deny the Allies the use of French communications facilities, including railways and ports, and he threatened to order a French division to barricade itself in Strasbourg and oblige the Allies to assist it. By now fully aware of the political importance the French attached to holding Strasbourg, Eisenhower formally backed down, earning the praise of Churchill.[92]

From a military perspective, as argued earlier by Devers and Patch, the line of the Vosges was actually less defensible than the forward positions held by American troops.[93] This proved to be the case in the defense of Strasbourg against the Germans' Operation *Sonnenwende* ("Solstice"), a southern pincer attack launched from the northern edge of the Colmar pocket toward the city on 7 January by the German Nineteenth Army. Originally intended to have started with Operation *Nordwind,* it sputtered out six days later in the face of resistance by the French 1st Infantry and 5th Armored Divisions.[94] Strasbourg was saved, but the entire crisis required de Lattre to walk a fine line between national and coalition loyalty. "To do everything possible to save Strasbourg was a categorical imperative," he observed, "but to do everything possible to safeguard Allied solidarity in the struggle and to avoid 'doing a Stalingrad' alone in the ruins of a besieged city were its logical complements."[95] For his pains, however, he received a patently unfair dressing-down from de Gaulle, who wrongly thought that de Lattre would not ultimately obey his national authority. Some even suggested that de Gaulle considered firing de Lattre.[96] For de Lattre to have shown such commitment to the Allies testifies to the overall effectiveness of American policy in handling a coalition partner, in which regard Devers even went so far as to disseminate Ultra intelligence to de Lattre.[97]

While it was obviously in the interests of the French to liberate their own country, it was also in the Americans' interest to use French forces for their own purposes, not least of which was to spare the lives of their own soldiers. Eisenhower's chief of staff, Bedell Smith, recognized this, recommending in late December 1944 that the simplest, quickest, and most economical way to raise additional divisions and augment American fighting strength was to equip the French divisions then being formed by the French government. He pointed out that the French were eager to do their share in the final struggle, but he accepted that it was not all altruism, clearly recognizing that casualties taken by French divisions in battle would reduce the number of American losses.[98] Since American replacements at the time were not meeting casualty rates, Smith even went so far as to propose using the equipment of one or two of the last U.S. divisions being formed to equip a corresponding number of French divisions; breaking up these American divisions would also have allowed their personnel to be used as replacements for divisions already in the line. He thought that with the addition of French units expected in the spring, this ought to be enough to finish the job.[99] Marshall saw another advantage: French divisions could be readied a good deal sooner than American ones, which would have had to be raised, trained, and shipped overseas.[100]

The French First Army launched its final attack on the Colmar pocket on 20 January with an assault by the I Corps on the southern flank of the salient, supported by Gerardot's 1st French Air Corps. The main effort conducted by the 4th Moroccan and 2nd Moroccan Infantry Divisions on the left aimed at Cernay, while the 9th Colonial Infantry Division on the right carried out a diversionary attack north of Mulhouse. The French 1st Armored Division supported the infantry but remained largely in reserve to exploit toward Neuf-Brisach and the bridge over the Rhine at Brisach. Launched in a driving snowstorm, the attack initially achieved tactical surprise, but German reactions and snow conditions limited the depth of the French penetration. It nonetheless accomplished its object of drawing in German armored reserves to stem the I Corps' advance. The II Corps' assault, supported by Saville's XII Tactical Air Command, then went in on 23 January, with the reinforced 3rd U.S. Infantry Division—flanked by the weaker 1st Free French Division on the left and the fatigued U.S. 28th Infantry Division on the right—conducting the main thrust to secure bridgeheads over the Colmar Canal for a final drive on Neuf-Brisach by the French 5th Armored Division. Crossing sites over the canal were not attained until 30 January, however, by which time the sorely tested 3rd Division was completely spent. On the southern front, subzero weather and German tenacity had also exhausted the infantry and depleted the limited artillery ammunition stocks of the I Corps.[101]

Meanwhile, having long held that he faced an eight-division German army in the Colmar pocket almost equal in size to his own command, de Lattre appealed to Devers for additional support.[102] Goaded by Eisenhower and equally eager to finish off the Germans west of the Rhine, Devers responded by placing Milburn's U.S. XXI Corps (reinforced with the U.S. 75th Infantry Division) under de Lattre's operational control on 25 January.[103] The U.S. 12th Armored Division had also been assigned for duty in the Strasbourg sector. On 28 January, the XXI Corps took over a sector between the French I and II Corps with the U.S. 3rd, 28th, and 75th Infantry Divisions under its command and the French 5th Armored Division in support. Exploiting the success of the 3rd Division in breaching Colmar Canal defenses, the 28th Division and CC4 liberated Colmar on 2 February while the 75th Division reached the outskirts of Neuf-Brisach. On 3 February, in accordance with de Lattre's wishes, the 12th Armored Division joined the XXI Corps and attacked south to link up with elements of the French I Corps at Rouffach two days later. With the fall of Neuf-Brisach on 6 February, the Colmar pocket was split four ways. As American forces now redeployed to the north—Eisenhower's goal all along[104]—the French First Army mopped up what remained of a German force that might more profitably have simply been masked. With the clearance of the Chalampe area of the Rhine on 9 February, the battle for the Colmar pocket finally ended.[105] In this superbly executed operation, the French suffered 16,000 casualties, twice those of the Americans. Still, Eisenhower insisted that next to weather, the French caused him more trouble than anything else, including landing craft.[106]

De Lattre now faced the challenge of crossing the Rhine, but here he had more to fear from his allies than the Germans. Eisenhower and SHAEF had made no plans for the French and were not disposed to share the invasion of Germany with any French army. To de Lattre, however, the battlefield performance of his 295,000-strong army had earned France the right to participate in the conquest of Germany. Taking possession of enemy soil was also the best way to demonstrate France's resurrection and ensure its future security after years of humiliating defeat and occupation. Therefore, de Lattre began to explore ways to get his army across the Rhine. Recognizing that it would be folly to attempt to cross the Rhine in his sector—which faced the Siegfried Line and the Black Forest—he sought to extend his boundary northward toward the Pforzheim gap between Karlsruhe and Speyer, which offered a natural avenue of approach into southern Germany.[107] On 10 March, when Devers invited de Lattre to support an attack of the U.S. Seventh Army on Wissembourg, de Lattre seized the opportunity to move the French First Army boundary north of Lauterbourg just below Karlsruhe.[108] In secret instructions to the commander of the 3rd Algerian Division, which would mount the supporting attack, he wrote, "Theoretically your front ends slantwise at the Lauter [River]; do anything so that it ends squarely."[109]

Having gained his first "loophole" on the Rhine, de Lattre now asked Devers to let his army accompany the Seventh into Germany. In response, Devers agreed to let the French II Corps enter Germany as a task force under the tactical control of Patch. He further agreed that the II Corps, on reaching the Erlen River, would revert to the French First Army. By 25 March, after having fought through the Siegfried Line, the French II Corps occupied a twelve-mile frontage on the left bank of the Rhine between the Lauter and Erlen. Two days later, de Lattre requested Devers to extend his boundary north to include Speyer. Since the Seventh Army had been drawn farther north yet again, Devers acceded to this request, running the west-east army boundary through Weisloch.[110] The French First Army was now in a position to cross the Rhine.

In aggressively pushing for his army to play a role in the invasion of Germany, de Lattre anticipated the strategic intentions of his government. On 29 March, he received a telegram from de Gaulle that did not mince words: "You must cross the Rhine even if the Americans are not agreeable and even if you have to cross it in boats. It is a matter of the greatest national interest. Karlsruhe and Stuttgart await you, even if they do not want you."[111] To de Gaulle, the only question of any import at this juncture was the part that France would play in the inevitable defeat of Germany and reordering of Europe, and what he desired most for his nation was a zone of occupation, perhaps even a client southern German state that could increase both the bargaining power and voice of France in diplomatic councils.[112] Indeed, Eisenhower had foreseen that the French were probably going to demand a section of Germany to occupy, which he hoped to avoid.[113] That the French

First Army was a political instrument of state should not have come as a shock to anyone. After all, this is exactly what the use of armed force is all about. Although de Gaulle's desire for France to field fifty divisions by the end of the war proved to be a totally unrealistic and unattainable goal, the French were well on their way to eighteen divisions by war's end.[114] Compared to the Canadian commitment of five divisions and two armored brigades, the French Army thus constituted the third most powerful ground force on the Western Front after the Americans and British.

On 28 March, Devers authorized de Lattre to launch a corps across the Rhine with the task of capturing Karlsruhe, Pforzheim, and Stuttgart. No time was set for the operation to begin, but because de Lattre worried that the Seventh Army striking east from Worms might cut into his sector below the Weisloch-Heilbronn boundary, he decided to attack on 31 March to prevent this from happening. According to Devers, de Lattre sensed the historical significance of crossing the Rhine and acted as though he were Napoleon himself.[115] Scraping together whatever bridging equipment was available from limited supplies, the French II Corps gamely crossed between Speyer and Germersheim.[116] While the 3rd Algerian Division innovatively infiltrated to the other side in a stealthy night operation, the 2nd Moroccan Division failed to cross with its artillery barrage and suffered heavy casualties when caught in open water in daylight. They nonetheless gained a permanent foothold, as did the 9th Colonial Division in the Leimersheim-Leopoldshafen area. When the French burst from their bridgeheads on 1 April, however, they encountered elements from the Seventh Army nine miles south in their sector, thus confirming de Lattre's original fears. Had he delayed crossing for twenty-four hours, the French First Army would have been relegated to following the Seventh through the Pforzheim gap.[117]

In accordance with Devers's original directive, de Lattre on 1 April issued orders for his II Corps to take Karlsruhe, capture Stuttgart as soon as possible, and then move on to Ulm on the Danube. The next day, however, he received a second directive from Devers ordering the French First Army not to advance more than nineteen miles beyond the Rhine along the west–east axis Leopoldshafen-Heidelsheim-Gochsheim-Landhausen. The French First Army was simply to cover the right flank of the Seventh Army and remain within its bridgehead positions. This was in keeping with Eisenhower's new direction for the 12th Army Group to wheel right, essentially shifting the southward movement of the French First Army farther west. By de Lattre's own admission—no doubt reflecting French national aspirations voiced earlier by de Gaulle—he chose to carry on with his own plans already set in train. By the evening of 4 April, he had 130,000 men and four divisions of the II Corps east of the Rhine, with Karlsruhe in his hands. The 9th Colonial Division now swept south to secure the east bank of the Rhine at Strasbourg so that the I Corps could cross in that vicinity. On 8 April, Pforzheim fell, and by 18 April, in a dramatic maneuver, both corps had converged on the town of Freudenstadt on the eastern edge of the Black Forest, which had been split across its width and from north to center by this maneuver. The French First Army had thus penetrated to the heart of the German Nineteenth Army and cut off Stuttgart from the south.[118]

De Lattre's intention from this point was to use his newly acquired central position to unleash two simultaneous encirclements, one by the II Corps around Stuttgart and another by the I Corps ringing the southern Black Forest. From there, he envisioned the II Corps enveloping the Schwäbische Alb from the north, while the I Corps closed from the south through Sigmaringen and Ulm. The problem was that in response to redirection by SHAEF to accommodate Bradley and Patton, Devers on 16 April gave the Seventh Army the task of advancing south up the Neckar Valley along the eastern slopes of the Black Forest to Lake Constance. The French First Army was charged only with clearing the eastern bank of the Rhine and attacking Stuttgart from the west. With the right wing of the Seventh still blocked in the Heilbronn area north of Stuttgart, however, de Lattre opted to "exceed" Devers's orders in the national interest of France. On 18 April, the French II Corps entered the newly assigned American sector to storm and capture Stuttgart by 22 April.[119] The large enveloping maneuver that took Stuttgart's defenses in the rear, in de Lattre's view, produced a resounding victory that "belonged to the military patrimony of France."[120]

Despite such machinations, Devers never lost faith in de Lattre as a fighter who displayed great personal courage, inspirational leadership, and complete unselfishness and dedication in carrying out assigned tasks.[121] Recognizing de Lattre's Stuttgart maneuver as an impressive feat of arms, Devers shifted the interarmy boundary to include Stuttgart in the French First Army's sector. On 23 April, however, he transferred the city back to the Seventh Army on the grounds that it needed the Stuttgart road network to sustain its southern advance. De Lattre objected, and considering the issue more political than military insofar as it related to gaining a French occupation

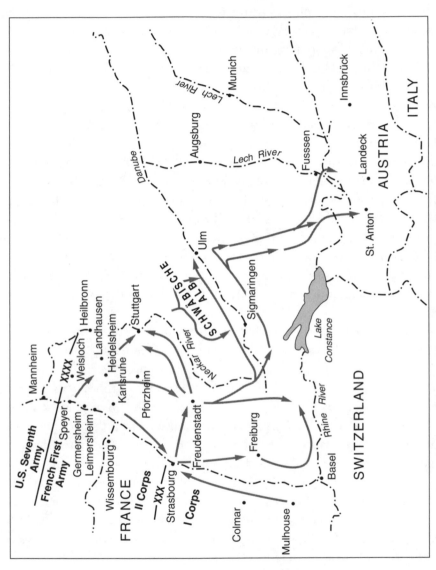

The Freudenstadt Maneuver and the Drive into Germany

zone, he exercised his right as a national commander to refer the matter to his government. De Gaulle reacted predictably by ordering him on 24 April to keep a French garrison in Stuttgart and set up a military government there at once. De Gaulle also told de Lattre to explain to the Americans that the orders of his government were to hold and administer the territories con- quered by French troops until the French zone of occupation had been set- tled.[122] Although SHAEF reiterated its order to the 6th Army Group on 26 April to occupy Stuttgart with the Seventh Army and establish a military government there, the French ultimately prevailed.[123] On 28 April, Eisen- hower regretfully accepted the status quo, which, in fact, did not prevent American troops from passing through Stuttgart.[124] For an Allied nation that had neither representation on the Combined Chiefs of Staff or SHAEF nor voice in the strategic direction of the war, this, too, was quite a feat.[125]

In the meantime, de Lattre's other operations to secure a French occupa- tion zone had yielded further territorial gains. To Devers's utter fury, he also sent his troops to capture Ulm in emulation of Napoleon's great maneuver victory of 1805, even though it meant crossing into the Seventh Army's zone in front of the VI Corps, which was driving on the Danube.[126] Fortunately, there was no collision, and on 24 April, the tricolour flew beside the Stars and Stripes above the city. For his Napoleonic venture, de Lattre received a laudatory telegram from Churchill. By 28 April, the Black Forest had been secured, and since Devers had earlier assigned the French First Army a fifty- mile frontage running between Lake Constance and Fussen on the Lech River, de Lattre's forces now raced the Americans into Austria. Reaching St. Anton on 7 May, they thus ensured that France would also be granted a zone of occupation in the western part of this country. From this perspective— that of restoring France to a position of prestige—it is quite unfair to describe the French First Army's operations in Germany and Austria during this period as "opera bouffe."[127] In spite of the substantial odds arrayed against them, nine divisions of the French First Army had by the time of the German surrender managed to seize a large chunk of the former Third Reich, leaving de Gaulle strongly positioned to negotiate French zones of occupation and a seat on the Allied Control Commission.[128]

To the end, de Lattre sought to re-establish France's place in the sun. In his view, neither the surrender of the German Nineteenth Army nor the capitulation of Army Group G to American commanders accorded sufficient respect to France, the prestige and status of which the French First Army had fought so hard to restore. He saw himself as the representative of France more than the commander of the French First Army, and he therefore refused to sign the text of the Army Group G surrender document sent to him by Devers. In de Lattre's view, the German Nineteenth Army, as the principal opponent of the French First Army, should have surrendered to him. To make matters worse, when de Lattre called for the surrender of what remained of the German Twenty-fourth Army, its commander, Gen. Hans Schmidt, impertinently terminated negotiations with the French First Army on the grounds that negotiations were in train with the 6th Army Group.[129] To his further chagrin, in attending the Soviet-orchestrated German capitulation in Berlin on 8 May as representative of France, he had to have a makeshift tricolour stitched together for the proceedings. In spite of such minor humiliations, however, the efforts of de Lattre and his army helped gain France a great-power seat on the Allied Control Council for the administration of defeated Germany. Stalin had also reluctantly agreed to British proposals at Yalta on 4–11 February that the French be granted an occupation zone in Germany, but he insisted that this zone and a corresponding sector of Berlin be carved out of zones and sectors allocated to the British and Americans. The French zone of occupation that resulted largely reflected the imprint of French boots already planted firmly on the ground.[130]

De Lattre's passion for promoting the prestige of France did not abate with the dissolution of the French First Army on 1 August 1945. In 1948, after serving as inspector general of the French forces, he assumed the appointment of commander in chief of Western Union Land Forces and developed a reputation for being an *enfant terrible* and haughty Anglophobe. The Western Union defense pact grew out of the Brussels Treaty signed on 17 March 1948 by Britain, France, Belgium, Luxemburg, and the Netherlands and aimed at producing concerted action against any Soviet move into Western Europe. Montgomery, the first chairman of the Commanders in Chief Committee, maintained that France had to be the military mainstay of the Western Union and accordingly recommended de Lattre for land force command. Much to Montgomery's surprise, however, de Lattre refused to take orders from a chairman, even after the Commanders in Chief Committee decreed that the chairman was to be regarded as supreme commander. De Lattre was fully aware, of course, that Montgomery conducted the entire Normandy battle as Allied ground force commander and had sought to continue in this capacity to the exclusion of Eisenhower. To

a certain extent, de Lattre played the role of a "super-Montgomery," object-
ing to whatever the latter proposed to the point of completely souring
relations. In the view of some, they deserved each other. De Lattre not only
manifested a more inflated vanity than Montgomery, but also handily
matched him in conceit and egotism. When a desperate Montgomery
finally offered an olive branch in May 1950, de Lattre accepted it with
tears of emotion. Weeping like a child, he was reportedly comforted by
Montgomery, who offered him his handkerchief. After their reconciliation,
de Lattre fully supported Montgomery.[131]

In early December 1950, de Lattre took over as high commissioner and
commander in chief of French troops in Indochina. Once again, he showed
his old flair, restoring flagging French morale, inflicting several defeats on the
Vietminh, and shoring up the deteriorating position of France as best he
could. Gen. Vo Nguyen Giap later remarked that de Lattre was the only
French general whom he ever feared.[132] De Lattre received a personal blow
on 29 May 1951, when his only son, Lt. Bernard de Lattre, was killed in
action, but like Patch before him, he bore his grievous loss with dignity and
no apparent loss of control, though it broke his heart. In a solemn mass in the
Cathedral of Hanoi for the repose of Bernard's soul, he again demonstrated
his mastership of form and protocol in a ceremony that accentuated the sacrifices of France.[133] In November 1951, after having been diagnosed with
cancer, de Lattre departed Indochina for France, leaving some to observe the
unhealthy sign that the steadying hand of discipline had been removed.[134] De
Lattre died in Paris on 11 January 1952, just short of his sixty-third birthday.
At his state funeral on 16 January, Montgomery and Eisenhower acted as pall-
bearers. He was taken home to Mouilleron-en-Pareds for burial. The marshal's baton posthumously awarded him now rests in the World War II section
of the *Musee de l'armee, L'Hotel national des Invalides*. While he more than lived
up to its inscription, *Terror belli, decus pacis*—"terror in war, ornament in
peace"—this baton, like all memorabilia at *Invalides* honoring the memory of
French soldiers, remains forever overshadowed by the dark brooding statue of
Napoleon high on the courtyard wall.

Conclusion

The foregoing survey of the forgotten Allied field army commanders of the Western Front has revealed more than the sum of their parts. These six men played an important and often critical role in the direction of military operations across the entire front. Uniquely responsible for coordinating air support and disseminating Ultra intelligence, they planned days and even weeks ahead to develop operational concepts and logistical plans at the military strategic level. They also coordinated the operations of corps—the highest tactical level—though their degree of involvement depended on the style of the individual army commander; whereas Crerar, Simpson, and Patch gave fairly loose rein to their corps commanders, Hodges and de Lattre kept theirs on tighter leashes. They influenced battles by ordering air strikes, committing reserves and additional artillery, regrouping formations, adjusting boundaries, and personally intervening to redirect units—and also by failing to act at key junctures.

Despite roughly similar backgrounds in training and education, no set career pattern or personality trait determined the selection of Allied field army commanders. Appointments depended on chance and patronage as much as military ability. If Lucian Truscott had not been tied up in Anzio, Patton likely would not have received command of the U.S. Third Army. Marshall's high opinion of Hodges, stubbornly shared by Eisenhower and Bradley, ensured that he rose to command the U.S. First Army and would never be replaced by the more competent J. Lawton Collins. Simpson came close to not getting command of the U.S. Ninth Army while Patch, de Lattre, and Dempsey were the personal choices of Devers, de Gaulle, and Montgomery, respectively. In contrast, Crerar essentially engineered his own advancement, with the ultimate support of the Canadian government.

Such random, even accidental, selection of higher field commanders was not necessarily at variance with the machine-like nature of modern mass armies. Army systems fundamentally rejected the idea of the indispensability of any individual regardless of rank. When any commander or general staff officer fell or left his post, another similarly trained officer took his place. The general staff system was designed to compensate for commanders' shortcomings, and a good staff could rescue a mediocre commander, as in the case of Hodges. This is not to suggest that commanders were no longer important or that one was not better than another, but simply that they were part of a larger machine that could function without them.

Unlike his fellow Allied army commanders, Crerar had already attained the top-ranking position in his own army before assuming field command. In this capacity, he laid the foundations of the largest Canadian field army in history, an accomplishment that few Canadians in military or civilian circles can even comprehend today. For this, he deserves more credit than he has been given. Even so, the country might have been better served had Crerar remained in Canada as the head of the wartime army with influence on national strategic policies and concerns. He could possibly have persuaded the Canadian government to push harder to gain a strategic voice within the Anglo-American alliance. Opting instead to pursue field command, Crerar led his 1 Corps to Italy, but after less than two months in the line vainly attempting to gain experience, he assumed command of a First Canadian Army that had ceased to be entirely Canadian. With more British troops than the Eighth Army had at Alamein, it was arguably the last British imperial army and, appropriately, was commanded by a Dominion soldier. Crerar hoped that his army would be able to repeat the performance of Sir Arthur Currie's Canadian Corps during World War I.

The closest Crerar and his army came to achieving this was during Operation Totalize, which, had it succeeded, would have resulted in a resounding victory cutting off the German Seventh Army from behind just as it plunged west. Unfortunately, the opportunity arose early in the campaign, whereas Currie's greatest feats occurred in the final days of World War I when he was most experienced. Only Crerar's intervention could have maintained the momentum of Totalize—by canceling the second-phase bombing, redirecting the uncommitted 3rd Division toward the east, or effecting another divisional flanking movement from the west via Claire Tizon. Fear of jeopardizing future air support from Bomber Harris, especially after having expended so much land and air staff effort in arranging heavy bomber strikes for Totalize, militated against canceling the bombing, and earlier clashes with Simonds in Italy and Crocker in Normandy may also have left him reluctant to overrule corps commanders during operations. From a man-management perspective, his dispute with Crocker appears to have been badly handled, particularly when compared to Patch's treatment of Truscott and Simpson's treatment of Middleton as sole corps commanders. After Totalize, there were not many opportunities for the First Canadian Army to shine, though to say it became the "Cinderella Army" of the Western Front ignores the trials of the U.S. First Army in the Huertgen Forest and the U.S. Seventh Army in the Vosges.

Crerar's declining health, coupled with his failure to assign one corps to clear the coast and the other to execute the opening of Antwerp, accounted for the ponderous performance of the First Canadian Army in the liberation of the Channel ports. After Crerar's medical evacuation, Simonds assumed command and directed the operations of the First Canadian Army in the Battle of the Scheldt, which opened Antwerp to Allied ships. Of all battles fought by the First Canadian Army, this constituted the greatest contribution to Allied victory in Europe. Simonds's performance in the Scheldt also indicated that he could easily have replaced Crerar as army commander.

Shortly after his return to the field, Crerar received his promotion to full general and went on to direct Operation Veritable, the largest military operation ever undertaken by Canadian arms, though Canadians comprised only a quarter of Crerar's total force. While Crerar performed creditably as an army commander in Veritable, especially with respect to logistical support, he tended to conduct the operation as two corps battles rather than a single army battle—that is, he let Horrocks run his own show and then allowed Simonds to conduct Blockbuster as the principal effort on the left flank. The problem was that Simonds ended up attacking where the Germans, having managed to mass artillery east of the Rhine, were strongest. His insistence on forcing the Hochwald gap rather than flanking it to the south—possibly out of personal pride or nationalistic reasons—also produced a costly battle of attrition. At this point, Crerar could have assigned Simonds the British 3rd Division, which was making headway on the 30 Corps' left and, with the necessary boundary adjustment, directed him to take the Hochwald in the rear through a southern turning movement. Again, as in Totalize, this would have meant overruling Simonds, which Crerar was still not prepared to do.

I n contrast, Miles Dempsey showed no such reluctance to intervene and provide on-the-spot direction. During the battle to secure the Normandy bridgehead, he instructed Crocker to position all of his armored reserves on the dominating high ground at Columby-sur-Thaon. He later seized on an opportunity to envelop Caen from the southwest by personally directing the 7th Armoured Division to drive on Villers-Bocage. If the corps commander had reacted as quickly as Dempsey and reinforced this drive, it most likely would have succeeded. That Dempsey had commanded at the brigade, division, and corps levels in active theaters of war made him one of the most experienced, if youngest, field army commanders. Before the battle for Normandy was over, he controlled the operations of five corps totaling more than fifteen divisions. As a protege of Montgomery, he also had the challenge of handling non-Monty men, two of whom were former army commanders themselves. Although quiet and unassuming, Dempsey rose to this leadership challenge and exercised a strong grip on the operations of the British Second Army. In his handling of Keller and subsequent sacking of Bucknall, Erskine, and Hinde, he also displayed an inner toughness not necessarily expected given his naturally friendly nature.

While Dempsey may have reacted overly cautiously to Ultra information and drawn an erroneous conclusion from the British artillery's defeat of a major panzer counterattack in Operation Epsom, he generally demonstrated a good feel for battle. The heavy cost of Epsom and Charnwood and the disbandment of British divisions for lack of manpower further drove Dempsey to propose an attack, Operation Goodwood, that utilized surplus tanks, economized on infantry, and was supported by heavy bombers. Since Montgomery had stipulated attacking without incurring undue losses and looked to launch Goodwood simultaneously with Cobra, the equally casualty-conscious Dempsey was able to sell his concept. In order to capitalize on a breakthrough if one developed, Dempsey prudently positioned his tactical headquarters well forward. Although Goodwood proved a tactical failure and cost fairly heavy infantry casualties, Dempsey correctly judged it a strategic success since it forced the overstretched Germans to concentrate their main strength and logistics against the British, who now posed an extremely grave threat to the Germans. Had Cobra been launched on 19 July as originally planned and drawn forces away from the British, Dempsey might have achieved a breakthrough.

That Montgomery took most of the blame for Goodwood and essentially shielded Dempsey from criticism reinforced the symbiotic relationship between them. In Operation Bluecoat, a two-corps attack Dempsey launched after ordering an impressive regrouping on extremely short notice, he still appears to have been ready to exploit a breakthrough. As it turned out, Bluecoat again forced the Germans to commit substantial reserves, including two panzer divisions that might have been turned against the Americans. After the closure of the Falaise pocket, Dempsey further demonstrated that he could conduct a rapid pursuit as the British Second Army raced some 300 miles to Brussels in ten days. Dempsey's performance in Operation Market Garden was also as good as could be expected in light of the fact that SHAEF's First Allied Airborne Army planned the Market airborne phase. Following Market Garden, Montgomery also accepted Dempsey's independent assessment that he lacked the forces to hold the Nijmegen bridgehead, eliminate the enemy on his right flank west of the Meuse, and continue to attack southeast between the Rhine and the Meuse. Significantly, Dempsey also backed Simpson in his demand of Montgomery that the U.S. Ninth Army not just provide an American corps for the British Second Army, but also participate as a separate army in Operation Plunder. The overwhelming success of the British Second Army in carrying out the lead role in Plunder further attested to the meticulous planning and execution conducted under the practical leadership of the widely respected Dempsey, who, in this operation, also coordinated the employment of the XVIII Airborne Corps. In his greatest moment since D-Day, he nonetheless remained overshadowed by the more flamboyant Montgomery, who commanded nearly a million men.

If Dempsey was a Monty man, Hodges was a Marshall man among Marshall men (a group that included both Eisenhower and Bradley). Having once commanded the Third Army and been seriously considered to lead it again in Normandy, Hodges assumed the appointment of deputy to Bradley when Bradley still commanded the First Army, with the understanding that Hodges would take over the First after Bradley left to head the 12th Army Group. Since Hodges inherited Bradley's staff, including its chief, he was never able to escape the shadow of his higher commander; described by Marshall as exactly the same class of man as Bradley, he might not have been inclined to do so. The most reclusive of Allied field army commanders, Hodges remained aloof from his larger staff, preferring to confide in an inner circle of senior advisers. This rendered him more remote and inaccessible as a commander while enhancing the position and power of his chief of staff, who many came to think actually ran the U.S. First Army. Hodges's relations with his corps commanders were also more fraught with tension than those of any other Allied field army commander. He never got on well with Corlett, who was highly regarded in certain quarters; endured stormy sessions with Gerow; and finally fired Milliken in the middle of the Remagen bridgehead battle. Collins proved the exception, though one suspects he received the most important roles to ensure Hodges's own success.

Lack of confidence in most of his corps commanders and an excessive fixation on low-level tactics seem to have driven Hodges to micromanage operations. Constantly badgering subordinates for detailed reports and exerting unrelenting pressure on them, he increasingly immersed himself in ongoing corps operations rather than retaining the longer-range perspective of an army commander. Yet while he insisted on knowing the locations of platoons in situation reports, he seldom visited units below divisional level on the rare occasions when he went forward between September 1944 and February 1945. One result was that he never became known to his troops. Another was that he never developed a feel for what was actually happening on the ground or gained any appreciation of the conditions facing his troops. This was especially the case in the Battle of the Huertgen Forest, where his approach of smashing ahead instead of relying on "tricky maneuver" foundered because attacks delivered piecemeal in insufficient depth could not generate enough combat power to overcome enemy reserves and countermoves. Once he had incurred troop losses, he faced the eternal commander's dilemma of either accepting that his men died in vain or continuing the attack in the hope that the enemy was on the verge of cracking. Unfortunately, Hodges precipitated battle on the enemy's terms in terrain that negated American advantages in air, armored mobility, and artillery. The Germans were capable of defending their own ground within the Huertgen but possessed little capacity to mount offensive operations from the forest. Had Hodges employed a plans section, he may have been persuaded to outflank the Huertgen by advancing through the Monschau corridor, which also offered the best route to secure the Roer dams. Yet even after Hodges recognized that German possession of the dams might impede the American advance across the Roer, he did not switch his main effort from the Stolberg corridor that drew him into the Heurtgen Forest and the most disastrously fought American battle in Europe.

Ironically, the First Army performed better in the Battle of the Bulge in the absence of direction from Hodges. Having driven himself to exhaustion in the advance on the Roer, he simply lost his grip in the face of the shattering German onslaught. The evidence further suggests that a combination of fatigue, sickness, and mental strain, exacerbated by shock, left him incapacitated for at least two days, during which time effective command of the army devolved to his chief of staff. In contrast to Hodges, Kean remained very much on top of the situation and, with his staff, set in train the initial countermoves of fighting formations and simultaneous displacement of logistical installations. He further reinforced Gerow's gallant and ultimately successful defense of the First Army's northern shoulder. Significantly, when Montgomery assumed operational control of the First, he dealt primarily with Kean, who had obviously been a pillar of strength during his army's greatest crisis. If there was any battle in which the chief of staff deserved greater credit for victory than his commander, the Battle of the Bulge qualifies as a prime example, even more so than Tannenberg in World War I.

Should Hodges have been fired as he fired Millikin? After observing conditions at First Army headquarters on 21 December, Eisenhower's deputy G-2, Brig. Gen. Thomas J. Betts, certainly thought so, but Montgomery, who had been authorized to relieve Hodges, chose not to do so. In view of Hodge's comparatively weak performance, however, it is difficult to dispute the assessment of one American historian that he should have, and would have, been sacked had it not been for coalition politics and the potentially adverse effect his removal might have had at a critical moment. In the event, shielded by his chief of staff and saved by the sheer valor of his troops under the direction of corps and divisional commanders, Hodges survived the ordeal of the Battle of the Bulge. He was never again seriously challenged as an army commander, and after the lucky seizure of the Ludendorff Bridge at Remagen, which generated enough excitement to eclipse his previously tarnished performance, he went on to become Eisenhower's "scintillating star."

Although Hodges remained historically overshadowed by Bradley, he never quite faded into the obscurity that shrouded Simpson, the most forgotten American field army commander of the Western Front. Hodges had always been considered for army command, whereas Simpson's ascendancy had never been so assured. In August 1944, Eisenhower toyed with making Patch's Seventh Army the fourth American army in his theater and suggested that if the formation of the Ninth Army was delayed, Bradley might opt to select an experienced corps commander instead of Simpson for this command. At that time, he proposed Gerow and Corlett since both had shown that they could handle large formations. There is also reason to believe that Eisenhower and Bradley would have preferred Collins rather than Simpson as the next field army commander in the 12th Army Group after Hodges and Patton. In October, Eisenhower confirmed as much when he told Marshall that if he had been able to foresee the actual development of command arrangements, he would probably have advanced a corps commander to take over the Ninth Army. Simpson apparently got the job only because Marshall wished to assure generals who had trained large formations in the U.S. that they would not be excluded from leading them in action overseas. For his part, Eisenhower accepted Simpson to command the Ninth Army simply because Simpson was on the ground and arrangements had gone so far that Eisenhower thought it best to follow through.

Simpson and his Ninth Army were never put to the test as were Hodges and his First Army, but Simpson appears to have been a more competent field army commander. Notably good-natured and imbued with a quick wit and earthy sense of humor, the unassuming and soft-spoken Simpson possessed a knack for making others feel comfortable in his presence. He got along well with his corps commanders and basically left them alone to do their jobs, assisting them as necessary with army-level assets. Like Hodges, he also relied heavily on his staff, but unlike Hodges, he enjoyed particularly cordial relations with all members of his headquarters. He also gave a great deal of latitude to his chief of staff, their extremely close relationship being likened to that of Hindenburg and Ludendorff in World War I.

Simpson has been criticized, however, for a questionable command approach. Instead of personally conducting a commander's estimate to determine the best course of action, he gave only general guidance to his staff to produce three plans from which he would select the best features. The problem with this approach was that without well-thought-out and clear command direction, much staff effort risked being fruitlessly dissipated in the production of plans that had scant hope of ever being adopted. Providing a commander had reliable intelligence and adequate information, his personal completion of the estimate was likely to produce the most focused and efficient use of staff in the development of operational plans. That being said, Simpson's approach certainly enabled him to avoid becoming mired in detail and gave him the freedom to look beyond the more immediate tactical concerns of current operations that seemed to consume, and often bring out the worst in, Hodges.

The main reason that Simpson has not been as well remembered as his American peers is that he remained in the shadow of the British for too long. His Ninth Army spent almost half of its operational life under Montgomery's command. Although Simpson personally suspected that being out of contact with Americans may have cost him promotion to four-star rank in theater, he considered it a blessing to be assigned to the 21st Army Group because this ensured that his army was built up to twelve divisions and maintained at that strength. Simpson and his chief of staff also got on exceedingly well with the British and held Montgomery in high esteem. Simpson later recalled that the field marshal had displayed great calm and complete self-possession during the Battle of the Bulge. In his postwar speeches, Simpson often referred to Montgomery as an example of professional excellence to be emulated. While Simpson liked the fact that Montgomery allowed him substantial freedom of action, both shared an affinity for meticulous planning and battlefield order.

Like Montgomery, Simpson was also casualty-conscious, preferring to send a shell in place of a man. When Simpson launched his attack in Operation Grenade, he unleashed the greatest weight of firepower ever concentrated by an American field army on the Western Front. In Simpson's estimation, Grenade was a classic example of skill in maneuver that unfolded exactly as intended because of painstaking planning at all levels. Arguably the most significant contribution of the Ninth Army to victory in Europe, Grenade vaulted Simpson into the first rank of American field army commanders. After crossing the Rhine and completing the encirclement of the Ruhr pocket by linking up with the First Army at Lippstadt, the Ninth Army reverted to the command of Bradley's 12th Army Group. Now directed by Bradley to reduce the northern half of the Ruhr pocket, Simpson continued to race east with roughly half his force to establish a secure bridgehead on the Elbe by 12 April. Still under the impression that he was to drive on Berlin, Simpson received orders to stand fast three days later. Whether Simpson could have captured Berlin before the Russians remains a matter of historical conjecture, but a dash by Simpson to secure the western outskirts of the capital could feasibly have gained the Allies a land route to their already-agreed occupation zones in Berlin. Had he remained under Montgomery, his entire army would have been hurled in that direction—a major factor that prompted the reassignment of the Ninth to Bradley.

If Simpson's historical obscurity can be attributed to his close connection with Montgomery and the British, Patch's association with the Mediterranean theater and Devers left him out of the Overlord inner circle. He may well have been the most underrated general of the war. More the choice of Marshall and Devers than Eisenhower, Patch headed the ground invasion of southern France in Operation Dragoon, which was also more the child of Marshall than Eisenhower. That Dragoon unfolded under British general Henry Maitland Wilson rather than Eisenhower arguably marginalized the feat, especially since most attention at the time focused on Patton's dash across France. Although nowhere nearly as contested as Overlord, Dragoon turned out to be an almost flawless amphibious operation. By 9 September, aided by Ultra intelligence indicating that the enemy was conducting a general withdrawal, Patch had projected a 300-mile advance north in some twenty-six days. While unable to cut off the retreating Germans in his rapid drive, partly because of logistical and air support restraints, he handled operations and his major ground commanders in commendable fashion. Indeed, his firm but sensitive treatment of the highly experienced and outspoken Truscott, at the time his sole corps commander, stands in marked contrast with Crerar's initial handling of Crocker. Patch also got on well with de Lattre, giving priority to his reduction of Toulon and Marseilles and placating him over the contentious division of French Army B during the advance north.

The transfer of the Seventh Army to Eisenhower on 15 September coincided with the establishment of the French First Army and the activation of the 6th Army Group under Devers. The decision to deploy the French First Army on the right of the line left Patch with only Truscott's VI Corps under his command to face the formidable Vosges Mountains. The grinding fight through the Vosges commenced on 20 September and continued after Haislip's XV Corps joined the Seventh Army nine days later. Patch suffered a heavy personal blow with the death of his only son in action on 22 October, but he bore his grievous loss with fortitude like Crocker and O'Daniel. Unfortunately, the slow progress of the Seventh Army during October apparently convinced Eisenhower that Devers's 6th Army Group was unlikely to make much of a contribution to the Allied advance in November; Eisenhower's intense personal dislike and mistrust of Devers may also have compelled him to draw this conclusion. The 6th Army Group's attack, launched on 13 November, saw the Seventh Army debouch from the Vosges to capture Strasbourg on the Rhine ten days later. When Eisenhower and Bradley visited Devers and Patch on 24 November, they found Seventh Army corps staffs busily planning to cross the Rhine into Germany itself. Eisenhower, who does not appear to have given much thought to the employment of Devers's forces, personally put a stop to this because of his concern about the slow progress of Patton. Stalled before Metz for all of October, Patton had managed only to inch his way forward in his Saar campaign. To assist him, Eisenhower directed Patch's Seventh Army to advance north in support of the Third Army rather than east.

The Germans' Ardennes offensive cast Patch's operations even farther into the shadow of Patton since it compelled the Seventh Army to suspend offensive operations for a second time, in this case to take over a large portion of the Third Army's front. While this enabled Patton to famously race to the rescue of the First Army, it left the Seventh Army overextended and vulnerable to German secondary counterattacks designed to protect the southern flank of their Ardennes penetration. The upshot was Operation *Nordwind,* which the Germans intended to break through the Seventh Army to facilitate an attack into the rear of Patton's Third. Fortunately, Patch had prepared for this contingency and successfully withstood *Nordwind* and a series of subsequent attacks during 5–25 January. In these battles, which largely escaped historical notice, Patch continued to display his careful, yet forceful style of command. Monitoring intelligence and troop dispositions, husbanding and reconstituting reserves, he offered advice to corps commanders but allowed them freedom of action. Although some did not always agree with him on certain issues, Patch was confident enough in his command to accept their arguments when they made sense. His relations with his staff were also good, but he expected them to assist the troops and implement direction rather than formulate options. While close to his chief of staff, he never allowed him the latitude of Kean. Patch further ruled that any staff officer could approve a subordinate commander's request, but only he, Patch, could say no. Essentially a team builder and player, the quietly competent Patch selflessly accepted assignments for the good of the Allied effort. During Operation Undertone, he raised no objections to Patton's request to enter his zone to round up more Germans. In support of the 12th Army Group's sweep across Germany, the Seventh Army received the secondary task of acting as a flank guard for Patton. In the end, Patch's Seventh Army also dutifully stepped aside to make room for Patton's Third Army to carry out the last great American offensive of the war.

The secondary tasks given to Patch reflected Eisenhower's September promise to Bradley that the Seventh Army would always be maneuvered to support the 12th Army Group. For this reason, he had also insisted on deploying the French First Army on the right of the line. Eisenhower's animosity toward Devers, exacerbated by their November clash over crossing the Rhine, further precluded giving a leading role to the 6th Army Group, except to reduce the Colmar pocket left sandwiched between the Seventh and French First Armies. Unfortunately for Devers, his slow progress in eliminating the pocket only increased Eisenhower's hostility toward him. Yet had the Seventh Army crossed the Rhine as suggested by Devers in November, it would have threatened the pocket in the rear and prevented the German reinforcement that occurred. Eisenhower's decision to instead turn the Seventh Army north to rescue Patton left Devers no alternative but to give the task of reducing the pocket to the French First Army, and prevented Devers from reinforcing the French formation with the VI Corps. When de Lattre launched a pincer attack on the pocket in December, it stalled after a week because of weather, lack of supply, and the sheer exhaustion of troops who had suffered heavy casualties in previous actions. In January, de Lattre attacked again, and with the reinforcement of the XXI Corps, he managed to clear the pocket by early February in a well-executed operation that cost the French twice as many casualties as the Americans. Eisenhower nonetheless told Marshall shortly thereafter that the French caused him more trouble in the war than any other factor, including weather.

The problem was that the Americans tended to view the French First Army as an alliance force, whereas the French intended it to be a national army serving the interests of a resurgent sovereign France. De Gaulle had agreed to place French forces under American command for Dragoon, but his quid pro quo was that an independent French army be established after the amphibious phase. Although the French had no representation on the Combined Chiefs of Staff or at SHAEF headquarters, it was obviously in the French interest to participate in the liberation of France and the occupation of a conquered Germany. At the same time, it was also in the American interest to equip and control French forces to spare the need to field more U.S. divisions. Given their growing strength, the French could likely have attained Anglo-American assent for an integrated headquarters to direct the operations of the French First Army, but de Gaulle accepted its service under a purely American army group headquarters. For the Americans, this essentially dictated leaving the Seventh Army under Devers rather than reassigning it to Bradley as Eisenhower once contemplated. The formal establishment of the French First Army, which left American troops outnumbered within the 6th Army Group, further required the reinforcement of the Seventh Army in order to show that Devers actually commanded an American army group. With the French First Army as part of the 6th Army Group, Devers commanded more French troops than any non-Frenchman in history. For this achievement and the considerable sagacity with which he handled the difficult de Lattre, Devers deserves fuller historical treatment than he has received to date—a task beyond the scope of this work.

De Lattre remains the most intriguing Allied field army commander of the Western Front. Although the Anglo-Americans would have preferred Juin because of his performance as commander of French forces in Italy, de Gaulle had no interest in keeping French troops there and selected the more idealistic de Lattre instead. He may also have preferred to "create" two successful field commanders, Juin *and* de Lattre, rather than a single famous one who could conceivably pose a challenge to his own authority. De Lattre's abiding hatred of Juin nicely complemented this divide-and-rule approach, which eventually saw Juin named chief of the Defense Staff. In de Lattre as head of the French First Army, de Gaulle had an inspired, if idiosyncratic, national commander who personally sought to emulate Napoleon in redeeming French prestige and resurrecting the greatness of France. Dynamic and debonair, de Lattre was also egotistical, theatrical, and volatile, liable to explode at the smallest perceived slight. At one moment, he could be absolutely charming and, at the next, burst into a tirade, loudly exposing contradictions in his impulsive temperament. Ruthlessly authoritarian, yet notoriously unpunctual and unpredictable, his autocratic and erratic method of command sorely tested his staff and created a tense atmosphere within his headquarters. Highly emotional and often melodramatic, he was certainly a difficult personality compared to his long-forgotten Allied peers. Yet in his passionate quest to redeem the honor and glory of France, de Lattre displayed a dedication and selflessness that transcended his eccentricities. Personally courageous and inspiring, he was also able to drive his troops relentlessly without much concern for casualties while receiving their adoration in return.

In the hotly contested battles for Toulon and Marseilles, de Lattre demonstrated that he was prepared to take risks as well as casualties to gain his objectives. That both ports fell a week earlier than expected confirmed the success of his field leadership. In contrast with Devers and Patch, who exercised loose control over subordinates, de Lattre kept a tight grip on his corps commanders, arguably getting too involved in tactics for an army commander. His firing of de Larminat, however, appears to have been as much linked to the latter's Free French roots as to tactical issues. On the other hand, de Lattre's relationship with fellow Vichyites Béthouart and de Monsabert withstood the test of battle for the rest of the war. They both performed extremely well in forcing the Belfort gap, which saw an astonishingly successful French First Army race to the Rhine—the first of all Allied armies to do so. The daring Burnhaupt maneuver that completed the subsequent annihilation of trapped enemy showed de Lattre to be an outstanding maneuverist in what may well have been his finest hour. An inability to influence the course of battle through the employment of artillery and air strikes may have compelled him to rely on maneuver to attain his operational aims. De Lattre also faced logistical and manpower problems unique to an essentially African army that was running out of replacements. As the metropolitan French did not readily identify with these troops, who in turn felt that they were bearing a comparatively heavier burden, de Lattre instituted a policy of *blanchissement,* or "whitening." Eventually, 137,000 FFI troops amalgamated with 250,000 soldiers of the French Empire to sustain the French First Army as a national instrument.

Eisenhower's decision during the Battle of the Bulge to have Devers evacuate Strasbourg and pull back to the line of the Vosges forced de Lattre to walk a fine line between coalition and national loyalty. Ordered by de Gaulle to defend Strasbourg at all costs, he laid plans to comply but at the same time sought to safeguard Allied solidarity. Fortunately, both Devers and Patch considered withdrawal unnecessary, and Eisenhower eventually backed down in the face of concerted French opposition. De Gaulle nonetheless reprimanded de Lattre, erroneously suspecting that the commander of the French First Army would not ultimately obey his national authority. In fact, in aggressively finding ways for the French First Army to cross the Rhine when Eisenhower and SHAEF had not planned for it to do so, de Lattre anticipated the direction of de Gaulle to take possession of enemy soil in the interests of France. De Lattre himself had a firm grasp of French interests, and the good relations he had nurtured with Devers enabled him to achieve them. When later direction from Eisenhower threatened to halt the advance of his army and squeeze it out of the line, de Lattre chose to carry out plans already in train and "exceed" Devers's orders by taking Stuttgart in the national interests of France. On being ordered to withdraw, he referred the matter to his government on the grounds that his conquest had political implications. De Gaulle ordered de Lattre to hold and administer all territory captured by French troops until Allied governments agreed on the French zone of occupation. Although de Lattre infuriated Devers by taking Ulm in symbolic imitation of Napoleon's famous victory, the subsequent thrust of the French First Army into Austria ensured the attainment of a French zone in the western part of that country and strongly positioned de Gaulle to negotiate a French role in the postwar settlement.

The performance of the French merely confirmed the nature of coalition warfare: all nations strive to get their way in alliances, and political aspects increase in importance as fighting draws to an end. This was as true of the British, who attempted to project a strong influence into northern Germany through Operation Plunder, as it was of the Americans, who sought to end the war in the west largely on their terms by not driving on Berlin. The British also wanted the French to have an occupation zone in Germany since they feared that the Americans might withdraw after two years; in this event, the French could help occupy the American zone and not leave the British alone to face a possibly resurgent Germany or predatory Soviet Union. Having been knocked out of the war in 1940, France had the more difficult challenge of fighting its way back into the position of a great power. They not only had to raise a field army for the liberation of France, negotiating equipment supply and command relationships with the Americans, but also suffered the disadvantage of not being party to the determinations of SHAEF. In this regard, Devers proved critical, and much of the credit for the artful manner with which the Americans handled the French as allies must go to him. Without the French First Army, there would not likely have been an American 6th Army Group, which added greatly to the overall perception of massive U.S. power projected on the Western Front.

Only the Canadians had as limited a strategic voice as the French, but this was a self-inflicted wound by a Canadian government that intentionally left all aspects of the higher direction of the war to Churchill and Roosevelt. Although Canada provided roughly 20 percent of the troops in the invasion of Normandy, the Canadian prime minister was not even notified of the operation until the day it took place. There was no Canadian representation on the Anglo-American Combined Chiefs of Staff Committee or any important Canadian staff integrated at SHAEF. That Canadian troops served under a SHAEF composed almost exclusively of Americans and Britons nonetheless accorded with Crerar's view that liaison with the Supreme Commander was properly his own responsibility as Canadian national commander. Had the Canadians not split their army between Italy and northwest Europe, Crerar would have had more clout, but Canadian troops would not then have seen major-formation action until 1944, long after the Americans, who joined the war late. In any case, Montgomery would never have been able to wield the influence that he did on the Western Front without the First Canadian Army, even though it remained half British almost to the end of the war. Indeed, until the last two months of the war, Crerar commanded more British troops than Montgomery had in his Eighth Army at Alamein. Similarly ironic, Montgomery's 21st Army Group at various times controlled more American troops than Devers.

In choosing to deal one-on-one with the British alone, the Americans played their cards well and showed themselves to be shrewd masters of coalition warfare. They not only gained privileged access to a global empire but also avoided having to contend with a common front of British Dominions and various other allied nations. In asserting their ultimate dominance of the alliance, they at the same time never lost sight of the paramount importance of the Russian contribution to winning the war. Since American preponderance on the Western Front took some time to develop, however, the British were able to exercise substantial operational influence from a position of troop strength, buttressed by Montgomery's role as ground force commander during the Battle of Normandy. On 1 July 1944, the Anglo-Canadians and Poles fielded thirteen divisions, as many as the number deployed by the Americans. By September 1944, there were twenty-eight American divisions on the Western Front, but another twenty-seven were non-American, including eighteen Anglo-Canadian–Polish divisions. American ground force strength reached forty-nine divisions in January 1945, but other Allies still fielded twenty-four—and often larger equivalents on the front line. By war's end, Eisenhower commanded sixty-one American and thirty non-American divisions, including twenty-one Anglo-Canadian–Polish divisions under Montgomery. Almost half of the combat aircraft supporting these ground forces were non-American, mainly Commonwealth.

Given such numbers, one can only conclude that America's allies had a perfect right to argue over Western Front strategy and act in their own national interests. The British had long realized, of course, that the only thing worse than fighting with allies was fighting without them; they had historically always required allies in order to win their wars. Their wartime experience and greater strength compared to other western powers initially induced the Americans to listen to their strategic voice. In arguing that it was logistically feasible to support only one major thrust into Germany, the British further articulated a good case for a northern drive that would not only eliminate threats from V1 and V2 rocket sites and submarine pens but also capture the industrial Ruhr and, ultimately, Berlin. The growing size of U.S. forces and American ascendancy within the Combined Chiefs of Staff Committee and SHAEF nonetheless ensured that Eisenhower's broad-front strategy prevailed over the single northern thrust preferred by the British. Yet with barely enough troops to carry out a broad-front strategy, Eisenhower could not even have envisioned such a concept without the immediate availability of non-American divisions. His four American armies could not have defeated the Germans on the Western Front without the support of Canadian, British, and French field armies. Significantly, too, these forces roughly approximated the number of U.S. divisions sent to the Pacific. In short, the celebrated two-ocean war fought by the United States could not have occurred without British Commonwealth and French support in Europe.

While the Eastern Front was unquestionably the most decisive theater of the war, the Western Front proved critical for the Allies. Here the seven field armies commanded by the generals discussed in this book fought and bled their way forward to achieve ultimate victory in the West. How these field army commanders performed reflected not just their own ability but also the quality of their subordinate-formation commanders and troops. Invariably, because of the position and operational circumstances of their armies in the line, they faced quite disparate situations and dissimilar challenges in the exercise of their command. Patton, for example, inherited the breakout from Cobra and the dash to Bastogne, both of which captured the imagination of the press and the public, while other field armies were left to conduct less glamorous operations in the Caen area, Scheldt Estuary, Huertgen Forest, Vosges Mountains, and Colmar pocket. Patton's more outgoing personality also contrasted sharply with the generally quiet and unassuming nature of his Anglo-American peers. Dempsey and Patch both considered it unprofessional to seek publicity, and Crerar and Simpson never attracted the limelight. Only the Napoleonic de Lattre approached the colorfulness of Patton, while Hodges basked briefly in the fame of Remagen after being saved by his staff and troops in the Battle of the Bulge. Unfortunately, the names of these six field army commanders, who collectively directed almost two million more troops than Patton, remain largely forgotten to history. In some sense, this is fitting since old soldiers who survive wars tend to fade away, but their accomplishments and the sacrifices of their troops deserve to be illuminated so that light can shine through the historical shadows of myth.

The Tactical Air Support of Allied Ground Troops

Both British and American tactical air support of ground troops evolved from the centralized air control system first set up by Coningham in the Desert Air Force supporting the Eighth British Army.[1] This system recognized the coequal status of land and air power and involved attaching independent air support control organizations to corps and divisions connected by wireless links to forward air tentacles through which ground troops passed air support requests. Quesada served in North Africa and paid tribute to Coningham for forcing the United States Army Air Forces (USAAF) to take part in the ground battle.[2] Joint army–air command meant exactly that, however, and no army officer at any level could order air support. The RAF as a separate independent service reserved the right to establish priorities and approve targets, and its main role remained to achieve and maintain air superiority over the battlefield. Contingent roles included the provision of air transport, operations with airborne forces, reconnaissance, and attacking ground targets. Reconnais-

---

1. Coningham and Montgomery got along famously during the Desert War, collocating their headquarters and working closely together, but had a serious falling out in Normandy over what appears to have been Coningham's jealously of the publicity showered on his army counterpart.
2. B. Michael Bechthold, "A Question of Success: Tactical Air Doctrine and Practice in North Africa, 1942–43," *Journal of Military History* 3 (July 2004): 821–51; Ian Gooderson, *Air Power at the Battlefront: Allied Close Air Support in Europe, 1943–45* (London: Frank Cass, 1998), 26; Max Hastings, *Overlord: D-Day and the Battle for Normandy* (London: Pan, 1985), 319; and Russell A. Hart, *Clash of Arms: How the Allies Won in Normandy* (Boulder: Lynne Reinner, 2001), 113. Quesada was less a creative genius than an adapter of innovations devised by others. He had virtually no operational experience before a stint in North Africa. Phillip S. Meilinger, "U.S. Air Force Leaders: A Biographical Tour," *Journal of Military History* (October 1998), 854–55.

sance included artillery reconnaissance carried out by artillery pilots in light observation aircraft, photographic reconnaissance, and tactical reconnaissance focused on German rear areas immediately opposite the field army concerned. In attacking ground targets, RAF doctrine attempted to distinguish between indirect and direct support. Indirect support aimed at isolating the battlefield by striking enemy lines of communication to hinder the forward movement of troops and supplies, while direct support encompassed attacks upon front-line and rearward enemy forces engaged in combat in the immediate battle area.[3] Doctrine further categorized direct support on the basis of urgency, between "pre-arranged" and "impromptu" ground force requests for air support. The most common way of projecting direct support into the German rear was armed reconnaissance by fighter-bombers ranging over an area behind enemy lines collecting intelligence and attacking targets of opportunity with bombs, rockets, or strafing. For direct support of frontline troops the Cab-rank system was most famously employed. This involved having a number of fighter-bombers, usually four Typhoons, but sometimes a whole squadron, circle a specific point just behind the front, available to swoop down upon an enemy target as soon as ground forces called for support.[4]

Field army and RAF composite air group headquarters formed a Joint Battle Room or, if physical limitations rendered this impractical, simply coordinated their separate staffs by constant telephone contact, meetings, or visits.[5] This consultation level constituted the heart of the tactical air support organization and allocated most direct support tasks as well as approved impromptu requests. The Group Control Centre (GCC), not usually collocated with either army or group headquarters, scrambled planes, vectored them to their

---

3. In today's terminology, direct support would include close air support (CAS) and battlefield air interdiction (BAI).

4. The RAF Second Tactical Air Force consisted of four RAF groups of several wings. Attack wings usually fielded three squadrons of three or four flights each. USAAF Tactical Air Commands usually consisted of two to three fighter wings of three or four fighter groups. Fighter groups usually included three fighter squadrons. Squadrons in both air forces consisted of twelve to twenty aircraft divided into flights of three or four aircraft.

5. When asked whether he would run a Joint Operations Room with the RAF, Maj. Gen. F. W. de Guingand, former chief of staff of the Eighth Army, replied that it was "ideal to have the whole thing together," but physical limitations often prevented it from happening. For this reason he found it better to have army and air force operations rooms separate. The RAF maintained a map of its own, which army headquarters updated. He added, however, that army and air headquarters should be abreast. CP, Vol 5, Notes on Lecture by Maj. Gen. F. W. de Guingand, CB, CBE, DSO, "Operation of Eighth Army HQ in the Field" given at Main HQ, First Canadian Army in the Field, 28 February 1944. Collocation also meant having to stay close to airfields on certain occasions.

targets, and ensured the maintenance of air superiority within the group area. To speed up the air request process without having to go through division and corps levels, Army Support Signals Units (ASSU) established dedicated air communication networks within each field army/air group—No. 1 ASSU for the First Canadian Army and No. 2 ASSU for the Second British Army. With the forward troops, vehicle-mounted ASSU tentacles commanded by artillery officers passed back leading battalion and brigade air requests via ASSU channels for approval by the Joint Battle Room and strike action by the GCC. As tentacle officers did not have any means of communicating directly with aircraft, they received confirmatory strike timings and target marking instructions. Each field army/air group additionally possessed a Forward Control Post (FCP) usually collocated with leading corps headquarters, but deployable to division in fluid operations. Mounted in two or three vehicles, the ten-man FCP included both an RAF pilot in the rank of wing commander and an army Air Liaison Officer (ALO) who together advised on the optimal employment of air support. Equipped with VHF wireless and capable of talking with overhead aircraft up to forty kilometers away, the FCP could directly monitor ASSU traffic and act on the most important impromptu requests by contacting the GCC or directing any available aircraft or Cab rank onto the target. The smaller five-man Visual Control Post (VCP), first deployed with the 29th Armoured Brigade in Operation Goodwood on 18 July,[6] was a normal tentacle mounted in a specially fitted tank augmented by an ALO and fighter-bomber pilot equipped with a VHF wireless set for communication with overhead aircraft. VCPs in each army/air group were capable of directing air strikes onto targets that they could see, but as positions offering good observation of targets were seldom available, they did not prove entirely successful. As a result, the VCP came to be employed as a miniature FCP normally sited with leading brigades.[7] Another tentacle variant introduced by

---

6. On 19 July, a tank-mounted air-ground cooperation party from IX TAC arrived at headquarters CCA, 2nd Armored Division, to participate in Operation Cobra. The next day, IX TAC issued instructions on the conduct of the new air-ground operations system. Michael D. Doubler, *Closing with the Enemy: How GIs Fought the War in Europe, 1944–1945* (Lawrence: University Press of Kansas, 1994), 69–70.

7. In Operation Totalize, ASSU tentacles were allotted to headquarters, 2nd Canadian Infantry Division, the 5th and 6th Canadian Infantry Brigades, the 2nd Canadian Armoured Brigade, and the 33rd, 153rd, and 154th Brigades of the 51st Highland Division. There was one VCP on the ASSU net. National Defence Headquarters (NDHQ), Ottawa, Ontario, Directorate of History, 693.013 (D2), Ops 2 Cdn Corps, 51 (H) Div OO No. 6 Operation Totalize, 6 Aug 44 and 2 Cdn Div OO No. 2 Operation Totalize, 7 Aug 44. See also RG 24, Vol. 14,052, War Diary, 4th Cdn Armd Bde, 9 Aug 44; James Allan Roberts, *The Canadian Summer: Memoirs* (Toronto: University of Toronto Bookroom, 1981), 97.

Broadhurst to determine the location of leading army elements on the ground so as to better control tactical reconnaissance aircraft was the Contact Car manned by an RAF reconnaissance pilot and ASSU wireless operator. Owing to its reconnaissance focus, however, the Contact Car was not always used in the forward control of air attacks.[8]

The major problem of army-air cooperation centered on the timeliness of fighter-bomber responses to impromptu ground force requests for air support. Pre-arranged air support laid on during alternate daily army/composite group conferences does not appear to have been similarly contentious. These conferences chaired by the army chief of staff and attended by composite group officers under the Senior Air Staff Officer (SASO) and members of the army general staff section, including the G (Ops) Air or G (Air) responsible for planning army air support, generally produced a consensus. The "bomb line" located forward of the actual front line—beyond which air forces were free to fire—was also determined at army level. For reasons of troop safety, air force engagements short of the bomb line required army permission. Although the First Canadian Army's chief of staff, Brig. C. C Mann, expressed outrage in July 1944 over an RAF pilot not knowing the location of the bomb line, he was far more upset by what he considered the inadequacies of the coequal joint command relationship between army and air. Mann, perhaps the most vociferous critic of Allied tactical air support, charged on 11 August that the practice of the air group cooperating with the First Canadian Army sabotaged rather than supported ground force action.[9] Neither could the joint system produce, within a matter of several hours, heavy or effective bombing attacks requiring resources beyond supporting air group

---

8. Paul Johnston, "2nd TAF and the Normandy Campaign: Controversy and Under-developed Doctrine" (Unpublished MA Thesis, Royal Military College of Canada, 1999), 24–48, 89 and his excellent "Tactical Air Power Controversies in Normandy: A Question of Doctrine," *Canadian Military History* 2 (Spring 2000): 59–71; and Gooderson, *Air Power at the Battlefront*, 26–31. See also "Impromptu Support" under Air Plan in British Army of the Rhine (BAOR) Battlefield Tour, Operation Veritable, Spectator's Edition, 24.

9. This could have been because Broadhurst's No. 83 Group, affiliated with the Second British Army, coordinated air support for the First Canadian Army up to 12 August. Although Broadhurst was deeply committed to the air support of ground forces, his first priority would naturally have been to his affiliated army. After Air Vice-Marshal Brown's newly formed No. 84 Group assumed full responsibility for supporting the First Canadian Army, Mann expressed praise for his cooperation, but he also remarked that relations between air group and army headquarters "were only on a cordial basis superficially." Mann recalled Brown saying that Coningham had relieved him in November 1944 for being too cooperative with the army. NAC, CP, Vol. 24, Lecture to the Canadian Staff Course, Royal Military College, Kingston, Ontario, by Maj. Gen. C. C. Mann, 25 July 1946.

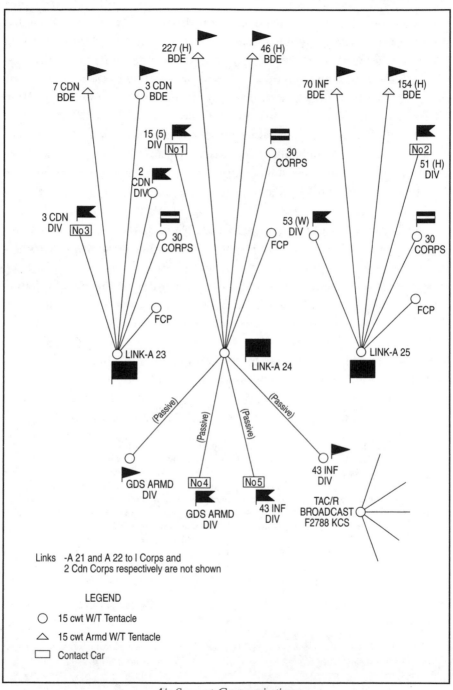

227 (H)
BDE

46 (H)
BDE

7 CDN
BDE

3 CDN
BDE

70 INF
BDE

154 (H)
BDE

15 (5)
DIV No 1

30
CORPS

No 2

51 (H)
DIV

2
CDN
DIV

3 CDN
DIV No 3

30
CORPS

53 (W)
DIV

FCP

30
CORPS

FCP

FCP

LINK-A 23

LINK-A 24

LINK-A 25

(Passive)

(Passive)

(Passive)

(Passive)

GDS ARMD
DIV

No 4

No 5

43 INF
DIV

GDS ARMD
DIV

43 INF
DIV

TAC/R
BROADCAST
F2788 KCS

Links -A 21 and A 22 to I Corps and
        2 Cdn Corps respectively are not shown

LEGEND

○ 15 cwt W/T Tentacle

△ 15 cwt Armd W/T Tentacle

▭ Contact Car

Air Support Communications:
Deployment of the 2nd Canadian ASSU in Operation Veritable

capacity.[10] Yet in retrospect, the accusation that the RAF was too slow and unresponsive to army requests for air support does not seem entirely fair. In some cases, impromptu requests filled by a composite group's own squadrons averaged about an hour from the request for an air strike to the appearance of aircraft on target. By other accounts, it took several hours unless a FCP or VCP was present.[11] If a Cab rank was available with an FCP or VCP, however, aircraft could be brought on target much more quickly, sometimes within minutes and faster than artillery response. The trouble was that Cab ranks were a costly means of employing air power. Given time for reloading and refueling as well as flying and loitering, keeping one Cab rank of four Typhoons on station required an entire wing of two dozen or more planes.[12]

With only six wings of Typhoons available in all of 2nd TAF, it is therefore understandable why the RAF preferred not to disperse the air effort by penny packeting Cab ranks out to every division or corps as they wanted them, but to use them mainly for critical junctures in the broader battle. Attacking targets that appeared to be favorable did not necessarily mean that they were vital in the overall scheme of things.[13] The difficulty of locating and attacking enemy frontline targets—often protected by antiaircraft fire— also posed a problem for fighter-bombers responding to impromptu requests with low-level strikes. Although clearly bolstering the morale of friendly troops while eroding that of the enemy, such direct air support incurred losses that did not appear to justify results. The RAF at least believed that

10. After the war, Mann recommended one unified commander for field army/air group level, suggesting that a qualified airman exercise such command initially supported by an army chief of staff and then rotating the two positions between services. This solution would neither have made the best use of air resources, however, nor solved the problem of obtaining air resources beyond those controlled by group. Mann illustrated this last problem by recounting the 2 Canadian Corps' request for a bomber attack on Oldenburg 14–17 April 1945. Here it took seventy-two hours to obtain air support beyond the resources of No. 84 Group, RAF, owing to disagreements over the suitability of targets for air attack, chain of command confusion, and Coningham's reluctance to comply. NAC, CP, Vol. 24, Lecture to the Canadian Staff Course, Royal Military College , Kingston, Ontario, by Maj. Gen. C. C. Mann, 25 July 1946; and CP, Vol. 3, Memorandum Concerning Targets for Air Attack on Oldenburg Beyond Resources of 84 Group RAF by Col. G. E. Beament to Chief of Staff, First Canadian Army, 17 April 1945.
11. Broadhurst produced a detailed breakdown to show that fifty minutes was the average time required to meet immediate requests without FCP facilities. Public Record Office (PRO), London, Air 55/112, AVM Sir Harry Broadhurst to AVM C.H.N. Guest, 17 October 1950.
12. Johnston, "2nd TAF," 37–38, 59, 63–70, 117. The US Army also complained that notification of the denial or cancellation of air support took too long, usually between four to six hours and, in one instance, nine hours. Unless a division knew by midnight what air support it was to receive, it was difficult to integrate air attack into the next day's operation. Gooderson, Air Power at the Battlefront, 47.
13. Johnston, "Tactical Air Power," 67.

armed reconnaissance in the German rear yielded better results at lower cost than the dedicated frontline intimate air support preferred by the army. The now widely recognized inaccuracy of bombs and rockets delivered by Typhoons, Spitfires, and American P-47 Thunderbolts has generally borne this out. It is therefore difficult to dispute the conclusion that armed reconnaissance was of far greater value to the Allied war effort than direct air support of ground troops. In any case, between June and August 1944, armed reconnaissance rose from 17 to 56 percent of the 2nd TAF's effort, while direct support ground attack declined to 15 from 25 percent.[14] Significantly, this was not out of step with the USAAF, which, except for focused operations, seldom allocated more than 15 percent of air forces available to what the Americans termed Third Phase Tactical Air Operations (the third priority role of close-in air cooperation with ground forces). The remaining 85 percent, less that required for bomber escort, was devoted to isolating the battlefield, preventing enemy movement, attacking airfields, supply dumps, bivouac areas, and miscellaneous targets, and other activities normally classified as First (air superiority) or Second Phase (interdiction) Air Operations.[15]

Joint staff planning within the IX, XIX, and XXIX TACs featured routine targeting conferences with army staff and flowed from an air Combat Operations Section to a field army/TAC Combined Operations Center, which both functioned closely with the Tactical Control Center (TCC)[16]

---

14. Johnston, "2nd TAF," 105–10; and Terry Copp, *Fields of Fire: The Canadians in Normandy* (Toronto: University Press, 2003), 92–96.
15. The Collections of the Manuscript Division, Library of Congress, Gen. James H. Doolittle Papers, "The Effectiveness of Third Phase Tactical Air Operations in the European Theater 5 May 1944–8 May 1945," Prepared by the Army Air Forces Evaluation Board in the European Theater of Operations, August 1945.
16. The XII TAC established an equivalent system, but at a lower level that allowed more direct contact with corps and divisions in controlling local air operations. In Italy, the XII TAC adopted the British Rover David system (after Group Capt. David Heysham's first use on 23 October 1943) that consisted of an air force officer and army officer, both operationally experienced, directing Cab-rank air strikes through an Air OP that identified and marked ground targets with artillery fire. The air force officer called up and guided attacking aircraft while the army officer controlled ground communications and monitored the bomb line and position of forward troops. The XII TAC took its variant to France. In this system, devised to accurately bomb targets inside the bomb line, a combat pilot acted as a forward air controller in a light observation aircraft referred to as a "horsefly." He was accompanied and advised by an army officer from the supported corps' or division's G3 Air staff who was familiar with the terrain and targets. Marshall Library, Marshall Papers, Lt. Gen. Jacob L. Devers to Marshall, 1 July 1944; CP, Vol. 8, Canadian Operations in the Mediterranean Area May-September 1944, Extracts from War Diaries and Memoranda (Series 28), paragraphs "Rover David, Cabrank, and Air Op cum Rover David"; Gooderson, *Air Power at the Battlefront* 28, 43–44; and Doubler, *Closing with the Enemy*, 74.

that, like the British GCC, controlled air formations. At corps level, an Air-Ground Cooperation Officer[17] (later Tactical Air Liaison Officer, or TALO), a pilot in the rank of lieutenant colonel, acted as the TAC commander's representative, offering air advice and assistance and evaluating the suitability of targets selected for air cooperation. His fourteen-man Air-Ground Cooperation Party (later Tactical Air Party) could also transmit air cooperation requests to TAC headquarters or take control of aircraft participating in a coordinated air-ground action. At division level, a five-man party headed by a pilot in the rank of major performed a similar function. Air-Ground Cooperation Officers worked closely with army G3 Air and artillery officers in a Combined Operations Office in both corps and division headquarters.[18] Ground Liaison Officers (GLOs) attached to air groups (British air wings) and squadrons performed essentially the same tasks as British ALOs. Air-ground cooperation officers submitted future "planned mission" requests originating in divisions through air cooperation communication channels to corps, where, after joint concurrence by the corps' air-ground cooperation officer and the army's G3 Air, they were sent on to the air Combat Operations Section. Here with the concurrence of the army G3, the mission was accepted or refused. Requests for "immediate" or impromptu missions originating in divisions followed the same channels, except where communications failed, in which case the division air-ground cooperation officer could send requests directly to the TCC.[19] As in the British system, response times were not always fast enough and greater reliance came to be placed on having armed reconnaissance pilots check in before proceeding on their main mission to engage "immediate" frontline targets of opportunity.[20]

The most often cited instance of effective U.S. air-ground cooperation[21] was the "armored column cover"—or more accurately "armoured *combat*

---

17. Or Air Support Party Officer (ASPO) or Tactical Air Party Officer (TAPO), depending on which TAC this represented. Gooderson, *Air Power at the Battlefront*, 42.
18. As most infantry and new armored divisions had no G3 Air, the G3 had to perform this staff function. Gooderson, *Air Power at the Battlefront*, 46.
19. Library of Congress, Quesada Papers, Headquarters, IX Tactical Air Command, Standing Operating Procedure for Air-Ground Cooperation Officers, 28 January 1945.
20. Gooderson, *Air Power at the Battlefront*, 42–52.
21. "Only on occasion is detailed evidence available of cooperation between tanks and their covering planes," stated one Ninth Air Force report that urged citing known episodes, which have been repeated since. DDE Library, Collection of 20th Century Military Records, 1918–50, Series I, Box 9, USAF Historical Studies, Air Forces Historical Studies No. 36, Ninth Air Force, April to November 1944, AAF Historical Office, Headquarters, Army Air Forces.

command column cover"—provided by Weyland's XIX TAC to Patton's Third Army as it advanced in three directions in August 1944. Given the dispersed and fast moving pace of operations, which rendered planned missions impossible, one TALO was deployed per infantry division and three with a spearhead armored division, one with each of its three combat commands. Initially, Weyland deployed non-flyers with special training for TALO duty, but later rotations resulted in experienced combat-pilot volunteers replacing them. In fact, the fluid nature of operations and absence of any German ground resistance or air threat enabled Weyland to operate fighter-bombers in "four-ship" flights in direct support of advancing ground elements.[22] They were told to attack any identified enemy target in front of army elements, which reinforced the later impression that they blazed a trail for the army. While this American equivalent of Cab rank covered the movement of armored spearheads, however, Weyland also conducted long-route and area armed reconnaissance in front of the advancing army on the lookout for enemy forces that might be taking up defensive positions. Armed reconnaissance additionally facilitated deep strikes against enemy airfields and communications to hamper reinforcement and withdrawal. All of this accorded with Patton's stated priorities, the highest of which was to protect the Third Army's vulnerable southern flank on the Loire. Assisting with armored column cover came a distant fourth, after maintaining air superiority and carrying out armed reconnaissance deep behind German lines.[23] Thus, much in the manner of their British compatriots, XIX TAC maintained a carefully considered balance between allotting aircraft to army request missions, including "immediate" requests, and attacking distant targets vital to the enemy in reestablishing a defense. Although not an independent air force like

---

22. Air Forces Historical Studies No. 36; Albert F. Simpson Historical Research Center, Air University, United States Air Force Oral History Program, Interview of Gen. O. P. Weyland by Dr. James C. Hasdorff, 19 November 1974 (San Antonio, Texas), 143–47. Four fighter-bombers relieved at thirty-minute intervals covered each column in daylight. Within CCA, 2nd Armored Division, the lieutenant colonel in charge of the ASPO rode in a tank and used an SCR 522 radio (the American version of the British TR1143 transceiver) to communicate with planes, while the army tank commander communicated with the CCA commander using his SCR 528 tank radio. DDE Library, Collection of 20th Century Military Records, 1918–50, Series II, Box 19, 12th Army Group, Battle Experiences No. 38, Air Support of Armored Columns, 3 September 1944.

23. USAF Academy Archives, Gen. Robert M. Lee Papers, Tactical Air Operations in Europe: A Report on the Employment of Fighter-Bombers, Reconnaissance and Night Fighter Aircraft by XIX Tactical Air Command, Ninth Air Force, in connection with the Third U.S. Army Campaign from 1 August 1944 to VE Day, 9 May 1945. Patton's fifth and last priority was the support of grounds troops in the reduction of the Brittany ports. Doubler, *Closing with the Enemy*, 72.

the RAF, the USAAF thought like one[24] and regarded the task of achieving air superiority as the greatest single factor contributing to the success of ground operations as it provided friendly forces security from enemy air attack, thus allowing them freedom of movement.

24. During the Korean War, U.S. Air Force chief of staff Hoyt Vandenberg remained absolutely opposed to army control of close air support. Marshall Library, Gen. James A. Van Fleet Papers, Box 83, Folder 12, Van Fleet to Gen. M. B. Ridgway, 20 December 1951; and Meilinger, "U.S. Air Force Leaders," 166–70, 181–82.

Notes

INTRODUCTION

1. The First Allied Airborne Army, commanded by Lt. Gen. Lewis H. Brereton, did not fight continuously in line as a formation. The U.S. Fifteenth Army, deployed in January 1945 under Lt. Gen. Leonard T. Gerow primarily to plan the occupation of Germany, briefly relieved Bradley's formations and played a minor part in the Battle of the Ruhr Pocket by actively patrolling across the Rhine. Russell F. Weigley, *Eisenhower's Lieutenants: The Campaign of France and Germany, 1944–1945* (Bloomington: Indiana University Press, 1981), 668, 678; and Omar N. Bradley, *A Soldier's Story* (New York: Henry Holt, 1951), 529.

2. Simpson, like Crerar, has rated a PhD dissertation, and Hodges was earlier the subject of an MA thesis.

3. Martin Blumenson, "Measuring Generalship," *Army* (March 1999), 12.

4. Dwight D. Eisenhower (DDE) Library, Abilene, Kansas, Jacob L. Devers Papers, Reel 2, Box 1, Brig. Gen. R. E. Jenkins to President, The General Board, US Forces, European Theatre, 30 October 1945; U.S. Army Military History Institute (USAMHI), Devers Diary, 8 September 1944; USAMHI, Reuben E. Jenkins Papers, Jenkins to Col. Robert N. Young, Command and Staff College, Fort Leavenworth, 28 January 1947; Jeffrey J. Clarke and Robert Ross Smith, *United States Army in World War II: The European Theater of Operations, Riviera to the Rhine* (Washington: Center of Military History, 1993), 577 (hereafter cited as Clarke and Smith, *Riviera to the Rhine*); Bradley, *Soldier's Story*, 222, 360; Omar N. Bradley and Clay Blair, *A General's Life: An Autobiography* (New York: Simon and Shuster, 1983), 283–84; and Weigley, *Eisenhower's Lieutenants*, 182–83. According to Jenkins, as the bulk of the problems at army group level were presented by staff officers and not the enemy, fewer staff officers meant fewer problems.

5. Stephen Ashley Hart, *Montgomery and "Colossal Cracks": The 21st Army Group in Northwest Europe, 1944–45* (Westport: Praeger, 2000), 131; National Defence Headquarters (NDHQ), Ottawa, Ontario, Directorate of History, 570.011 (D1), Address by Gen. H. D. G. Crerar, "Reminiscences of 1939–45," 2; West Point Archives, Matthew B. Ridgway Papers, Interview of Ridgway by Maj. Matthew P. Caulfield, USMC, and Lt. Col. Robert

M. Elton, U.S. Army, 29 August 1969; David W. Hogan, *A Command Post at War: First Army Headquarters in Europe, 1943–1945* (Washington: Center of Military History, 2000), 285; and Sir Brian Horrocks with Eversley Belfield and Maj. Gen. H. Essame, *Corps Commander* (New York: Charles Scribner's Sons, 1977), 31.

6. Clarke and Smith, *Riviera to the Rhine,* 87–89, 420, 502–3, 580; F. H. Hinsley, *British Intelligence in the Second World War,* abridged ed. (Cambridge: University Press, 1993), 23, 490–99, 505–11, 563–66; Bradley and Blair, *General's Life,* 291–92, 350–52. In the case of the First Canadian Army, Crerar, his chief of staff, and six other senior staff officers had access to Ultra. Terry Copp, *Cinderella Army: The Canadians in Northwest Europe, 1944–1945* (Toronto: University Press, 2006), 89, 350. Devers also provided de Lattre with Ultra information as required. From at least late December 1944, de Lattre sent Ultra communications to his two corps commanders and de Gaulle. Service historique de l'armee de terre, Chateau Vincennes, De Lattre Papers, Ultra Secret de Lattre a Monsabert, le 31 Decembre 1944; Ultra Secret General commandant la Iere Armee Française a General de Gaulle, le 3 Janvier 1944; and Ultra Secret Telegramme Officiel General commandant la Iere Armee Francaise a General commandant le 1er C.A., le 10 Janvier 1945.

7. The Allied Expeditionary Air Force dissolved after the establishment of the 12th Army Group. Leigh-Mallory served as SHAEF's air commander in chief until 15 October 1944.

8. Coningham was an Australian-born New Zealander, Brown a South African, and Hudleston an Australian.

9. Lt. Gen. Lewis H. Brereton commanded the U.S. Ninth Air Force up to 7 August 1944. DDE Library: Collection of 20th Century Military Records, 1918–50, Series I, Box 9, USAF Historical Studies, Ninth Air Force Tactical Commands, 1 June and 30 November 1944. Quesada apparently expected to replace Brereton, and although he worked amicably with Vandenberg, there always seemed to be tension between them. Phillip S. Meilinger, *Hoyt S. Vandenberg: The Life of a General* (Bloomington: Indiana University Press, 1989), 50.

10. SHAEF promulgated the formal authorization of the multinational First Tactical Air Force on 6 April 1945. Vandenberg did not hold Royce in high regard and thought his tactical ideas "ridiculous." Meilinger, *Vandenberg,* 49.

11. DDE Library, Oral History OH-184, James M. Gavin, by Ed Edwin 20 January 1967, Columbia University Oral History Project.

12. National Archives of Canada (NAC), Crerar Papers (CP), "Operational Policy—2 Cdn Corps" signed Lt. Gen G. G. Simonds, 17 February 1944.

13. A typical combat command comprised tank, armored infantry, and self-propelled artillery battalions, a cavalry reconnaissance troop, and engineer company. The assistant division commander usually commanded CCA, a tank unit commander CCB, and an infantry unit commander CCR, although other variations occurred. James Jay Carafano, *After D-Day: Operation Cobra and the Normandy Breakout* (Boulder: Lynne Reinner, 2000), 45–47; and Keith E. Bonn, *When the Odds Were Even: The Vosges Mountains Campaign, October 1944–January 1945* (Novato, CA: Presidio, 1994), 56–61. The French, who were equipped and structured like the Americans, numbered their combat commands (CC1, CC2, etc.), although the French 2nd Armored Division used the letters of the last names of their commanders (CCD, CCL, CCV, except for CCR) and formed two task forces, each under CCD and CCL. Clarke and Smith, *Riviera to the Rhine,* 126, 371–72, 408. The British paired their tank-equipped divisional reconnaissance regiment with the motorized infantry battalion of the armored brigade to produce the fourth battle group; the other three resulted from pairing the three tank regiments (U.S. battalion equivalents) of the armored brigade with the three infantry battalions of the infantry brigade. The

Americans retained two heavy armored divisions, the 2nd and the 3rd, that had one infantry and two tank regiments (totaling six tank battalions); heavy on armor with some 400 tanks, these did not have the ideal one-to-one tank-infantry ratio of the standard American armored division. See also Roman Johann Jarymowycz, *Tank Tactics: From Normandy to Lorraine* (Boulder: Lynne Rienner, 2001), 93–94, 213–14.

14. Marshall Library, Gen. Walton Walker Papers, Box 3, Folder 1, The Story of XX Corps, 1–2.

15. The average strength of the U.S. VII Corps after 6 June was 70,000 men. MP, Box 67, Folder 2, Eisenhower to Marshall, 9 April 1945.

16. Horrocks, *Corps Commander,* xiv, 31–32; USAMHI, Senior Officers Oral History Program, Project 72–1, Interview Gen. J. Lawton Collins by Lt. Col. Charles C. Sperow, 1972; Eversley Belfield and H. Essame, *The Battle for Normandy* (London: Pan, 1983), 48–49; John A. English, *The Canadian Army and the Normandy Campaign: A Study of Failure in High Command* (New York: Praeger, 1991), 16, 144–45, 238; Harold R. Winton, *Corps Commanders of the Bulge: Six American Generals and Victory in the Ardennes* (Lawrence: University of Kansas Press, 2007), 2, 7–8; and Dr. Robert H. Berlin, *U.S. Army World War II Corps Commanders: A Composite Biography* (Fort Leavenworth; Combat Studies Institute, 1989), 1–3. The British used the orders format: information, intention, method, administration, and intercommunication, while the Americans used situation, mission, execution, service support, and command and signal. NATO's adoption of the latter eventually triggered endless "mission analyses" of what a commander's intention might actually be. In the World War II British system, the commander simply stated what his intention was in the intention paragraph of his orders. Any commander unable to make his intention crystal clear in one simple sentence was probably not worth his salt.

17. The classic example is that of Lt. Col. Richard Hentsch, who after personal deliberation on behalf of his commander, Moltke the Younger, ordered the commanders of the First and Second German armies, against the wishes of the former, to break off action and withdraw during the Battle of the Marne in September 1914. Theodore Ropp, *War in the Modern World* (New York: Collier, 1962), 240–41; and Walter Goerlitz, *History of the German General Staff, 1657–1945,* trans. Brian Battershaw (New York: Praeger, 1957), 161–62.

18. Oberst i.G. Christian O. E. Millotat, *Understanding the Prussian-German General Staff System* (Carlisle: U.S. Army War College Strategic Studies Institute, 1992), 37. In 1938, it was decreed that commanders alone were responsible externally and internally, but that the general staff officer remained accountable for the relevance of his advice, which he was to offer as if he were jointly rather than just internally responsible himself. Millotat, *Understanding,* 46; Ropp, *War in the Modern World,* 241.

19. Millotat, *Understanding,* 1, 19–21, 23, 27–31, 41–43, 46, 59–60; Goerlitz, *German General Staff,* 164–66; 173. Hindenburg apparently later stated that had the battle been lost it would have been crystal clear who the commander was.

20. Common doctrine being loosely defined as the fundamental precepts by which the various parts of military forces are guided in the attainment of objectives.

21. Michael Howard, *The Franco-Prussian War: The German Invasion of France, 1870–1871* (London: Methuen, 1981), 11–12, 18–26; Michael Howard, *War in European History* (Oxford: University Press, 1992), 100; Arden Bucholz, *Moltke and the German Wars, 1864–1871* (New York: Palgrave, 2001), 59, 119–21, 132–33, 191; Col. T. N. Dupuy, *A Genius for War: The German Army and the General Staff, 1807–1945* (London: Macdonald and Jane's, 1977), 38, 17–109; John Masters, *The Road Past Mandalay: A Personal Narrative* (New York; Bantam, 1979), 87–88; and John A. English, *Marching through Chaos: The Descent of Armies in Theory and Practice* (Westport: Praeger, 1996), 50–53.

22. J. D. Hittle, *The Military Staff: Its History and Development* (Harrisburg, PA: Military Service, 1949), 214–21; Maj. Marc B. Powe, "A Great Debate: The American General Staff (1903–16)," *The Military Review* 4 (April, 1975), 71–89; Hogan, *Command Post at War,* 4–16, 25–35, 273; and Timothy K. Nenninger, "'Unsystematic as a Mode of Command': Commanders and the Process of Command in the American Expeditionary Forces, 1917–1918," in *The Journal of Military History* 64 (July 2000): 739–68. See also Maj. Gen. Otto L. Nelson Jr., *National Security and the General Staff* (Washington: Infantry Journal, 1946). The 1942 authorized strength of an American army headquarters was 228 officers, 23 warrant officers, and 508 enlisted personnel. Hogan, *Command Post at War,* 298–99.

23. Maj. Gen. J. F. C. Fuller, *The Army in My Time* (London: Rich and Cowan, 1935), 107–10, 117; John Gooch, *The Prospect of War: Studies in British Defence Policy, 1847–1942* (London: Frank Cass, 1981), 32–130 and "The Creation of the British General Staff, 1904–1914," *JRUSI* 662 (June 1971), 50–53; and English, *Canadian Army,* 89–106.

24. As a rule, the GSO1 or G1 of a division called upon to make a decision had to make one that could be put into operation that day; a corps chief of staff had twice that time; a field army chief of staff had about four days; and an army group chief of staff had to be thinking a week ahead. Maj. Gen. Harold E. Pyman, *Call to Arms* (London: Leo Cooper, 1971), 93–94. Pyman served as chief of staff of the British 30 Corps and chief of staff of the British Second Army to the end of the war.

25. NAC, RG 24, Vol. 13,711, Minutes of Conference Held by General Montgomery, HQ 21 Army Group, 0930 hrs 13 Jan 44; CP, Vol. 4, Crerar to Chief of Staff, CMHQ, 28 Feb 45 and Vol. 9, Memorandum on the Organization of Command, the Functioning of the Staff, Services, Mess Appointments at HQ, First Canadian Army by Brig. C.C. Mann, chief of staff, 1 Feb 45 (first edition 1 Jan 44 destroyed).

26. English, *Marching through Chaos,* 51–52, 65; and English, *Canadian Army,* 91–94, 104.

27. Operations must work closely with intelligence, which in the British (and German) staff structure fell under operations. As combat intelligence usually requires some indication from operations as to what essential elements of information are needed, this made some practical sense. Another view was that intelligence should be free of operations influence in a separate equal branch. Anyone who has worked in a G3/G2 setting can attest, however, to the growth of interbranch rivalry, even to the extent of G2 often viewing G3 as an "enemy" and declining to offer worthwhile intelligence assessments for fear of being found wrong. Hogan, *Command Post at War,* 288. Bradley's aide, Maj. Chester B. Hansen, recorded that the British intelligence sysytem was superior because of its regular intelligence corps. USAMHI, Chester B. Hansen Papers, War Diary, 1 January 1944.

28. CP, Vol.2, Beaver III Notes on Commanders.

29. USMA West Point, Bradley Papers, Address by Lt. Gen. Omar N. Bradley, Commanding General, First United States Army, to Officers of the Headquarters Staff, 15 April 1944, 1600 hours, at Bristol, England.

30. Royal Military College of Canada Archives, Gen. H. D. G. Crerar Papers, The Responsibilities of the Comd, the Staff and the Services, HQ, 1 Canadian Corps, 11 Dec 43; and John A. Macdonald, "In Search of Veritable: Training the Canadian Army Staff Officer, 1899 to 1945" (Unpublished MA Thesis, Royal Military College, 1992), 44–46.

31. The "C" in ABC definitely did not stand for Canada. Most probably it stood for conversations or conference, or possibly even Commonwealth. Col. Stanley W. Dziuban, *Military Relations between the United States and Canada, 1939–1945* (Washington: Office of the Chief of Military History, 1959), 103. The full title of ABC-1 was "United States-British Staff Conversations, Report." Dziuban, *Military Relations,* 103, 106; Steven T. Ross, *U.S. War Plans, 1939–1945* (Malabar, Florida: Kreiger, 2000), 18–20, 131–33; and Christopher

Thorne, *Allies of a Kind: The United States, Britain, and the War against Japan, 1941–1945* (Oxford: University Press, 1978), 77–78.

32. On 29 August 1941, Roosevelt approved ABC-22, a Canadian-American defense plan conforming with ABC-1. Ross, *U.S. War Plans, 1939–1945,* 20–21; and John Alan English, "Not an Equilateral Triangle: Canada's Strategic Relationship with the United States and Great Britain, 1939–1945" in *The North Atlantic Triangle in a Changing World: Anglo-American-Canadian Relations, 1902–1956,* eds. B. J. C. McKercher and Lawrence Aronsen (Toronto: University Press, 1996), 164–67.

33. A point not lost on Adolf Hitler, which may explain why he immediately declared war on the United States after Pearl Harbor.

34. Robert E. Sherwood, *The White House Papers of Harry L. Hopkins* (London: Eyre and Spottiswoode, 1948), 1:467.

35. Three other combined boards emerged from the Arcadia Conference: the Munitions Assignments Board that operated directly under the Combined Chiefs of Staff coordinating the allocation of weapons and equipment to various theatres of war; the Combined Shipping Adjustment Board; and the Combined Raw Materials Board. A Combined Food Board and Combined Production and Resources Board were later set up in June 1942. C. P. Stacey, *Arms, Men, and Governments: The War Policies of Canada, 1939–1945* (Ottawa: Information Canada, 1974), 162, 167–78; and Alex Danchev, *Very Special Relationship: Field Marshal Sir John Dill and the Anglo-American Alliance, 1941–44* (London: Brassey's, 1986), 82–83.

36. The Joint Chiefs of Staff comprised the American army and navy chiefs and the commanding general of the U.S. Army Air Force and functioned directly under Roosevelt, who was commander in chief of the U.S. armed forces. From July 1942, the personal chief of staff to the president, Adm. William D. Leahy, acted as chairman of the Joint Chiefs of Staff and provided balance by being the second naval member. This action, which removed the military chiefs from the departmental control of the two civilian service secretaries, eventually enabled the Joint Chiefs to wield unprecedented power in the areas of diplomacy, politics, and economics. They became, in Samuel P. Huntington's words, "next to the President, the single most important force in the overall conduct of the war." While the State Department watched from the sidelines, the Joint Chiefs acted as "executors of the national will." Samuel P. Huntington, *The Soldier and the State* (Cambridge: Harvard University Press, 1979), 317–29, 337.

37. Churchill assumed his created portfolio of minister of defence, one unemcumbered by a working department, to chair the British Chief of Staff Committee using members of his cabinet secretariat as his staff and making their head, Gen. Sir Hasting Ismay, his personal chief of staff and the fourth member of the committee. The British Joint Staff Mission reflected the committee and comprised the British Admiralty Delegation, the RAF Delegation, and the British Army Staff. Danchev, *Very Special Relationship,* 10, 12–16, 19–25, 58; Stacey, *Arms, Men, and Governments,* 161–62; and English, "Not an Equilateral Triangle," 158–59.

38. Queen's University Archives, C. G. Powers Papers, Minutes of the Cabinet War Committee, 11 March 1942 and 4 June 1942; and Stacey, *Arms, Men, and Governments,* 162–68, 180–83, 186–87, 200–201, 354–57; and Danchev, *Very Special Relationship,* 82–83.

39. Stacey, *Arms, Men, and Governments,* 154, 180–81.

40. Ross, *U.S. War Plans, 1939–1945,* 131.

41. Eisenhower explained this strategy as follows: "the only profitable plan is to hustle all our forces up against the Rhine, including Devers's forces, build up our maintenance facilities and our reserves as rapidly as possible and then put one sustained and unremitting advance

against the heart of the enemy country." DDE Papers, Principal File, Box 80, Eisenhower to Marshall, 14 September 1944.

42. Charles B. MacDonald, *The Mighty Endeavor: American Armed Forces in the European Theater in World War II* (New York: Oxford University Press, 1969), 291, 406, 513; Weigley, *Eisenhower's Lieutenants,* 356, 571, 667–68, 727; and Carlo D'Este, *Decision in Normandy* (London: Collins, 1983), 262–64. Of eighteen divisions in Italy, only seven were American. The British reinforced the Western Front with five divisions from Italy in February 1945 (the British 1st, 5th, and 46th and 1st and 5th Canadian). Field Marshal The Viscount Montgomery of Alamein, *Normandy to the Baltic* (London: Hutchinson, 1946), 197–98.

43. Maj. L. F. Ellis with Lt. Col. A. E. Warhurst, *Victory in the West,* vol. 2, *The Defeat of Germany* (London: Her Majesty's Stationery Office, 1968), 406–7; and DDE Library, General Harold R. Bull Papers, Box 1, Summary of Strength of Army Personnel on Continent up to 30 April 1945. According to Weigley, at the end of March 1945, there were 1,617,000 American soldiers serving under Bradley, Devers, and Montgomery. The total strength of Western Allies serving on the continent numbered 2,553,000. In the European theater U.S. forces totaled 3,051,000, including 458,000 in the U.S. Army Air Forces and 633,000 in the Communications Zone. *Eisenhower's Lieutenants,* 667–68, 727.

44. The armored brigade (one of which was disbanded) fielded some 223 tanks in three tank regiments. The Americans established independent tank battalions of about 68 tanks each for attachment to infantry divisions.

45. The American infantry division had eighteen additional M3 105mm infantry howitzers in regimental "cannon companies" that were usually attached to divisional artillery units equipped with heavier M2 105mm howitzers. Joseph Balkoski, *Beyond the Beachhead: The 29th Infantry Division in Normandy* (Mechanicsburg, PA: Stackpole Books, 1989), 115, 306; and Michael D. Doubler, *Closing with the Enemy: How GIs Fought the War in Europe, 1944–1945* (Lawrence, KS: University Press of Kansas, 1994), 301–3.

46. USAMHI, Oral History: The General James A. Van Fleet Papers, Senior Officers Debriefing Program Conversations between General James A. Van Fleet and Lieutenant Colonel Bruce H. Williams (1973). Van Fleet made the observation in Korea, stating that the British had the best artillery and a "Time on Target" (TOT) fire direction system far superior to what was taught at Fort Sill. He actually took a group of visiting US artillery officers out to the British front and asked them to pick out far distant targets to demonstrate the point, which the British Commonwealth divisional artillery invariably did, concentrating the fire of all available artillery in a matter of seconds. "We cannot do that in American units," said Van Fleet, who described the Commonwealth Division as one of his best. It used the World War II Anglo-Canadian "Uncle" artillery fire system.

47. Maj. Gen. E. L. M. Burns, *Manpower in the Canadian Army, 1939–1945* (Toronto: Clarke, Irwin, 1956), 18–24; and Balkoski, *Beyond the Beachhead,* 98–105, 123–36. The heavy 2nd and 3rd U.S. Armored Divisions each fielded 14,620 personnel and 252 medium and 158 light tanks. Weigley, *Eisenhower's Lieutenants,* 17–24.

48. DDE Papers, Principal File, Box 80, Eisenhower to Marshall, 31 August 1944.

CHAPTER ONE
In the Shadow of Sir Arthur: Gen. H. D. G. Crerar, First Canadian Army

1. J. L. Granatstein, *The Generals: The Canadian Army's Senior Commanders in the Second World War* (Toronto: Stoddart, 1993), 83.

2. Paul Dickson, *A Thoroughly Canadian General: A Biography of General H. D. G. Crerar* (Toronto: University Press, 2007).

3. Ten days after the Canadians captured Vimy Ridge the British in a resolution of the Imperial War Conference formally recognized Canada as an autonomous nation within an imperial Commonwealth. Canada's population in the summer of 1914 was a little less than eight million, of whom considerably over two million were French-Canadians who largely refused to fight. C. P. Stacey, *Canada and the Age of Conflict* (Toronto; Macmillan, 1977), 170, 235, 238.

4. Paul D. Dickson, "The Politics of Army Expansion: General H. D. G. Crerar and the Creation of First Canadian Army, 1940–41," *The Journal of Military History* 60 (April 1996), 280; and Paul D. Dickson, "The Hand that Wields the Dagger: Harry Crerar, First Canadian Army Command and National Autonomy," *War and Society* 2 (October 1995), 117.

5. National Archives of Canada (NAC), MG 30, E157, General H.D.G Crerar Papers (CP), Vol. 21, Crerar to Colonel C.P. Stacey, 10 October 1952; and Granatstein, *Generals,* 84–86.

6. Granatstein, *Generals,* 86–92; "Biography of General The Honourable Henry Duncan Graham Crerar, P.C., C.H., C.B., D.S.O.," *Quadrant* 1 (June 1989), 11, 13; CP, file 958C.009 (D30), Memorandum, 17 October 1939, Letter Major-General T.V. Anderson to Crerar, 25 September 1939, and Memorandum Crerar to C.G.S. of 30.9.37.

7. Granatstein, *Generals,* 91–98; Dickson, "Politics," 295, and Dickson, "Hand," 115–121; English, *Canadian Army,* 67–69; and Frederick W. Gibson and Barbara Robertson, eds., *Ottawa at War: The Grant Dexter Memoranda, 1939–1945* (Winnipeg: Manitoba Record Society, 1994), 174, 176–78, 196, 227–29.

8. Stacey, *Arms, Men, and Governments,* 146–50, 155–56, 180–84.

9. Stacey, *Arms, Men, and Governments,* 45. Following occupation duty in Iceland, the 2nd Canadian Infantry Division arrived in October 1940 to join the 1st Division already in Britain. The 1st Canadian Tank Brigade (later designated the 1st Canadian Armoured Brigade) disembarked in June 1941 and the 3rd Canadian Infantry Division in the autumn of that year. By November 1941, the 5th Canadian Armoured Division had completed its movement overseas and the 4th Canadian Armoured Division arrived in the summer of 1942. With the shipment of the 2nd Canadian Army Tank Brigade to Britain in June 1943, five months after the establishment of Headquarters 2 Canadian Corps, the fielding of 1 and 2 Canadian Army Groups Royal Artillery (AGRA) concluded the deployment.

10. English, *Canadian Army,* 64–69. AGRA usually comprised three medium regiments, one field regiment, a heavy antiaircraft regiment, and a rocket and a radar battery. The adoption of the name AGRA avoided having to use the acronym RAG that would have resulted from the more sensible designation, Royal Artillery Group. NAC, McNaughton Papers, Vol. 156, The Employment of Army Groups Royal Artillery.

11. Crerar's wife, Verse, described as stunningly beautiful and coming from a distinguished and wealthy London, Ontario, family, seems also to have promoted his career. The influential *Winnipeg Free Press* political reporter, Grant Dexter, thought fit to record lunching with "Mrs. Crerar, wife of H. D. G Crerar and some years ago the toast of the town. She may still pass as a joy forever but there's no denying she works pretty hard at it. She was painted and enamelled, curled and eye-dropped. I gathered that H. D. G. has been pestered of late with beauteous Nazi female spies. But I didn't take this seriously. More interesting she was markedly anti-British." Queen's University Archives (QUA), Grant Dexter Papers, Grant Dexter to George S. Currie, 2 October 1943; and Granatstein, *Generals,* 86.

12. Gibson and Robertson, 135, 177, 196.

13. Crerar later recorded that McNaughton had suffered a "breakdown." CP, Vol. 2, Notes re: Enclosed Correspondence with C.-in-C. South-Eastern Command—1Cdn Corps Comd Feb 1942–May 1943.

14. English, *Canadian Army,* 126–27; and Granatstein, *Generals,* 93–94, 99–101.

15. For details see English, *Canadian Army,* 127–30.

16. Field Marshal Lord Alanbrooke, *War Diaries, 1939–1945,* eds. Alex Danchev and Daniel Todman (London: Weidenfeld and Nicolson, 2001), 388.

17. Luckily escaping censure on both counts. See Paul Dickson, "Crerar and the Decision to Garrison Hong Kong," *Canadian Military History* 3 (Spring 1994): 97–110; and Dominick Graham, *The Price of Command: A Biography of General Guy Simonds* (Toronto: Stoddart, 1993), 291–96. Also see entries for 10 February, 31 March, and 18 June 1943 in Alanbrooke, *War Diaries,* 381, 391, 422.

18. English, *Canadian Army,* 136–37, 144–52; Granatstein, *Generals,* 98–108; J. L. Granatstein, *Canada's Army: Waging War and Keeping the Peace* (Toronto: University Press, 2002), 195, 205–6; and Daniel G. Dancocks, *The D-Day Dodgers: The Canadians in Italy, 1943–1945* (Toronto: McClelland and Stewart, 1991), 131.

19. Jeffery Williams, *The Long Left Flank: The Hard-Fought Way to the Reich, 1944–1945* (Toronto: Stoddart, 1988), 18.

20. Montgomery did not obsess over dress and apparently issued an order on the subject only once. This was prompted by the occasion of a bare-chested Canadian soldier leaning out of his truck and doffing a top hat in salute as the army commander drove by. After a good laugh, Montgomery promulgated a one-line order: "Top hats will not be worn in Eighth Army." Carlo D'Este, *Bitter Victory: The Battle for Sicily, 1943* (London: Collins, 1988), 102.

21. CP, Vol. 15 Comd 1 Cdn Corps War Diary, 8,10, and 17 Dec 43 and 18–19 Jan 44 and Vol. 21, Crerar to Stacey, 28 August 1952; English, *Canadian Army,* 143–44, 148–51, 181–82, 186–89; and Granatstein, *Generals,* 106–7, 160–62.

22. CP, Vol. 7, GOC-in-C 6-10-11 (958C.009 (D180)) Montgomery to Crerar, 21-12-43.

23. Stacey, "Canadian Leaders of the Second World War," *CHR* 1 (March 1985): 68, 72; Granatstein, *Generals,* 85, 101, 106, 109, 114; and Hart, *Montgomery and "Colossal Cracks,"* 160.

24. Tony Foster, *Meeting of Generals* (Toronto: Methuen, 1986), 394.

25. CP, Vol. 8, Crerar to COS, CMHQ, 28 Mar 44, COS, CMHQ to Crerar, 1 May 44, and Crerar to COS, CMHQ, 3 May 44; and Hart, *Montgomery and "Colossal Cracks,"* 165–66.

26. The appreciation, described as an orderly sequence of reasoning leading logically to the best solution of an operational or administrative problem, was actually the heart of Anglo-Canadian doctrine. The sequence included defining the object or aim to be obtained, squeezing sensible deductions from all factors affecting the attainment of the aim, selecting and assessing courses open to one's own side and the enemy side, and, finally, setting forth a workable plan. Whether presented verbally or in writing, the appreciation followed the formal format: aim, factors, courses open, and plan.

27. CP, Vol. 1, GOC 3-6 Memorandum Crerar to BGS and DA&QMG dated 24 Jun 1944. Crerar also passed copies of his corps "Aide Memoire for Orders" to his divisional commanders. Royal Military College of Canada, Kingston, Ontario, Crerar Papers, "Aide Memoire for Orders."

28. Dickson, *Thoroughly Canadian General,* 256–57. In the senior mess they dined well with wine and drinks, white tablecloths, and silver service. Crerar regularly enjoyed a gin with lunch and one scotch before and another after dinner. Ibid., 311.

29. Crerar said he had to be where he could get information quickest in the centre of communications and within a limited number of miles from air group headquarters. CP, Vol. 8, Report of Press Conference for General Crerar, 7 August 1945; and CP, Vol. 3, Wireless Diagram of Tac HQ First Canadian Army, 5 Sep 44.

30. Carried out by supply and transport, medical, ordnance, electrical and mechanical engineer, works engineering, chaplain, dental, postal, provost, salvage, labor, legal, catering, education, graves registration, civil affairs, and air liaison sections. According to Dickson, Lister was later court-martialed for black market activities. *Thoroughly Canadian General,* 441.

31. John A. Macdonald, "In Search of Veritable: Training the Canadian Army Staff Officer, 1899 to 1945" (Unpublished MA Thesis, Royal Military College of Canada, 1992), 163, 195, 215, 220–21, 258–64; Dickson, *Thoroughly Canadian General,* 290, 308–9; Hart, *Montgomery and "Colossal Cracks,"* 166–67; and Col. C. P. Stacey, *Official History of the Canadian Army in the Second World War, The Victory Campaign: The Operations in North West Europe, 1944–1945* (Ottawa: Queen's Printer, 1966), 32–33. All told, there were 471 vehicles and 97 motorcycles on the First Canadian Army headquarters establishment, with 29 vehicles and 3 motorcycles in tactical headquarters. By November 1944, total strength reached 2,420 personnel, not including signals. Dickson, *Thoroughly Canadian General,* 371.

32. By August 1944 there were over 17,000 Canadian aircrew in the RAF compared with under 10,000 on strength of overseas units and formations designated RCAF. Stacey, *Arms, Men, and Governments,* 301.

33. No. 84 Group comprised fifteen Spitfire, three Mustang, and eight Typhoon squadrons, including three RAF reconnaissance squadrons and two air observation post squadrons. Henry Probert, "84th Composite Group," and John Terraine, "Second Tactical Air Force" in *D-Day Encyclopedia,* 201, 500–501.

34. The 1st Polish Division was almost a permanent component of the First Canadian Army and the 1st Belgian Infantry Brigade and the Royal Netherlands Brigade (Princess Irenes's) came under temporary command in August 1944 and again before final victory. The 1st Czechoslovak Independent Armoured Brigade Group also served in the army for several weeks in August. Stacey, *Victory Campaign,* 642.

35. Crerar followed Montgomery's direction on collocation to the letter. CP, Vol. 3, Montgomery to Crerar, 4 May 1944. Marked maps with full information about current operations were maintained only in army operations, the joint battle room, and Q operations. CP, Vol. 3, Security Instructions for HQ First Cdn Army on and after D-Day, 30 May 44.

36. Stacey, *The Victory Campaign,* 40–41, 202; Henry Probert, "Brown, L.O." in *The D-Day Encyclopedia* (New York: Simon and Schuster, 1994), 125–26, 201; and Mike Bechthold, "Air Support in the Breskens Pocket: The Case of First Canadian Army and 84 Group Royal Air Force," *Canadian Military History* 3 (Autumn, 1994), 53–62.

37. NAC, CP, Vol. 24, Lecture to the Canadian Staff Course, Royal Military College, Kingston, Ontario, by Major General C. C. Mann, 25 July 1946; and National Defence Headquarters (NDHQ), Directorate of History and Heritage Biographical File, New Air Commander on Western Front, AVM Hudleston, CBE, 9/12/44 No. 34. Montgomery was incensed by Coningham's removal of Brown and wrote Crerar "Coningham has told the Air Ministry that your A.O.C. [Brown] is no good, that you do not like him, and you want him changed. So far as I remember you have always spoken very well of Brown and his work, and have a high regard for him. I therefore feel that this is a piece of real dirty work on the part of Coningham, who does not like Brown himself. " CP, Vol. 7, Montgomery to Crerar, 6-7-45. Coningham remained just as jealous of the Broadhurst-Hudleston duo as he did of Broadhurst-Brown however. Nigel Hamiliton, *Monty: The Field Marshal, 1944–1976* (London: Hamish Hamilton, 1986), 393. According to Probert, Brown at the time of his removal was not in the best of health.

38. National Archives of Canada (NAC), RG 24, Vol. 10,800, Report on "Spring" 25 July 1944 by Lieutenant Colonel McLellan, GSO1 (Liaison), 3rd Canadian Infantry Division.

39. Public Record Office 70473, CAB 106/1064, Crerar Diary, Notes on Conference given by C-in-C 21 Army Group on 22 June 1944; and CP, Vol. 2, Notes on Conference C-in-C—GOC-in-C First Cdn Army, 24 Jun 44.

40. Imperial War Museum, Montgomery of Alamein Papers (MAP), BLM 126, M511 Montgomery to Brooke, 14-7-44; and Liddell Hart Centre for Military Archives, King's College, London (LHC), Alanbrooke Papers, 14/28 Montgomery to Brooke, 14 July 1944.

41. MAP, BLM 126, M508 Montgomery to Brooke 7 July and BLM 1/101 Brooke to Montgomery 11 July 1944. Earlier, Alanbrooke had noted that he had full confidence that Crerar would not let him down. Alanbrooke, *War Diaries,* 535–36.

42. For detailed coverage of the dispute see English, *Canadian Army,* 191–94. On examining the Crerar-Crocker dispute through a map study, I concluded that Crerar was actually more at fault than his corps commander. Crerar later alleged that Crocker had resented competing with him in the development of tactics and techniques for the Normandy assault landing. CP, Vol. 21, Crerar to Stacey, 12 August 1957.

43. CP, Vol. 8, Montgomery to Crerar 26th July 1944; and "Thoughts on Command in Battle," *British Army Review* 69 (December 1981), 5.

44. CP, Vol. 8, Crocker to Crerar, 28.3.45.

45. CP, Vol. 2, Remarks to Senior Officers, Cdn Army Operation "Totalize" by GOC-in-C First Cdn Army 051100, August 1944.

46. CP, Vol. 21, Crerar to Col. C. P. Stacey, 7 June 1952 and 12 August 1957; and CP, Vol. 3, Tactical Directive by Comd, First Cdn Army, 22 July 1944.

47. CP, Vol. 2, Remarks to Senior Officers, Cdn Army Operation "Totalize" by GOC-in-C First Canadian Army 051100, August 1944 and CP, Vol 2, Crerar to Ralston, 1 September 1944 (report upon the initial phase of operations of First Canadian Army during the campaign in France 7–23 August 1944); English, *Canadian Army,* 267–68; and Hart, *Montgomery and "Colossal Cracks,"* 157.

48. LHC, Alanbrooke Papers, 14/29 Montgomery to Brooke, 9–8–44.

49. USMA West Point Archives, Thomas R. Goethals Papers, Extracts from Telephone Journal Seventh German Army, 8–9 August 1944; and John S. D. Eisenhower, *The Bitter Woods* (New York: Da Capo, 1995), 55.

50. RG 24, Vol. 10,808, Operation Totalize Appreciation by Lt. Gen. G. G. Simonds, 1 August 1944.

51. English, *Canadian Army,* 263–66, 269–70; and British Army of the Rhine (BAOR) Battlefield Tour Operation Totalize: 2 Canadian Corps Operations Astride the Road Caen-Falaise 7–8 August 1944, Spectator's Edition (1947), 1–16.

52. English, *Canadian Army,* 265–67, 269–73; and BAOR Totalize, 6–15.

53. Neither Air Chief Marshal Sir Arthur Harris's Bomber Command nor Lt. Gen. Carl A. "Tooey" Spaatz's U.S. Strategic Air Forces were willing to take orders from Leigh-Mallory, however. To resolve this difficulty, it was agreed that direction of all Overlord air command would be vested in the Supreme Allied Commander, to be exercised by his deputy, Air Chief Marshal Sir Arthur Tedder.

54. Initial details were fleshed out on 4 August in a meeting at First Canadian Army headquarters attended by Crerar, Leigh-Mallory, Coningham, Broadhurst, and Brown. Brig. C. C. Mann, chief of staff of the First Canadian Army, flew to England the next day with Brig. C. L. Richardson, 21st Army Group (Plans), for a conference at Allied Expeditionary Air Force headquarters chaired by Leigh-Mallory and attended by the Senior Air Staff Officer (SB) of Bomber Command, Air Vice-Marshall R. D. Oxland. Tedder, Spaatz, and Broadhurst were also in attendance. On 6 August, Mann visited Bomber Command

headquarters to personally convince "Bomber" Harris of the feasibility of night bombing in support of ground troops. Stacey, *Victory Campaign,* 211–13; and CP, Vol. 15, GOC-in-C War Diary, 6 Aug 44.

55. English, *Canadian Army,* 268–69; and BAOR Totalize, 12–13.

56. RG 24, Vol. 10,800, "Immediate Report" on Operation Totalize, 7–9 August 1944; and Stephen Hart, *Road to Falaise* (Stroud: Sutton, 2004), 41–47.

57. English, *Canadian Army,* 273–74; and BAOR Totalize, 17–22. Brigadier Wyman, commanding the 2nd Armoured Brigade, signaled at 0615 hours that the forward area was securely held and that the situation appeared to be entirely suitable for further operations to begin. Jody Perrun, "Best Laid Plans: Guy Simonds and Operation Totalize, 7–10 August 1944," *Journal of Military History* 1 (January 2003), 164–65.

58. RG 24, Vol. 10,797, GOC's Activities, 0700, 8 August 1944.

59. "The enemy really had little to do with limiting the success of the [4th Armoured] Division on 8 August." Brig. Gen. E. A. C. (Ned) Amy, "Normandy: 1 Squadron Canadian Grenadier Guards, Phase 2 Operation Totalize 7/8 August 1944," unpublished paper dated 21 February 1993.

60. The Corps reconnaissance unit, the 12th Manitoba Dragoons armored car regiment had been placed under command of the 4th Armoured Division, in sensible anticipation of a more fluid, fast-moving situation developing. It was later employed on the division's right flank. RG 24, Vol 10, Simonds Draft of Lessons, 1 July 1944; and English, *Canadian Army,* 228–30, 241–48, 271, 274.

61. Dwight D. Eisenhower (DDE) Library, Abilene, Kansas, J. Lawton Collins Papers, Box 5, Operation Cobra, Chapter I: VII Corps Operations (24–31 Jul 44); Carafano, *After D-Day,* 185–86, 192–203, 221, 262–63; Weigley, *Eisenhower's Lieutenants,* 155–64; D'Este, *Decision in Normandy,* 404; and Eisenhower, *Bitter Woods,* 45.

62. The bomb line ran from the north edge of Robertmesnil along the north edge of Gaumesnil to the south edge of the quarry west of Gaumesnil.

63. RG 24, Vol. 10,797, GOC's Activities, 1245, 8 August 1944 and RG 24, Vol. 13,712, Main HQ 2 Cdn Corps War Diary, 8 Aug 44. As has been pointed out, the Eighth Air Force bomber strike could also have been cancelled in flight up to 1100 hours. Brian A. Reid, *No Holding Back: Operation Totalize, Normandy, August 1944* (Toronto: Robin Brass, 2005), 130. Earlier arrangements had also provided for postponing the 1400 strike up to 2000 if army headquarters so requested before 0900 hours, but weather predictions indicated that the strike had to go in before 1300 or not at all. In short, it was probably easier to cancel the bombing than wait for it. PRO, Air 25–704, First Canadian Army Operation "Totalize" Request for Air Support, Part III—The Air Plan, 4 Aug 44.

64. Carl von Clausewitz, *On War,* ed. and trans. Michael Howard and Peter Paret (Princeton: University Press, 1976), 357–59, 379–80, 488; and English, *Marching through Chaos,* 75–76.

65. English, *Canadian Army,* 276–78; BAOR Totalize, 25–27; and RG 24, Vol. 10,800, "Immediate Report" Totalize.

66. CP, Vol. 21, Crerar to Stacey, 3 December 1958.

67. CP, Vol. 29, Report on Survey of Reinforcement Situation—Canadian Army Overseas by Lieutenant General E. W. Sansom, 29 March 1945.

68. Amy, 5. At 0710 Simonds ordered both armored divisions to feed forward. RG 24, Vol. 10,797, COS 2 Cdn Corps Handwritten Telephone Notes, 8 August 1944.

69. English, *Canadian Army,* 277–78.

70. Hubert Meyer, *The History of the 12. SS-Panzerdivision "Hitlerjugend,"* trans. H. Harri Henschler (Winnipeg: Fedorowicz, 1994), 170–80.

71. English, *Canadian Army,* 279–80.

72. CP, Vol. 21, Crerar to Stacey, 10 January 1958.

73. English, *Canadian Army,* 277–78, 291, 297–98, 303 (n. 28), 301 (n. 7).

74. CP, Vol. 21, Crerar to Stacey, 23 Jul 47.

75. English, *Canadian Army,* 274–78, 290; Hart, *Montgomery and "Colossal Cracks,"* 158; and CP, Vol. 21, Crerar to Stacey, 23 Jul 47 and 10 January 1958.

76. CP, Vol. 21, Crerar to Stacey, 10 January 1958; and CP, Vol. 15, GOC-in-C First Canadian Army War Diary, 14 Aug 44. In fact, Crerar ended up observing more fratricidal bombing than occurred during Totalize.

77. English, Canadian Army, 299–300; Stacey, *Victory Campaign,* 236–64.

78. Stacey, *Victory Campaign,* 279–97, 308; Williams, *Long Left Flank,* 27–32; and Gen. George C. Marshall Papers (MP), Box 67, Folder 12, Eisenhower to Marshall, 24 August 1944. Eisenhower stressed driving hard to size V Bomb sites in the Pas de Calais area.

79. PRO, Crerar Diary, 1–4 September 1944; Royal Military College of Canada Archives (RMC), Crerar Papers, Directive Crerar to Comd 1 Brit Corps and Comd 2 Cdn Corps, 1 September 1944; Stacey, *Victory Campaign,* 297–304; Hart, *Montgomery and "Colossal Cracks,"* 169; Graham, *Price of Command,* 178–79; and Terry Copp and Robert Vogel, "'No Lack of Rational Speed': 1st Canadian Army Operations, September 1944," *Journal of Canadian Studies* 16 (Fall/Winter, 1981), 147. The 2nd Infantry Division halted at Dieppe to absorb a thousand reinforcements. In attending the memorial parade there Crerar missed Montgomery's planning conference of 3 September attended by Bradley, Hodges, and Dempsey. On receiving a rather severe "ticking off" from Montgomery, Crerar remonstrated that he had acted in his capacity as a Canadian national commander and was prepared to take the matter up with his government if necessary. In the end, on learning that Crerar had not received his last message in sufficient time, Montgomery apologized for his reaction.

80. Copp and Vogel, "'No Lack of Rational Speed,'" 152, 155. The port eventually received 7,000 tons per day. Ostend fell on 9 September, and its port opened on the twenty-eighth. Allied divisions required maintenance supply in the order of 650–700 tons per day.

81. DDE Library, Eisenhower Principal File, Eisenhower to Marshall, 14 September 1944.

82. Martin Blumenson, *United States Army in World War II, The European Theater of Operations: Breakout and Pursuit* (Washington: Office of the Chief of Military History, 1961), 632, 655–56; Maj. Gen. J. F. C. Fuller, *The Second World War, 1939–1945: A Strategical and Tactical History* (London: Eyre and Spottiswoode, 1948), 332; and Maj. Gen. J. L. Moulton, *Battle for Antwerp: The Liberation of the City and the Opening of the Scheldt, 1944* (New York: Hippocrene, 1978), 74–78, 228. Cherbourg fell on 27 June, but was not mopped up until 1 July; it took another month to open the port to Allied shipping. Brest was not taken until 20 September. Le Havre opened to Allied shipping on 9 October.

83. Stacey, *Victory Campaign,* 310, 312, 329–31; Moulton, *Battle for Antwerp,* 50–51; and Hamilton, *Monty: The Field Marshal,* 47, 103–6.

84. MAP, Montgomery to Crerar, 13 September 1944; and Stacey, *Victory Campaign,* 310, 329–31, 336, 358–359.

85. MAP, Crerar to Montgomery, 13 September 1944.

86. PRO, Crerar Diary, 15 Sep 44, Appendix F, Army Commander's Directive to Corps Commanders, 15 Sep 44; Stacey, *Victory Campaign,* 357–60; and Copp and Vogel, "'No Lack of Rational Speed,'" 150–51. With a population of 160,000 in 1936, Le Havre was second only to Marseilles as a ranking French port before the Second World War. Its population at the time of capture was about 50,000. In the 1 Corps' attack, code-named Operation

Astonia, heavy strategic bombers and numerous specialized armored fighting vehicles, including flail and Crocodile flamethrowing tanks, and Kangaroo APCs were used.

87. Dunkirk was subsequently masked by the 4th Special Service (Commando) Brigade and the 154th Brigade of the 51st (Highland) Division. On 9 October the 1st Czechoslovak Independent Armoured Brigade assumed the task, eventually receiving the German garrison's surrender. Stacey, *Victory Campaign,* 368.

88. PRO, Crerar Diary, Appendix G, Directive to 1 Brit and 2 Cdn Corps Commanders, 19 Sep 44; Stacey, *Victory Campaign,* 359–61; and Copp and Vogel, "'No Lack of Rational Speed,'" 153.

89. When the GOC 2 Canadian Corps complained about this on 22 September, the 2nd Canadian Infantry Division was placed under command of 1 British Corps effective 26 September. Stacey, *Victory Campaign,* 367.

90. Stacey, *Victory Campaign,* 331–54.

91. W. A. B. Douglas and B. Greenhous, *Out of the Shadows* (Toronto: Oxford University Press, 1977), 200. Other critics include H. Essame, *The Battle for Germany* (New York: Bonanza, 1969), 29; and R. W. Thompson, who wrote, "On the Channel coast the Canadians were investing Boulogne and Calais as though there was all the time in the world, and without a trace of imagination." *The Eighty Five Days: The Story of the Battle of the Scheldt* (London: Hutchinson, 1957), 60.

92. Over 11,000 Germans garrisoned Le Havre, compared to roughly 10,000 at Boulogne. The two divisions at Le Havre suffered 388 casualties; the two brigade groups at Boulogne, 634, which only went to show once again the truth of the old military adage: "the more you use the fewer you lose." Attacking force size may, of course, have been calculated on the basis of pre-war peacetime populations; Le Havre's 160,000 rating two divisions (six brigades) and Boulogne's 51,000 a proportionately less two brigades.

93. Stacey, *Victory Campaign,* 343–56; and Copp and Vogel, "'No Lack of Rational Speed,'" 150–51.

94. CP, Vol. 21 Crerar to Stacey, 3 December 1958; Copp and Vogel, "'No Lack of Rational Speed,'" 282–83, 145; and MAP, Crerar to Montgomery, 13 Sep 44.

95. Moulton, *Battle for Antwerp,* 69; Williams, *Long Left Flank,* 37–38; and CP, Vol. 15, GOC-in-C First Cdn Army War Diary, 13 and 15 Sep 44.

96. Dickson, *Thoroughly Canadian General,* 257, 289–90, 307–8, 327, 334, 338, 351, 353–54.

97. Hart, *Montgomery and "Colossal Cracks,"* 160, 170; Granatstein, *Generals,* 287; CP, Vol. 15, GOC-in-C War Diary, 19, 21, 24–27 Sep 44; C. P. Stacey, *A Date with History: Memoirs of a Canadian Historian* (Ottawa: Deneau, 1982), 237; and Graham, *Price of Command,* 179.

98. RG 24, Vol. 10,799, Simonds's comments on the aim of the G Plan appreciation.

99. Hart, *Montgomery and "Colossal Cracks,"* 166.

100. CP, Vol. 15, GOC-in-C First Cdn Army War Diary, 22, 25, and 26 Oct and 7 Nov 44; Hart, *Montgomery and "Colossal Cracks,"* 170; and Granatstein, *Generals,* 172.

101. Stacey, *Date with History,* 236.

102. Stacey, *Victory Campaign,* 426–30, 438.

103. PRO, Crerar Diary, 7 February 1945 and Remarks by GOC-in-C to Warcos—7 Feb 45 as "Off Record" Background to Operation "Veritable."

104. PRO, Crerar Diary, 8–16 December 1944; Hart, *Montgomery and "Colossal Cracks,"* 176–77; Macdonald, "In Search of Veritable," 174–177; and Stacey, *Victory Campaign,* 427, 437–38.

105. PRO, Crerar Diary, GOC-in-C 1-0-7/11 Operation "Veritable" dated 14 Dec 44 to Comd 1 Brit Corps, 2 Cdn Corps, and 30 Brit Corps and Remarks by GOC-in-C First Canadian Army on Operation "Veritable" to Staff Officers HQ First Canadian Army/84 Group RAF, 16 Dec 44.

106. PRO Crerar Diary, Memorandum GOC-in-C 1-0-4/1 Crerar to COS, 19 Dec 44 and Notes on Conference Held at Tac HQ 21 Army Group 1100 hrs by C-in-C with Comds First Canadian and Second British Armies, 20 Dec 44; Stacey, *Victory Campaign,* 437–42; and Macdonald, "In Search of Veritable," 2, 176–77, 200, 218 (n. 41).

107. PRO, Crerar Diary, 19 and 25 January 1944, Appendix 2, Address to Senior Officers First Canadian Army 22 January 1945; Appendix 2a, Notes on Conference held by C-in-C 21 Army Group at Tac, 21 Army Group 1130–1300 hrs, 23 January 45; and 4 February 1945, Appendix 3, Notes on Conference held by C-in-C 21 Army Group at his Tac HQ 1115 hrs, 4 February 1945 and Notes for [Crerar's] Remarks—C-in-C's Conference 4 Feb 1945; Stacey, *Victory Campaign,* 455–56, 460–64; and BAOR Battlefield Tour Operation Veritable: 30 Corps Operations between the Rivers Maas and Rhine, 8–10 February 1945, Spectator's Edition, 2–3 (hereafter cited as BAOR Veritable).

108. Stacey, *Victory Campaign,* 464–65; Horrocks, *Corps Commander,* 173–89; Macdonald, "In Search of Veritable," 159, 201; and BAOR Veritable, 14–15, 37.

109. PRO, Crerar Diary, 1 February 1945 and Appendix 3, Notes on Conference held by C-in-C 21 Army Group at his Tac HQ 1115 hrs, 4 February 1945 and Notes for [Crerar's] Remarks—C-in-C's Conference 4 Feb 1945 Stacey, *Victory Campaign,* 465, 467; Hart, *Montgomery and Colossal Cracks,* 157; and BAOR Veritable, 19–22.

110. Stacey, *Victory Campaign,* 465–466; and BAOR Veritable, 23–25.

111. Between 0945 and 1600 barrages were fired in support of the 2nd Canadian, 15th (Scottish), and 53rd (Welsh) division attacks that commenced at 1030. The 51st (Highland) Division, which attacked at the same time on the right, opted instead for supporting concentrations and stonks.

112. Stacey, *Victory Campaign,* 468–74; and BAOR Veritable, 45–51.

113. Stacey, *Victory Campaign,* 457–58, 471, 475–77; BAOR Veritable, 53–55.

114. Essame, *Battle for Germany,* 153–57; and Horrocks, *Corps Commander,* 187.

115. Stacey, *Victory Campaign,* 476–80; BAOR Veritable, 57–58; and Horrocks, *Corps Commander,* 173–89.

116. Hart, *Montgomery and "Colossal Cracks,"* 174.

117. Horrocks was "a born leader such as I had never met before," observed one senior Canadian officer, adding that "most Canadian commanders felt like cheering when the general completed the outline of his plan and intentions." James Alan Roberts, *The Canadian Summer: Memoirs* (Toronto: University Press, 1981), 108.

118. Horrocks, *Corps Commander,* 31, 182–83; Williams, *Long Left Flank,* 65, 208; and W. Denis Whitaker and Shelagh Whitaker, *Rhineland: The Battle to End the War* (Toronto: Stoddart, 1989), 111. Crerar was aloft every day from 8 February until weather prevented flying on 15 February. Between 21 February and 10 March, he flew forward daily some dozen times. PRO, Crerar Diary, 8 February-10 March 1945. Apart from nagging subordinates about current traffic congestion, there was little a lone airborne commander, bereft of artillery and air advisers, could do to influence the close or distant battle.

119. CP, Vol. 4, Crerar to COS, CMHQ, 28 Feb 45, and Immediate Message Canmilitry to Defensor, 021705A Mar 45. Crerar also recommended Beament's promotion to brigadier.

120. PRO, Crerar Diary, 7 February 1945 and Remarks by GOC-in-C to Warcos; Macdonald, "In Search of Veritable," 199, 202; CP, Vol 27, Address by Gen. H. D. G. Crerar on "Principles and Policies of the First Canadian Army"; and Stacey, *Victory Campaign,* 480–81.

121. Stacey, *Victory Campaign,* 482–86, 489–91; Whitaker and Whitaker, *Rhineland,* 140–51.

122. Stacey, *Victory Campaign,* 491–93; and Williams, *Long Left Flank,* 221–22.

123. Stacey, *Victory Campaign,* 495–96, 508–9; Williams, *Long Left Flank,* 221–24, 233, 238; and Whitaker and Whitaker, *Rhineland,* 219, 223.

124. PRO, Crerar Diary, 25 February 1945 and Appendix 4, Directive GOC-in-C 1-0-7/11 dated 25 Feb 45 to Comds 2 Canadian Corps and 30 Corps.
125. Whitaker and Whitaker, *Rhineland,* 220–21, 224, 231; Williams, *Long Left Flank,* 240; Macdonald, "In Search of Veritable," 218; and Stacey, *Victory Campaign,* 438–39, 494, 508–9.
126. Stacey, *Victory Campaign,* 496–514; Whitaker and Whitaker, *Rhineland,* 194–207, 221–43; and Williams, *Long Left Flank,* 224–32, 237–43. 28 February was the only day on which the Second Tactical Air Force was able to provide air support on a large scale. Williams, *Long Left Flank,* 252.
127. The 52nd Division captured a deserted Weeze on 2 March and the Well locality on the night of 3 March. The bridge was completed three days later. Stacey, *Victory Campaign,* 494, 514.
128. Whitaker and Whitaker, *Rhineland,* 195–96, 219, 222, 224, 228–29; Graham, *Price of Command,* 203; and Williams, *Long Left Flank,* 245.
129. Some 10,330 of these were British, but Canadian losses of 5,304—of which 3,638 occurred in Blockbuster—were also heavy. Stacey, *Victory Campaign,* 522.
130. CP, Vol. 6, Personal Message from the Army Commander, 20 July 1945.
131. CP, Vol. 7, Montgomery to Crerar, 6-7-45.
132. CP, Vol. 6, Personal Message from Army Commander, 20 July 1945; Stacey, *Victory Campaign,* 522, 530–619; Williams, *Long Left Flank,* 257–91; Granatstein, *Generals,* 114–15; Dickson, *Thoroughly Canadian General,* 441–65; and CP, Vol. 24, Eisenhower to Mrs. H. D. G. Crerar, 6 April 1965. According to Canadian military historian, Desmond Morton, beyond a pension, Crerar's chief reward after the war was discreet removal from a Hull jail cell and the dropping of drunk driving charges. Desmond Morton, *Understanding Canadian Defence* (Toronto: Penguin/McGill, 2003), 172.

CHAPTER TWO
In the Shadow of Montgomery: Gen. Miles C. Dempsey, British Second Army

1. Keegan, ed., *Churchill's Generals* (London: Weidenfeld and Nicolson, 1991). Brian Horrocks, Neil M. Ritchie, and Richard O'Connor are all classed among Churchill's generals, but not Dempsey. Similarly, though Dempsey appears on the jacket of Raymond Callahan's *Churchill and His Generals* (Lawrence, KS: University Press of Kansas, 2007), he rates only cursory mention. According to Horrocks, the larger Second Army never captured the imagination of the public as did the smaller Eighth, with the result that Dempsey remained almost completely unknown. Horrocks, *Corps Commander,* 22.
2. Stephen Ashley Hart, *Montgomery and "Colossal Cracks."*
3. Liddell Hart Centre for Military Archives (LHC) London, General Sir Harold Pyman Papers, 6/6/7, Dempsey to Pyman, 16 September 1947.
4. Peter Caddick-Adams, "General Sir Miles Christopher Dempsey (1896–1969): 'Not a Popular Leader'" in *RUSI Journal* 5 (October, 2005): 66–72; Nigel Hamilton, *Monty: Master of the Battlefield, 1942–1944* (London: Hamish Hamilton, 1983), 697; and LHC, LH1/230, Obituaries in The *Times* and *Telegraph,* 7 June 1969, and Selwyn Lloyd letter to the editor, *The Times,* 10 June 1969. Dempsey refused to comment on remarks made by Patton in his battle memoirs. Pyman Papers, 6/6/10, Dempsey to Pyman, 20 November 1947.
5. LHC, Pyman Papers, 6/6/2, Dempsey to Pyman, 24 July 1948, and Pyman Papers, 4/15, An Account of the Operations of Second Army in Europe 1944–1945 (2 volumes with map section 1–18), ed. Major-General H.E Pyman, CBE, DSO. Pyman's "Secret Copy #8" was signed by Dempsey, who also wrote the Introduction dated 5 August 1945. Dempsey had told his staff to prepare the account, intended to be valuable to future his-

torians, setting the facts down in writing. He for his part intended to add his own notes to it, showing why the various operations were undertaken, how and why they were initiated and what their objects were. His appointment to another theatre prevented him from doing so.

6. PRO, CAB 106/1061, Operation Goodwood, Interview with Gen. Sir Miles Dempsey by Lt. Col. G. S. Jackson, 8 March 1951 and Notes made by Capt. B. H. Liddell Hart on his interview with Gen. M. C. Dempsey, 28.3.52.

7. Caddick-Adams, "General Sir Miles Dempsey," 66–67; Hart, *Montgomery and "Colossal Cracks,"* 134; and Selwyn Lloyd letter to the editor, *The Times,* 10 June 1969.

8. Brooke noted that Franklyn handled his division admirably in the retreat to Dunkirk. LHC, Field Marshal The Viscount Alanbrooke Papers (AP), Box 1, File 1(a), 3/C/VI/11, Strategy and Personality.

9. On the disbandment of Second Army headquarters in June 1945, Montgomery wrote that Dempsey had been at his side through Sicily, Italy, and northwest Europe and that he had never regretted his choice. PRO 70423, WO 285/23 Personal Message from the C-in-C to Headquarters, Second Army by Field Marshal B. L. Montgomery, June 1945.

10. LHC, LH 1/230. Obituary by Frank MacGarry, *Daily Express,* 7 June 1969. Dempsey received the nickname "Lucky" because he took his 13th Infantry Brigade out of Dunkirk and led the 13 Corps ashore in Sicily. Ironically, "Lucky" was also the American code name for Patton's headquarters. Dempsey never said how he got the nickname "Bimbo," but supposedly used to blush when asked the question. Carlo D'Este, *Decision in Normandy,* 60.

11. LHC, Obituary Gen Sir Miles Dempsey, *The Times,* 7-6-69; Caddick-Adams, "General Sir Miles Dempsey," 67–68; John Swettenham, *McNaughton,* vol. 2, *1939–1943* (Toronto: Ryerson Press, 1969), 121–22, 179; and Ronald Lewin, *Montgomery as Military Commander* (New York: Stein and Day, 1971), 191–92. Montgomery originally suggested to Brooke that Lt. Gen. Sir Oliver Leese take the British Second Army and Dempsey the First Canadian Army on the grounds that Canadians would, initially at least, gladly accept a British general whom they knew and trusted rather than have their troops mishandled by an inexperienced general of their own. LHC, AP, 14/24, Montgomery to Brooke, 28–12–43. Brooke fired back that he had about one and a half intimate years with the Canadians in the last war and knew well what their feelings were: that they would insist on Canadian forces being commanded by Canadians. MAP, BLM 1/101 Brooke to Montgomery 11 July 1944. Montgomery said of Leese: "he has done splendidly as a corps commander in my army—he is easily the best I have." AP, 14/24, Montgomery to Brooke, 29-9-43.

12. Hart, *Montgomery and "Colossal Cracks,"* 142; and PRO 70519, WO 285/16 Main Army—27 Nov [1944] Notes.

13. Gen. Sir Harold E. Pyman, *Call to Arms,* 61, 98–99; Stephen Badsey, "Crocker, J.T." in *D-Day Encyclopedia,* eds. Davis G. Chandler and James Lawton Collins, Jr. (New York: Simon and Shuster, 1994), 170–71; D'Este, *Decision in Normandy,* 18, 60–61, 512; and NAC, CP, GOC-in-C First Cdn Army, 21 October 44. Field Marshal Lord Carver said to serve Crocker "was an education in itself." The Editor, British Army Review, described him as: "A man of legendary personal courage and absolute integrity, he had the unusual gift of being as fine a staff officer as he was a commander in battle." "Thoughts on Command in Battle," *British Army Review* 69 (December, 1981), 5. According to Pyman, "Honest John" Crocker possessed an outstanding command of the English language. *Call to Arms,* 99.

14. Brooke had high praise for Crocker, who had been his general staff officer, grade 1, and he never lost faith in Ritchie, who had been his BGS and stood by him "always calm, never rattled, with a good sense of humour" in "dark Dunkirk days." Brooke maintained

that Ritchie's appointment by Gen. Sir Claude Auckinleck to command the Eighth Army was a major blunder, and unfair to Ritchie who was young and had no experience commanding anything larger than a brigade; to jump him up to command an army, especially one locked in battle, was folly. AP, Box 1, File 1(a), 3/C/VI/11, Strategy and Personality and 12/XII/1–2, Interview with M. C. Long.

15. Alanbrooke, *War Diaries,* 538; D'Este, *Decision in Normandy,* 193–94; and Hamilton, *Monty: Master of the Battlefield,* 427.

16. In December 1943, Montgomery suggested that O'Connor take over the Eighth Army from Leese. LHC, AP, 14/24, Montgomery to Brooke, 28-12-43.

17. Hart, *Montgomery and "Colossal Cracks,"* 136–37, 142–43; D'Este, *Decision in Normandy,* 60–62; Alanbrooke, *War Diaries,* 509; John Baynes, "O'Connor, Richard N." in *D-Day Encyclopedia,* 403–4; and Brig. Peter Young, *World War, 1939–1945* (London: Pan, 1966), 109–12. In 1950, O'Connor wrote, "I have never for a moment thought myself good enough to defeat Rommel had I remained, and I am sure no one else did either! Moreover, any thoughts in my own mind that I could have done some of the things Monty did never entered my mind. He is my superior in every way, and has qualities I have never possessed. He is a wonderful man to serve." MAP, Montgomery Collections: Ancillary Collections 9, General Sir Richard O'Connor to Arthur Bryant , 7 February 1950. Montgomery allowed O'Connor to be poached after the latter steadfastly refused to support the firing of Maj. Gen. Lindsay Silvester, commander of the U.S. 7th Armored Division. Bradley fired Silvester. Marshall Library, Lexington, Virginia, Marshall Papers, Eisenhower to Marshall, 18 November 1944; and Hart, *Montgomery and "Colossal Cracks,"* 162.

18. No. 83 Group consisted of roughly ten wings of some twenty-nine squadrons, including fifteen designated RCAF and one RAAF (Royal Australian Air Force). Of these, thirteen flew Spitfires, six the long-range Mustang, and ten the Typhoon. Henry Probert, "83d Composite Group" and John Terraine, "Second Tactical Air Force" in *D-Day Encyclopedia,* 207, 500–501.

19. MAP, Personal Diary, 18–19 June 1944 and letter Montgomery to Dempsey, Crerar, Bradley, and Patton, 4 May 1944. "I fear that Chilton is not really fit to be COS to a large army; however, we will have to teach him," observed Montgomery. MAP, Montgomery to Major General Frank Simpson, 19-6-44. Pyman, chief of staff of the 30 Corps, became Dempsey's chief of staff on 15 January 1945. Pyman, *Call to Arms,* 78.

20. D'Este, *Decision in Normandy,* 219–22; Henry Probert, "Broadhurst, Harry" in *D-Day Encyclopedia,* 123–24; and Ian Gooderson, *Air Power at the Battlefront: Allied Close Air Support in Europe, 1943–45* (London: Frank Cass, 1998), 35–36, 39–40. Broadhurst flew as his personal aircraft a captured German Storch painted bight yellow. In 1945, Montgomery had to overcome RAF opposition to get Broadhurst knighted for his wartime service.

21. D'Este, *Decision in Normandy,* 112, 120–45; Stacey, *Victory Campaign,* 115–17, 121; Hart, *Montgomery and "Colossal Cracks,"* 141; and John A. English, "I Corps" in *D-Day Encyclopedia,* 242–43.

22. Quoted in D'Este, *Decision in Normandy,* 160.

23. D'Este, *Decision in Normandy,* 73–75, 141–50, 156–57; English, *Canadian Army,* 203, 219; and F. H. Hinsley, *British Intelligence,* 471–74.

24. Russell A. Hart, *Clash of Arms: How the Allies Won in Normandy* (Boulder: Lynne Rienner, 2001), 250, 307, 387–90.

25. Hart, *Clash of Arms,* 329.

26. PRO 70473, WO 285/9–11, Dempsey Diary (DD), 12 Jun 44.

27. D'Este, *Decision in Normandy,* 174–98; DD, 13–14 Jun 44; and MAP, Personal Diary, 14 June 1944.

28. MAP, Personal Diary, 15, 18 June and 24 June-2 July 1944; and Hart, *Montgomery and "Colossal Cracks,"* 103, 114.

29. DD, 19–30 Jun and 1 Jul 44; D'Este, *Decision in Normandy*, 235–44; Stacey, *Victory Campaign*, 147–49; and Hart, *Montgomery and "Colossal Cracks,"* 95.

30. CP, Vol. 3, Crocker to Dempsey, 5 July 1944 and Dempsey to Montgomery, 6 July 1944; and DD, 1–5 Jul 44. The direct and plain-speaking Crocker had also castigated Maj. Gen. Charles W. Ryder and his U.S. 34th Infantry Division during the 9 Corps' operations in Tunisia. Although press leakage of the incident upset the Americans, Bradley later admitted that Ryder overlooked the shortcomings of ineffective subordinates and thus penalized his division as well as himself. Bradley, *Soldier's Story*, 67–68, 100; and Rick Atkinson, *An Army at Dawn* (New York: Henry Holt, 2003), 470–78.

31. Montgomery, while concurring in Dempsey's assessment, left the decision of what to do with Keller to Crerar and the Canadian chain of command. MAP, Personal Diary, 4 and 8 July 1944; and NAC, CP, Vol. 3, Montgomery to Crerar, 8 July 1944. Crerar had been a long time supporter of Keller, even recommending him for corps command at one point, and in passing the matter to Simonds suggested that it "was quite possible Crocker's handling of Keller had not brought out the best in the latter." At the time, Simonds was also dealing with a request by Keller to fire one of his 3rd Division brigade commanders. In a 27 July letter to Dempsey, Simonds recommended against the immediate removal of Keller on the grounds that it would have undermined the morale of the 3rd Division, which had not been out of the line since D-Day and had incurred 5,500 casualties. English, *Canadian Army*, 189–90, 217, 226–27, 234 (n. 27), 251–52, 261 (n. 34). Brooke expressed concern that Keller had been nominated to replace the 1 Canadian Corps commander in Italy who had been found wanting. MAP, BLM 1 /101 Brooke to Montgomery 11 July 1944.

32. Dempsey flew with Broadhurst in his Storch to observe the bombing and alerted the former to the fact that they were being shot at. After Broadhurst put the Storch down, he confirmed that they had been hit eleven times. D'Este, *Decision in Normandy*, 314.

33. DD, 7–9 Jul 44; English, *Canadian Army*, 217–22; D'Este, *Decision in Normandy*, 305–6, 309–18; and Stacey, *Victory Campaign*, 153–64.

34. D'Este, *Decision in Normandy*, 242–44, 260–63; Stacey, *Victory Campaign*, 149, 163, 166; Hart, *Montgomery and "Colossal Cracks,"* 49–61, 64, 145; DD, 10 Jul 44; and Eversley Belfield and H. Essame, *The Battle for Normandy* (London: Pan, 1983), 144–45.

35. PRO 70519, WO 285/16, Main Army Speaking Notes, 27 November 1944.

36. LHC, LHI/230/22, Dempsey to Liddell Hart, 28 March 1952 covering "Operation Goodwood," 18 July 1944, Dempsey's expansion (18.3.52) of the notes he wrote down in brief form 21.2.52; Liddell Hart to Dempsey, 31 March 1952, covering amended notes; and Dempsey to Liddell Hart, 16 April 1952; DD, 12 Jul 44; Hart, *Montgomery and "Colossal Cracks,"* 70, 145; and D'Este, *Decision in Normandy*, 354–59.

37. PRO, WO 205/5D, D.O. Correspondence of C-in-C, Montgomery to Eisenhower (M.508), 8-7-44; MAP, Personal Diary, 2 July 1944 Summary; Martin Blumenson, *Breakout and Pursuit*, 189; D'Este, *Decision in Normandy*, 355–57; Stacey, *Victory Campaign*, 165–69; and Hart, *Montgomery and "Colossal Cracks,"* 68–69, 86, 99.

38. MAP, Notes on Second Army Operations 16 July–18 July dated 15-7-44 and Personal Diary, 13–18 July 1944; and Stacey, *Victory Campaign*, 168.

39. D'Este, *Decision in Normandy*, 352–55. Selwyn Lloyd also stated that Dempsey, who loved music and played the piano, possessed a first-class intellect. LHC, Selwyn Lloyd letter, *The Times*, 10 June 1969. Lloyd had been Dempsey's Colonel General Staff heading the army headquarters G branch and accompanied him to Normandy on the destroyer HMS *Impulsive*.

40. West Point Archives, Original Patton Diary, 1 June 1944.

41. Pyman, Dempsey's brilliant chief of staff, considered it the perfect combination. LHC, Pyman Papers, LH1/587, Pyman to Liddell Hart, 6 December 1949. Though Montgomery's chief of staff offered that Montgomery would never have accepted Alexander commanding him in Sicily and Italy as he commanded Dempsey. DDE Papers, Principal File, Box 34, Francis de Guingand to Eisenhower, 20 January 1949.

42. Hart, *Montgomery and "Colossal Cracks,"* 132–35; D'Este, *Decision in Normandy,* 60, 133, 353–54; Horrocks, *Corps Commander,* 23–24, Ronald Lewin, *Montgomery as Military Commander,* 191–92, 275, 341; DD, 7 Jul 44; Belfield and Essame, *Battle for Normandy,* 47; and LHC, LH 1/230, Selwyn Lloyd letter, *The Times,* 10 June 1969 and obituaries in the *Times, Telegraph, Daily Mail,* and *Daily Express,* 7 June 1969. Pyman thought the self-assured yet modest Dempsey to be the "perfect British Officer, without peer." His powers of leadership were boundless and he really understood the British soldier. Pyman, *Call to Arms,* 68, 83.

43. CP, Vol. 2, M510 Directive, Montgomery to Bradley, Dempsey, Patton, and Crerar, 10-7-44; MAP, Personal Dairy, 10 June 1944; English, *Canadian Army,* 182, 208; CP, Vol. 21, Crerar to Stacey, 7 June 1952; RG 24, Vol. 10,799, WD GS 2 Cdn Corps, Operation "Axehead" 8 May 1944 and CP, Vol. 9, Ops/1-6-4 Operation "Pintail" 18 May 1944. From Epsom up to Cobra, 520–725 panzers continuously deployed against the British sector, whereas during the same period the Americans rarely faced more than 190. On 25 July 1944, the Germans had an estimated 30,000 fighting men and 150–180 tanks in the area north of Coutances between the Vire River and the ocean. Most of these belonged to the 2nd SS "Das Reich" Panzer Division, which had come from the south. DDE Library, J. Lawton Collins Papers, Box 7, Selected Intelligence Reports, Vol. 1, June 1944–November 1944, Office of the AC of S, G2, First United States Infantry Division, Germany (6 December 1944), 25.

44. This was in line with what Eisenhower had urged Montgomery to do. While acknowledging Montgomery's plan to hold firmly on the left, attracting enemy armor, while striving to advance in the west, Eisenhower pointed out that because the US "advance on the right has been slow and laborious," the British should attempt a "major full dress attack." DDE Papers, Principal File, Box 83, Eisenhower to Montgomery, 7 July 1944.

45. PRO, CAB 106/1061, Operation Goodwood, Interview with Gen. Sir Miles Dempsey, 8 March 1951, by Lt. Col. G. S. Jackson. Dempsey's order directed the 8 Corps to seize the triangular area Bretteville-sur-Laize–Vimont–Agence–Falaise. Montgomery reversed the triangle to Bourguebus–Vimont–Bretteville-sur-Laize. The only mention of Falaise was that armored cars should push towards that location, spread alarm and despondency, and discover the "form." To ensure that this was clear, Montgomery gave Dempsey written Notes on Second Army Operations 16 July–18 July dated 15-7-44, a copy of which Dempsey gave to O'Connor along with his own instructions. It was the first and last time that Montgomery gave such a written directive. MAP, Notes on Second Army Operations 16 July–18 July dated 15-7-44; PRO 70375, CAB 106/1041 Second Army Operations (commencing 18 July) dated 17 July 44 covering Second Army Operations 18/19 July Notes Given to BGS 8 Corps by Army Comd; and D'Este, *Decision in Normandy,* 294, 354, 362–64, 396.

46. "If circumstances are favourable, the drive on FALAISE is to continue—tempered with common sense. Whether the Corps can drive SOUTH or not largely depends on whether the Cdns succeed in establishing a firm base and a Cl 40 br in the area of Vaucelles." PRO 70375, CAB 106/1041, Second Army Operations 18/19 July, Notes Given to BGS 8 Corps by Army Comd, under cover Second Army Operations (commencing on 18 July) signed by Dempsey 17 July 44.

47. Interestingly, Bradley later produced evidence to show that Montgomery had not misled Ike into believing that he, Monty, had made a fundamental change in strategy—as some historians also suggest. Ike knew full well that the original Overlord strategy was still the guiding policy, that Goodwood was designed to support Cobra, the main breakout effort, and not the other way around. Bradley and Blair, *General's Life,* 274–75.

48. Hart, *Montgomery and "Colossal Cracks,"* 81–82, 86, 139, 147, 314–15; D'Este, *Decision in Normandy,* 361–67; and Lewin, *Montgomery as Military Commander,* 274–75. In asking Eisenhower on 12 July for the whole weight of airpower on the day, Montgomery wrote, "My whole eastern flank will burst into flames on Saturday. The operation on Monday may have far reaching results." Eisenhower enthusiastically approved Goodwood, offering that "O'Connor's plunge into his vitals will be decisive." D'Este, *Decision in Normandy,* 361.

49. PRO 70375, CAB 1041, Second Army Operations (commencing on 18 July) dated 17 July 44; D'Este, *Decision in Normandy,* 357–58, 370–72, 377; Chester Wilmot, *The Struggle for Europe* (London: Fontana/Collins, 1974), 409–11; and DD, 12–13 Jul 44.

50. Hinsley, *British Intelligence,* 501. Dempsey was aware that the restricted bridgehead posed a challenge, which is why he advised against using it in June. DD, 18 Jun 44. Good staff work, especially tight movement control, was the only if not entirely satisfactory solution.

51. This is hard to square with O'Connor's later account that he had earlier requested the conversion of self-propelled artillery pieces into armored personnel carriers so that infantry could keep up with tanks in relative safety from small arms fire. According to O'Connor, Dempsey turned his request down. D'Este, *Decision in Normandy,* 389–90.

52. D'Este, *Decision in Normandy,* 373–85; Stacey, *Victory Campaign,* 169–70; Lewin, *Montgomery as Military Commander,* 273–74; Interview with Dempsey, 8 March 1951; and DD, 18–19 Jul 44.

53. LHC, LH1/230/22, Dempsey to Liddell Hart, 28 March 1952, covering Dempsey's expansion (18.3.52) of the notes he wrote down in brief form 21.2.52.

54. D'Este, *Decision in Normandy,* 367, 374, 385–88; and Hart, *Clash of Arms,* 316.

55. Although Montgomery hedged his bets in orders, he did foolishly announce, prematurely, that a breakthrough had occurred. Tedder, one of Montgomery's harshest critics, stated after Goodwood that he had no faith in returning to the original plan of holding on the left and leading the enemy to believe that an advance to Falaise-Argentan was intended so that a break out could be effected on the American right. DDE Papers, Principal File, Box 115, Tedder to Eisenhower, 23 July 1944.

56. MAP, Personal Diary, 28 July 1944. American press charges that US troops were doing more fighting and suffering more casualties than the British prompted Brooke to urge Montgomery that Dempsey attack at the earliest possible moment on a large scale to prevent German forces from moving to the US front. MAP, Personal Diary, 9, 19, and 25 July 1944 and BLM 1/102 Brooke to Montgomery, 29 July 1944.

57. DD, 25–29 Jul 44; BAOR Battlefield Tour, Operation Bluecoat: 8 Corps Operations South of Caumont 30–31 July 1944, Spectator's Edition (1947), 1–14; Hart, *Montgomery and "Colossal Cracks,"* 39, 82, 98, 139–40; D'Este, *Decision in Normandy,* 422; and Hart, *Clash of Arms,* 317, 335.

58. Dempsey grouped the 7th Armoured Division and 43rd (Wessex) and 50th (Northumbrian) Infantry Divisions under Bucknall and the 11th Armoured Division and 15th (Scottish) Infantry Division supported by the 6th Guards Tank Brigade under O'Connor.

59. DD, 30 Jul-3 Aug 44; Montgomery, *Normandy to the Baltic,* 89–94; Lewin, *Montgomery as Military Commander,* 287–89; PRO 70375, CAB, 106/1041, Dempsey's Instructions to

Commander 30 Corps, 3 August 1944; BAOR Bluecoat, 17–22; Belfield and Essame, *Battle for Normandy,* 208–9; and D'Este, *Decision in Normandy,* 422–24; Stacey, *Victory Campaign,* 203–4; Weigley, *Eisenhower's Lieutenants,* 168–69; and Hinsley, *British Intelligence,* 505. Montgomery admitted that he made a mistake in his choice of Bucknall, whom he characterized as careful and meticulous, but nearly always 24 hours too late. MAP, BLM 119/13, Report on Lt. Gen. Bucknall, 2 August 1944.

60. Dempsey possessed a three to one superiority in tanks, but had no great advantage in infantry, which was most required in fighting through bocage. Lewin, *Montgomery as Military Commander,* 288.

61. Stacey, *Victory Campaign,* 259, 266–68, 280–83; DD, 17, 19 Aug 44; Weigley, *Eisenhower's Lieutenants,* 241–47; USAMHI, Bradley Papers, *Daily Telegraph* and *Morning Post,* 5 Sep 44; DDE Papers, Principal File, Box 13, Bradley to Eisenhower, 10 September 1944; Hart, *Montgomery and "Colossal Cracks,"* 148; and D'Este, *Decision in Normandy,* 474–75. According to Weigley, Dempsey was "one Briton whom the Americans could rarely accuse of trying to hog the headlines." *Eisenhower's Lieutenants,* 169.

62. "Some Administrative Problems Encountered During the Advance of Second Army from Falaise to Brussels, 24 Aug to 3 Sep 44," Current Reports From Overseas, 68 (20 December, 1944), 6–8; DD, 23–27 Aug 44; Lewin, *Montgomery as Military Commander,* 300; and Weigley, *Eisenhower's Lieutenants,* 254–55. The British Second Army advanced 300 miles in ten days from Falaise to Brussels, an average of 40 miles per day.

63. LHC, 1/230/30, Liddell Hart to Dempsey, 4 February 1953; and Pyman, 74.

64. Stacey, *Victory Campaign,* 296–303; Lewin, *Montgomery as Military Commander,* 300; D'Este, *Decision in Normandy,* 353; and Weigley, *Eisenhower's Lieutenants,* 255, 274.

65. W. Denis Whitaker and Shelagh Whitaker, *Tug of War: The Canadian Victory that Opened Antwerp* (Toronto: Stoddart, 1984), 18–43; Moulton, *Battle for Antwerp,* 28–42, 66–9; Richard Lamb, *Montgomery in Europe, 1943–45: Success or Failure?* (New York: Franklin Watts, 1984), 199, 201–7; Maj. Gen. Pip Roberts, *From the Desert to the Baltic* (London: William Kimber, 1987), 206–11. Horrocks later stated that the 30 Corps still possessed 100 liters of petrol per vehicle, plus a further day's supply within reach. He also stressed that his troops were not exhausted and would have been able to go on. Horrocks, *Corps Commander,* 79–81.

66. Weigley, *Eisenhower's Lieutenants,* 260. By the beginning of September, Patton had crossed the Meuse and flung patrols forward to the Moselle near Metz and Nancy. Yet, as intelligence reports confirmed, the Germans had by early September also concentrated the strongest German army in the west against him. The German First Army, under General der Panzertruppen Otto von Knobelsdorff, had been built up into a force of three panzergrenadier divisions (the 3rd, 15th, and reconstituted 17th SS), four and a half infantry divisions (including the 553rd and 550th Volksgrenadier), and the 106th Panzer Brigade equipped with Panther tanks. Patton's Third Army in early September had only two armored and four infantry divisions. With his front swarming with Germans by 3 September, Patton's advance stalled three days later before Metz, which did not capitulate until 25 November. Weigley, *Eisenhower's Lieutenants,* 257, 265.

67. Moulton, *Battle for Antwerp,* 68. Weigley ventured that Montgomery was a commander of greater audacity than Americans sometimes liked to admit. *Eisenhower's Lieutenants,* 175.

68. Graham, *Price of Command,* 180; and Stacey, *Victory Campaign,* 359. Montgomery specifically mentioned Rotterdam in his Market Garden order.

69. Alanbrooke, *War Diaries,* 600. Chester Wilmot contended that the Canadian Army might have been spared "a long and bloody campaign" had the necessity for it have been foreseen. He suggested that immediately after the capture of Antwerp an amphibious force

could have landed at the mouth of the Scheldt without any great difficulty. Following the Normandy invasion, however, most landing craft were reassigned to the Pacific or to the Mediterranean for landings in southern France. *Struggle for Europe,* 623.

70. MacDonald, *Mighty Endeavor,* 332

71. B. H. Liddell Hart, *History of the Second World War* (London: Pan, 1973), 591.

72. Lewin, *Montgomery as Military Commander,* 301. Montgomery frankly admitted that he made "a bad mistake" in underestimating "the difficulties of opening up the approaches to Antwerp," adding that "I reckoned that the Canadian Army could do it while we were going for the Ruhr. I was wrong." Field Marshal The Viscount Montgomery of Alamein, *Memoirs* (London: Collins, 1958), 297. DD, 7 Sep 44.

73. Fuller, *Second World War,* 339.

74. Graham and Bidwell, *Coalitions, Politicians, and Generals,* 238.

75. Lamb, *Montgomery in Europe,* 216–17. Although Adm. Sir Bertram Ramsey, Allied naval commander in chief, had warned both SHAEF and the 21st Army Group on 3 September that Antwerp would be useless without the clearance of its sea approaches, Eisenhower at the time placed no special emphasis on the Scheldt. Moulton, *Battle for Antwerp,* 47–49; and Stephen E. Ambrose, *Eisenhower: Soldier, General of the Army, President-Elect, 1890–1952* (New York: Simon and Schuster, 1983), 350. Gen. James M. Gavin, former commander of the 82nd Airborne Division, which seized the bridge at Nijmegen, placed full blame on Eisenhower for failing to open Antwerp: "I cannot understand how a historian can avoid placing the responsibility [for failing to open Antwerp] on Eisenhower . . . [as] he, more than anyone else, had a keen awareness of the critical nature of the logistics situation in his armies." Gen. James M. Gavin, *On to Berlin: Battles of an Airborne Commander, 1943–1946* (New York: Bantam, 1981), 154. Gavin also wondered why actions of Allied naval forces were not coordinated with those of the 21st Army Group to deal with the problem and partly attributed the oversight to the remoteness of Eisenhower in his distant Granville headquarters. Ibid., 155, 223–24.

76. Operation Comet, which postulated capturing Nijmegen and Arnhem by starting 30 Corps from Antwerp on 7 September and the Airborne Corps dropping two or three airborne brigades that morning to get the bridges. Like most airborne operations after Normandy, it was cancelled. DD, 4 and 8 Sep 44.

77. Stacey, *Victory Campaign,* 310–16; and Cornelius Ryan, *A Bridge Too Far* (London: Book Club Associates, 1975), 74–76. Wesel had one less river to cross and, according to Alistair Horne, was also Montgomery's first choice, but the air barons vetoed Wesel on the grounds that concentrated flak fire from the Ruhr would make aircraft losses prohibitively high. Alistair Horne with David Montgomery, *Monty: The Lonely Leader, 1944– 1945* (New York: Harper Collins, 1994), 287. Lamb suggests Dempsey exerted less influence than Browning on Montgomery, which may well have been true after Goodwood, with the result that he impulsively chose Arnhem over Wesel. *Montgomery in Europe,* 214–16.

78. DD, 9 Sep 44.

79. Dempsey Papers, WO 285/29, letter Dempsey to Major L. F. Ellis, 18 June 1962.

80. DD, 10–13 Sep 44.

81. Ryan, *Bridge Too Far,* 81, 96–97, 118–20, 122.

82. It is now generally accepted that this catchphrase was never actually uttered by Browning. Horne, *Monty,* 287.

83. Hinsley, *British Intelligence,* 544–46; Lamb, *Montgomery in Europe,* 222–51; Geoffrey Perret, *There's a War to Be Won: The United States Army in World War II* (New York: Ballantine, 1991), 371–73; and DD, 17–28 Sep 44.

84. PRO, WO285/29, Dempsey to Maj. L. F. Ellis, 18 June 1962. Although he stated that he could not say how much responsibility for faulty planning lay with the Airborne Corps, Dempsey seems to have manifested more faith in Browning, with whom he had previously worked, than in Urquhart. PRO, WO285/29, Dempsey to Ellis, 28 June 1962.

85. PRO, WO285/29, Dempsey to Ellis, 18 June 1962 and Ellis to Dempsey, 20 June 1962. Dempsey also suggested that the 1st Airborne Division failed to appreciate the importance of reaching back to link up at Elst, where he would have liked to drop a parachute brigade had it not been for lack of airlift. Lewin, *Montgomery as Military Commander,* 307.

86. PRO, WO 285/29, Dempsey to Ellis, 7 July 1966. Urquhart's book *Arnhem* (London, 1958) likely rankled Dempsey.

87. Lewin, *Montgomery as Military Commander,* 306; Horne, *Monty,* 287; Lamb, *Montgomery in Europe,* 238, 247–48; and Gavin, *On to Berlin,* 165–66.

88. Although Dempsey on discussing the operation with Horrocks on 15 September noted that "coordination with Airborne Forces is going well, and the necessary commanders and staff officers have been here to make final arrangements." DD, 15 September 1944.

89. The commander of the 101st Division, Maj. Gen. Maxwell Taylor, appalled that the airborne plan did not allot him sufficient lift to attack the Zon bridge from both sides, appealed directly to Montgomery to overrule the decision. Brereton refused Montgomery's request on the grounds that it was too late to alter the plan in any respect, with the result that further delay occurred in the construction of a Bailey over the crossing at Zon. Lamb, *Montgomery in Europe,* 218, 220, 222, 226, 231, 246–47.

90. PRO, WO285/29, Dempsey to Ellis, 28 June 1962; Weigley, *Eisenhower's Lieutenants,* 318; Lewin, *Montgomery in Europe,* 306–7; Ryan, *Bridge Too Far,* 79–80, 85–106, 190. Lt. Col. John Frost, who commanded the battalion holding Arnhem bridge, later stated that the worst mistake was failure to give priority above all to the seizure of the Nijmegen road bridge on D-Day when resistance was less. Gavin could only spare one battalion for this task, however, as he had been told to secure Groesbeek Heights, where Browning's headquarters was later sited. Lamb, *Montgomery in Europe,* 243–47.

91. Horrocks, *Corps Commander,* 23.

92. DD, 18–23 September 1944.

93. PRO 70375, WO 285/24, Dempsey's Handwritten Speaking Notes for Address to Army Troops of Second Army, "Nijmegen."

94. Horrocks expressed the same sentiment to Bedell Smith. Smith replied that if he had his way Horrocks would be an army commander. DDE Library, Walter Bedell Smith Papers, Box 8, Horrocks to Smith, 21 September 1944 and Smith to Horrocks 3 October 1944.

95. Gavin, *On to Berlin,* 204. Gavin also wrote that if Eisenhower "had kept Patton halted on the Meuse, and given full logistic support to Hodges and Dempsey after the capture of Brussels, the operation in Holland could have been an overwhelming triumph." Ibid., 217. Gavin opposed Eisenhower's broad-front approach, preferring a single concentrated thrust, and charged that Eisenhower did not support Montgomery with adequate troops and resources. Tolerating Patton's attempt to make a main effort himself, a reconnaissance in force, ensured that both efforts failed. "I can't help but feel that historically this will never stand the test of accurate analysis without it looking unfavourable to General Eisenhower," stated Gavin. DDE Library, Columbia University Oral History Project, Oral History OH-184, Interview James M. Gavin by Ed Edwin, 20 January 1967. Weigley also argued that Market Garden could have succeeded. *Eisenhower's Lieutenants,* 317–18.

96. DD, 6–7 October 1944.

97. PRO 70519, WO 285/16 C-in-C Top Secret Note dated 7 October 1944.

98. MAP, Eisenhower to Montgomery, 13 October 1944. The Combined Chiefs of Staff had urged Eisenhower as far back as 12 September to make energetic efforts to open Antwerp. Noting that his report on Operation Market Garden presented intelligence about the Scheldt, but made no mention of Antwerp, they decided to send him a telegram drawing his attention to the importance of opening up northwest ports, particularly Antwerp and Rotterdam, before bad weather set in. While urging the neutralization, preferably by air attack, of the defence of the Scheldt resulting from the massing of German forces on the islands guarding the port of Antwerp, they also pointed to the advantages of a northern approach into Germany. Stacey, *Victory Campaign,* 312, 330–31; and Hinsley, *British Intelligence,* 541. Eisenhower's directive of 13 September nonetheless still referred to opening up Brest. Blumenson, *Breakout and Pursuit,* 346–47, 632–33.

99. Stacey, *Victory Campaign,* 316, 378–79, 387–91, 655–56; DD, 7–27 Oct 44; PRO 70519, WO 285/16, Dempsey verbal order notes to Comds 8, 12, and 30 Corps, 9 Oct 44; and Moulton, *Battle for Antwerp,* 119–21.

100. DD, 31 Oct-7 Dec 44 and 16 Dec 44–18 Jan 45; and Stacey, *Victory Campaign,* 428–29, 438, 455, 530.

101. Winston S. Churchill, *The Second World War: Triumph and Tragedy* (Boston: Houghton Mifflin, 1953), 455. The British now recognize this as more of a political war than a military one, observed Eisenhower. USAMHI, Chester B. Hansen Diary, 12 April 1945.

102. Alanbrooke, *War Diaries,* 657. Churchill told Brooke that the President had said Americans would only remain in Germany for two years after the end of the war, which had serious implications for the occupation of a possible resurgent Germany and defence against Russia. For this reason the British wanted to project as much strength as possible and have the French involved in the occupation. Brooke had also proposed as far back as 27 July 1944 that Germany be gradually built up and converted into an ally to meet the Russian threat. Alanbrooke, *War Diaries,* 575.

103. BAOR Battlefield Tour, Operation Plunder: Operations of 12 British Corps Crossing the River Rhine, on 23, 24 and 25 March 1945, Spectator's Edition (1947), 1, 7–18, 55, 77–78, 85, 91–92; and Lewin, *Montgomery in Europe,* 322. The Second Army calculated that a grand total of 3,411 guns, including 853 antitank and 1,038 antiaircraft guns and rocket projectors, supported its five corps. Stacey, *Victory Campaign,* 532–33. Dempsey thought highly of his staff and said so. PRO 70519, WO 285/16, GOC-in-C Talk to Main Army Headquarters 27 Nov 44.

104. DD, 12, 14, and 20 Feb 45. Montgomery insisted on having the XVIII US Airborne Corps rather than the 1st British Airborne Corps for reasons of superior signals communications and combat experience. Weigley, *Eisenhower's Lieutenants,* 647.

105. DD, 22–23, 25 and 27 February 1945; Stacey, *Victory Campaign,* 532–37; Weigley, *Eisenhower's Lieutenants,* 647–48. Horrocks's 30 Corps reverted to Dempsey's command on 8 March.

106. Lewin, *Montgomery as Military Commander,* 320–21, 331; Stacey, *Victory Campaign,* 530–34; Weigley, *Eisenhower's Lieutenants,* 640–41; and Lamb, *Montgomery in Europe,* 358–59.

107. DD, 2–24 March 1945.

108. The still dangerous 1st Parachute Army held the east bank to the Rhine between Emmerich and Kreveld and did not appear ready to throw in the towel.

109. DD, 27 March 1945; and PRO 70375, WO 285/24, Dempsey's Speaking Notes, "Preparations for Rhine to Baltic." Leaving Simpson out seemed to waste Ninth Army's accumulation of bridging equipment, the fine quality of which greatly impressed Dempsey. DD, 30 Apr 45.

110. Of this second occasion serving in battle under Dempsey, Ridgway recorded that he had "never had more satisfying professional service in combat, nor more agreeable personal relations" than with the British Second Army. DDE Library, Hodges Papers, Box 29, Headquarters XVIII Corps (Airborne), Summary of Operations the Elbe to the Baltic 27 April 1945 to 3 May 1945 dated 20 May 1945.

111. BAOR Plunder, 53–56; Lewin, *Montgomery as Military Commander,* 323, 333; Lamb, *Montgomery in Europe,* 360–64, 371–93; and Hamilton, *Monty: The Field Marshal,* 470–71, 479–500; Gavin, *On to Berlin,* 316–17; Weigley, *Eisenhower's Lieutenants,* 719–23; and MAP, Personal Diary Campaign in N.W. Europe 24 March 1945–28 April 1945. The assertion that the British had to be reminded about the need to beat the Russians into Denmark seems questionable but may be related to Churchill's fear that advocating turning aside to clear Denmark and the Hanseatic port of Lubeck would seriously weaken the British case for driving with maximum force on Berlin rather than Leipzig. DDE Papers, Principal File, Box 80, Eisenhower to Marshall, 27 April 1945; and Churchill, *Triumph and Tragedy,* 461, 515–16.

112. Alanbrooke, *War Diaries,* 702.

113. MAP, BLM 1/108, Brooke to Montgomery, 10 April 1945.

114. PRO 70423, WO 285/23 Personal Message from the C-in-C to Headquarters, Second Army by Field-Marshal B. L. Montgomery, June 1945 and PRO 70375, WO 285/24 Dempsey Speaking Notes to Services.

115. LHC, Selwyn Lloyd letter, *The Times,* 10 June 1969; and Lamb, *Montgomery in Europe,* 398. Seeing Dempsey at a surrender ceremony moved one British field officer to observe, "He is a most unassuming man." LHC, PP/MCR/292 Papers of Major N. Whitaker, Officer Commanding, Second Army Headquarters Defence Company, diary entry 12 May 45.

116. Hamilton, *Monty: The Field Marshal,* 678.

117. "The best decision of my life," he wrote. DDE Papers, Principal File, Box 34, Dempsey to Eisenhower, 29 December 1948.

118. LHC, LH1/587, The Rhine Crossing and Advance Across North West Germany.

119. LHC, LH1/230/26 B.H. Liddell Hart to Dempsey, 1 July 1952; and LH 1/230/27 Dempsey to Hart, 8 July 1952. Hart apparently forfeited forty shillings on a bet that Dempsey would be brought back as chief of the Imperial General Staff.

120. LHC, LH1/230/44, Dempsey to Liddell Hart, 23 December 1955.

121. LHC, LH1/230, Obituaries in *The Times, Telegraph, Daily Mail,* and *Daily Express,* 7 June 1969.

CHAPTER THREE
In the Shadow of Bradley: Gen. Courtney H. Hodges, First U.S. Army

1. Dwight D. Eisenhower (DDE) Library, Abilene, Kansas, Courtney Hicks Hodges Papers (HP), Box 20, Biography: Gen. Courtney Hicks Hodges.

2. HP, Box 25, William Walton, cabled draft of *Time* cover story on General Hodges, p. 2. Hodges, who had had drinks with Walton on 4 October 1944, apparently did not like the cabled version, which was considerably revised for publication. National Archives and Records Administration (NARA), Archives II, College Park, Maryland, Maj. William C. Sylvan Diary (SD), 4 and 24 October 1944. Late in the war, Maj. Chester B. Hansen recorded that Hodges looked slight and undistinguished next to Bradley, who was a tall, powerfully built man. U.S. Army Military History Institute (USAMHI) Archives, Chester B. Hansen Papers, War Diary (HD), 9 March 1945. Sylvan was Hodges's aide, and Hansen was Bradley's aide.

3. Marshall Library, Lexington, Virginia, George C. Marshall Papers (MP), Box 66, Folder 54, Eyes Only Message Marshall to Eisenhower, 28 December 1943. Hodges's G-2 also said Hodges was much like Bradley, describing him as a "tall [if 5'9" is tall], quiet infantryman, shy of publicity, unpretentious and a lover of hunting and fishing. He rarely raised his soft Georgia voice, but his blue eyes would at times flare fire." USAMHI, Col. Benjamin A. Dickson Papers, G-2 Journal Algiers to the Elbe. Bradley was six years younger than Hodges.

4. Bradley, *Soldier's Story*, 226. Bradley preferred Hodges over Patton. In his late eighties, Bradley stated that he "would not have included Patton in Overlord [as he] had shown in Sicily that he did not know how to run an army." Bradley and Blair, *General's Life*, 218–19, 222–23; Stephen T. Wishnevsky, *Courtney Hicks Hodges: From Private to Four-Star General in the United States Army* (Jefferson, NC: McFarland, 2006).

5. USAMHI, General Omar N. Bradley Papers, "I Remember" oral history, 1966 transcript of taped interview by Kitty Buhler, second wife of Bradley and Hollywood screenwriter/reporter.

6. D'Este, *Patton,* 468. Weigley, *Eisenhower's Lieutenants,* 84–85, 384, 602, 630–631.

7. Blumenson, *Patton Papers,* 367. West Point Archives, Original Patton Diary, 14 July 1944. Martin Blumenson, *The Battle of the Generals: The Untold Story of the Falaise Pocket—The Campaign That Should Have Won World War II* (New York: William Morrow, 1993), 241.

8. Williamson Murray and Allan R. Millett, *A War to be Won: Fighting the Second World War* (Cambridge: Belknap Press of Harvard University Press, 2000), 418. They and Carlo d'Este are also highly critical of the jealous, suspicious, unimaginative, and narrowminded Bradley, who, though virtually canonized by war correspondent Ernie Pyle as a plain spoken "soldier's general," was anything but; his soldiers hardly knew him well enough to identify with him. D'Este, *Patton,* 467.

9. Carlo D'Este, *Eisenhower: A Soldier's Life* (New York: Henry Holt, 2002), 627.

10. MacDonald, *Mighty Endeavor,* 354–55.

11. The description was apparently coined by Ernest Hemingway, then an accredited war correspondent. G. Patrick Murray, "Courtney Hodges: Modest Star of World War II," *American History Illustrated* VII, No. 9 (January 1973), 20; and Charles B. MacDonald, *The Battle of the Huertgen Forest* (Philadelphia: J.B. Lippincott, 1963), 4. Hemingway once reputedly referred to himself as "Old Ernie Hemorrhoid, the Poor Man's Pyle."

12. SD, 30 July 1944.

13. Hogan, *Command Post at War,* 121, 161–62, 229–30, 288. This is an absolutely outstanding work of military history.

14. Richard G. Stone, Jr., "Hodges, Courtney Hicks," in *Dictionary of American Military Biography,* eds. Roger J. Spiller, Joseph G Dawson III, and T. Harry Williams (Westport: Greenwood Press, 1984), II:482.

15. USAMHI, The Hodges Story File, "Reflections on General Courtney Hodges," Oral History Project 73–5 (1973), Interview of Col. Charles G. Patterson, First Army Chief of Anti-Aircraft Artillery, by Capt. G. Patrick Murray, p. 2.

16. HP, Box 3, Lt. Gen. Lesley J. McNair, Army Ground Forces, to Lt. Gen. Courtney H. Hodges, Third Army, 10 March 1943; Hodges to McNair, 8 April 1943; and Record of Important Telephone Call, Hodges to McNair, 4 June 1943. In his report on the 93rd Division stationed at Fort Huachuca, Hodges elaborated upon the limited ability of coloured junior officers and enlisted personnel, recommending that they focus more on their profession rather than the question of social equality.

17. HP, Box 1, Bibliographical Note and Biography Lt. Gen. Courtney H. Hodges; Box 3, Biography Courtney Hicks Hodges; Box 20, Biography: Gen. Courtney Hicks Hodges;

and Benjamin Franklin Miller, "A Forgotten Soldier: Courtney Hodges and the Second World War" (unpublished MA Thesis, Georgia Southern University, 1995), 1–21; Clayton R. Newell, "Hodges, Courtney H.," in *The D-Day Encyclopedia* (New York: Simon and Schuster, 1994), 296–97; and "Hodges, Courtney Hicks," in *Webster's American Military Biographies* (Springfield, Mass.: G. & C. Merriam, 1978), 178.

18. Biography Courtney Hicks Hodges; and Miller, "A Forgotten Soldier," 14–15. When Marshall, senior instructor with the Illinois National Guard, learned of his promotion to brigadier general, effective 1 October 1936, he asked whether Hodges would consider being detailed in his place with the headquarters of the 33rd Division in Chicago. HP, Box 3, Major E.N. Slappey to Lt. Colonel Courtney Hodges, 8 September 1936.

19. HP, Hodges to Maj. Gen. John L. DeWitt, Commandant, Army War College, Washington, 12 February 1938; and DeWitt to Hodges, 21 April 1938.

20. Eisenhower Library, DDE Collection, Pre-Presidential Papers: 1916–1952, Principal File, Box 57, Courtney Hodges Folder, Eisenhower to Hodges, 1 May 1940.

21. Marshall Library, F. C. Pogue interview with Hodges at San Antonio, 7 November 1957.

22. HP, Box 7, Subject: Carolina Maneuvers, November 1941, report to the Adjutant General, Washington, D.C. by Maj. Gen. Courtney H. Hodges, Chief of Infantry.

23. HP, Box 7, Report of a Visit to North African Theater of Operations, submitted by Hodges to Commanding General, Army Ground Forces, Washington, D.C.

24. According to D'Este, Hodges thought he was to take the Third Army to England in early 1944 and only found out otherwise on accidentally receiving a letter addressed to Patton as commanding general of the Third. *Patton,* 571–72.

25. Col. Robert S. Allen, *Lucky Forward: The History of Patton's Third U.S. Army* (New York: Vanguard, 1947), 12–14; and Charles M. Province, *Patton's Third Army: A Daily Combat Diary* (New York: Hippocrene, 1992), 11–13.

26. Eisenhower had earlier considered Hodges a candidate for army group command, possibly for reasons of seniority. DDE Papers, Principal File, Box 132, Messages 8781 and 8792 Eisenhower to Marshall, 29 December 1943.

27. This was after the "Knutsford Indident" of 25 April 1944, in which Patton created a furor by predicting in a speech that Britain and the U.S. were destined to rule the world after the war. DDE Papers, Principal File, Box 91, Message from Eisenhower to Marshall, 30 April 1944.

28. Hogan, *Command Post at War,* 27–28, 44; and SD, 11 June–31 July 1944.

29. The 1st, 2nd, 4th, 9th, 28th, 29th, and 30th Infantry and the 2nd and 3rd Armored. The 5th and 35th were earmarked to revert to the Third Army. SD, 1 August 1944.

30. Of initially 228 officers, 23 warrant officers, and 508 enlisted personnel (later slightly expanded).

31. Hogan, *Command Post at War,* 5, 26, 29–34, 298–99; and Miller, "A Forgotten Soldier," 28–29. The special staff sections provided tactical and technical advice, handled technical details, and coordinated their work with the rest of the staff. The most important of these were the artillery, engineer, signals, and supply. Hogan, *Command Post at War,* 34. On 18 July 1944 SHAEF raised civil affairs sections to army general staff status (G5). Hogan, *Command Post at War,* 103.

32. HD, 2 June 1944.

33. HD, 28 March 1945; and Hogan, *Command Post at War,* 24, 123–24, 288–91, 295.

34. Although "his clothes seemed to rumple when things went badly." Weigley, *Eisenhower's Lieutenants,* 297.

35. HD, 11–12 February 1945.

36. Hodges was apparently a light drinker who enjoyed wine with meals. His spirit preference was a Dubonnet cocktail (of bourbon, Dubonnet, vermouth, and a dash of bitters),
which he usually mixed himself. Miller, "A Forgotten Soldier," 32.

37. Miller, "A Forgotten Soldier," 31–33; and Hogan, *Command Post at War,* 28–35, 121–23,
288.

38. HD, 28 March 1945.

39. Miller, "A Forgotten Soldier," 31; Hogan, *Command Post at War,* 123, 289; and Bradley,
Soldier's Story, 360.

40. Only Patch, also from the Pacific, sought him out. According to Corlett, Patch traveled
from Italy to England and spent two days talking about his Anvil assault plans to Corlett.
USAMHI, Charles H. Corlett Papers, "One Man's Story, Some of it About War," MS by
Charles H. Corlett, 231–32, and "Cowboy Pete: The Autobiography of Major General
Charles H. Corlett," 246 (later published as *Cowboy Pete: An Autobiography of Major General
Charles H. Corlett,* ed. William Farrington [Santa Fe, NM: Sleeping Fox Publishers, 1974]).

41. Hogan, *Command Post at War,* 53–56, 91–94, 161; Weigley, *Eisenhower's Lieutenants,* 358;
Max Hastings, *Overlord,* 287; and Sylvan Diary, 19 July 1944. On 11 July Corlett was
bedridden with a kidney infection. Sylvan Diary, 11 July 1944.

42. Hogan, *Command Post at War,* 53, 104–5, 160–61, 292–93. Patch apparently thought
Collins too aggressive on Guadalcanal and the Marine Corps not aggressive enough.
William K. Wyant, *Sandy Patch: A Biography of Lt. Gen. Alexander M. Patch* (New York:
Praeger, 1991), 64.

43. Weigley, *Eisenhower's Lieutenants,* 431. Eisenhower and Bradley also suggested that Gerow
and Corlett were better bets for field army command than Simpson. MP, Eisenhower to
Marshall, 31 August 1944. Collins received command of a Normandy assault corps after
it became apparent that Maj. Gen. Lucian K. Truscott could not be released from the
Mediterranean theatre. MP, Eisenhower to Marshall, 29 January 1944. Collins was a 1917
West Point graduate; Corlett graduated in 1913. On U.S. corps commanders, see Berlin,
U.S. Army World War II Corps Commanders; and Winton, *Corps Commanders of the Bulge.*

44. USAMHI, "Reflections on General Courtney Hodges," Oral History Project 73–5,
Interview of J. Lawton Collins by Capt. G. Patrick Murray, 41.

45. Hogan, *Command Post at War,* 53, 122, 245, 253–54, 288, 293; Murray, "Courtney
Hodges," 17; Weigley, *Eisenhower's Lieutenants,* 602; Winton, *Corps Commanders of the
Bulge,* 31–35, 44–48, 353–55; and Stone, "Hodges," 484.

46. Normally Hodges received verbal orders from Bradley several days before the latter's
written version arrived, which allowed Hodges to give earlier guidance to his staff.
Hogan, *Command Post at War,* 135.

47. Hogan, *Command Post at War,* 122, 125, 293; and USAMHI, "Reflections on General
Courtney Hodges," Oral History Project 73–5, Interview of Lt. Gen. Charles E. Hart by
Capt. G. Patrick Murray, 42–43.

48. Significantly, Hodges had visited Dempsey's British Second Army's tactical headquarters
the day before (Montgomery was the first to introduce the concept of the small "Tac
HQ" in British Commonwealth armies). Hodges "Tac" initially contained 25 officers and
200 enlisted men. Sylvan Diary, 4–5 and 8 August 1944; and Hogan, *Command Post at
War,* 125–27.

49. MacDonald, *Battle of the Huertgen Forest,* 24; and Hogan, *Command Post at War,* 97–99,
192.

50. MP, Eisenhower Message Fwd 18341 to Marshall, 30 March 1945; and Weigley, *Eisenhower's Lieutenants,* 158, 172. According to Maj. Gen. John S. Wood, Patton had no part in
the breakthrough as Wood's 4th Armored Division was part of the First Army when it

advanced on Avranches. Wood further stated that Patton did not take charge until the 4th Armored reached Rennes on 1 August. LHC, Maj. Gen. J. F. C. Fuller Papers, IV/7, John S. Wood to Liddell Hart, 5 December 1948.

51. DDE Library, J. Lawton Collins Papers, Box 5, Operation Cobra, Chapter I: VII Corps Operations (24–31 Jul 44); Carafano, *After D-Day,* 13, 84, 94–95. Hodges spent the morning and afternoon of the 25 July looking for the body of Gen. Lesley J. McNair, who had been killed when U.S. bombers dropped short. Carafano, *After D-Day,* 116.

52. Miller, "A Forgotten Soldier," 28–29; Geoffrey Perret, *There's a War to Be Won,* 333–34; and d'Este, *Decision in Normandy,* 408–13. In its dash to Le Mans, the XV Corps covered seventy-two miles in five days. Eisenhower, *Bitter Woods,* 49.

53. Of 2nd Panzer and 1st, 2nd, and 116th SS Panzer Divisions.

54. The XV Corps consisted of the French 2nd Armored and 5th Armored Divisions with the 79th and 90th Infantry Divisions.

55. HP, Box 25, Operational History of the First United States Army in World War II, 9–10; D'Este, *Decision in Normandy,* 408–21; Hogan, *Command Post at War,* 128–30; Weigley, *Eisenhower's Lieutenants,* 202–3; Eisenhower, *Bitter Woods,* 50–55; Miller, "A Forgotten Soldier," 34–37; and Perret, *There's a War to Be Won,* 333–39.

56. The 90th Division under Maj. Gen. Raymond S. McLain and the 2nd French Armoured Division under the already legendary Maj. Gen. Jacques Philippe Leclerc (the *nom de guerre* adopted by Philippe Francois Marie de Hautecloque to protect his family when he first joined Free French forces in West Africa in 1940). They were reinforced by the 80th Division under Maj. Gen. Horace L. McBride. Haislip was a graduate of the French Army's *Ecole Superieure de Guerre.* Weigley, *Eisenhower's Lieutenants,* 201, 209–10.

57. Weigley, *Eisenhower's Lieutenants,* 208, 211–13; Hogan, *Command Post at War,* 131–32; and Blumenson, *Battle of the Generals,* 234–38. Bradley had ordered Patton to form a provisional corps headquarters to direct the three divisions when Haislip's XV Corps headed east. Patton sent his chief of staff, Maj. Gen. Hugh J. Gaffey, with four officers to do so. Gaffey ordered an attack for 1000 hours on 17 August and was in the process of working out details when Gerow arrived. Gerow had not been told of this arrangement and could not confirm his authority until midday on 17 August. He then postponed the attack until the next day to prepare his own plan and bring up his corps artillery. Clearly, Bradley had overestimated the time necessary for Gerow to take command. Hogan, *Command Post at War,* 132.

58. Operational History, 12; Hogan, *Command Post at War,* 131–32; Weigley, *Eisenhower's Lieutenants,* 239–43.

59. SD, 17–27 August 1944; and Weigley, *Eisenhower's Lieutenants,* 241–47. Dempsey personally called on Hodges on 22, 24, 25, and 27 August. Hodges visited Dempsey on 26 August. PRO 70473, WO 285/9, Dempsey Diary, 22, 24, 25, 26, 27 Aug 44.

60. Hogan, *Command Post at War,* 139; Weigley, *Eisenhower's Lieutenants,* 246–47, 262–63, 273–75; and Blumenson, *Battle of the Generals,* 256–58.

61. Patton made a longhand note in his diary that "The British radio, BBC, said this morning that Patton's Third Army had taken Paris. Poetic justice. It will be refuted, but no one will pay any attention." West Point Archives, Original Patton Diary, 24 August 1944.

62. The Americans would have preferred to bypass Paris, but de Gaulle wanted the city liberated from without rather than within by largely communist resistance forces that could have constituted a threat to his government.

63. SD, 21–25 August 1944; Hogan, *Command Post at War,* 138–39; Weigley, *Eisenhower's Lieutenants,* 201, 249–52; Miller, "A Forgotten Soldier," 42–44; Eisenhower, *Bitter Woods,* 68–70. In the matter of the military governorship of Paris the First Army G-5 (civil affairs)

recommended recognizing the French authority, while Kean backed Gerow. Hogan, *Command Post at War*, 138–39.

64. SD, 6 September 1944; DDE Library, Collins Papers, War Diary, 2–6 Sep 44 and HP, Box 25, Memorandum Corlett to Hodges, 6 September 1944; Hogan, *Command Post at War*, 139–43, 149; and Weigley, *Eisenhower's Lieutenants*, 273–77.

65. Weigley, *Eisenhower's Lieutenants*, 276–77, 281–82, 297–99;and Hogan, *Command Post at War*, 143–48.

66. Hogan, *Command Post at War*, 147–49, 157; MacDonald, *Battle of the Huertgen Forest*, 27–86; Weigley, *Eisenhower's Lieutenants*, 301–4, 320–25; 365–66; and SD, 11–26 September 1944.

67. Hogan, *Command Post at War*, 160–62; and Weigley, *Eisenhower's Lieutenants*, 357.

68. USAMHI, Corlett Papers, Box 1, "One Man's Story," 253, 277–78, 282; and "Cowboy Pete," 270, 296–97.

69. DDE Papers, Principal File, Bradley to Eisenhower, Relief of Major General Charles H. Corlett, 19 October 1944; Hogan, *Command Post at War*, 165–66, 169–71; Weigley, *Eisenhower's Lieutenants*, 350, 356–64, 755; "One Man's Story," 282–83; and "Cowboy Pete," 301–2. According to Corlett, he was forward at one of his divisional command posts when his chief of staff came up and handed him a slip of typewriter paper, an order from First Army, which said he had been relieved of command. When he called Hodges, the latter said, "Oh, I had intended to get down to see you before that order arrived." "One Man's Story," 279–80; and "Cowboy Pete," 279.

70. Hogan, *Command Post at War*, 171, 181–84; and Weigley, *Eisenhower's Lieutenants*, 383–84.

71. SD, 1 November 1944; Hogan, *Command Post at War*, 184–85; and Weigley, *Eisenhower's Lieutenants*, 365–66.

72. SD, 1–8 November 1944; MacDonald, *Battle of the Huertgen Forest*, 88–120; Hogan, *Command Post at War*, 185; and Weigely, *Eisenhower's Lieutenants*, 366–68.

73. SD, 7 November 1944.

74. Weigley, *Eisenhower's Lieutenants*, 413–14; MacDonald, *Battle of the Huertgen Forest*, 121–87; and Hogan, *Command Post at War*, 161–62, 186.

75. Weigley, *Eisenhower's Lieutenants*, 381–83, 412–13; and Hogan, *Command Post at War*, 185–86.

76. Weigley, *Eisenhower's Lieutenants*, 414–17; and MacDonald, *Battle of the Huertgen Forest*, 137–48.

77. SD, 16 November 1944

78. SD, 17 November 1944.

79. SD, 20 November 1944.

80. Weigley, *Eisenhower's Lieutenants*, 417.

81. SD, 21 and 23 November 1944.

82. SD, 27 and 28 November 1944; DDE Papers, Principal File, Box 80, Eisenhower to Marshall, 5 December 1944; and MacDonald, *Battle of the Huertgen Forest*, 173–87. Maj. Gen. John W. O'Daniel also lost an only son.

83. Weigley, *Eisenhower's Lieutenants*, 366, 368, 418–23; and MacDonald, *Battle of the Huertgen Forest*, 58, 86, 120, 172, 180, 187, 196–204; and MacDonald, *Mighty Endeavor*, 355–56; and Hogan, *Command Post at War*, 187–90.

84. SD, 10 December 1944.

85. There were seven Roer dams, three located on tributaries rather than the Roer itself. The most important were the concrete Urfttalsperre, on the Urft River between Gemund and Ruhrberg, and the earthern, concrete-core Schwammenauel on the Roer roughly three kilometers southeast of Schmidt. The Urfttalsperre enabled the Germans

to increase the amount of water behind the Schwammenauel downstream. These two dams controlled the Roer and provided hydroelectric power; the other dams mainly regulated the flow of the river. Weigley, *Eisenhower's Lieutenants,* 434.

86. MacDonald, *Mighty Endeavor,* 352–55.

87. Hogan, *Command Post at War,* 286–87. On 2 October, four days before the 9th Division attacked into the Huertgen, the division G2 warned that regulating dam discharge could produce destructive flood waves and that demolition could flood the Roer Valley as far as the Meuse and into Holland. First Army dismissed this report. Weigley, *Eisenhower's Lieutenants,* 434.

88. Weigley, *Eisenhower's Lieutenants,* 365, 413, 432; and MacDonald, *Battle of the Huertgen Forest,* 141–42, 197–204.

89. MacDonald, *Battle of the Huertgen Forest,* 205. Gavin also maintained that it was battle that should not have been fought. He further charged that higher commanders had fought the battle on maps, and battles are not won on maps. Gavin, *On to Berlin,* 298–99.

90. SD, 27 November and 8 December.

91. Hogan, *Command Post at War,* 192–93; MacDonald, *Battle of the Huertgen Forest,* 193–94, 201; Weigley, *Eisenhower's Lieutenants,* 434–35; and SD, 13–14 December 1944.

92. Hodges later wrote that while lack of strength in defending the Ardennes was risky, it was also necessary to take such a risk in order to ensure the success of the Allied offensive along the Aachen-Cologne axis and in the Saar region. The Ardennes area was furthermore not considered particularly vulnerable. HP, Box 9, Hodges's "Short Study of the Ardennes Campaign" forwarded under cover letter Hodges to the Command and Staff School, Military Review, Fort Leavenworth , Kansas, 13 August 1946.

93. SD, 16 December 1944.

94. Hogan, *Command Post at War,* 205, 209, 211–12; Weigley, *Eisenhower's Lieutenants,* 448, 461, 465, 471; and Charles B. Macdonald, *A Time for Trumpets: The Untold Story of the Battle of the Bulge* (New York: William Morrow, 1985), 180, 261.

95. Hogan, *Command Post at War,* 194, 212. According to the Sylvan diary entry for 17 December, General Simpson, General Quesada, and several others gathered in Hodges's office, but the only entrance to his office was through Kean's.

96. Gavin was the acting commander of the XVIII Airborne Corps, the SHAEF reserve, placed under command of the First Army from 17 December. While the 101st Division deployed to Bastogne, the 82nd went to Werbomont west of St. Vith. The XVIII Corps eventually occupied a sector between the V and VIII Corps, taking command of the 30th Infantry and 7th Armored divisions in addition to the 82nd.

97. Gavin, *On to Berlin,* 227–28.

98. Hogan, *Command Post at War,* 212, 222.

99. SD, 30 December 1944; HP, "Short Study of the Ardennes Campaign"; Hogan, *Command Post at War,* 205, 213–15; and Bradley, *Soldier's Story,* 475, 478.

100. The command echelon went to Spa, the supply echelon to Micheroux, six miles east of Liege. Hogan, *Command Post at War,* 215.

101. First developed by Montgomery as "J" service, which listened in to wireless reports from British commanders of all grades all over the battlefield to enable him to ascertain the true situation within his own forces. "J" service complemented "Y" service, which monitored enemy wireless traffic in low and medium grade cyphers to build up the enemy picture. Phantom units were originally formed in 1939 to pinpoint forward troop locations for the RAF and though absorbed by "J" service gave their name to its operation. Phantom detachments intercepted divisional and brigade wireless traffic and sent it back immediately to army headquarters. Stephen Brooks, ed., *Montgomery and Eighth Army*

(The Bodley Head: Army Records Society, 1991), 308, 383, 388–89; and David French, *Raising Churchill's Army: The British Army and the War against Germany, 1919–1945* (Oxford: University Press, 2001), 253. Patton's 6th Cavalry Group performed a similar function for him. The group, which encompassed a number of reconnaissance platoons formed into troops under two squadron commands, ranged far and wide and bypassed usual channels of communications to keep the army commander in touch with scattered units and subordinates. Weigley, *Eisenhower's Lieutenants,* 242.

102. Hogan, *Command Post at War,* 217, 229–30, 286; and Sylvan Diary, 18 December 1944. A SHAEF visitor to Chaudfontaine later recalled the staff barely knew their own location much less the location of friendly or enemy troops. Hogan, *Command Post at War,* 221–22.

103. As even admitted by Hodges. HP, Box 20, Operational Highlights of the First Army Speech for General Courtney H. Hodges, 17. See also Eisenhower, *Bitter Woods,* 464–65.

104. The 30 Corps then included the Guards Armoured Division and the 43rd, 51st, and 53rd divisions with three armored brigades.

105. Hogan, *Command Post at War,* 219, 221–22, 225–27; SD, 26 December 1944; and MP, Box 1, Folder 7, Lt. Gen. W. B. Smith to Lt. Gen. Thomas Handy, War Department, Washington, 28 December 1944.

106. SD, 20 December 1944.

107. DDE Principal File, Box 83, Message M-384 Montgomery to Eisenhower, 20 December 1944. Montgomery transferred the 51st (Highland) Division and 6th Guards Tank Brigade to Ninth Army to replace the 2nd US Armored Division, which along with the 84th and later 75th Infantry Divisions concentrated under Collins. DDE Principal File, Box 83, Message M-385 Montgomery to Eisenhower, 21 December 1944. The 3rd Armored Division was also earmarked for Collins. Eisenhower, *Bitter Woods,* 351.

108. "I was placed practically under Monty's command . . . he superseded Hodges so far as my corps was concerned. The moves that were made up there were good, sound moves" said Collins. HP, "Reflections of General Courtney Hodges," Interview J. Lawton Collins by Capt. G. Patrick Murray, 45.

109. MAP, Personal Diary, 20 December 1944.

110. "Hodges is the quiet reticent type and does not appear as aggressive as he really is," Eisenhower wrote, with the qualifier that "*unless he becomes exhausted* [author's italics] he will always wage a good fight." He concluded by asking Montgomery to inform him instantly "if any change needs to be made on United States side." DDE Principal File, Box 83, Message S71982, Eisenhower to Montgomery, 22 December 1944; Hogan, *Command Post at War,* 220–21; Weigley, *Eisenhower's Lieutenants,* 538; and Pogue, *Marshall,* 509–10. On 22 December, Montgomery signaled Eisenhower that "Hodges was a bit shaken early on and needed moral support and was very tired. He is doing better now and I see him and Simpson every day." DDE Principal File, Box 83, Message M-389 Montgomery to Eisenhower, 22 December 1944.

111. DDE Library, Oral History OH-397, Interview with Brig. Gen. Thomas J. Betts, by Dr. Maclyn Burg, 16 August 1976.

112. Both Collins and Ridgway considered Montgomery's liaison officers more intrusive than informative, but others saw the Phantom and liaison officer system as a tremendously valuable asset. USAMHI, George I. Forsythe Papers, Oral History Project 74–1, Interview with Lt. Gen. (Retired) George I. Forsythe by Lt. Col. Frank L. Henry (1974), 191–92.

113. Hogan, *Command Post at War,* 219–20. Gavin observed that the First Army's staff obviously liked Montgomery and respected his professionalism. In contrast, they deeply resented Patton getting all the publicity. *On to Berlin,* 270–71.

114. Sylvan Diary, 22–23 December 1944.

115. MAP, Memo DMO/BM/705, DMO to CIGS, 31 December 1944.

116. Hogan, *Command Post at War,* 224; Eisenhower, *Bitter Woods,* 393–403.

117. On the Eastern Front, reserves concentrating in the area of cornerston. were invariably exposed to the full weight of Russian guns, which didn't even have move to bring fire to bear, and were battered to a pulp. The more prudent course was to start flanking attacks against Russian bulges much farther back, where German flanks were less exposed to Red Army counterattack and were outside the range of less mobile Russian artillery. Maj. Gen. F. W. von Mellenthin, *Panzer Battles,* trans. H. Betzler (Norman, OK: University of Oklahoma Press, 1983), 300.

118. Hogan, *Command Post at War,* 227. Eisenhower, like Montgomery, recognized that the Germans could have retained mobile forces expressly to deal with Allied counterattacks against the salient. DDE Principal File, Box, 83, draft letter Eisenhower to Montgomery, 29 December 1944 (probably not sent). See also Winton, Corps *Commanders of the Bulge,* 203–4.

119. The power of every attack diminishes until a point is reached at which forces remaining are only capable of maintaining a defense. This is the culminating point, the correct judgment of which is as critical as it is difficult to gauge. This is simply because beyond the culminating point the scale turns, often producing a violent reverse much greater than that of the original attack.

120. Hogan, *Command Post at War,* 223–27; and Winton, *Corps Commanders of the Bulge,* 216–35, 340–45.

121. SD, 27–31 December 1944 and 2–5 January 1945; DDE Principal File, Box 83, Message M423 Montgomery to Eisenhower, 31 December 1944; and Hogan, *Command Post at War,* 227.

122. Collins stated that Montgomery used to come to the VII Corps every other day and that Ridgway would come over and join him. Collins couldn't remember Hodges visiting. USAMHI, "Reflections on General Courtney Hodges," Oral History Project 73-5, Interview of J. Lawton Collins by Capt. G. Patrick Murray, pp. 48, 53.

123. On 15 January, Major General Huebner took over command of the V Corps from Gerow, who assumed command of the U.S. Fifteenth Army.

124. SD, 6–23 January 1945; Hogan, *Command Post at War,* 227–28; Weigley, *Eisenhower's Lieutenants,* 562; and Eisenhower, *Bitter Woods,* 429–30.

125. Ridgway's powerful personality resulted in his staff holding him in such awe that during his frequent absences from his headquarters, they tended to wait for his return to make even routine decisions. Eisenhower, *Bitter Woods,* 298. On Gerow and Ridgway, see also Winton, *Corps Commanders of the Bulge,* 112–36, 172–86, 250–68, 282–84, 310.

126. With the VII Corps' attack, the Germans began to withdraw; on 9 January, Hitler himself ordered the Sixth Panzer Army to withdraw.

127. Hogan, *Command Post at War,* 229–30; and Eisenhower, *Bitter Woods,* 412–30.

128. Eisenhower, *Bitter Woods,* 462; and Weigley, *Eisenhower's Lieutenants,* 523.

129. Hogan, *Command Post at War,* 289.

130. This was done to support the U.S. Ninth Army's attack across the Roer (planned for 9 February) by removing the menace of the dams discharging destructive flooding on US lines. On 4 February, the Urfttalsperre dam fell to the 9th Infantry Division of Huebner's V Corps, but the drive by the 78th Division on Schmidt and the Schwammenauel bogged down. Hodges attributed this to poor management, and with an aching back exacerbating his irritation, he ordered Huebner to the 78th Division to take personal charge of the situation. He also pushed the 9th Division through the 78th to accelerate the attack. By the time the Schwammenauel was finally captured on 9 February, however,

the Germans had jammed open the sluiceways, which produced a controlled flooding and sustained overflowing of the Roer that held up the Ninth US Army's crossing until 23 February. Hogan, *Command Post at War,* 244–45; Weigley, *Eisenhower's Lieutenants,* 599–603; and SD, 4–9 and 21 February 1945.

131. Hogan, *Command Post at War,* 249–52; SD, 3–8 March 1945; and Weigley, *Eisenhower's Lieutenants,* 617–19, 626–31.

132. SD, 12 March 1945. "Millikin's biggest problem," in Hogan's view, "was that he was not J. Lawton Collins, the man the First Army headquarters openly wished had received the windfall." Hogan, *Command Post at War,* 254.

133. It was Weigley's assessment that Hodges was "as sure to turn in a pinch to his strongest corps commander as he was to hector and often remove less favoured subordinates." *Eisenhower's Lieutenants,* 632. Millikin later commanded a division, never really receiving the credit he deserved for his performance in the Bulge. Winton, *Corps Commanders of the Bulge,* 359, 459–60.

134. By this time, three other bridges had been pushed across the river and three ferries were running. Operational History, 24; Hogan, *Command Post at War,* 253–54; Weigley, *Eisenhower's Lieutenants,* 631–32; and SD, 8–17 March 1945. Hodges lack of confidence in Millikin may have been related to old army interbranch and personal feuds. Patton professed delight in sending Millikin to the First Army, adding that "Millikin has done a good job, but I don't like him and never have." West Point Archives, Original Patton Diary, 10 February 1945.

135. Operational History, 26; SD, 19 March–18 April 1945; Hogan, *Command Post at War,* 255–62; and Weigley, *Eisenhower's Lieutenants,* 671–80.

136. Eisenhower, *Bitter Woods,* 443–45; Hogan, *Command Post at War,* 260–62, 270; and SD, 5–27 April.

137. Weigley, *Eisenhower's Lieutenants,* 758–59. Bradley ranked the 6th Army Group's commander, Jacob L. Devers, twenty-first, just behind Corlett.

138. MP, Eisenhower to Marshall, 26 March 1945. On the War Department list of generals of the army and generals dated 1 September 1945 Hodges rated relative number 12, Patton 11, Bradley 9, Devers 5, Eisenhower 3 (after Macarthur 2), and Marshall 1. DDE Library, Maj. Reith M. Briggs Papers, War Department, Office of the Adjutant General, List of Officers Holding Permanent or Temporary Grade of General of the Army, General, Lieutenant General, Major General, or Brigadier General, Including Retired Officers on Active Duty, 1 September 1945.

139. MP, Eisenhower to Marshall, 12 March 1945. On 1 February 1945, Eisenhower rated Patton fourth on a list that showed Gerow eighth, Collins ninth, Patch tenth, Hodges eleventh, and Simpson twelfth. Weigley, *Eisenhower's Lieutenants,* 758.

140. MP, Message Fwd 18341, Eisenhower to Marshall, 30 March 1945.

141. "With respect to Four Star appointments," Eisenhower had signaled Marshall, "the selection of Hodges and Patton should not create resentment here because of length of time these two officers have been bearing the burden of army command and because of their fine records. MP, Eyes Only Message, Eisenhower to Marshall, 9 April 1945.

142. Bradley, *Soldier's Story,* 226. In his late eighties, however, Bradley recalled to Clay Blair, "I had always liked and admired Courtney Hodges, but now, as he became my subordinate, I began to fret privately. Courtney seemed indecisive and overly conservative. I hoped that my veteran First Army staff—Bill Kean in particular—would keep a fire under him." Bradley and Blair, *General's Life,* 218.

143. D'Este, *Patton,* 468. By mid-July, Sylvan recorded, five general officers and countless regimental officers had been relieved. SD, 13 July 1944.

144. Patton himself admitted "that those low bastards, the Germans, gave me my first bloody nose when they compelled us to abandon our attack on Fort Driant in the Metz area." Library of Congress, Doolittle Papers, Box 16, Reproduced from the Collections of the Manuscript Division, demi-official letter from Lt. Gen. G. S. Patton Jr. to Lt. Gen. J. H. Doolittle, Headquarters Eighth Air Force, 19 October 1944.

145. HP, Box 21, Courtney H. Hodges, "Remagen: The Bridge that Changed the War."

146. DDE Principal File, Box 57, Eisenhower to Hodges, 5 February 1948; Hodges to Eisenhower, 26 February 1948; and Eisenhower to Hodges, 2 March 1948.

CHAPTER FOUR
In the Shadow of Britannia: General William H. Simpson, Ninth U.S. Army

1. The U.S. Fifteenth Army deployed after the Ninth Army, but followed the advance of the front line armies, occupying, organizing, and governing the Rheinprovinz, Saarland, Pfalz, and a portion of Hessen. Commanded by Lt. Gen. Leonard T. Gerow from 15 January 1945, the Fifteenth also prepared plans for the Bremen Enclave and the Berlin District. It additionally received, trained, and equipped newly arrived formations and rehabilitated, re-equipped, and reinforced various units that had suffered heavy losses in the Battle of the Bulge. On 7–8 May the Fifteenth Army received the surrender of German forces in the Lorient–St. Nazaire pocket, which it had contained since April 1945. USMA West Point Archives, Gen. Omar N. Bradley Papers, History of the Fifteenth United States Army 21 August 1944 to 11 July 1945 (Fort Bliss, Texas: Learning Resources Center, US Army Sergeants Major Academy), Foreword; Weigley, *Eisenhower's Lieutenants,* 668, 678; and Bradley, *A Soldier's Story,* 529.

2. SP, Box biography, Speeches Folder. Simpson was also present at the Hammersmith St. Paul's School when Montgomery used what Simpson called a splendid terrain model to deliver a masterly briefing to the king, Churchill, Eisenhower, and other senior Allied military leaders on the Normandy invasion.

3. Roger J. Spiller, Joseph G. Dawson III, and T. Harry Williams (eds.), *Dictionary of American Military Biography,* 3 vols. (Westport: Greenwood Press, 1984).

4. Thomas R. Stone, "1630 Comes Early on the Roer," *Military Affairs* 53 (October 1973): 3–21, and "General William Hood Simpson: Unsung Commander of US Ninth Army," *Parameters* XI, No.2 (June 1981): 44–45; and Thomas R. Stone, "He Had the Guts to Say No: A Military Biography of General William Hood Simpson" (unpublished Ph.D. thesis, Rice University, 1974). See also chapter 4 in J. D. Morelock, *Generals of the Ardennes: American Leadership in the Battle of the Bulge* (Honolulu: University Press of the Pacific, 2003), 153–227.

5. Maj. Gen. E. N. Harmon with Milton MacKaye and William Ross MacKaye, *Combat Commander: Autobiography of a Soldier* (Englewood Cliffs, NJ: Prentice-Hall, 1970), 211–12, 216. When Harmon paid a farewell call to Hodges after a battle, Hodges chastised him for not complying with a recent order to wear green patches under his shoulder insignia, a distinguishing mark reserved for officers with commands as opposed to those without. Harmon inwardly fumed at the absurdity of scolding a general who had just successfully concluded a crucial combat assignment for a trivial irregularity in his uniform. He further offered that Hodges did little without the advice and support of Collins and unnecessarily destroyed three gallant divisions in the Huertegn Forest battle. Harmon also said he was more pleased to receive a congratulatory sentence penned by Montgomery on a formal letter of commendation from Hodges than the letter itself. Ibid, 207–8, 225, 247–49.

6. USAMHI, William H. Simpson Papers (SP), Wolfgang Saxon, Obituary, *New York Times,* Sunday, 17 August 1980; War Correspondent Frank Conniff Interview with General Simpson; and Robert H. Shoemaker, "Simpson . . . Soldier's Soldier."

7. SP, *Life,* 12 March 1945. At first glance the head seemed "so cadaverously lean that you think of it as a friendly skull." Ibid.

8. Allen, *Lucky Forward,* 159. Although apparently startled, Simpson joined in the laugh.

9. USAMHI, Oral History Interview of Simpson by Lt. Col. Thomas R. Stone, 22 April 1971.

10. USAMHI, Alvan C. Gillem Papers, Simpson to Gillem, 24 August 1954.

11. Interview of Simpson by Lt. Col. Thomas R. Stone, 22 April 1971.

12. Some say this is where Simpson received the nickname "Big Simp," but equally likely, he received it in his regiment to distinguish him from another Simpson called "Little Simp." Simpson's other nicknames were "Texas Bill" and the "Doughboy General" appellation of the U.S. press. SP, Wolfgang Saxon, Obituary, *New York Times,* Sunday, 17 August 1980; Bradley and Blair, *General's Life,* 340; and Stone, "Guts," 3. Hodges joined West Point with Simpson, but failed out after a year.

13. SP, Biography of General William Hood Simpson; Trevor N. Dupuy, Curt Johnson, and David L. Bongard, *The Harper Encyclopedia of Military Biography* (Edison, NJ: Castle Books, 1995), 687; *Webster's American Military Biographies* (Springfield, MA: G. & C. Merriam, 1978), 391–92; and SP, extract copy Current Biography 1945, Simpson William H(ood) entry.

14. Ibid.

15. Stone, "Guts," 1–27.

16. Marshall Library, Lexington, Virginia, Marshall Papers (MP), Box 67, Folder 12, Eisenhower to Marshall, 31 August 1944.

17. Weigley, *Eisenhower's Lieutenants,* 431. Although in July Marshall changed the policy to allow theater commanders to select battle experienced commanders over those proposed on Washington lists. MP, Box 19, Folder 4, Marshall to Maj. Gen. Emil F. Reinhardt, CG, IX Corps, Fort McPherson, Georgia, 6 July, 1944.

18. Stone, "Guts," 109, 130 (fn. 13) (quoting letter Eisenhower to Marshall, 1 October 1944). Eisenhower further suggested that Marshall have "Simpson's commission as a lieutenant general regularized by the Senate." In mid-January 1945 when Marshall asked him if he still felt that Simpson should be a lieutenant general, Eisenhower said yes. Stone, "Unsung," 50. Significantly, on 1 December 1944, Bradley ranked Simpson sixteenth on a proposed promotion list of thirty-two general officers, ahead of Corlett (20) and Devers (21), but behind Middleton (14) and Patch (15) and well behind Collins (7), Gerow (8), Patton (6), and Hodges (3). In his list of 1 February 1945, Eisenhower rated his chief of staff third, Patton fourth, Truscott sixth, Doolittle seventh, Gerow eighth, Collins ninth, Patch tenth, Hodges eleventh, and Simpson twelfth. Weigley, *Eisenhower's Lieutenants,* 758–59.

19. SP, Biography of General William Hood Simpson and "Ninth Army's Operations in the European Theater" written by Simpson; and Stone, "Guts," 32–43.

20. USAMHI, SP, "Ninth Army's Operations in the European Theater"; *Conquer: The Story of the Ninth Army 1944–1945* (Washington: Infantry Journal Press, 1947), 21–40; and Stone, "Guts," 47–81. Weigley harshly condemned the Brittany campaign and siege of Brest for diverting troops and supplies from operations beyond the Seine. Brittany sucked in some 80,000 troops, substantial air resources, and a large quantity of supplies. Bradley on 10 September even gave Middleton priority in supply over formations advancing on Germany. In the end, the VIII Corps suffered 9,831 casualties and ended up with 25,000 tons of surplus ammunition. Weigley, *Eisenhower's Lieutenants,* 283–86. See also A. Harding Ganz, "Questionable Objective: The Brittany Ports, 1944" in *The Journal of Military History* 1 (January 1995): 77–95.

21. *Conquer,* 30, 78–79, 152–53; DDE Library, Collection of 20th Century Military Records, 1918–50, Series I—USAF Historical Studies, Box 9, Line diagram XXIX TAC dated 30 November 1944; and Donald J. Porter, "Fully combat tested by war's end, the XXIX TAC was a unit 'born and bred' in the combat zone," *Military History* 2 (June 1995): 20–24. "Conquer" was the code name for the U.S. Ninth Army.
22. Gillem Papers, Gillem to Simpson, 19 January 1945. On 31 December 1944 the 29th Division asked if it were possible to get air support parties down to regiments for "air-ground talking," pointing out that this would require two or three parties per division. SP, Personal Calendar, Headquarters Diary, Notes on Two Conferences Between General Simpson, General Gillem, General Gerhardt, and General Keating, 31 December 1944.
23. MP, Box 67, Folder 13, Eisenhower to Marshall, 18 September 1944.
24. Simpson placed his command post in Arlon because Luxembourg City was too far forward for an army headquarters. Both he and his chief of staff said it was mistake for Bradley to put his 12th Army Group headquarters there prior to the Battle of the Bulge. USAMHI, James E. Moore Papers, Senior Officers Oral History Program, Project 84–19, Interview of Gen. James E. Moore by Lt. Col. Larry F. Paul, 1984; and Marshall Library, Interview of Lt. Gen. William H. Simpson by F. C. Pogue, 12 April 1952.
25. Stone, "Guts," 57, 88, 102–13; SP, "Ninth Army's Operations in the European Theater"; *Conquer,* 52–69; and Bradley, *Soldier's Story,* 435–37.
26. Gillem Papers, Simpson to Gillem, 24 August 1954.
27. USAMHI, Gillem Papers; and Berlin, *U.S. Army World War II Corps Commanders,* 3, 8, 10, 11, 13.
28. Cited as "an outstanding example of joint Anglo-American effort" by Simpson. SP, Personal File, letter Simpson to Dempsey 28 November 1944. See also Horrocks, *Corps Commander,* 148–56.
29. Stone, "Guts," 120–128; USAMHI, SP, "Ninth Army's Operations in the European Theater"; *Conquer,* 71–113; and Weigley, *Eisenhower's Lieutenants,* 381–82, 423–31.
30. Bradley, *Soldier's Story,* 422, 528.
31. Col. Charles P. Bixel served as G-2 from 22 May 1944 until 22 February 1945; his replacement, Col. Harold D. Kehm, served from 3 March to 10 October 1945. Col. Armistead D. Mead Jr. was G-3, and Col. Roy V. Rickard, G-4. Moore was later promoted to major general in the position of chief of staff.
32. SP, General Simpson's Contemplated Biography, The Army Commander and his Staff under covering letter from Col. James P. Abbot to Simpson, 12 May 1963; Senior Officers Oral History Program, Project 84-19, Interview of Gen. James E. Moore by Lt. Col. Larry F. Paul, 1984; and Stone, "Unsung," 46.
33. Perret, *There's a War to Be Won,* 569 (n. 32). Moore had been Simpson's chief of staff in the 35th and 30th Divisions and the XII Corps.
34. Col. Daniel H. Hundley was G-1. When G5 was added to the general staff, Col. Carl A. Kraege assumed the appointment of assistant chief of staff, G5 (for civil affairs in liberated territory and military government in enemy territory). *Conquer,* 19, 107.
35. Horrocks considered the morning conference, at which each staff branch presented a status report, to be a complete waste of valuable time as he usually took no more than ten minutes to conduct an update with his chief of staff before heading forward to the front. Horrocks, *Corps Commander,* 152.
36. Abbott, The Army Commander and his Staff; and Stone, "Unsung," 45, 48.
37. D'Este, *Patton,* 596.
38. MAP, Deposit 5, Personal Diary, Montgomery to Maj. Gen. Frank "Simbo" Simpson, Director of Military Operations, War Office, 12 December 1944. In fundamentals Patton

and Montgomery "were curiously very much alike" noted General Charles H. Bonesteel, a former US planner with the 21st Army Group. USAMHI, Senior Officers Oral History Program, Project 73–2, Interview Gen. Charles H. Bonesteel III by Lt. Col. Robert St. Louis.

39. NAC, RG 24, Vol. 13,711, Minutes of Conference Held by General Montgomery, HQ 21 Army Group, 0930 hrs 13 Jun 44. Collins also adhered to this approach: "I first blocked out the attack . . . personally, on the map" with the chief of staff, G3, G2, G4, and artillery and engineer advisors present. After thrashing out the corps plan in central discussion, Collins then called in the division commanders and he, not the G3, "personally outlined" the plan. "I personally did it," he stressed, adding that, "this is where we sometimes make a mistake in my judgment because the commander has to do this, not some staff officer." After a final thrashing out and appropriate adjustments to general satisfaction, he issued a field order based upon the agreed plan. USAMHI, Senior Officers Oral History Program, Project 72–1, Interview with Gen. J. Lawton Collins by Lt. Col. Charles C. Sperow, 1972.

40. Allen, *Lucky Forward,* 287. Bradley later stated that Simpson's staff was in some respects superior to others. Bradley and Blair, *General's Life,* 395.

41. SP, Simpson to Lt. Gen. James E. Moore, 4 April 1957.

42. The soft-spoken Simpson later offered that Patton was courteous and polite as a cadet, but little by little "picked up swearing, obscenity as marks of distinction" Marshall Library, Oral History, Interview of Lt. Gen. William H. Simpson by F. C. Pogue, 12 April 1952.

43. Stone, "Unsung," 46–49; and Abbott, Staff Officers-General and Special.

44. Marshall Library, Oral History Interview with Lt. Gen. William H. Simpson by F. C. Pogue, 12 April 1952.

45. SP, "Ninth Army's Operations in the European Theater" and Notes on Two Conferences between General Simpson, General Gillem, General Gerhardt, and General Keating, 31 December 1944; and *Conquer,* 117–29.

46. The river rose five feet and widened from 400 to 1200 yards, with flow velocity increasing to 10.5 feet per second, well over the maximum for the installation of floating bridges. Conquer, 162; and DDE Papers, Principal File, Box 80, Eisenhower to Marshall, 20 February 1945.

47. SP, "Ninth Army's Operations in the European Theater" and "An Account of the Ninth US Army Operation 'Grenade'" (delayed by the Bulge); MAP, Personal Diary, 20, 22 December 1944, 17–18 January and 4, 7 February 1945; *Conquer,* 133–66; and MacDonald, *Mighty Endeavor,* 352–55, 417–19.

48. Interview with Simpson by F.C. Pogue, 12 April 1952. Liddell Hart Centre for Military Archives (LHC), King's College, London, Alanbooke Papers, 14/3 DMO to CIGS 3 December 1944.

49. Interview with Simpson by F.C. Pogue, 12 April 1952; and DDE Library, Interview with Gen. William H. Simpson by Dr. Maclyyn P. Burg, 5 November 1972.

50. SP, Interview with Simpson by Lt. Col. Thomas R. Stone, 22 April 1971; and "Ninth Army's Operations in the European Theater." In the Stone interview Simpson remarked that Dempsey was "a very able army commander" and that Monty's system of employing ten to twelve bright young liaison officers to seek out and pass information was not a bad one. He further added that Eisenhower visited him two or three times but that he saw little of Bradley.

51. Moore described Montgomery as "a feisty little somebody and he pulled things together down there for First Army during the Battle of the Bulge." USAMHI, Interview Gen. James E. Moore by Lt. Col. Larry F. Paul, 1984.

52. *Conquer,* 160; and Stone, "Guts," 157.

53. Stone, "Unsung," 47.

54. Harry Yeide, *The Longest Battle: September 1944 to February 1945, From Aachen to the Roer and Across* (St Paul, MN: Zenith, 2005), 104. The first Allied supply convoy reached Antwerp on 28 November 1944, but intense V1 and V2 attacks that delivered a total of 1,214 rockets from mid-October restricted the offloading of ammunition. Moulton, *Battle for Antwerp,* 230–31.

55. MAP, Personal Diary, 13 November 1944.

56. SP, Personal Calendar, 19 January 1945.

57. Under Brig. Gen. John F. Uncle, the 34th Field Artillery Brigade consisted of three battalions of 240-millimeter howitzers and one battalion of 8-inch guns. *Conquer,* 167.

58. *Conquer,* 75, 91, 154. A "unit of fire" of artillery ammunition was a specific number of rounds for each type of weapon, based on average daily expenditure in typical operations. For the European theater this was roughly 125 rounds for the 105-millimeter howitzer, 75 rounds for the 155-millimeter howitzer and 4.5-inch gun, 50 rounds for the 155-millimeter gun and 8-inch howitzer, 25 rounds for the 240-millimeter howitzer, and 35 rounds for the 8-inch gun (not including certain additions for special types of fuzes and ammunition). Thus, on the first day of Grenade, the XIII Corps' allocation was 375 rounds per 105-millimeter howitzer. *Conquer,* 28. By way of comparison, the Canadians dumped 750 rounds per gun for Totalize. Moore admitted that the British "took care of their people better" in respect of ammunition supply. Interview Gen. James E. Moore by Lt. Col. Larry F. Paul, 1984. In October 1944, Patton decided that ammunition would be listed in rounds per gun (rpg) per day (the British system) and not in units of fire, which meant nothing to anyone. West Point Archives, Original Patton Diary, 9 October 1944.

59. Weigley, *Eisenhower's Lieutenants,* 607–8.

60. SP, "Notes Written in General Simpson's Hand" attached to copy of "Ninth Army's Operations in the European Theater." Simpson always aimed to have a quarter or a third of his force in reserve. Patton boasted that he only ever retained a platoon in reserve.

61. The entry recorded in Simpson's personal calendar for Monday 15 January reads: "The FM tossed a bombshell ... the Ninth was to carry the ball for the western front drive—be the Main Effort, while the First Army would assume a holding mission on our south and after the breakthru [sic], protect the Ninth's south flank. That 'protect the Ninth's flank' would be the greatest and most satisfying crack at the Grand Old Armie possible! How all here would love to see that in print!" SP, Personal Calendar, HQ Diary, 15 january 1945. Moore later stated that the First Army G3 said the northerly thrust of the Ninth Army in Grenade would never work. USAMHI, Senior Officers Oral History Program, Project 84–19, Interview of Gen. James E. Moore by Lt. Col. Larry F. Paul, 1984

62. SP, "Ninth Army's Operations in the European Theater"; Lt. Gen. William H. Simpson, "Rehearsal for the Rhine: An Account of the Ninth United Sates Army Operation 'Grenade,'" *Military Review* XXV (1945): 20–28; Stone, "Guts," 134–67; Weigley, *Eisenhower's Lieutenants,* 607; and Whitaker and Whitaker, *Rhineland,* 77–79. Nugent apparently disliked Quesada.

63. Montgomery visited Ninth US Army at 1500 hours on 21 February and recorded: "Bill Simpson could not decide whether to launch 'GRENADE'; it was a very fine day, the country was drying fast, the river had fallen, the engineers could do bridging, and the weather forecast was good. So I decided for him, and ordered 'GRENADE' to be launched at 0330 hrs on 23 February." MAP, Personal Diary, 21 February 1945. Simpson had previously agonized over postponing the planned 10 February start date for Grenade as Veritable had started on 8 February. Stone, "Guts," 158–63.

64. SP, "Ninth Army's Operations in the European Theater"; Lieutenant General William H. Simpson, "Rehearsal for the Rhine: An Account of the Ninth United Sates Army Operation 'Grenade,'" *Military Review* XXV (1945): 20–28; *Conquer,* 169–91; Weigley, *Eisenhower's Lieutenants,* 606, 609–14; and Whitaker and Whitaker, *Rhineland,* 174–91, 244–55.

65. SP, Folder, Ninth Army in Europe Papers; Comments on Recent Operations (Lessons learned); and "Rehearsal for the Rhine." Simpson's thorough planning and detailed staff work very much resembled the Montgomery approach.

66. *Conquer,* 114.

67. Stacey, *Victory Campaign,* 522.

68. Williams, *Long Left Flank,* 244–51. As Crerar wrote, "We have drawn in all, or portions of, eleven enemy divisions, including four of the Para variety, and have captured 12,000 of them to date. Simpson's task , which commenced yesterday, should be notably lightened and the enemy's problems very importantly increased." NAC, CP, Crerar to Lt. Gen. Richard McCreery, GOC-in-C, Eighth Army, 24 February 1945.

69. "Veritable is drawing most of the immediately available reserves up north," wrote Montgomery, which is "excellent and exactly what we want." DDE Library, DDE Principal File, Box 83, Message M555 Montgomery to Eisenhower, 12 Feb 45. See also Bradley and Blair, *General's Life,* 599; MacDonald, *Mighty Endeavor,* 420–25; and Hamilton, *Monty: The Field Marshal,* 374–76, 386–90, 395–96, 402–6.

70. PRO 70473, CAB 106/1064, Crerar Diary, Notes on Conference held between C-in-C 21 Army Group—GOC-in-C First Canadian Army at TAC HQ 21 Army Group, 1200–1300 hrs 16 Jan 45.

71. PRO 70473, CAB 106/1064, Crerar Diary, Notes on Conference held by C-in-C 21 Army Group at his Tac HQ 1115 hrs 4 February 1945; MacDonald, *Mighty Endeavor,* 424–25; Weigley, *Eisenhower's Lieutenants,* 615, 639–40.

72. SP, Interview Lt. Gen. William H. Simpson by F. C. Pogue, 12 April 1952. The involvement of two armies not surprisingly produced, in Simpson's words, one of the knottiest problems we had to solve. Inevitably, squabbles arose over road movement as each army vied to feed troops rapidly forward over limited routes and bridges. The vital bridge at Wesel proved a particular bone of contention as Ninth Army forces had been promised a five-hour credit, but ended up waiting for the seemingly infinite passage of Second Army elements, which so angered Simpson that he thought his forward flow was intentionally being blocked by the British. In response to his protests, Montgomery on 31 March assigned the Ninth Army control of the bridge, with the British Second Army retaining crossing rights for five hours each day. SP, Personal Calendar, 27, 29, and 31 March 1945.

73. MP, Box 67, Folder 21, Eisenhower to Marshall 26 March 1945. In certain situations, Eisenhower added, Patton "has no equal, but by and large, it would be difficult indeed to choose between him, Hodges and Simpson for Army command." Days earlier, Eisenhower had told Marshall, "I believe that our successful Army commanders should eventually be promoted to four star rank, but I would consider it unwise at this time to imply a comparison to the discredit of Hodges, Patch, and Simpson by making Patton on a separate list ahead of them." MP, Box 67, Folder 20, Eisenhower to Marshall, 12 March 1945.

74. SP, "Ninth Army's Operations in the European Theater"; *Conquer,* 213–68; and Weigley, *Eisenhower's Lieutenants,* 644–51. The 2,070 guns deployed by Ninth Army in *Plunder* included tank, antitank, and antiaircraft weapons over and above 624 artillery pieces of 105-millimeter or larger size. Stacey, *Victory Campaign,* 533. One suspects that this was also the case in Grenade. For actual Ninth Army ammunition expenditures see *Conquer,* 389–91.

75. SP, "Ninth Army's Operations in the European Theater" and memorandum "Crossings of the Elbe"; and *Conquer,* 289–304. Gillem later stated that he was 48 miles from Berlin on 12 April, the day Roosevelt died, and had advance parties east of the Elbe. He said he could have been in Berlin, a day and a half march away, before the Russians as there was no German resistance. USAMHI, Gillem Papers, Interview of Gillem by Eugene Miller (1972), 43.

76. Eisenhower had said that, "Clearly, BERLIN is the main prize. . . . There is no doubt whatsoever, in my mind, that we should concentrate all our energies and resources on a rapid thrust to Berlin. Our strategy, however, will have to be coordinated with that of the Russians, so we must also consider alternate objectives." Imperial War Museum, Montgomery of Alamein Papers (MAP), GCT 370–31/Plans Eisenhower to Montgomery, 15 September 1944; and DDE Library, Jacob L. Devers Papers, Eisenhower to Devers, 15 September 1944.

77. DDE Papers, Principal File, Box 83, Message M562 Montgomery to Eisenhower, 27 March 1945; MAP, Montgomery to "Simbo" Simpson, 8–4–45; MacDonald, *Mighty Endeavor,* 477; Weigley, *Eisenhower's Lieutenants,* 681–87; and Hamilton, *Monty: The Field Marshal,* 439–48. Brooke noted in his diary on 3 April 1945 that Eisenhower's deputy, Air Marshal Sir Arthur Tedder, explained to him "that Ike was forced to take immediate action with Stalin as Monty had issued a directive Ike did not agree with!" Brooke recorded that he "was astonished that Ike found it necessary to call in Stalin in order to control Monty!" Alanbrooke, *War Diaries,* 680–81. Eisenhower later said that Berlin had become nothing but a geographical location. DDE Papers, Principal File, Box 83, Message FWD 18389 Eisenhower to Montgomery, 31 March 1945.

78. SP, Folder 1, Simpson to The Editor, *New York Times Book Review,* 30 April 1966. Simpson wrote this letter to rebut inaccuracies in S. L. A. Marshall's book review, "Berlin, April, 1945," *New York Times Book Review,* 71 (27 March 1966), which dismissed assertions in John Toland, *The Last 100 Days* (New York: Random House, 1966), and Cornelius Ryan, *The Last Battle* (New York: Simon and Schuster, 1966), that Simpson could have captured Berlin had Eisenhower not stopped him. What probably galled Simpson the most was Marshall's claim that "General Simpson's statement of how his troops stood when the halt was called is categorically wrong." Both Toland and Ryan urged Simpson to write the rebuttal to S. L. A. Marshall in the *New York Times.* Toland added that some German generals had secretly agreed to let U.S. forces through so that their German forces could go fight the Reds. SP, John Toland to Simpson, 12 March 1966; and Cornelius Ryan to Simpson, 12 March 1966.

79. In his estimation, leading elements of the 2nd Armored Division could have reached the outskirts of Berlin by darkness on 17 April and elements of the XIII Corps by darkness on 19 April or earlier. Gillem Papers, "Situation of the Ninth US Army on the Elbe River on 15 April 1945" by W.H. Simpson, 29 March 1945.

80. SP, Folder 1, Maj. Gen. Armistead D. Mead to Simpson 4 May 1966; and Simpson to The Editor, *New York Times Book Review.*

81. SP, Folder 1, Colonel Barry F. Phillips to Simpson 27 May 1966; Gen. I. D. White to Simpson 15 March 1966; and Simpson to The Editor, *New York Times Book Review.*

82. Weigley, *Eisenhower's Lieutenants,* 697–99.

83. Donald E. Shepardson, "The Fall of Berlin and the Rise of a Myth," in *The Journal of Military History* 1 (January 1998): 135–53; Essame, *Battle for Germany,* 198; and Weinberg, *World at Arms,* 824–30.

84. Shepardson's "Fall of Berlin" article relies heavily upon S. L. A. Marshall's book review and makes no mention of Simpson's letter to the editor rebuttal.

85. SP, "Ninth Army's Operations in the European Theater."
86. NAC, Crerar Papers, Amon G. Carter, Publisher, *Fort Worth Star-Telegram,* to Crerar, 2 July 1945.
87. SP, Personal File, Simpson to Dempsey, 1 May 1946; and *Conquer,* 361–64. The Ninth Army had a life span of sixteen months, nineteen days. *Conquer,* 364.
88. SP, Special Order No.153 under covering letter Maj. Gen. John A. Klein, Adjutant General, to Simpson, 4 August 1954. In October 1945 Simpson had appeared fourth on a list headed by Patch for permanent promotion to brigadier general. Hodges ranked second on a list of ten for permanent promotion to major general. MP, Box 67, Folder 29, Marshall to Eisenhower, 4 October 1945.
89. Dupuy et al., *Harper Encyclopedia of Military Biography,* 687; *Webster's American Military Biographies,* 391–92; SP, Wolfgang Saxon, Obituary, *New York Times,* 17 August 1980; and Stone, "Unsung," 52 (n. 40).

CHAPTER FIVE
In the Shadow of Patton: Lt. Gen. Alexander M. Patch Jr., U.S. Seventh Army

1. Terrence Poulos, *Extreme War: The Military Book Club's Encyclopedia of the Biggest, Fastest, Bloodiest, and Best in Warfare* (Garden City, NY: The Military Book Club, 2004), 367–88.
2. Macdonald, *Mighty Endeavor,* 407.
3. Perret, *There's a War to Be Won,* 232. Wyant, *Sandy Patch.* Lt. Col. William K. Wyant Jr. was Patch's general staff secretary. West Point Archives, Patch Papers, Box 6, Roster of HQ Personnel.
4. Weigley, *Eisenhower's Lieutenants,* 758–59. When Bradley rated generals at Eisenhower's request on 1 December 1944, Patch ranked fifteenth, just ahead of Simpson at sixteenth, but behind Middleton at fourteenth, Kean at twelfth, Collins at seventh, Patton at sixth, Truscott at fifth, Quesada at fourth, and Hodges at third.
5. Marshall Library, Marshal Papers (MP), Eisenhower to Marshall, 26 March 1945. Eisenhower had been impressed by Simpson's performance during Grenade.
6. MP, Box 67, Folder 29, Marshall to Eisenhower, 4 October 1945. Hodges who was on a separate list for promotion to the permanent grade of major general ranked second, just ahead of Devers.
7. MP, Box 67, Folder 12, Eisenhower to Marshall, 31 August 1944
8. MP, Box 66, Folder 54, Eisenhower to Marshall, 17 December 1943; Dwight David Eisenhower (DDE) Library, Abilene, Kansas, DDE Papers, Principal File, Box 132, Message W8550 Eisenhower to Marshall 25 Dec 43 and Jacob L. Devers Papers, Marshall to Devers, 28 December 1943; Pogue, *George C. Marshall: Organizer of Victory, 1943–1945,* 373–76; Bradley and Blair, *General's Life,* 217; and Clarke and Smith, *Riviera to the Rhine,* 29–30, 574–76.
9. Devers Papers, Reel 2, Box 1, Devers to Marshall, 1 July 1944; and Wayne Michael Dzwonchyk, "General Jacob L. Devers and the First French Army" (unpublished MA thesis, University of Delaware, 1975), 10, 17–20. In earlier discussions regarding senior appointments, Marshall had proposed Devers for army group command with Bradley and Hodges under him. Pogue, *George C. Marshall: Organizer of Victory, 1943–1945,* 374. Devers got on extremely well with Wilson, whom he considered an outstanding soldier. United States Army Military History Institute (USAMHI) Carlisle, Pennsylvania, Devers Diary, 9 September 1944.
10. DDE Library, Maj. Ruth M. Briggs Papers, List of Officers Holding Permanent or Temporary Grade of General of the Army, General, Lieutenant General, Major General, or Brigadier General, Including Retired Officers on Active Duty, 1 September 1945. Eisen-

hower was not happy about Marshall's promotion of Devers. Bradley and Blair, *General's Life,* 404.

11. Devers Papers, Reel 2, Box 1, Biographical Sketch of Maj. Gen. Jacob L. Devers, Chief of the Armored Force; and Reel 4, Box 1, Biographical Material: Lt. Gen. Jacob L. Devers, Headquarters Sixth Army Group, Public Relations Section; and "Devers, Jacob Loucks" in *Webster's American Military Biographies* (Springfield, MA: G&C Merriam, 1978), 100.

12. Capt. Harry C. Butcher, *My Three Years with Eisenhower* (New York: Simon and Schuster, 1946), 379–80.

13. West Point Archives, Original Patton Diary, 12 February 1944. When Patton recorded Eisenhower's comment in his diary, he added, "I rather concur, but some others are not over .32 caliber themselves."

14. Patton Diary, 21 September 1944. Patton Diary, 5 February 1945.

15. Bradley and Blair, *General's Life,* 210; and Perret, *There's a War to Be Won,* 382, 564. Bedell Smith later told Forrest Pogue that neither Eisenhower nor he had any confidence in Devers, though he was probably better than they gave him credit for being. USAMHI, Interview of Gen. Walter B. Smith by F. C. Pogue, 13 May 1947; and DDE Papers, Principal File, Box 109, WBS note to Eisenhower, 13 January 1945.

16. MP, Box 63, Marshall to Devers, 6 May 1940.

17. Devers Papers, Brig. Gen. Reuben E. Jenkins to President, The General Board, US Forces, European Theater, 30 October 1945. This report outlined the operation of the 6th Army Group headquarters, which was modeled on the British 15th Army Group that once ran efficiently with as few as eighty-five officers before it became bloated like the 12th Army Group headquarters. Jenkins was Devers's highly capable G3 whose absolutely brilliant analytical staff papers can still be read with profit. See also Weigley, *Eisenhower's Lieutenants,* 183, 345.

18. And he later wrote an article indicating as much. Gen. Jacob L. Devers, "Major Problems of a Theater Commander in Combined Operations," *Military Review* 27 (October 1947), 3–15.

19. Devers Papers, Marianne Clay, *York Daily Record,* 25 September 1987. Devers gave his papers to the Historical Society of York County, Pennsylvania, his home and place of birth. Ironically, the DDE Library also holds nine reels of Devers Papers on microfilm.

20. Like Dempsey, Devers apparently vowed not to write a book, whereas Bradley, Patton, and Eisenhower all did. As this work was being prepared for publication, David P. Colley's *Decision at Strasbourg: Ike's Strategic Mistake to Halt the Sixth Army Group at the Rhine in 1944* (Annapolis, MD: Naval Institute Press, 2008) appeared. It presents a long-overdue and strong defense of Devers.

21. Devers Papers, Reel 1, Box 1, Patch to Devers, 1 June 1945.

22. West Point Archives, Patch Papers, War Department Biography, up to date as of 22 November 1945 and West Point Assembly obituary; and Wyant, *Sandy Patch,* 13–30.

23. Wyant, *Sandy Patch,* 31–44.

24. Wyant, *Sandy Patch,* 45–69, 213; and Perret, *There's a War to Be Won,* 55, 232–35.

25. Wyant, *Sandy Patch,* 13, 25, 40, 58, 63, 70–89, 214.

26. Report on Operations: The Seventh United States Army in France and Germany 1944–1945, 3 vols. (Heidelberg: Aloys Graf, 1946), I:1–3.

27. DDE Library, Oral History Interview of Gen. Mark W. Clark by John Luter, 4 January 1970; Clarke and Smith, *Riviera to the Rhine,* 30–31; Pogue, *George C. Marshall: Organizer of Victory, 1943–1945,* 373–76; and Weigley, *Eisenhower's Lieutenants,* 221–22.

28. MP, Box 66, Folder 54, Eisenhower to Marshall, 17 December 1943 and Message Marshall to Eisenhower, 28 December 1943; DDE Papers, Principal File, Box 132, Message

R-8213 Marshall to Eisenhower, 17 Jan 44; and Pogue, *George C. Marshall: Organizer of Victory, 1943–1945*, 376–77.

29. Perret, *There's a War to Be Won*, 349. Smith, who described Patch as "nervous, tense, and brave," was a close friend. USAMHI, Interview of Devers by F. C. Pogue and Interview of Gen. Walter B. Smith by F. C. Pogue, 13 May 1947.

30. Wyant, *Sandy Patch*, 89; Devers Papers, Devers to Marshall, 20 June 1944 and Patch to Devers, 1 June 1945. Devers later said that he selected Patch. DDE Library, Oral History Interview of Gen. Jacob Devers by Dr. Maclyn P. Burg, 2 July 1975, 179–80.

31. Devers Papers, Devers to Marshall, 20 June 1944.

32. Lt. Col. G. W. L. Nicholson, *Official History of the Canadian Army in the Second World War, Volume II, The Canadians in Italy, 1943–1945* (Ottawa: Queen's Printer, 1956), 181–83 (hereafter cited as Nicholson, *Canadians in Italy*); Clarke and Smith, *Riviera to the Rhine*, 5–7; Alan F. Wilt, *The French Riviera Campaign of August 1944* (Carbondale: Southern Illinois University Press, 1981), 1–5; and Pogue, *George C. Marshall: Organizer of Victory, 1943–1945*, 195, 199, 417, 650.

33. Clarke and Smith, *Riviera to the Rhine*, 7–11; Devers Papers, Reel 2, Box 1, Marshall to Devers, 27 January 1944; and Graham and Bidwell, *Coalitions, Politicians, and Generals*, 171–74, 180–81.

34. Although, as pointed out by General Vorshilov, the Russian chief military adviser at Tehran, "Stalin did not insist on an operation against the south of France." Wilt, *French Riviera Campaign*, 19. Clearly, Stalin was interested primarily in Overlord.

35. Clarke and Smith, *Riviera to the Rhine*, 11–12; Wilt, *French Riviera Campaign*, 1–13; Nicholson, *Canadians in Italy*, 180–83, 387.

36. Clarke and Smith, *Riviera to the Rhine*, 13–16.

37. Devers Papers, Reel 22, Box 1, Marshall to Devers, 27 January 1944 and Devers to Marshall, 1 July 1944, 9 August 1944, and 21 August 1944; MP, Box 63, Folder 52, Marshall to Devers, 24 September 1943; and USAMHI, Devers Diary, 20–21 August 1944.

38. Graham and Bidwell, *Coalitions Politicians, and Generals*, 5, 174–96; and Pogue, *George C. Marshall: Organizer of Victory, 1943–1945*, 191, 195, 199. It is hard to imagine that Marshall did not know that no Americans, only French and British officers, were included in the signing of the 1918 armistice agreement. David R. Woodward, *Trial by Friendship: Anglo-American Relations, 1917–1918* (Lexington, KY: The University Press of Kentucky, 1993), 219.

39. In fact, Anvil was too far away to contribute logistically to the Normandy battle. The great Channel storm of 19 June, which destroyed the American Mulberry harbor off Omaha, did not turn out to be the disaster anticipated since the Americans ultimately moved more supplies directly across the beaches than they could have through the Mulberry. Cherbourg fell on 27 June but was not mopped up until 1 July, after which it took another month to open the port to Allied shipping. When Eisenhower said that he needed ports on 19 August, he was looking to Brittany, especially Brest, the investiture of which on 25 August coincided with his decision to pursue beyond the Seine. Optimistic hopes of attaining Channel ports and even Rotterdam and Antwerp, however, caused SHAEF on 3 September to abandon plans to use the ports of Lorient, Quiberon Bay, St. Nazaire, and Nantes. By 5 September, Eisenhower's eyes were firmly fixed on opening the ports of Le Havre and Antwerp as the Allies advanced. On 14 September, SHAEF decided not to use Brest, which was thoroughly demolished when taken on 20 September. When Eisenhower turned his back on the Brittany ports, he unbalanced his forces logistically, a situation exacerbated by mismanagement in his Communications Zone. It is true that southern ports, controlled by the Mediterranean theater until November, han-

dled over a quarter of Allied supplies by September and over a third of tonnage during October and November, but most of this supply went to the 6th Army Group. The logistical benefit of Anvil thus seems to have been an afterthought for SHAEF. John A. English, "Cinderella Campaign: The Genesis and Conduct of First Canadian Army Operations Leading to the Opening of the Scheldt Estuary," in *World War II in Europe: The Final Year,* ed. Charles F. Brower (New York: St. Martin's Press, 1998), 183–86, 202; and Wilt, *French Riviera Campaign,* 167–71.

40. Clarke and Smith, *Riviera to the Rhine,* 17–21; Wilt, *French Riviera Campaign,* 17–20, 46–60; and Pogue, *George C. Marshall: Organizer of Victory, 1943–1945,* 335–41, 409–20.

41. The XII Tactical Air Command eventually came under the First Tactical Air Force, commanded by Maj. Gen. Ralph Royce, which accorded the 6th Army Group its own coordinating air headquarters. This headquarters also controlled the First French Air Corps eventually paired with the First French Army. Weigley, *Eisenhower's Lieutenants,* 345; and DDE Papers, Principal File, Box 80, Eisenhower to Marshall, 31 August 1944. In February 1945, Brig. Gen. Glenn O. Barcus replaced Saville and remained in command until he returned to the U.S. in August 1946. Barcus had previously commanded the 64th Fighter Wing in Naples, Italy, from April 1944. Wyant, *Sandy Patch,* 179, 184.

42. White was eventually promoted to major general and all his operations (G) staff to full colonel. West Point, Patch Papers, Roster of Personnel as of 27 April 1945.

43. Patch also retained an aide, Capt. G. Gordon Bartlett Jr., who spoke fluent French. Wyant, *Sandy Patch,* 174; and Clarke and Smith, *Riviera to the Rhine,* 216–17.

44. Wyant, Sandy Patch, 82, 90–91, 139, 183–85.

45. Some said Patch resembled the actor Gary Cooper, but when the actress Mary Martin saw him on a beach in wet shorts, she supposedly exclaimed, "Good Lord, its Mahatma Ghandi!" Wyant, *Sandy Patch,* 86. See also Wilt, *French Riviera Campaign,* 23.

46. After the war Mrs. Patch was apparently concerned that Patch was drinking excessively with Quinn and put a stop to it. Wyant, *Sandy Patch,* 210. He correctly thought it a mistaken idea of many junior officers that being a good scout and sympathizing with the hardships the men must undergo was an indication of good leadership. An officer who asks his men to drink with them, Patch wrote, will find them quick to respond, but the next day in the field or garrison he will also learn that they are equally quick to take advantage of that proffered friendship. Maj. Gen. Alexander M. Patch, "Some Thoughts on Leadership," *Military Review* XXII (December, 1943).

47. Wyant, *Sandy Patch,* 2–4, 5, 17, 59, 82–85, 90–91, 137, 139; and *Time,* 28 August 1944, 22–24. In some trench foot cases, it was found that men had not removed their boots for three to four days or more. Devers Papers, Memorandum Devers to Patch, 27 November 1944.

48. Devers Papers, Reel 2, Box 1, Devers to Marshall, 22 March 1944; and MP, Box 63, Folder 57, Devers to Marshall, 13 June 1944.

49. Clarke and Smith, *Riviera to the Rhine,* 42–45.

50. Wilt, *French Riviera Campaign,* 2, 64–71, 87; Wyant, *Sandy Patch,* 105–9; Clarke and Smith, *Riviera to the Rhine,* 42–45, 92.

51. Clarke and Smith, *Riviera to the Rhine,* 32–34, 45.

52. Truscott had participated in the Dieppe Raid, led the 60th Infantry Regiment in an amphibious assault in Morocco, and commanded the 3rd Infantry Division in the Sicily landing. Born in 1885, he graduated from the Oklahoma Normal School in 1911 and the Command and General Staff School in 1936. He did not attend the War College. He had been slated to command an assault corps in the Normandy landing, but on his posting to the Mediterranean, Collins took his place. MP, Box 67, Eisenhower to Marshall, 5 December 1943, 29 January 1944, and 9 February 1944. (For some reason, neither Patch

nor Patton wanted Collins. USAMHI, Interview of Gen. Walter B. Smith by F. C. Pogue, 13 May 1947.) Had Truscott been available at the time of the "Knutsford Incident" of April 1944, it is likely that Eisenhower would have given him command of the Third Army before Patton. DDE Papers, Principal File, Box 91, Message S-50965, Eisenhower to Marshall, 30 April 1944. Eisenhower had told Marshall that he thought Lucas would command a combat corps most successfully. MP, Box 66, Folder 53, Eisenhower to Marshall, 24 August 1943.

53. In Devers's view the SSF had "reached the limit of its usefulness and should be organized into a special Ranger battalion, releasing Canadians" as replacements for their army. Devers Dairy, 25 January 1944.

54. Clarke and Smith, *Riviera to the Rhine,* 76–125; Wilt, *French Riviera Campaign,* 88–109; and MacDonald, *Mighty Endeavor,* 321–22.

55. Truscott had stated before the landing that he did not like the arrangement whereby CC1 had to revert to de Lattre on D+3 in condition to fight. He wanted no restrictions and said he preferred a combat command from the U.S. 1st Armored. Truscott Papers, Truscott to Patch, 21 July 1944; and Devers Papers, Devers to Patch, 23 November 1944.

56. The Germans had no intention of counterattacking, but were instead attempting to buy time for their withdrawal up the Rhone.

57. Clarke and Smith, *Riveria to the Rhine,* 141–70, 194–95.

58. Clarke and Smith, *Riveria to the Rhine,* 126–43, 194. Devers Diary, 30 August 1944. Wilson did not think much of Mark Clark. Devers Papers, Reel 1, Box 1, Devers to Maj. Gen. Thomas Handy, Operations Division, War Department, General Staff, Washington, 9 September 1944.

59. Clarke and Smith, *Riveria to the Rhine,* 171–78.

60. Truscott Papers, Box 12, Folder 7, Truscott to Patch, 2 September 1944.

61. Clarke and Smith, *Riveria to the Rhine,* 181–83, 195, 213–15.

62. Ibid., 186–95, 223–24.

63. Devers Diary, 4–18 September 1944.

64. Truscott Papers, Truscott to Patch, 15 September 1944.

65. In a telephone call of 16 September he nonetheless frankly told Truscott that his letter was ill-advised and less than credible. Truscott Papers, Telephone Conversation Between General Patch and General Truscott, 1830, 16 September 1944.

66. Clarke and Smith, *Riveria to the Rhine,* 224–32. According to Douglas Porch, Eisenhower ran out of ideas after Market Garden and chose simply to push forward on a broad front to seize ground from the Germans rather than seeking to destroy them by striking through vulnerable points like the Belfort Gap to turn the Vosges from the south. Douglas Porch, *The Path to Victory: The Mediterranean Theater in World War II* (New York: Farrar, Straus and Giroux, 2004), 600.

67. Clarke and Smith, *Riveria to the Rhine,* 226, 231–54; and Weigley, *Eisenhower's Lieutenants,* 345–46. "If Jake Devers gets the XV Corps," Patton angrily remarked to Bradley, "I hope his plan goes sour." When the transfer was officially announced, he wrote in his diary, *"May God rot his guts."* Clarke and Smith, *Riveria to the Rhine,* 254; and West Point Archives, Original Patton Diary, 22 and 28 September 1944. Devers saw Patton for a few minutes on 21 September and noted in his diary that "he seemed subdued and not too friendly. For this I am sorry." Devers Diary, 21 September 1944.

68. Clarke and Smith, *Riveria to the Rhine,* 256–70; Weigley, *Eisenhower's Lieutenants,* 343–47, 383–97, 402–3.

69. Bradley and Blair, *General's Life,* 396–97; Perret, *There's a War to Be Won,* 415; and Max Hastings, *Armageddon: The Battle for Germany, 1944–1945* (New York: Vintage, 2005), 420.

70. Gregory L. Owen, "Across the Bridge: The World War II Journey of Cpt. Alexander M. Patch, III, the son of Lt. Gen. Alexander M. Patch, Jr.," A Manuscript for the George C. Marshall Foundation, Lexington, Virginia (1995), 49–51.

71. MP, Eisenhower to Marshall, 5 December 1944.

72. Wyant, *Sandy Patch,* 150.

73. Owen, "Across the Bridge," 51–52.

74. Devers Diary, 1 November 1944.

75. Clarke and Smith, *Riveria to the Rhine,* 272–96.

76. Ibid., 311–33.

77. Ibid., 334–45. The 442nd Regimental Combat Team composed primarily of American citizens of Japanese descent joined the 36th Division on 15 October. Ibid, 313.

78. West Point Archives, Original Patton Diary, 22 and 28 September.

79. Clarke and Smith, *Riveria to the Rhine,* 349–53.

80. Ibid., 352–55.

81. Ibid., 363–405; and Weigley, *Eisenhower's Lieutenants,* 401–6.

82. Weigley, *Eisenhower's Lieutenants,* 402; and Blumenson, *Patton Papers,* 576.

83. Clarke and Smith, *Riveria to the Rhine,* 418–19, 433–38, 533, 556.

84. Ibid., 437–40, 563. "All the current operations in [Devers's] region," according to Eisenhower, were "merely for the purpose of cleaning up that flank as a preliminary to turning the bulk of the Seventh Army north to make with Patton a converging attack upon the great salient in the Seigfried Line west of the Rhine." MP, Eisenhower to Marshall, 27 November 1944.

85. Devers Diary, 26 November 1944.

86. Clarke and Smith, *Riveria to the Rhine,* 444–62.

87. Maj. Gen. Robert T. Frederick assumed command of the 45th Division on 4 December after Eagles was wounded when his jeep hit a mine.

88. Clarke and Smith, *Riveria to the Rhine,* 464–90. Devers attributed the rapid drive of VI Corps to the personal leadership and exceptionally fine battle sense of Brooks. Devers Diary, 17 December 1944.

89. Devers Diary, 19 December 1944.

90. Devers Diary, 27 December–1 January 1945; Riviera, 444–445, 490–500; and Franklin Louis Gurley, "Policy versus Strategy," in *The Journal of Military History* 58 (July 1994), 486–90.

91. Devers Papers, Summary of Directions in Chronological Order Concerning Holding Strasbourg or Not Holding Strasbourg, 3 January 1945 and de Gaulle to Eisenhower, 3 January 1945; USAMHI, The 100th Infantry Division Papers, Franklin L. Gurley, "The Relationship between Jean de Lattre de Tassigny and Jacob L. Devers, 1944–1945" given on 26 March 1994 at the Sorbonne at the two day colloquim "Jean de Lattre and the Americans 1943–1952"; Clarke and Smith, *Riveria to the Rhine,* 511–12, and Gurley, "Policy versus Strategy," 491–513.

92. Clarke and Smith, *Riveria to the Rhine,* 493–95, 498–504.

93. Ibid., 504–10, 564–65.

94. Ibid., 513–28.

95. "Right now and very secretly," Eisenhower informed Montgomery, " I am directing some troops to Devers to clean out the Colmar Pocket and to get the line of the Rhine south of the Siegfried Line. If we can accomplish this quickly, we can turn over the whole Alsace plain to French forces. This would allow Seventh Army to take over all the defensive areas up to and including the Moselle." DDE Papers, Principal File, Box 83, Eisenhower to Montgomery, 17 January 1945.

96. Clarke and Smith, *Riveria to the Rhine,* 532–35, 547–60; and Weigley, *Eisenhower's Lieutenants,* 550–51, 596–99, 633.

97. Berlin, *U.S. Army World War II Corps Commanders,* 5–6, 8, 11–13, 18–20; Wyant, *Sandy Patch,* 10, 182–83; and Weigley, *Eisenhower's Lieutenants,* 201.

98. Weigley, *Eisenhower's Lieutenants,* 633–39; Wyant, *Sandy Patch,* 181; and Bradley, *Soldier's Story,* 515–21. Of this affair, Devers recorded, "Patton, I am afraid, is up to his old tricks of suggesting certain things and I believe is willing to go to some lengths to cross us up." Devers Diary, 17 March 1945.

99. MP, Message FWD 18815 Eisenhower to Marshall, 9 April 1945 and Eisenhower to Marshall, 15 April 1945.

100. Weigley, *Eisenhower's Lieutenants,* 654, 685, 701–4; Wyant, *Sandy Patch,* 184, 187–88; and MacDonald, *Mighty Endeavor,* 450–51, 466, 475–76.

101. Wyant, *Sandy Patch,* 187–91; Weigley, *Eisenhower's Lieutenants,* 704–9; Bradley, *Soldier's Story,* 543; and Bradley and Blair, *General's Life,* 430–431.

102. Devers Papers, Devers to Patch, 22 April 1945 and Dever's Note to File, 27 April 1945.

103. Devers Papers, Message B13391Devers to Lattre, 24 April 1945.

104. Weigley, *Eisenhower's Lieutenants,* 711–13; MacDonald, *Mighty Endeavor,* 490–92, and Wyant, *Sandy Patch,* 192–95.

105. Weigley, *Eisenhower's Lieutenants,* 713–16, 725–26; Wyant, *Sandy Patch,* 196–202. Foertsch impressed Devers. Devers Diary, 5 May 1945. Unlike Eisenhower and Crerar who refused to meet with German generals, Patch spent hours talking with captured Field Marshal Gerd von Rundstedt whom he had admired since reading the latter's writings. Wyant, *Sandy Patch,* 204. Dever's Chief Liaison Officer provided a riveting record of the surrender ceremony. Massachusetts Historical Society, Henry Cabot Lodge Papers, Narrative of Lt. Col. Henry Cabot Lodge Jr., former U.S. Senator from Massachusetts, Chief of Liaison Section 6th Army Group on the German capitulation on 5 May.

106. Clarke and Smith, *Riveria to the Rhine,* 577–78; and Wyant, *Sandy Patch,* 163.

107. Wyant, *Sandy Patch,* 206–16. By Public Law 83–508, Patch received posthumous promotion to general, effective 19 July 1954.

CHAPTER SIX
In the Shadow of Napoleon: Gen. Jean de Lattre de Tassigny, First French Army

1. Among others, Bernard Simiot, *De Lattre* (Paris: Flammarion, 1994); Jean-Luc Barre, *De Lattre* (Paris: Perrin, 1990); Pierre Darcourt, *De Lattre au Viet-nam: Une Annee de Victoires* (Paris: La Table Ronde, 1965); and Pierre Pellissier, *De Lattre* (Paris: Perrin, 1998).

2. Maj. Gen. Sir Guy Salisbury-Jones, *So Full a Glory: A Biography of Marshal de Lattre de Tassigny* (London: Weidenfeld & Nicolson, 1954), Anthony Clayton, *Three Marshals of France: Leadership after Trauma* (London: Brassey's, 1992), and Jean de Lattre de Tassigny, *The History of the French First Army,* trans. Malcolm Barnes (London: Allen and Unwin, 1952). La Marechale de Lattre asked Eisenhower to introduce the book after the death of her husband. The Dwight D. Eisenhower (DDE) Library, Abilene, Kansas, DDE Papers, Principal File, Box 34, La Marechale de Lattre to Eisenhower, 6 April 1952 and Eisenhower to La Marechale de Lattre, 26 April 1952.

3. Clayton, *Three Marshals of France,* 116

4. Salisbury-Jones, *So Full a Glory,* 1–13; Clayton, *Three Marshals of France,* 22–27; and Pellissier, *De Lattre,* 15–42, 555.

5. DDE Library, Jacob L. Devers Papers, Reel 1, Box 1, Biographies of French Generals under cover of memorandum by Colonel Edward J.F Glavin, 22 February 1944; Biographical Note on General de Lattre de Tassigny under cover AG 201.35/011 LIA-0 dated

9 August 1944; and Biographical Sketch of General de Lattre de Tassigny, Commanding the First French Army; Salisbury-Jones, *So Full a Glory,* 14–30; Clayton, *Three Marshals of France,* 22–27; and Pellissier, *De Lattre,* 43–70, 555–56.

6. Devers Papers, Biographical Note on General de Lattre de Tassigny and biographical sheet, "De Lattre de Tassigny, Jean" under cover of Colonel L. Higgins, Chief, Liaison Section AFHQ, memorandum to Deputy C-in-C, 25 February 1944"; Pellisier, *De Lattre,* 71–186, 555–56; and Salisbury-Jones, *So Full a Glory,* 33–92.

7. Devers Papers, Biographical Note on General de Lattre de Tassigny; letter H.R. Stark, United States Naval Forces in Europe, London, to Devers, 15 November 1943 covering attachment "General De Lattre de Tassigny"; and biographical note "General Lattre de Tassigny"; Pellisier, *De Lattre,* 193–268; and Salisbury-Jones, *So Full a Glory,* 97–121.

8. Public Record Office, 70519, FO 371/36106 "Most Secret" letter signed by W. H. B. Mack, 18 October 1943. Douglas Porch says he was sprung from prison by Special Operations Executive. Porch, *Path to Victory,* 594.

9. The metropolitan army was conscript with service limited to the homeland unless the soldier agreed to serve elsewhere. The Army of Africa comprised of white and indigenous troops existed to garrison North Africa and provide strategic reserves for the metropole. *La Colonial*—of indigenous and some white regiments—existed to garrison colonies other than North Africa. Troops of the Army of Africa and *La Colonial* could be used anywhere. The cadres, officers and NCOs, of the Army of Africa were metropolitan personnel, spending tours, sometimes whole careers, in North Africa, while those of *La Colonial* served their entire careers in colonial soldiering. Anthony Clayton, *The Wars of French Decolonization* (London: Longman, 1994), 4.

10. Marcel Vigneras, *United States Army in World War II: Special Studies: Rearming the French* (Washington,: US Government Printing Office, 1957), 7–9.

11. In November 1945, he formally changed his family name to Leclerc de Hauteclocque. Clayton, *Three Marshals of France,* 42, 123.

12. Vigneras, *Rearming the French,* 10; Clayton, *Three Marshals of France,* 46–53; Porch, *Path to Victory,* 584–86; and Biographies of French Generals under cover of memorandum by Col. Edward J. F Glavin, 22 February 1944.

13. Vigneras, *Rearming the French,* 11–12; Pogue, *Marshall: Organizer of Victory,* 231; and Col. Adolphe Goutard, "Marshal Alphonse Juin," in *The War Lords: Military Commanders of the Twentieth Century,* ed. Field Marshal Sir Michael Carver (Boston: Little, Brown, 1976), 599–600.

14. Vigneras, *Rearming the French,* 1, 12–17, 117; Weinberg, *World at Arms,* 432–33; and Porch, *Path to Victory,* 343–66. By 1 September 1944, the Army of Africa totaled 560,000 men. Vigneras, *Rearming the French,* 194.

15. Vigneras, *Rearming the French,* 14–15, 31–32, 36–44; and Pogue, *Marshall: Organizer of Victory,* 231–40.

16. Devers Papers, Brig. Gen. H. F. Loomis, Chairman Joint Rearmament Committee NATOUSA, to Devers 17 January 1944. The divisions were: 1st Free French Motorized, 2nd Moroccan, 3rd Algerian, 4th Moroccan Mountain, 7th Algerian, 8th Algerian (recommended by De Gaulle and Giraud to be eliminated from the program), and 9th Colonial Infantry Divisions and the 1st, 2nd, 3rd, and 5th Armored Divisions.

17. Vigneras, *Rearming the French,* 71, 82, 94–97, 105–8, 115–16, 121–27, 155, 158; and de Lattre, *French First Army,* 25–28. These were the 1st, 2nd, and 5th Armoured divisions and the 1st Free French Motorized Infantry, 2nd Moroccan Infantry, 3rd Algerian Infantry, 4th Moroccan Mountain, and 9th Colonial Infantry Divisions.

18. Devers Papers, Devers to Marshall, 13 February 1944.

19. Vigneras, *Rearming the French,* 22, 78–80, 86–87, 96, 98, 118, 151–53.

20. Vigneras, *Rearming the French,* 124–25.

21. Ibid., 150. See also Pogue, *Marshall: Organizer of Victory,* 229–30, 235–39.

22. Vigneras, *Rearming the French,* 119–20, 149–51; and Jean Lacoture, *De Gaulle: The Ruler, 1945–1970* (New York: W.W. Norton, 1993), 8, 40.

23. Robert Speaight, *Vanier: Soldier, Diplomat, and Governor General* (Toronto: Collins, 1970), 197–98, 258–59, 269–70, 295–96. Vanier's wife was apparently a cousin to Leclerc, who seems to have been favored over de Lattre. Ibid, 219.

24. USAMHI, Devers Diary, 13 December 1943.

25. Lattre, *French First Army,* 23–25.

26. Devers Papers, Memorandum on Command of French Army from Major General F.G. Beaumont-Nesbitt, Chief of Liaison Section, Allied Forces Headquarters to COS, AFHQ, 13 June 1944.

27. Devers Papers, Devers to Marshall, 13 February 1944.

28. PRO 70519, FO 371/36106, Most Secret letter dated 18 October 1943 by signed W. H. B Mack.

29. De Lattre's dinner partner was the Commissioner of War and Air, Andre Le Troquer, another difficult personality regarded as dangerous by Devers and his staff. Le Troquer and de Lattre appeared to be on the most intimate and friendly terms. Devers Papers, "Comments made by General de Lattre de Tassigny" private memo from "D.G." to Bedell Smith, 9 January 1944. Le Troquer lost an arm in the World War I and joined the Resistance early. An admirer of the British, he blamed the General Staff for the French collapse and believed the French had a duty to redeem themselves by fighting. Devers Papers, Reel 1, Box 1, Colonel L. Higgins to Deputy Commander-in-Chief, 16 January 1944.

30. Clayton, *Three Marshals of France,* 52, 73–76; and Porch, *Path to Victory,* 586–87.

31. Speaight, *Vanier,* 269. Juin had nothing good to say about le Troquer either. Ibid, 284.

32. A Group of Moroccan Tabors comprised three Tabors, each equivalent in strength to a battalion. Each Tabor consisted of three Goums, each of some 200 mainly infantrymen. Moroccan *goumiers* were irregular Berber mountaineers who wore woolen gaiters with distinctive long striped *djellba* overcoats and fought in their own manner.

33. Vigneras, *Rearming the French,* 69–73, 82, 111–113, 178–79.

34. Devers Diary, 16 May 1944; and Devers Papers, Devers to Marshall, 9 May 1944.

35. Vigneras, *Rearming the French,* 111, 119, 125; Clayton, *Three Marshals of France,* 53–58, 77–87; and Porch, *Path to Victory,* 592.

36. "I am quite sure that there is bitter hatred between Leclerc . . . and de Lattre" recorded Devers, Devers Diary, 15 December 1944.

37. Devers Papers, Conversation between General de Gaulle and General Sir Henry Maitland Wilson, Monday 17 January 1944.

38. Not all Allied staff agreed, however, as Beaumont-Nesbitt offered that de Lattre, as an idealist ready to give everything in the cause of France, was a better choice than Juin, who tended to be more cynical and prone to let things take their course. On the other hand, he also noted that Juin lacked the excitability, verbosity, and vehemence so characteristic of Frenchmen—qualities de Lattre possessed in abundance. Devers Papers, Memorandum on Command of French Army from Major General F.G. Beaumont-Nesbitt, Chief of Liaison Section, Allied Forces Headquarters to COS, AFHQ, 13 June 1944.

39. Also included were fourteen motor transport groups, ten companies of muleteers, a 5,000-strong woman's army element, and numerous signals and quartermaster units.

40. Devers Diary, 7 November 1944. Getting our thoughts across to de Lattre, observed Devers, was a major operation and he had to be careful to use a good interpreter and have

others present so as to avoid misunderstandings due to his lack of French and de Lattre's poor understanding of English. On occasion he had to insist on meeting de Lattre alone with just two interpreters present. In this regard, Devers was extremely well served by Lt. Col. Henry Cabot Lodge Jr., who possessed an almost perfect understanding of French and French sensitivities.

41. Marcel Carpentier, Valluy, de Linares, and Andre Demetz. The code name for the command post of the First French Army was *Hirondelle* (Swallow). De Lattre, *French First Army,* 505.

42. Clayton, *Three Marshals of France,* 101–2, 117–18; Salisbury-Jones, *So Full a Glory,* 125, 204–5; and Devers Diary, 7 September 1944. Leclerc thought de Lattre's command style outmoded, with undue attention paid to elaborate routine and paper work handled by elegant staff and liaison officers. Clayton, *Three Marshals of France,* 62.

43. Bullitt had warned Roosevelt about the Soviet threat and fallen from grace as a result. He joined the Free French in May 1944 and landed with de Lattre as a French army major on his staff. Devers had Cabot Lodge exercise control over his influence beyond de Lattre's circle. Marshall Library, Interview of Devers by F. C. Pogue; and de Lattre, *French First Army,* 92, 236. Devers Diary, 28 September 1944.

44. Salisbury-Jones, *So Full a Glory,* 203–5.

45. Devers Diary, 8 October 1944.

46. Vigneras, *Rearming the French,* 101, 112, 159, 163, 180–86; de Lattre, *French First Army,* 28, 34–35; Clayton, *Three Marshals of France,* 86, 101–4; Marshall Library, Interview with Devers by F. C. Pogue; and Porch, *Path to Victory,* 594–95.

47. Devers Papers, Devers to Marshall, 13 February 1944.

48. Clarke and Smith, *Riviera to the Rhine,* 27.

49. De Lattre, *French First Army,* 31–32. Other Americans thought the French would be "insufferable" if given command of US troops. Truscott Papers, T. J. C. to Truscott, 20 July 1944.

50. Marshall Papers, Box 63, Folder 55, Devers to Marshall, 22 March 1944.

51. Devers Papers, letter Maj. Gen. Lowell W. Rooks, Deputy COS, AFHQ, to Devers, 16 April 1944, outlining Minutes of a Conversation between General Wilson and General Bethouart.

52. Clarke and Smith, *Riviera to the Rhine,* 27–28.

53. De Lattre, *French First Army,* 52–56, 71–75; Clarke and Smith, *Riviera to the Rhine,* 123–24, 131–34, 137.

54. De Lattre, *French First Army,* 71–114; Clarke and Smith, *Riviera to the Rhine,* 138–42.

55. De Lattre, *French First Army,* 76–101; Clarke and Smith, *Riviera to the Rhine,* 139–40; and Clayton, *Three Marshals of France,* 104, 106.

56. Devers Papers, Biographies of French Generals, General de Larminat, by Col. Edward J. F. Glavin, 22 February 1944; Devers to Larminat, 12 May 1945; and DDE Library, Oral History Interview with Gen. Jacob Devers by Dr. Maclyn P. Burg (2 July, 1975), 191–193. Born in 1895, de Larminat, was wounded three times and mentioned in dispatches three times during World War I. He committed suicide in 1962.

57. Clarke and Smith, *Riviera to the Rhine,* 171–73, 181–83.

58. Massachusetts Historical Society (MHS), Cabot Lodge Papers, Memorandum of "Conversation with General de Lattre at Luncheon" dated 8 September 1944 written by Lt. Col. Henry C. Lodge Jr., Senior Liaison Officer, 6th Army Group; and Lodge to Devers, 26 August 1944.

59. Clarke and Smith, *Riviera to the Rhine,* 224–26, 231.

60. Devers Papers, Brig. Gen. Reuben E. Jenkins to Devers, 24 February 1947; and West Point Archives, Original Patton Diary, 11 September 1944. According to Clarke and Smith, however, first contact occurred between elements of the 1st French Infantry Division and a patrol from the 6th US Armored Division. Clarke and Smith, *Riviera to the Rhine,* 223.

61. Devers Papers, Biographies of French Generals, Marie Emile Bethouart and General Bethouart, by Col. Edward J. F. Glavin, 22 February 1944; and Atkinson, *Army at Dawn,* 107–8. Essame described Bethouart as a gallant and most intelligent soldier. H. Essame, *Patton: A Study in Command* (New York: Charles Scribner's Sons, 1974), 49. Bethouart did not impress Alanbrooke who described him as "a grey putty faced, flabby sort of chap with a doleful countenance." Alanbrooke, *War Diaries,* 555.

62. MP, Devers to Marshall, 9 May 1944; and Devers Diary, 16 May 1944.

63. Oral History Interview with Gen. Jacob Devers by Dr. Maclyn Burg (2 July, 1975), 191; Devers Diary, 18 January 1945; Wilt, 128; and Dominick Graham and Shelford Bidwell, *Tug of War: The Battle for Italy: 1943–45* (London: Hodder & Stoughton, 1986), 297–327.

64. Clarke and Smith, *Riviera to the Rhine,* 431, 577–78.

65. De Lattre, *French First Army,* 288–90, 296, 367–68, 379. The French also had seventy-two World War I 155–millimeter howitzers that used powder charges no longer available. DDE Library, Principal File, Box 34, Devers to Eisenhower, 23 January 1945.

66. Vigneras, *Rearming the French,* 211–12; Weigley, *Eisenhower's Lieutenants,* 345; and de Lattre, *French First Army,* 224, 293, 345.

67. Devers Diary, 22 December 1944.

68. Devers Diary, 30 January 1945. De Lattre mentioned the French Air Corps only six times and Gerardot only four in his memoirs. De Lattre, *First French Army,* 206, 224, 293, 323, 330, 345, 494.

69. Clarke and Smith, *Riviera to the Rhine,* 231–32, 238–39, 252, 298–99, 301–8; MP, Truscott Papers, Truscott to de Goislard de Monsabert, 2 October 1944; and de Lattre, *French First Army,* 204–5, 213–15.

70. MHS, Cabot Lodge Papers, Report of 6 October by Lt. Col. H. C. Lodge Jr., Senior Liaison Officer, 6th Army Group.

71. Vigneras, *Rearming the French,* 188, 337; de Lattre, *French First Army,* 27, 194; and Clarke and Smith, *Riviera to the Rhine,* 294, 299–301, 355, 432. Base 901, belatedly activated on 1 August 1944, was attached to the U.S. Coastal Base Section organized in July 1944 to support Franco-American forces in Anvil. When the Americans set up a Continental Advance Section (CONAD) at Dijon in October, a detachment of Base 901 joined them. On 23 October Lattre announced that CONAD would take over direct responsibility for the supply of the French First Army and authorized its American commander to appoint French officers from Base 901 to various staff sections and commands within CONAD. On 20 November 1944, a new headquarters, Southern Line of Communications (SOLOC), took over the entire American supply system in southern France. The French commander of Base 901 was named deputy to the American commanding general of SOLOC, which included integrated French officers who worked mainly under American command at all levels. Vigneras, *Rearming the French,* 187–88.

72. Devers Papers, Box 1, Reel 4, Devers to Eisenhower, 19 October 1944. Plans called for the integration of 51,000 FFI personnel in October, using 15,000 white FFI to replace a like number of black personnel—9,200 in the 9th Colonial and 6,000 in the 1st Infantry divisions. The Americans were meanwhile just beginning to introduce black platoons into their combat arms. Devers Papers, Brig. Gen. B.O. Davis to Maj. Gen. Charles H. Bonesteel, Chief General Inspectorate Section, HQ, ETOUSA, 25 April 1945 and Lieutenant General Ben Lear, Deputy Theatre Commander ETOUSA, to Devers, 10 February 1945.

73. Speaight, *Vanier,* 268.

74. Clarke and Smith, *Riviera to the Rhine,* 355–57, 463; de Lattre, *French First Army,* 169–80; Porch, *Path to Victory,* 600–603; and Devers Papers, Box 1, Reel 4, Devers to Eisenhower, 19 Oct 44.

75. The Alpine sector eventually came under the direct command of Devers, thus relieving Lattre of this responsibily. Devers Papers, Smith to Devers, 18 January 1945.

76. Clarke and Smith, *Riviera to the Rhine,* 357–60, 419, 431–32, 464, 488, 579; and de Lattre, *French First Army,* 219–20.

77. De Lattre, *French First Army,* 205–6, 213–16, 224–25; Clarke and Smith, *Riviera to the Rhine,* 301–2, 407–8, 413.

78. Both French armored divisions fielded three brigade-sized combat commands: CC1, CC2, and CC3 in the French 1st Armored Division and CC4, CC5, and CC6 in the French 5th Armored Division. Each comprised roughly 4,000–4,500 men and included a reconnaissance squadron, tank regiment, infantry battalion, and tank destroyer squadron, with motorized artillery, engineer, signals, transport, and supply elements. Leclerc's 2nd Armored used the letters of commander's last names to designate some combat commands. In one instance, CCD and CCL were each further subdivided into two smaller task forces; CCV remained in reserve, as did CCR based on the division's permanent reconnaissance element. Clarke and Smith, *Riviera to the Rhine,* 126, 371–72, 408; and de Lattre, *First French Army,* 54, 318–25, 379.

79. DeLattre, *French First Army,* 229–38; Clarke and Smith, *Riviera to the Rhine,* 412–416.

80. De Lattre, *French First Army,* 239–57; Clarke and Smith, *Riviera to the Rhine,* 406, 416–25.

81. De Lattre, *French First Army,* 269–84; Clarke and Smith, *Riviera to the Rhine,* 428–31. The 4th Moroccan Division had been released from the Alpine Front having been replaced by the newly raised 27th Alpine Infantry Division.

82. Speaight, *Vanier,* 295.

83. Clarke and Smith, *Riviera to the Rhine,* 434–42, 464.

84. Devers Papers, Devers to de Lattre, 18 December 1944.

85. USAMHI, Devers Diary, 15 December 1945 and 31 January 1945; and DDE Papers, Principal File, Box 34, Devers to Eisenhower, 18 December 1944, Leclerc to Devers, 14 December 1994, and Devers to Leclerc, 18 December 1944. Devers eventually posted Leclerc back to Seventh Army and XV Corps. Devers Diary, 11 February 1945 and Devers Papers, Devers to Juin, 12 April 1945. Leclerc seems also to have dragged his heels in attacking south to support de Lattre's operations against Colmar. Devers thought Leclerc had to strength to overcome the resistance he was facing and told him so. Devers Papers, Devers to Leclerc, 18 December 1944.

86. "Lattre is in one of his temperamental moods at the moment," observed Devers, "and it always takes some time to get him started again." Devers Papers, Devers to Marshall, 11 December 1944.

87. Clarke and Smith, *Riviera to the Rhine,* 484–91, 510; de Lattre, French First Army, 287–300.

88. Interestingly, Stalin expressed the same sentiment, stating that while Strasbourg was not necessarily of military value its recapture by the Germans would give them great political and psychological capital. Marshall Library, Gen. Thomas T. Handy Papers, Box 1, Folder 7, Memorandum of Conference with Marshal Stalin, 15 January 1945. Handy was Marshall's Chief of the Operations Division.

89. De Gaulle wrote to Lattre: "Dans l'eventualitie ou les Forces alliees se retireraient de leurs positions actuelles au Nord du dispositif de la 1ere Armee Française, je vous prescris de prendre a votre compte et d'assurer la defense de STRASBOURG." Vincennes Papers,

De Gaulle to Lattre, 1 January 1945; and DDE Library, Principal File, Box 34, De Gaulle to Eisenhower, 3 January 1945.

90. Marshall Library, General Thomas Handy Papers, Box 1, Folder 7, Beddell Smith to Handy, 12 January 1945; Clarke and Smith, *Riviera to the Rhine,* 490–91, 495–97; de Lattre, *French First Army,* 301–13; and Devers Papers, Summary of Directions in Chronological Order Concerning Holding Strasbourg or Not Holding Strasbourg, 3 January 1945.

91. It is not clear that he actually said this at the time as reported. DDE Library, Principal File, Box 34, Resume of a Conversation between General Eisenhower and General de Gaulle 25 January 1945.

92. DDE Library, Principal File, Box 80, Eisenhower to Marshall, 12 January 1945; PGurley, "Policy," 500–507; Eisenhower, *Bitter Woods,* 400–401; Ambrose, *Eisenhower,* 377–78.

93. Devers Diary, 28 December 1944; Clarke and Smith, *Riviera to the Rhine,* 497, 511–12; and MacDonald, *Mighty Endeavor,* 397.

94. Pellisier, *De Lattre,* 375–76; Lacoture, *De Gaulle,* 35–39; Clarke and Smith, *Riviera to the Rhine,* 511–18; de Lattre, *French First Army,* 313–25.

95. De Lattre, *French First Army,* 310.

96. USAMHI, The 100th Division Papers, Gurley, "The Relationship between Jean de Lattre and de Tassigny and Jacob L. Devers," 8.

97. In turn, de Lattre sent it on to his corps commanders. Service historique de l'armee de terre, Chateau de Vincennes, Ultra Secret Telegramme Officiel de Lattre a de Monsabert, le 3 Janvier 1945; Ultra Secret Telegramme Officiel General commandant Iere Armee Francais a General commandant 2eme C.A., le 6 Janvier 1945; Ultra Secret Telegramme General commandant Iere Armee Francaise a General commandant le 1 er C.A., 10 Janvier 1945.

98. Handy Papers, Box 1, Folder 7, Bedell Smith to Handy, 28 December 1944.

99. Handy agreed with Smith's assessment of using the French, but pointed out that no more US divisions were to be formed. Handy Papers, Box 1, Folder 7, Handy to Smith, 4 January 1945.

100. Vigneras, *Rearming the French,* 124.

101. Clarke and Smith, *Riviera to the Rhine,* 535–47; de Lattre, *French First Army,* 334–65; and Devers Papers, de Lattre to Devers, 18 January and 22 January 1945.

102. When it became apparent that the First French Army had lost its punch in December the Germans strongly reinforced the Colmar Pocket. Devers Papers, Jenkins to Devers, 24 February 1947. Devers nonetheless insisted that Lattre outnumbered the Germans in infantry by five to one. Devers Papers, Devers to de Lattre, 23 January, 1945. The training of French infantry inductees left much to be desired, however, and, as all infantrymen know, terrain can swallow infantry surprisingly fast especially in inclement weather.

103. Including, as well, artillery, chemical, engineer, tank destroyer, and antiaircraft elements. Devers Papers, Troop List of US Units Under Operational Control of First French Army, 29 January 1945.

104. MP, Eisenhower to Marshall, 27 November 1944.

105. Devers Papers, de Lattre to Devers, 21 and 27 January 1945; Devers to Milburn, 12 February 1945; de Lattre, *French First Army,* 358–60, 365–401; Clarke and Smith, *Riviera to the Rhine,* 420, 547–51, 556; and Weigley, *Eisenhower's Lieutenants,* 596–99.

106. DDE Library, Principal File, Box 80, Eisenhower to Marshall, 20 February 1945.

107. De Lattre, *French First Army,* 407–20.

108. Devers remained supportive of de Lattre, arranging for the artillery of the French I and II Corps to train jointly with the U.S. VI and XV corps to learn American artillery methods. Devers Papers, Box 1, Reel 4, Devers to Patch, 26 February 1945.

109. De Lattre, *French First Army,* 410.

110. Ibid., 407–20.

111. Ibid., 421.

112. Lacoture, *De Gaulle,* 29–31, 43–65; Clayton, *Three Marshals of France,* 114.

113. DDE Library, Principal File, Box 80, Eisenhower to Marshall, 25 September 1944.

114. Porch, *Path to Victory,* 603, 607.

115. Marshal Library, Interview with Devers by F.C. Pogue. "Crossing the Rhine was Napoleonic—he was Napoleon and he was going to cross the Rhine as Napoleon had," recounted Devers.

116. Devers Papers, de Lattre to Devers, 31 March 1945.

117. De Lattre, *French First Army,* 419–29; Weigley, *Eisenhower's Lieutenants,* 658.

118. De Lattre, *French First Army,* 429–56

119. Ibid., 458–66; Weigley, *Eisenhower's Lieutenants,* 711–12; Clayton, *Three Marshals of France,* 115; and MacDonald, *Mighty Endeavor,* 490.

120. Devers Papers, de Lattre to Lieutenant Colonel du Souzy, Chief of the French Military Liaison Mission, 6th Army Group, 22 April 1945.

121. Devers Diary, 18 November 1944.

122. Devers Papers, Message 5A/25 Lattre to Devers, 25 April 1945; and de Lattre, *French First Army,* 490.

123. Devers Papers, Message B13538 Devers to de Lattre, 26 April 1945 and Message B13539 Devers to SHAEF Forward Personal for General Smith, 26 April 1945.

124. De Lattre, *French First Army,* 488–92; Devers Papers, de Lattre to Devers, 26 April 1945; and DDE Library, Principal File, Box 34, Eisenhower to de Gaulle, 28 April 1945 and de Gaulle reply to Eisenhower, undated.

125. The looting and raping carried out by French troops marred the Stuttgart victory. An NBC reporter who observed firsthand the "frightful" French occupation of Karlsruhe and Baden-Baden said neither could compare to what went on in Stuttgart, where rape was publicly rampant throughout the city. According to him, French authorities expressed little sympathy for the Germans and shrugged him off with the comment, "What can you do with the Moroccans?" Other observers reported that French white troops also indulged in an orgy of looting. Since observations and reports confirmed as much to Devers, he convened an investigation and ordered Patch to intervene. When Devers visited Stuttgart on 27 April, he found that the French had everything under control. As reported to the American acting secretary of war, twelve French soldiers were shot for rape. Devers Papers, Devers to Patch, 22 March 1945; Remarks dictated by General Devers on morning 27 April 1945; Sworn statement by Maj. Charles L. Leven and 1st Lt. Richard C. Simonson on Behavior of French Troops in Stuttgart to Commanding General, 100th Infantry Division, 28 April 1945; and Robert P. Patterson, Acting Secretary of War to Senator James O. Eastland, 30 July 1945.

126. De Lattre sent a letter to Devers explaining that on 20 October 1805 Napoleon by forced marches enveloped the Austrian Army at Ulm and compelled it to capitulate. On the bottom of the letter Devers wrote, "This letter will not be answered. General de Lattre violated directly my orders and moved an armored division across the front of VI Corps, thereby delaying the rapid advance of the VI Corps to the south and jeopardizing the lives of American and French soldiers. His act was that of an unbalanced man." Devers Papers, de Lattre to Devers, 24 April 1945. Devers Papers, Message B-13333 Devers to Lattre, 23 April 1945; Message 524/OP 3 Lattre to Devers, 24 April 1945; Message B-13391 Devers to Lattre, 24 April 1945; Message B-13400 Devers to Lattre, 24 April 1945; and MHS, Lodge Papers, de Lattre to Devers, 24 April 1945.

127. De Lattre, *French First Army,* 467–501; Weigley, *Eisenhower's Lieutenants,* 710–15; and MacDonald, *Mighty Endeavor,* 510.

128. Including the 10th Division, which lacked major items of equipment. Each of the other eight divisions also received an additional regiment of infantry. The 14th Division was also available. Devers Papers, Box 1, Reel 4, Bedell Smith to Devers, 18 January 1945.

129. Devers Papers, Lattre to Devers, 7 May 1945.

130. The question of the occupation of Germany had been seriously addressed during the summer of 1943. A committee headed by Deputy Prime Minister Clement Attlee drew up a memorandum spelling out British views on the allocation of occupation zones in Germany. The proposed boundaries placed the British in the northwest, the Americans in the southwest, and the Russians in the east. There was no mention of the French. When Roosevelt was asked about the British proposal on his way to the Cairo Conference, however, he signaled his reluctance to accept responsibility for southern Germany. He suggested instead that Prussia and Pomerania go to the Russians, Hamburg and Hanover to the Americans, and Baden, Wurttemberg and Bavaria to the British. The discussion over zones continued through the first half of 1944 with Roosevelt insisting that he wanted no responsibility for southern Germany and Churchill holding out for a British northwestern zone. Not until the second Quebec Conference of September 1944 did Roosevelt relent. There he agreed to accept the British proposal so long as Americans would have right of access to their southern zone through enclaves at Bremen and Bremerhaven. The Americans formally approved arrangements just before the Yalta Conference where the Russians, who had accepted the British proposals a year earlier, also gave their final assent. The British wanted a French zone as they feared that the Americans might withdraw from their zone, in which case the French could occupy it. Pogue, *Marshall: Organizer of Victory,* 460–65; and Weinberg, *World at Arms,* 803–5, 817.

131. Hamilton, *Monty,* 3:730–68.

132. "Lattre de Tassigny, Jean de," entry by Anthony Clayton in *Reader's Guide to Military History,* ed. Charles Messenger (London: Fitzroy Dearborn, 2001), 319–20; and Bernard Fall, *Street Without Joy* (New York: Schocken, 1972), 36–40, 47, 105.

133. PRO 70519, FO371/92453 letters H. A. Graves to J.D. Murray, South East Asia Department, Foreign Office, 2 June 1951 and 10 July 1951.

134. FO371/101083 Letter H.A. Graves to The Right Honourable Anthony Eden, MC, MP, Foreign Office, 30 January 1952.

Bibliography

PRIMARY SOURCES
Government Records, Personal Papers, and Manuscript Collections
Current Reports from Overseas.
Dwight D. Eisenhower (DDE) Library, Abilene, Kansas: DDE Collection, Pre-Presidential Papers: 1916–1952, Principal File, Courtney Hicks Hodges Papers, Jacob L. Devers Papers, J. Lawton Collins Papers, Harold R. Bull Papers, Ruth M. Briggs Papers, Walter Bedell Smith Papers, Oral History and Columbia University Oral History Interviews
Imperial War Museum (IWM), London: Montgomery of Alamein Papers
Library of Congress Manuscript Division, Washington: James H. Doolittle Papers
Liddell Hart Centre for Military Archives (LHC) King's College, London: Sir Basil Liddell Hart Papers, J.F.C. Fuller Papers, Alanbrooke Papers, Sir Miles Dempsey Papers, Sir Harold Pyman Papers
Marshall Library, Lexington, Virginia: George C. Marshall Papers, Lucien K. Truscott Papers, Thomas T. Handy Papers, James A. Van Fleet Papers, Walton Walker Papers
Massachusetts Historical Society, Boston, Massachusetts: Henry Cabot Lodge Papers
National Archives and Records Administration (NARA), Archives II, College Park, Maryland: copy William C. Sylvan Diary
National Archives of Canada (NAC): Record Group 24, National Defence 1870–1981, and H.D.G. Crerar Papers
National Defence Headquarters (NDHQ), Directorate of History and Heritage: Miscellaneous documents
Public Record Office (PRO), London: Cabinet Office Historical Section files (CAB Series), War and Foreign Office (FO) records, 21st Army Group Papers (WO205), Dempsey Papers (WO285), and Crerar Diary (CAB 106)
Queen's University Archives (QUA), Kingston, Ontario: C.G. Powers Papers, Grant Dexter Papers
Royal Military College of Canada (RMC), Kingston, Ontario: Crerar Papers

United States Army Military History Institute (USAMHI), Carlisle Barracks, Pennsylvania: Omar N. Bradley Papers, Jacob L. Devers Papers, William H. Simpson Papers, James E. Moore Papers, Alvan C. Gillem Papers, Chester B. Hansen Papers, Benjamin A. Dickson Papers, Charles H. Corlett Papers, Reuben E. Jenkins Papers, George I. Forsythe Papers, the 100th Infantry Division Papers, and Oral History Interviews.
United States Military Academy, West Point, New York: Omar N. Bradley Papers, Thomas R. Goethals Papers, George S. Patton, Jr. Papers, Alexander M. Patch Papers, Matthew B. Ridgway Papers
Service historique de l'armee de terre, Chateau de Vincennes: General de Lattre de Tassigny Papers and First French Army documents.

Memoirs, Journals, and Accounts

Allen, Col. Robert S. *Lucky Forward: The History of Patton's Third U.S. Army.* New York: Vanguard, 1947.
Alanbrooke, Field Marshal Lord. *War Diaries, 1939–1945.* Edited by Alex Danchev and Daniel Todman. London: Weidenfeld & Nicolson, 2001.
Bradley, Omar N. *A Soldier's Story.* New York: Henry Holt, 1951.
Bradley, Omar N., and Clay Blair. *A General's Life: An Autobiography by General of the Army Omar N. Bradley.* New York: Simon and Schuster, 1983.
Butcher, Capt. Harry C. *My Three Years with Eisenhower.* New York: Simon and Schuster, 1946.
Churchill, Winston S. *The Second World War: Triumph and Tragedy.* Boston: Houghton Mifflin, 1953.
Conquer: The Story of the Ninth Army, 1944–1945. Washington: Infantry Journal Press, 1947.
De Lattre de Tassigny, Jean. *The History of the French First Army.* Translated by Malcolm Barnes. London: Allen and Unwin, 1952.
Dexter, Grant. *Ottawa at War: The Grant Dexter Memoranda, 1939–1945.* Gibson, Frederick W., and Barbara Robertson (eds.) Winnipeg: Manitoba Record Society, 1994.
Fuller, Maj. Gen. J. F. C. *The Army in My Time.* London: Rich and Cowan, 1935.
Gavin, Gen. James M. *On to Berlin: Battles of an Airborne Commander, 1943–1946.* New York: Bantam, 1981.
Harmon, Maj. Gen. E. N., with Milton MacKaye and William Ross MacKaye. *Combat Commander: Autobiography of a Soldier.* Englewood Cliffs, NJ: Prentice-Hall, 1970.
Horrocks, Sir Brian, with Eversley Belfield and Maj. Gen. H. Essame. *Corps Commander.* New York: Charles Scribner's Sons, 1977.
Mellenthin, Maj. Gen. F. W. von. *Panzer Battles.* Translated by H. Betzler. Norman: University of Oklahoma Press, 1983
Meyer, Hubert. *The History of the 12. SS-Panzerdivision "Hitlerjugend."* Translated by H. Harri Henschler. Winnipeg: J. J. Fedorowicz, 1994.
Montgomery, Bernard Law. *Memoirs.* London: Collins, 1958.
———. *Normandy to the Baltic.* London: Hutchinson, 1946.
Pyman, Gen. Sir Harold E. *Call to Arms.* London: Leo Cooper, 1971.
Roberts, James Alan. The *Canadian Summer: Memoirs.* Toronto: University Press, 1981.
Roberts, Maj. Gen. Pip. *From the Desert to the Baltic.* London: William Kimber, 1987.
Sherwood, Robert E. *The White House Papers of Harry L. Hopkins.* 2 vols. London: Eyre and Spottiswoode, 1948.
Stacey, C. P. *A Date with History: Memoirs of a Canadian Historian.* Ottawa: Deneau, 1982

Official Histories

Clarke, Jeffrey J., and Robert Ross Smith. *United States Army in World War II, The European Theater of Operations: Riviera to the Rhine.* Washington: Center of Military History, 1993.

Dziuban, Col. Stanley W. *Military Relations between the United States and Canada, 1939–1945.* Washington: Office of the Chief of Military History, 1959.

Blumenson, Martin. *United States Army in World War II, The European Theater of Operations: Breakout and Pursuit.* Washington: Office of the Chief of Military History, 1961.

Ellis, Maj. L. F., with Lt. Col. A. E. Warhurst. *Victory in the West.* Vol. 2, *The Defeat of Germany.* London: Her Majesty's Stationery Office, 1968.

Hinsley, F. H. *British Intelligence in the Second World War: Abridged Version.* New York: Cambridge University Press, 1993.

Hogan, David W. *A Command Post at War: First Army Headquarters in Europe, 1943–1945.* Washington: Center of Military History, United States Army, 2000.

Nicholson, Lt. Col. G. W. L. *Official History of the Canadian Army in the Second World War.* Vol. 2, *The Canadians in Italy, 1943–1945.* Ottawa: Queen's Printer, 1956.

Report on Operations: The Seventh United States Army in France and Germany, 1944–1945. 3 vols. Heidelberg: Aloys Graf, 1946.

Stacey, C. P. *Official History of the Canadian Army in the Second World War.* Vol. 3, *The Victory Campaign: The Operations in North West Europe, 1944-1945.* Ottawa: Queen's Printer, 1966.

Stacey, C. P. *Arms, Men, and Governments: The War Policies of Canada, 1939–1945.* Ottawa: Information Canada, 1974.

Vigneras, Marcel. *United States Army in World War II: Special Studies: Rearming the French.* Washington: U.S. Government Printing Office, 1957.

SECONDARY SOURCES
Books

Ambrose, Stephen E. *Eisenhower: Soldier, General of the Army, President-Elect, 1890–1952.* New York: Simon and Schuster, 1983.

Atkinson, Rick. *An Army at Dawn: The War in North Africa, 1942–1943.* New York: Henry Holt, 2003.

Balkoski, Joseph. Beyond *the Beachhead: The 29th Infantry Division in Normandy.* New York: Dell, 1989.

Belfield, Eversley, and H. Essame. *The Battle for Normandy.* London: Pan, 1983.

Berlin, Robert H. *U.S. Army World War II Corps Commanders: A Composite Biography.* Fort Leavenworth: Combat Studies Institute, 1989.

———. *The Battle of the Generals: The Untold Story of the Falaise Pocket—The Campaign That Should Have Won World War II.* New York: William Morrow, 1993.

Blumenson, Martin. *The Patton Papers, 1940–1945.* Boston: Houghton Mifflin, 1974.

Bonn, Keith E. *When the Odds Were Even: The Vosges Mountains Campaign, October 1944–January 1945.* Novato, CA: Presidio, 1994.

Brooks, Stephen. *Montgomery and Eighth Army.* The Bodley Head: Army Records Society, 1991.

Brower, Charles F. *World War II in Europe: The Final Year.* New York: St. Martin's Press, 1998.

Bucholz, Arden. *Moltke and the German Wars, 1864–1871.* New York: Palgrave, 2001.

Burns, Maj. Gen. E. L. M. *Manpower in the Canadian Army, 1939–1945.* Toronto: Clarke, Irwin, 1956.

Callahan, Raymond. *Churchill and His Generals.* Lawrence, KS: University Press of Kansas, 2007.

Carafano, James Jay. *After D-Day: Operation Cobra and the Normandy Breakout*. Boulder, CO: Lynne Rienner, 2000.

Carver, Field Marshal Sir Michael. *The War Lords: Military Commanders of the Twentieth Century*. Boston: Little, Brown, 1976.

Chandler, David G., and James Lawton Collins Jr. *The D-Day Encyclopedia*. New York: Simon and Shuster, 1994.

Clausewitz, Carl von. *On War*. Edited and translated by Michael Howard and Peter Paret. Princeton, NJ: Princeton University Press, 1976.

Clayton, Anthony. *Three Marshals of France: Leadership after Trauma*. London: Brassey's, 1992.

———. *The Wars of French Decolonization*. London: Longman, 1994.

Colley, David P. *Decision at Strasbourg: Ike's Strategic Mistake to Halt the Sixth Army Group at the Rhine in 1944*. Annapolis, MD: Naval Institute Press, 2008.

Copp, Terry. *Cinderella Army: The Canadians in Northwest Europe, 1944–1945*. Toronto: University Press, 2006.

Danchev, Alex. *Very Special Relationship: Field Marshal Sir John Dill and the Anglo-American Alliance, 1941–44*. London: Brassey's, 1986.

Dancocks, Daniel G. *The D-Day Dodgers: The Canadians in Italy, 1943–1945*. Toronto: McClelland and Stewart, 1991.

D'Este, Carlo. *Bitter Victory: The Battle for Sicily, 1943*. London: Collins, 1988.

———. *Decision in Normandy: The Unwritten Story of Montgomery and the Allied Campaign*. London: Collins, 1983.

———. *Eisenhower: A Soldier's Life*. New York: Henry Holt, 2002.

———. *Patton: A Genius for War*. New York: Harper Collins, 1995.

Dickson, Paul. *A Thoroughly Canadian General: A Biography of General H. D. G. Crerar*. Toronto: University Press, 2007.

Doubler, Michael D. *Closing with the Enemy: How GIs Fought the War in Europe, 1944–1945*. Lawrence, KS: University Press of Kansas, 1994.

Douglas, W. A. B., and B. Greenhous. *Out of the Shadows*. Toronto: Oxford University Press, 1977.

Dupuy, Trevor N. *A Genius for War: The German Army and the General Staff, 1807–1945*. London: Macdonald and Jane's, 1977.

Dupuy, Trevor N., et al. *The Harper Encyclopedia of Military Biography*. Edison, NJ: Castle Books, 1995.

Eisenhower, John S. D. *The Bitter Woods: The Battle of the Bulge*. New York: Da Capo, 1995.

English, John A. *The Canadian Army and the Normandy Campaign: A Study of Failure in High Command*. New York: Praeger, 1991.

———. *Marching through Chaos: The Descent of Armies in Theory and Practice*. Westport: Praeger, 1996.

Essame, H. *The Battle for Germany*. New York: Bonanza, 1969.

———. *The Battle for Normandy*. London: Pan, 1983.

———. *Patton: A Study in Command*. New York: Charles Scribner's Sons, 1974.

Fall, Bernard. *Street without Joy*. New York: Schocken, 1972.

Foster, Tony. *Meeting of Generals*. Toronto: Methuen, 1986.

French, David. *Raising Churchill's Army: The British Army and the War against Germany, 1919–1945*. Oxford, England: Oxford University Press, 2001.

Fuller, Maj. Gen. J. F. C. *The Second World War, 1939–1945: A Strategical and Tactical History*. London: Eyre and Spottiswoode, 1948.

Goerlitz, Walter. History *of the German General Staff, 1657–1945*. Translated by Brian Battershaw. New York: Praeger, 1957.

Gooch, John. *The Prospect of War: Studies in British Defence Policy, 1847–1942*. London: Frank Cass, 1981.

Gooderson, Ian. *Air Power at the Battlefront: Allied Close Air Support in Europe, 1943–45*. London: Frank Cass, 1998.

Graham, Dominick. *The Price of Command: A Biography of General Guy Simonds.* Toronto: Stoddart, 1993.

Graham, Dominick, and Shelford Bidwell. *Coalitions, Politicians and Generals: Some Aspects of Command in Two World Wars.* London: Brassey's, 1993.

———. *Tug of War: The Battle for Italy: 1943–45.* London: Hodder & Stoughton, 1986.

Granatstein, J. L. *Canada's Army: Waging War and Keeping the Peace.* Toronto: University of Toronto Press, 2002.

———. *The Generals: The Canadian Army's Commanders in the Second World War.* Toronto: Stoddart, 1993.

Hart, Russell A. *Clash of Arms: How the Allies Won in Normandy.* Boulder, CO: Lynne Rienner, 2001.

Hart, Stephen Ashley. *Montgomery and "Colossal Cracks": The 21st Army Group in Northwest Europe, 1944–45.* Westport, CT: Praeger, 2000.

———. *Road to Falaise.* Stroud, England: Sutton, 2004

Hamilton, Nigel. *Monty: The Field Marshal, 1944–1976.* London: Hamish Hamilton, 1986.

———. *Monty: Master of the Battlefield, 1942–1944.* London: Hamish Hamilton, 1983.

Hastings, Max. *Armageddon: The Battle for Germany, 1944–1945.* New York: Vintage, 2005.

Hittle, J. D. *The Military Staff: Its History and Development.* Harrisburg, PA: Military Service, 1949.

Horne, Alistair, with David Montgomery. *Monty: The Lonely Leader, 1944–1945.* New York: Harper Collins, 1994.

Howard, Michael. *The Franco-Prussian War: The German Invasion of France, 1870–1871.* London: Methuen, 1981.

———. *War in European History.* Oxford: University Press, 1992.

Huntington, Samuel P. *The Soldier and the State.* Cambridge, MA: Harvard University Press, 1979.

Jarymowycz, Roman Johann. *Tank Tactics: From Normandy to Lorraine.* Boulder, CO: Lynne Rienner, 2001.

Keegan, John. *Churchill's Generals.* London: Weidenfeld and Nicloson, 1991.

Lacoture, Jean. *De Gaulle: The Ruler, 1945–1970.* New York: W. W. Norton, 1993.

Lamb, Richard. *Montgomery in Europe, 1943–45: Success or Failure?* New York: Franklin Watts, 1984.

Larrabee, Eric. *Commander in Chief: Franklin Delano Roosevelt, His Lieutenants, and Their War.* New York: Simon and Schuster, 1987.

Lewin, Ronald. *Montgomery as Military Commander.* New York: Stein and Day, 1971.

Liddell Hart, Basil H. *History of the Second World War.* London: Pan, 1973.

MacDonald, Charles B. *The Battle of the Huertgen Forest.* Philadephia: J.B. Lippincott, 1963.

———. *The Mighty Endeavor: American Armed Forces in the European Theater in World War II.* New York: Oxford University Press, 1969.

———. *A Time for Trumpets: The Untold Story of the Battle of the Bulge.* New York: William Morrow, 1985.

Masters, John. *The Road Past Mandalay: A Personal Narrative*. New York; Bantam, 1979.

McKercher, B. J. C., and Lawrence Aronsen. *The North Atlantic Triangle in a Changing World: Anglo-American-Canadian Relations, 1902–1956*. Toronto: University of Toronto Press, 1996.

Meilinger, Phillip S. *Hoyt S. Vandenberg: The Life of a General*. Bloomington, IN: Indiana University Press, 1989.

Messenger, Charles. *Reader's Guide to Military History*. London: Fitzroy Dearborn, 2001.

Millotat, Christian O. E. *Understanding the Prussian-German General Staff System*. Carlisle, PA: U.S. Army War College Strategic Studies Institute, 1992.

Morelock, J. D. *Generals of the Ardennes: American Leadership in the Battle of the Bulge*. Honolulu: University Press of the Pacific, 2003.

Morton, Desmond. *Understanding Canadian Defence*. Toronto: Penguin/McGill, 2003.

Moulton, Maj. Gen. J. L. *Battle for Antwerp: The Liberation of the City and the Opening of the Scheldt, 1944*. New York: Hippocrene, 1978.

Murray, Williamson, and Allan R. Millett. *A War to Be Won: Fighting the Second World War*. Cambridge, MA: Harvard University Press, 2000.

Nelson, Maj. Gen. Otto L. *National Security and the General Staff*. Washington: Infantry Journal, 1946.

Pellissier, Pierre. *De Lattre*. Paris: Perrin, 1998.

Perret, Geoffrey. *There's a War to Be Won: The United States Army in World War II*. New York: Ballantine, 1991.

Pogue, Forest C. *George C. Marshall: Education of a General, 1880–1939*. New York: Viking, 1963.

———. *George C. Marshall: Organizer of Victory, 1943–1945*. New York: Viking, 1973.

Porch, Douglas. *The Path to Victory: The Mediterranean Theater in World War II*. New York: Farrar, Straus and Giroux, 2004.

Poulos, Terrence. *Extreme War: The Military Book Club's Encyclopedia of the Biggest, Fastest, Bloodiest, and Best in Warfare*. Garden City, NY: The Military Book Club, 2004.

Province, Charles M. *Patton's Third Army: A Daily Combat Diary*. New York: Hippocrene, 1992.

Reid, Brian A. *No Holding Back: Operation Totalize, Normandy, August 1944*. Toronto: Robin Brass, 2005.

Ropp, Theodore. *War in the Modern World*. New York: Collier, 1962.

Ross, Steven T. *American War Plans, 1890–1939*. London: Frank Cass, 2002.

———. *U.S. War Plans, 1939–1945*. Malabar, FL: Kreiger, 2000.

Ryan, Cornelius. *A Bridge Too Far*. London: Book Club Associates, 1975.

Salisbury-Jones, Maj. Gen. Sir Guy. *So Full a Glory: A Biography of Marshal de Lattre de Tassigny*. London: Weidenfeld & Nicolson, 1954.

Speaight, Robert. *Vanier: Soldier, Diplomat and Governor General*. Toronto: Collins, 1970.

Spiller, Roger J., et al. *Dictionary of American Military Biography*. Westport: Greenwood Press, 1984.

Stacey, C. P. *Canada and the Age of Conflict*. Toronto; Macmillan, 1977.

Stoler, Mark A. *Allies and Adversaries: The Joint Chiefs of Staff, the Grand Alliance, and U.S. Strategy in World War II*. Chapel Hill: University of North Carolina Press, 2000.

Swettenham, John. *McNaughton*. Vol. 2, *1939–1943*. Toronto: Ryerson Press, 1969.

Thompson, R. W. *The Eighty Five Days: The Story of the Battle of the Scheldt*. London: Hutchinson, 1957.

Bibliography

Thorne, Christopher. *Allies of a Kind: The United States, Britain, and the War against Japan 1945*. Oxford: University Press, 1978.

Weigley, Russell F. *Eisenhower's Lieutenants: The Campaign of France and Germany, 1944–1945*. Bloomington, IN: Indiana University Press, 1981.

Weinberg, Gerhard L. *A World at Arms: A Global History of World War II*. Cambridge: University Press, 1994.

Weingartner, Steven. *The Greatest Thing We Have Ever Attempted: Historical Perspectives on the Normandy Campaign*. Wheaton: Cantigny First Division Foundation, 1998.

Whitaker, W. Denis, and Shelagh Whitaker. *Rhineland: The Battle to End the War*. Toronto: Stoddart, 1989.

———. *Tug of War: The Canadian Victory that Opened Antwerp*. Toronto: Stoddart, 1984.

Williams, Jeffery. *The Long Left Flank: The Hard Fought Way to the Reich, 1944–1945*. Toronto: Stoddart, 1988.

Wilmot, Chester. *The Struggle for Europe*. London: Fontana/Collins, 1974.

Wilt, Alan F. *The French Riviera Campaign of August 1944*. Carbondale: Southern Illinois University Press, 1981.

Winton, Harold R. *Corps Commanders of the Bulge: Six American Generals and Victory in the Ardennes*. Lawrence, KS: University of Kansas Press, 2007.

Wishnevsky, Stephen T. *Courtney Hicks Hodges: From Private to Four-Star General in the United States Army*. Jefferson, NC: McFarland, 2006.

Woodward, David R. *Trial by Friendship: Anglo-American Relations, 1917–1918*. Lexington, KY: University Press of Kentucky, 1993.

Wyant, William K. *Sandy Patch: A Biography of Lt. Gen. Alexander M. Patch*. New York: Praeger, 1991.

Yeide, Harry. *The Longest Battle: September 1944 to February 1945, From Aachen to the Roer and Across*. St. Paul, MN: Zenith, 2005.

Theses, Manuscripts, and Studies

British Army of the Rhine (BAOR) Battlefield Tour, Operation Totalize: 2 Canadian Corps Operations Astride the Road Caen-Falaise 7–8 August 1944, Spectator's Edition (1947).

BAOR Battlefield Tour, Operation Bluecoat: 8 Corps Operations South of Caumont 30–31 July 1944, Spectator's Edition (1947).

BAOR Battlefield Tour, Operation Veritable: 30 Corps Operations between the Rivers Maas and Rhine, 8–10 February 1945, Spectator's Edition (1947).

BAOR Battlefield Tour, Operation Plunder: Operations of 12 British Corps Crossing the River Rhine, on 23, 24, and 25 March 1945, Spectator's Edition (1947).

Dzwonchyk, Wayne Michael. "General Jacob L. Devers and the First French Army." Unpublished MA thesis, University of Delaware, 1975.

Macdonald, John A. "In Search of Veritable: Training the Canadian Army Staff Officer, 1899 to 1945." Unpublished MA thesis, Royal Military College of Canada, 1992.

Miller, Benjamin Franklin. "A Forgotten Soldier: Courtney Hodges and the Second World War." Unpublished MA thesis, Georgia Southern University, 1995.

Owen, Gregory L. "Across the Bridge: The World War II Journey of Cpt. Alexander M. Patch, III, the son of Lt. Gen. Alexander M. Patch, Jr." A manuscript for the George C. Marshall Foundation, Lexington, Virginia, 1995.

Stone, Thomas R. "He Had the Guts to Say No: A Military Biography of General William Hood Simpson." Unpublished dissertation, Rice University, 1974.

Articles

Amy, Brig Gen. E. A. C. "Normandy: 1 Squadron Canadian Grenadier Guards, Phase 2 Operation Totalize 7/8 August 1944." Unpublished paper dated 21 February 1993.

Bechthold, Mike. "Air Support in the Breskens Pocket: The Case of First Canadian Army and 84 Group Royal Air Force." *Canadian Military History* 3 (Autumn 1994): 53–62.

"Biography of General The Honourable Henry Duncan Graham Crerar, P.C., C.H., C.B., D.S.O." *Quadrant* 1 (June 1989): 11, 13.

Blumenson, Martin. "Measuring Generalship." *Army* (March 1999): 8–12.

Caddick-Adams, Peter. "General Sir Miles Christopher Dempsey (1896–1969): 'Not a Popular Leader.'" *RUSI Journal* 5 (October 2005): 66–72

Copp, Terry, and Robert Vogel, "'No Lack of Rational Speed': 1st Canadian Army Operations, September 1944." *Journal of Canadian Studies* 16 (Fall–Winter, 1981): 145–55.

"The Creation of the British General Staff, 1904–1914." *JRUSI* 662 (June 1971): 50–53.

Devers, Gen. Jacob L. "Major Problems of a Theater Commander in Combined Operations." *Military Review* 27 (October 1947): 3–15.

Dickson, Paul D. "Crerar and the Decision to Garrison Hong Kong." *Canadian Military History* 3 (Spring 1994): 97–110.

———. "The Hand that Wields the Dagger: Harry Crerar, First Canadian Army Command and National Autonomy." *War and Society* 2 (October 1995): 113–41.

———. "The Politics of Army Expansion: General H. D. G. Crerar and the Creation of First Canadian Army, 1940–41." *Journal of Military History* 60 (April 1996): 271–98.

French, David. "Colonel Blimp and the British Army: British Divisional Commanders in the War against Germany, 1939–1945." *English Historical Review* 111, No. 444 (November 1996): 1,182–1,201.

Ganz, A. Harding. "Questionable Objective: The Brittany Ports, 1944." *Journal of Military History* 1 (January 1995): 77–95.

Gurley, Franklin Louis. "Policy versus Strategy." *Journal of Military History* 58 (July 1994): 481–514.

Kimball, Warren F. "Stalingrad: A Chance for Choices." *Journal of Military History* 60 (January 1996): 89–114.

Nenninger, Timothy K. "'Unsystematic as a Mode of Command': Commanders and the Process of Command in the American Expeditionary Forces, 1917–1918." *Journal of Military History* 64 (July 2000): 739–68.

Patch, Maj. Gen. Alexander M. "Some Thoughts on Leadership." *Military Review* 22 (December 1943): 5–7.

Perrun, Jody. "Best Laid Plans: Guy Simonds and Operation Totalize, 7–10 August 1944." *Journal of Military History* 1 (January 2003): 137–73.

Powe, Maj. Marc B. "A Great Debate: The American General Staff (1903–16)." *Military Review* 4 (April 1975): 71–89.

Shepardson, Donald E. "The Fall of Berlin and the Rise of a Myth." *Journal of Military History* 1 (January 1998): 135–53.

Simpson, Lt. Gen. William H. "Rehearsal for the Rhine: An Account of the Ninth United Sates Army Operation 'Grenade.'" *Military Review* 25 (1945): 20–28.

Stone, Thomas R. "1630 Comes Early on the Roer." *Military Affairs* 53 (October 1973): 3–21.

———. "General William Hood Simpson: Unsung Commander of US Ninth Army." *Parameters* 11, No.2 (June 1981): 44–45.

"Thoughts on Command in Battle." *British Army Review* 69 (December, 1981): 5.

Acknowledgments

In researching and writing this book, I received support from many quarters.

In Britain over the years, Patricia Methven, Kate O'Brien, and Vicky Holtby of King's College London offered absolutely outstanding assistance, and I remain grateful to the trustees of the Liddell Hart Centre for Military Archives for permission to use quotations from the Alanbrooke, Fuller, Liddell Hart, and Pyman papers. Likewise, Roderick W. A. Suddaby, the Keeper of the Department of Documents at the Imperial War Museum, and his staff went out of their way to make my visits there pleasantly worthwhile. I am further grateful to the trustees of the Imperial War Museum for allowing me access to the Montgomery Collections and to The Right Honorable The Viscount Montgomery of Alamein, CMG, CBE, for permission to use quotations from them. As always, the Public Record Office staff at Kew proved most helpful with my research in London.

In France, I was graciously welcomed by Phillippe Schillinger, Conservateur en chef, Chef de la Division Archives, and assisted at every turn by the hardworking staff of the Service historique de l'armee de terre at Chateau de Vincennes.

In the United States, I received excellent service from the National Archives and Records Administration II in College Park, Maryland, and I remain especially beholden to Timothy K. Nenninger for taking great pains in providing me with pertinent research material. At the Dwight D. Eisenhower

Library in Abilene, Kansas, I was extremely fortunate in being looked after by Dwight E. Strandberg, who pointed me in the right direction on more than one occasion. During my research visit to the George C. Marshall Foundation Library and Archives in Lexington, Virginia, the late Dr. Larry I. Bland accorded me every courtesy, and I owe Marti Gansz a special word of thanks for her wonderful southern hospitality and many kindnesses. Thanks to Marti, I was put in touch with Gregory L. Owen of Staunton, Virginia, who kindly shared with me his vast knowledge of Gen. Sandy Patch of the U.S. Seventh Army. I remain grateful to Dr. Richard J. Sommers of the U.S. Army Military History Institute, Carlisle Barracks, Pennsylvania, and especially to David Keough, who sent me away with material that I would never have discovered by myself. I am further indebted to Bill Fowler, director of the Massachusetts Historical Society in Boston, and Peter Drummey and Carrie Foley for their personal assistance. I would also like to express my appreciation to Judy Sibley of the Special Collections of the U.S. Military Academy Library at West Point, and thank Col. Cole Kingseed for his warm hospitality during my visit there.

I would also like to acknowledge the unflagging support I received from the staff of the Naval War College (NWC) Library in Newport, Rhode Island; they never failed to respond to my continuous requests for interlibrary loans of books, theses, and dissertations. I owe an enormous debt to Prof. George Baer, who as chairman of the NWC's policy and strategy department, supported me to the hilt in my studies and research trips. I was further encouraged and supported by my colleague Stephen Ross, the NWC's William V. Pratt Chair, who provided a wealth of information and sage advice. To my other colleagues in the policy and strategy department, especially Col. Phillip Meilinger, who shared his research with me, I offer my sincere thanks for their comradeship and highly intellectual insights. I am additionally obliged to my students at the NWC who studied the commanders in this book along with me: Maj. James R. Blackburn Jr., Maj. John C. Garrett, Capt. Michael J. Gould, Maj. Michael A. Salvi, Lt. Col. Jacob A. Van Goor, Lt. Cmdr. Brett F. Bonifay, Lt. Cmdr. Timothy G. Craven, Maj. Dewey A. Granger, Lt. Cmdr. Douglas E. Heady, Lt. Cmdr. Patrick T. Holub, Maj. Charles K. Hyde, Lt. Cmdr. Bernard W. Kasupski, Lt. Col. Mark A. Milley, Lt. Col. Keith A. Seiwell, Maj. Andrew H. Smith, Lt. Col. Colby B. Smith, Russell E. Smith, Lt. Col. Brian W. Storck, Lt. Cmdr. Steven A. Swittel, Maj. Nicholas P. Chronis, Maj. Kent C. Curtsinger, Maj. Robert W. DeJong, Maj. Fred R. Eastwood III, Lt. Cmdr. Michael A. Giardino, Lt. Col. Kevin G. Herrmann, Lt. Col. Edward M. McCue III, Maj. Scott L. McLennan, Maj.

Christopher C. Miller, and Lt. Col. Lawrence R. Roberts. It was indeed an honour to serve with such fine officers as these.

In Canada, I would like to thank Serge Campion and his staff at the Fort Frontenac Library of the Canadian Land Forces Command and Staff College; they proved once again to be a personal mainstay. David Willis in particular offered especially valuable assistance, and I cannot thank him enough. I am similarly grateful to Benoit Cameron and the staff of the Royal Military College's Massey Library, who, as always, provided service above and beyond the norm. As I have often said before, the holdings of these two libraries together constitute the foremost repository of rare and contemporary military literature in Canada. For additional helpful support in archival research, I am further indebted to the staff of the National Archives of Canada in Ottawa and the Queen's University Archives in Kingston, Ontario. As a final accolade to my home and native land, I might add that without the generous financial support of the Social Sciences and Humanities Research Council of Canada, I would not have been able to complete the research required to write this book. Sincere thanks are also due to Prof. J. L. Granatstein, Prof. Marc Milner, Prof. Donald F. Bittner, Prof. David J. Bercuson, Prof. Martin Blumenson, and the late Prof. Gunther E. Rothenberg for their academic support.

I must likewise express my sincere gratitude to Mitch Kryzanowski for offering invaluable criticism and sound counsel possible only from one possessing unsurpassed historical knowledge and analytical skills. Special thanks are also due to Bob Caldwell of the Directorate of History and Terry Poulos of the University of Chicago for reading chapters and suggesting fresh perspectives and approaches. I am additionally grateful to John Selkirk for taking time out of his busy schedule to review drafts and make suggestions. I owe an enormous debt, as well, to Stephen Hart of the Royal Military Academy Sandhurst for sharing his research on Gen. Miles Dempsey and Gen. Harry Crerar and to David Hogan of the U.S. Army Center for Military History for his work and advice on Gen. Courtney Hodges. I would also like to thank Chris Evans and Dave Reisch at Stackpole Books for their editorial guidance and most efficient transformation of my manuscript into book form.

Finally, on the home front—as always—I was excused garden duty and sustained in my endeavors by the most appreciated support of my wife and daughters, to whom this volume is lovingly dedicated.

All errors of fact, omissions, and misinterpretations rest squarely on my shoulders alone.

Index

Page numbers in italics indicate illustrations